ZAGATSURVEY.

2001

PARIS
RESTAURANTS

Editor: Audrey Farolino

**Local Editors: Alexander Lobrano,
Mary Deschamps, François Simon**

Local Coordinator: Elizabeth d'Hémery

Published and distributed by
ZAGAT SURVEY, LLC
4 Columbus Circle
New York, New York 10019
Tel: 212 977 6000
E-mail: paris@zagat.com
Web site: www.zagat.com

Distributed in France by
Flammarion
26, rue Racine
75006 Paris
Tel: 01 40 51 31 00

Acknowledgments

We would especially like to thank the following people for their support:

George Balkind, Axel Baum, Odile Berthemy, Jean-Manuel Bourgois, Sabine and Patrick Brassart, Catherine Bret and Gilbert Brownstone, Mathilde Casimir, Frédéric Cassegrain, Sylvie Chadelaud, Jacques Dehornois, Alexandra Ernst and Dean Garret Siegel, Barbara and Peter Georgescu, Miki Goudsmit, Jack D. Gunther, Jr., Andrew Hibbert, Mark Kessel, M. L. Lewis, Vannina Maestracci, Sylvie Maurat, Anne and Gérard Mazet, Bruno Midavaine, Michelle Moss, Flore and Amaury de la Moussaye, Virginia and Jean Perrette, Anne de Ravel, Juliette Rey, Deirdre and Alfred J. Ross, Robert J. Sisk, Anne Thomas, Robert C. Treuhold, Dagmar and François de la Tour d'Auvergne, Charlotte and Franck Ullmann, Yveline le Cerf Vaucher, Martine Vermeulen, Denise and Alexandre Vilgrain, Jennifer and Sebastien Vilgrain, Stanislas Vilgrain, Stephen R. Volk, Lawrence A. Weinbach.

This guide would not have been possible without the exacting work of our staff:

Phil Cardone, Erica Curtis, Laura du Pont, Jeff Freier, Sarah Kagan, Natalie Lebert, Mike Liao, Dave Makulec, Jefferson Martin, Andrew O'Neill, Robert Seixas, Zamira Skalkottas, LaShana Smith.

Contents

About This Survey 4
What's New 5
Key to Ratings and Symbols 6
Map 8
Most Popular 9
Top Ratings
  • Food and by Cuisine and Arrondissement...... 10
  • Decor, Garden, Historic, Romantic, Room,
    Terrace, View, Waterside.................... 14
  • Service.................................... 15
Best Buys.................................... 16
ALPHABETICAL DIRECTORY,
RATINGS AND REVIEWS..................... 17
INDEXES
  • **Cuisines**............................... 184
  • **Locations**............................. 196
  • **Special Features:**
  • Breakfast 206
  • Brunch 206
  • Business Dining 206
  • Caters................................... 209
  • Dancing/Entertainment 210
  • Dining Alone 211
  • Expense Account 214
  • Family Appeal 215
  • Fireplace 217
  • Game in Season 217
  • Historic Interest......................... 218
  • Hotel Dining 220
  • "In" Places 220
  • Jacket/Tie Recommended 221
  • Jacket/Tie Required 221
  • July/August Dining...................... 221
  • Late Late – After 12:30 222
  • Meet for a Drink 223
  • Modish Intelligentsia 223
  • Noteworthy Newcomers 225
  • Outdoor Dining.......................... 225
  • Outstanding View....................... 228
  • Parking/Valet........................... 229
  • Parties & Private Rooms 230
  • People-Watching 234
  • Power Scene............................ 234
  • Quick Fix 235
  • Quiet Conversation...................... 236
  • Romantic 240
  • Saturday – Best Bets 242
  • Sunday – Best Bets 243
  • Singles Scene 245
  • Sleepers................................ 246
  • Special Occasion 246
  • Teenagers & Other Youthful Spirits 247
  • Teflons................................. 248
  • Theme Restaurant 249
  • Transporting Experience 249
  • Winning Wine List 249
  • Young Children.......................... 250
Notes 251

About This Survey

Here are the results of our *2001 Paris Restaurant Survey* covering over 950 restaurants in Paris and its surroundings.

By regularly surveying large numbers of local restaurant-goers, we have achieved a uniquely current and reliable guide. More than 1,260 people participated. Since the participants dined out an average of 3.2 times per week, this *Survey* is based on about 209,664 meals per year.

We want to thank each of our participants. They are a widely diverse group in all respects but one – they are food lovers all. This book is really "theirs."

Of the surveyors, 86% are French, 14% are other nationalities; 45% are women, 55% are men; the breakdown by age is 10% in their 20s, 19% in their 30s, 23% in their 40s, 26% in their 50s and 22% in their 60s or above.

To help guide our readers to Paris' best meals and best buys, we have prepared a number of lists. See, for example, Paris' Most Popular Restaurants (page 9), Top Ratings (pages 10–15) and Best Buys (page 16). On the assumption that most people want a quick fix on the places at which they are considering eating, we have provided handy indexes.

We are particularly grateful to our coordinator, Elizabeth d'Hémery, who pulled this project together, as well as to our editors: Alexander Lobrano, a food and travel writer, and Mary Deschamps, a freelance writer specializing in lifestyle and cultural subjects. We would also like to thank journalist François Simon for his help and advice.

We invite you to be a reviewer in our next *Survey*. To do so, simply send a stamped, self-addressed, business-size envelope to ZAGAT SURVEY, 4 Columbus Circle, New York, NY 10019, or e-mail us at paris@zagat.com, so that we will be able to contact you. Each participant will receive a free copy of the next *Paris Restaurant Survey* when it is published.

Your comments, suggestions and even criticisms of this *Survey* are also solicited. There is always room for improvement with your help.

New York, NY
August 22, 2000

Nina et Tim Zagat

What's New

A resurgent French economy is giving a la-vie-en-rose blush of health to the Paris dining scene, which is being reshaped by a spate of new openings and chef shuffles.

In an echo of the Belle Epoque, when many top restaurants were found in hotels, the city's 'grand palaces' are again exciting dining destinations. The new Le Cinq at the Four Seasons George V poached chef Philippe Legendre from the mighty Taillevent, which in turn lured Michel del Burgo away from the Bristol hotel. The Bristol then pulled off its own coup by hiring young chef Eric Fréchon to take his place. And at press time, the town was abuzz over the news that Alain Ducasse was leaving his townhouse digs in the 16th to take over the former Le Régence space in the Hotel Plaza-Athénée. Renamed Alain Ducasse au Plaza-Athénée, his Parisian flagship is to re-open in mid-September 2000.

While Parisians remain demanding diners, they increasingly expect restaurants to provide them with more than just a meal. No one understands dining-out-as-entertainment better than the Costes brothers. Their latest – Georges in the Pompidou Center and Café de l'Esplanade in the 7th – follow the same formula as such Costes hits as Café Beaubourg and Café Marly, featuring dramatic decor and a hip ambiance that keep the beautiful people rolling in regardless of the food. Other fashionable new entries: Bon, co-owned by designer Philippe Starck, with a très Starck setting in the 16th, and Rue Balzac, near the Etoile, co-owned by chef Michel Rostang and singer Johnny Hallyday.

As always, Paris remains a lure for chefs from the provinces. Among the latest arrivals: Jean-Yves Bath from Clermont-Ferrand, serving modernized Auvergnat fare at Bath's near the Champs-Elysées; Hélène Darroze, showcasing French Southwestern cuisine at her eponymous restaurant near Sèvres-Babylone; and Bernard Loiseau, who keeps his perch in Saulieu, La Côte d'Or, while extending his Parisian family of *tantes* (aunts) with Tante Jeanne in the 17th.

Though Parisians groan about prices, paying an average of 299 francs for a meal, it's unlikely they'll cut back their restaurant spending anytime soon given a tempting group of upcoming openings. Chef Ghislaine Arabian, ex Ledoyen, is opening a new venture in fall 2000; Ladurée tearooms are planned for the 16th and Saint-Germain; and Maison Prunier is expected to become a caviar house under the auspices of Pierre Bergé (president of YSL). And rumors continue that Joël Robuchon will renounce his restive retirement and make a grand comeback with a new Paris restaurant.

Paris, France   Alexander Lobrano
August 22, 2000

Key to Ratings/Symbols

This sample entry identifies the various types of information contained in your Zagat Survey.

(1) Restaurant Name, Address, Métro Stop & Phone Number

(2) Hours & Credit Cards

(3) ZAGAT Ratings

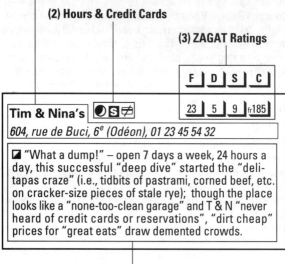

F	D	S	C
23	5	9	fr185

Tim & Nina's ◑ 🅂 ⊅

604, rue de Buci, 6ᵉ (Odéon), 01 23 45 54 32

◪ "What a dump!" – open 7 days a week, 24 hours a day, this successful "deep dive" started the "deli-tapas craze" (i.e., tidbits of pastrami, corned beef, etc. on cracker-size pieces of stale rye); though the place looks like a "none-too-clean garage" and T & N "never heard of credit cards or reservations", "dirt cheap" prices for "great eats" draw demented crowds.

(4) Surveyors' Commentary

The names of restaurants with the highest overall ratings, greatest popularity and importance are printed in **CAPITAL LETTERS**. Address and phone numbers are printed in *italics*.

(2) Hours & Credit Cards

After each restaurant name you will find the following courtesy information:

◑ .... *serving after 11 PM, Monday–Thursday*

🅂 .... *open on Sunday*

⊅ .... *no credit cards accepted*

6

(3) ZAGAT Ratings

Food, Decor and **Service** are each rated on a scale of **0** to **30**:

F	D	S	C

F .... *Food*
D .... *Decor*
S .... *Service*
C .... *Cost*

23	5	9	fr185

  0 - 9 .... *poor to fair*
10 - 15 .... *fair to good*
16 - 19 .... *good to very good*
20 - 25 .... *very good to excellent*
26 - 30 .... *extraordinary to perfection*

▽ 23	5	9	fr185

▽ .... **Low number of votes/less reliable**

The **Cost (C)** column reflects the estimated price of a dinner with one drink and tip. Lunch usually costs 25% less.

A restaurant listed without ratings is either an important **newcomer** or a popular **write-in**. The estimated cost, with one drink and tip, is indicated by the following symbols.

–	–	–	VE

I .... *below 200 Fr*
M .... *200 Fr to 350 Fr*
E .... *351 Fr to 500 Fr*
VE .... *more than 500 Fr*

(4) Surveyors' Commentary

Surveyors' comments are summarized, with literal comments shown in quotation marks. The following symbols indicate whether responses were mixed or uniform.

◪ .... *mixed*
◼ .... *uniform*

Most Popular

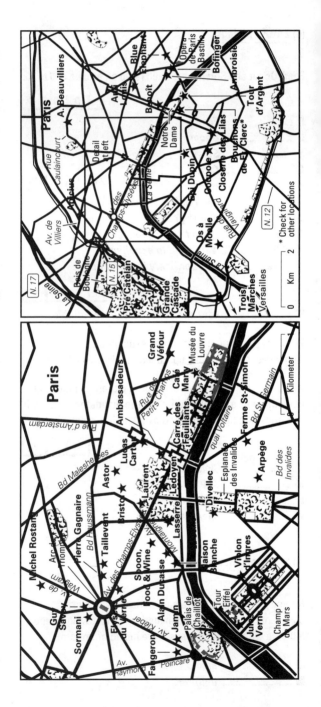

Most Popular

Each of our reviewers has been asked to name his or her five favorite restaurants. The 42 spots most frequently named, in order of their popularity, are:

1. Taillevent
2. Arpège
3. Ambroisie
4. Alain Ducasse
5. Grand Véfour
6. Pierre Gagnaire
7. Lucas Carton
8. Tour d'Argent
9. Guy Savoy
10. Carré des Feuillants
11. Jules Verne
12. Epi Dupin
13. Apicius
14. Ambassadeurs
15. Laurent
16. Grande Cascade
17. Blue Elephant
18. Bristol*
19. Ami Louis
20. Violon d'Ingres
21. Lasserre
22. Pré Catelan
23. Jamin
24. Maison Blanche
25. Michel Rostang*
26. Spoon, Food & Wine
27. Astor
28. Bouchons de Fr. Clerc
29. Café Marly
30. Sormani
31. Divellec
32. Elysées du Vernet
33. Bofinger
34. Ledoyen
35. Os à Moelle*
36. Faugeron
37. Beauvilliers (A.)
38. Trois Marches*
39. Closerie des Lilas
40. Benoît
41. Coupole*
42. Ferme St-Simon

It's obvious that many of the restaurants on the above list are among the most expensive, but Parisians also love a bargain. Were popularity calibrated to price, we suspect that a number of other restaurants would join the above ranks. Thus, we have listed over 80 Best Buys on page 16.

---

* Tied with the restaurant listed directly above it.

Top Ratings*

Top 40 Food Ranking

28	Taillevent	23	Goumard
27	Alain Ducasse		Lasserre
	Arpège		Comte de Gascogne
	Grand Véfour		Tour d'Argent
	Pierre Gagnaire		Marée
	Ambroisie		Astor
26	Lucas Carton		Pré Catelan
	Guy Savoy		Montparnasse 25
	Michel Rostang	22	Espadon
25	Gérard Besson		Laurent
	Bristol		Kinugawa
	Carré des Feuillants		Ledoyen
	Jamin		Divellec
24	Trois Marches		Os à Moelle
	Elysées du Vernet		Faucher
	Apicius		Tang
	Duc		Clos Morillons
	Faugeron		Beauvilliers (A.)
	Violon d'Ingres		Jacques Cagna
	Ambassadeurs		Epi Dupin

Top Food by French Cuisine

Bistro (Contemporary)
22 Os à Moelle
Epi Dupin
Avant Goût
19 Brézolles
Ardoise
Bistrot de l'Etoile Lauriston

Bistro (Traditional)
22 Ami Louis
Villaret
21 Biche au Bois
Benoît
20 Allobroges
Michel (Chez)

Bouillabaisse
23 Goumard
20 Port Alma
19 Dôme
Marius et Janette
Marius
18 Jarasse

Brasserie
17 Bœuf Couronné
16 Petit Lutétia
15 Sébillon Neuilly
Marty
Bofinger
Julien

Burgundy
19 Récamier
18 Tante Marguerite
17 Tante Louise
16 Ma Bourgogne (4e)
15 Ma Bourgogne (8e)
Crus de Bourgogne

Cassoulet
25 Carré des Feuillants
22 Trou Gascon
21 Benoît
18 Chez Eux
17 Sousceyrac
16 Fontaine de Mars

Caviar
21 Maison Prunier
19 Petrossian
Caviar Kaspia
17 Maison du Caviar
Flora Danica
13 Comptoir du Saumon

Cheese
23 Montparnasse 25
17 Androüet
Ambassade d'Auvergne
16 Ferme St-Hubert
Soufflé

---

* Excluding restaurants with low voting.

Top Food

Confit
22 Ami Louis
20 Oulette
    Paul Chêne
18 Truffe Noire
17 Ambassade du Sud-Ouest
13 Ami Jean

Haute Cuisine
28 Taillevent
27 Alain Ducasse
    Grand Véfour
    Ambroisie
26 Lucas Carton
    Michel Rostang

Haute Cuisine (Contemporary)
27 Arpège
    Pierre Gagnaire
26 Guy Savoy
25 Bristol
    Carré des Feuillants
23 Astor

Lyons
19 Bellecour
    René
17 Moissonnier
16 Auberge Bressane
    Rôtisserie du Beaujolais
    Assiette Lyonnaise

Provence
24 Elysées du Vernet
20 Casa Olympe
    Bastide Odéon
18 Campagne et Provence
    Olivades
15 Sud

Seafood
24 Duc
23 Goumard
    Marée
22 Divellec
    Gaya Rive Gauche
21 Ecaille et Plume

Shellfish
19 Dôme
    Huitrier
18 Pétrus
    Jarasse
17 Rech
    Pichet

Southwest
23 Comte de Gascogne
22 Trou Gascon
21 Hélène Darroze
20 Oulette
18 Truffe Noire
17 Ambassade du Sud-Ouest

Steakhouse
19 René
    Denise (Chez)
18 Relais de Venise
    Gourmets des Ternes
    Rôtisserie d'en Face
    Chez Eux

Wine Bar/Bistro
17 Willi's Wine Bar
16 Vin sur Vin
15 Enoteca
    Ma Bourgogne (8e)
14 Bacchantes
    Juvenile's

Top Food by Other Cuisines

Asian
22 Tang
20 Tan Dinh
    Blue Elephant
18 Erawan
    Diep
17 Kambodgia

Chinese
21 Chen
19 Vong (8e)
17 Tsé-Yang
    Délices de Szechuen
    FocLy
16 Passy Mandarin

Italian
22 Sormani
21 Ostéria
20 Grand Venise
    Conti
    I Golosi
    Romantica

Japanese
24 Isami*
22 Kinugawa
20 Benkay
19 Shozan
18 Orient-Extrême
17 Inagiku*

---

* Low votes.

Top Food

Mediterranean
19 Mavrommatis
   Délices d'Aphrodite*
   Fakhr el Dine
18 Al Diwan
16 Al Dar
   Noura Pavillon

North African
20 Timgad
19 Mansouria
   Wally Le Saharien
   Oum el Banine
18 Atlas
17 404

Top Food by Special Feature

Breakfast
25 Bristol
24 Ambassadeurs
18 Fontaines
16 Dalloyau
15 Ladurée
13 Bernardaud

See and Be Seen
18 Voltaire
13 Emporio Armani Caffé
   Costes
10 Alcazar
 9 Colette
 – Bon

Hotel Dining
27 Alain Ducasse
   Pierre Gagnaire
25 Bristol
24 Trois Marches
   Elysées du Vernet
   Ambassadeurs

Sunday Dining
25 Bristol
24 Trois Marches
   Ambassadeurs
23 Tour d'Argent
22 Espadon
13 Fouquet's

Late-Night
19 Denise (Chez)
18 C'Amelot
   Vong (1er)
17 "Pierre"/Fontaine Gaillon
   Maison du Caviar
16 Yvan, Petit

Tea & Desserts
16 Dalloyau
   Mariage Frères
15 Ladurée
13 A Priori Thé
   Bernardaud
   Deux Abeilles

Newcomers (Rated)
21 Cinq*
   Hélène Darroze
20 Aimant du Sud
   Cave Gourmand
   Il Baccello
19 Petrossian

Wine Lists**
29 Taillevent
27 Alain Ducasse
   Tour d'Argent
26 Grand Véfour
   Lucas Carton
   Arpège

Newcomers (Unrated)
   Atelier Berger
   Bon
   Café de l'Esplanade
   Georges
   Rue Balzac
   Tante Jeanne

---

* Low votes.
** Rated for their wines.

Top Food by Arrondissement

1st & 2nd
27 Grand Véfour
25 Gérard Besson
   Carré des Feuillants
23 Goumard
22 Espadon
21 Drouant

3rd & 4th
27 Ambroisie
22 Ami Louis
21 Ostéria
   Benoît
19 Orangerie
   Vieux Bistro

5th & 6th
23 Tour d'Argent
22 Jacques Cagna
   Epi Dupin
   Relais Louis XIII
21 Hélène Darroze
20 Bastide Odéon

7th
27 Arpège
24 Violon d'Ingres
22 Divellec
   Jules Verne
   Gaya Rive Gauche
21 Ecaille et Plume

8th
28 Taillevent
27 Alain Ducasse
   Pierre Gagnaire
26 Lucas Carton
25 Bristol
24 Elysées du Vernet

9th & 10th
21 Table d'Anvers
20 Casa Olympe
   Restaurant Opéra
   I Golosi
19 Wally Le Saharien
15 Julien

11th, 12th & 13th
22 Trou Gascon
   Avant Goût
   Villaret
21 Biche au Bois
   Amognes
20 Oulette

14th & 15th
24 Duc
23 Montparnasse 25
22 Os à Moelle
   Clos Morillons
   Philippe Detourbe
21 Chen

16th
25 Jamin
24 Faugeron
23 Pré Catelan
22 Tang
   Relais d'Auteuil
21 Grande Cascade

17th
26 Guy Savoy
   Michel Rostang
24 Apicius
22 Faucher
   Sormani
21 Petit Colombier

18th, 19th & 20th
22 Beauvilliers (A.)
20 Allobroges
17 Bœuf Couronné
15 Dagorno
14 Wepler
11 Ay!! Caramba!!

Outlying Areas
24 Trois Marches (Versailles)
23 Comte de Gascogne (Boulogne)
20 Romantica (Clichy)
19 Potager du Roy (Versailles)
18 San Valero (Neuilly)
   Cazaudehore (St-Germain/Laye)

Top 40 Decor Ranking

29 Grand Véfour	Maison de l'Amérique Latine
28 Tour d'Argent	Laurent
27 Jules Verne	Beauvilliers (A.)
Train Bleu	Espadon
26 Ambassadeurs	China Club
Taillevent	Orangerie
Grande Cascade	23 Coupe-Chou
25 Ambroisie	Elysées du Vernet
Maxim's	Café Marly
Trois Marches	Restaurant Opéra
Bristol	Costes
Lucas Carton	Toupary
24 Pré Catelan	22 Cazaudehore La Forestière
Alain Ducasse	Buddha Bar
Lasserre	Pavillon Montsouris
Blue Elephant	Altitude 95
Rest. du Musée d'Orsay	Fermette Marbeuf 1900
Ledoyen	Man Ray
Lapérouse	Jardins de Bagatelle
Maison Blanche	404

Garden

Grande Cascade	Maison de l'Amérique Latine
Laurent	Pré Catelan
Ledoyen	Trois Marches

Historic

Ambassadeurs	Lapérouse
Fermette Marbeuf 1900	Maxim's
Grand Véfour	Restaurant Opéra

Romantic

Beauvilliers (A.)	Coupe-Chou
Blue Elephant	Lasserre
China Club	Orangerie

Room

Alain Ducasse	Espadon
Ambroisie	Lucas Carton
Bristol	Taillevent
Elysées du Vernet	Train Bleu

Terrace

Café de Flore	Closerie des Lilas
Café Les Deux Magots	Fouquet's
Café Véry	Ile

View

Café Marly	Rest. du Musée d'Orsay
Jules Verne	Toupary
Maison Blanche	Tour d'Argent

Waterside

Cap Seguin	Plage Parisienne
Gégène	Quai Ouest
Guinguette de Neuilly	River Café

Top 40 Service Ranking

28 Taillevent
26 Alain Ducasse
Grand Véfour
25 Ambassadeurs
Arpège
Pierre Gagnaire
Ambroisie
24 Bristol
Tour d'Argent
Lasserre
Michel Rostang
Lucas Carton
Jamin
Guy Savoy
23 Laurent
Trois Marches
Ledoyen
Carré des Feuillants
22 Espadon
Faugeron

21 Elysées du Vernet
Pré Catelan
Grande Cascade
Orangerie
Restaurant Opéra
Gérard Besson
20 Marée
Relais d'Auteuil*
Jacques Cagna
Goumard
Astor
Apicius
Comte de Gascogne
Jules Verne
Violon d'Ingres
Drouant
19 Célébrités
Relais Plaza
Tire-Bouchon
Maison Prunier

---

* Tied with the restaurant listed directly above it.

Best Buys

40 Top Bangs for the Buck

This list reflects the best dining values in our *Survey*. It is produced by dividing the cost of a meal into the combined ratings for food, decor and service.

1. Crêperie de Josselin
2. Cosi
3. Chartier
4. A Priori Thé
5. Café Véry
6. Restaurant des Beaux Arts
7. Lina's
8. Ay!! Caramba!!
9. Mariage Frères
10. Perraudin
11. Café Beaubourg
12. Marianne
13. Café Charbon
14. Mathusalem
15. Polidor
16. Biche au Bois
17. Omar
18. Tire-Bouchon
19. Bouillon Racine
20. Dame Tartine
21. Impatient
22. Café Flo
23. 404
24. Petit Lutétia
25. Avant Goût
26. Bistrot St. Ferdinand
27. Astier
28. Atlas
29. Café de l'Industrie
30. Allobroges
31. Epi Dupin
32. Café du Commerce
33. Ma Bourgogne
34. Gamin de Paris
35. Angelina
36. Denise
37. Paul
38. Bacchantes
39. Bistro de la Grille
40. Rubis

Additional Good Values

(A bit more expensive, but worth every penny)

Affriolé
Alsaco
Ami Jean
Amognes
Anahï
Ardoise
Armand au Palais Royal
Atelier Maître Albert
Bascou
Bastide Odéon
Bistro du 17ème
Bistrot de l'Etoile Lauriston
Bistrot de l'Etoile Troyon
Bistrot du Dôme
Bookinistes
Brézolles
Café Bleu
Café de la Musique
Cap Seguin
Casa Alcalde
Colette
Contre-Allée
Ebauchoir
Enoteca
Ferme St-Hubert
Gallopin
Il Barone
Kambodgia
Kiosque
Livio
Manufacture
O à la Bouche
Petit Bofinger
Petit Niçois
Philippe Detourbe
Repaire de Cartouche
Rôtisserie d'en Face
Square Trousseau
Verre Bouteille
Wally Le Saharien
Willi's Wine Bar
Yvan, Petit

Alphabetical
Directory

Abélard 🖫   – | – | – | M

1, rue des Grands-Degrés, 5ᵉ (Maubert-Mutualité),
01 43 25 16 46; fax 01 43 29 66 55

Just across the Seine from Notre Dame in the 5th, this
French old-timer with Louis XIII decor wins praise for its
"warm welcome, excellent meat" and "good wine list",
but some feel it's on the "expensive" side and find the
"flowered tablecloths a bit too flashy"; good-value prix
fixe lunch menus are an economical way to go.

Absinthe (L')   13 | 12 | 13 | fr266

24, place du Marché St-Honoré, 1ᵉʳ (Tuileries),
01 49 26 90 04; fax 01 49 26 08 64

◪ Diners appreciate "the charm" of the Place du Marché
Saint-Honoré, the right bank setting of this "pretty" bistro
near the Tuileries run by chef Michel Rostang, and while
most also commend its "good, well-conceived" French
fare, a few carp that it's "heavy" and "lacking in originality";
still, no one can fault the "pleasant terrace" and a majority
considers it "a good buy."

A et M Le Bistrot   13 | 13 | 13 | fr260

136, bd Murat, 16ᵉ (Porte de St-Cloud), 01 45 27 39 60;
fax 01 45 27 69 71
105, rue de Prony, 17ᵉ (Péreire), 01 44 40 05 88; fax 01 44 40 05 89

■ These bistros "à la mode" in the 16th and 17th, from
Jean-Pierre Vigato of Apicius and François Grandjean of
Marius, get a thumbs-up from most voters for their "pretty
good", "inventive" modern bistro cooking and "fair prices";
"friendly service", "original" decor and a "trendy", "young
atmosphere" add to their popularity, but a few are less
impressed: "a lot of noise for nothing", "good PR agent."

Affriolé (L')   14 | 11 | 13 | fr226

17, rue Malar, 7ᵉ (Ecole Militaire/Invalides), 01 44 18 31 33;
fax 01 44 18 91 12

◪ The arrival of new chef Thierry Verola might be good
news for those who found the cooking "irregular" at this
little Left Bank bistro near Les Invalides with Pompeian red
walls and mosaic-topped tables; "good value for interesting
food" that "incites you to return" is the word from supporters,
with further praise for the "warm welcome" and "amiable"
service, but some wish they'd "rethink that decor."

Agape (L')   ▽ 17 | 5 | 13 | fr159

281, rue Lecourbe, 15ᵉ (Boucicaut/Convention),
01 45 58 19 29

◪ While the decor at this bistro serving "grand French
classics" in the "outer reaches of the 15th" is a bit "banal",
even "sad", admirers don't mind since they come here
"for what's on the plate", namely "refined" cuisine that's a
"very good value" – it's a "surprise to find such well-
executed cooking for the price"; service is "smiling", if
a bit "slow."

Aiguière (L') ▽ 16 17 13 fr286
37 bis, rue de Montreuil, 11ᵉ (Faidherbe-Chaligny),
01 43 72 42 32; fax 01 43 72 96 36
■ Tucked away in the 11th, this auberge with Gustavian decor pleases the few surveyors who know it with its "pleasant ambiance" and prix fixe deals, especially the tasting menu that includes a "different glass of wine with each dish" – "very satisfying" say fans who praise the "beautiful association" of food and wine created by chef Pascal Viallet (ex Hôtel Lutétia) and owner/maître sommelier Patrick Masbatin; "good service" is also lauded.

Ailleurs 7 16 9 fr228
26, rue Jean Mermoz, 8ᵉ (Franklin D. Roosevelt),
01 53 53 98 00; fax 01 53 53 98 01
◪ This "trendy" International off the Champs-Elysées boasts a "hip" crowd and a "good-looking", red-walled setting, but punster critics say that "for cuisine, it's better to look *ailleurs* [elsewhere]", citing "uneven" fare that's "expensive" for what you get (though the "sublime" chocolate tart has fans); some claim "the waitresses are recruited for their looks", since service has "attitude" and can be slow.

Aimant du Sud (L') ● – – – M
40, bd Arago, 13ᵉ (Les Gobelins), 01 47 07 33 57; fax 01 43 31 61 86
Frédéric Llorca, ex Fous d'en Face, has taken over what used to be Le Rhône, in the 13th but not far from Montparnasse, and is offering a regularly changing modern French menu with a sunny Provençal tint; some rave "superb, not to be missed", while others say "the cooking isn't up to the decor", but gentle prices and a large terrace work in its favor.

ALAIN DUCASSE AU PLAZA-ATHÉNÉE 27 24 26 fr842
Hôtel Plaza-Athénée, 25, av. Montaigne, 8ᵉ (Alma-Marceau/
Franklin D. Roosevelt), 01 53 67 65 00; fax 01 47 27 31 22
■ All of Paris will be holding its breath to find out what happens when Alain Ducasse's haute cuisine stunner reopens in mid-September after moving to the posh Hôtel Plaza-Athénée in the 8th; if the multi-Michelin-star chef's track record is any indication, it will remain "an out-of-body experience" with "sublime" food and "wonderful" service (rated No. 2 in both categories) and, *bien sûr*, "staggeringly expensive" prices.

Albert (Chez) ▽ 13 7 12 fr283
43, rue Mazarine, 6ᵉ (Mabillon/Odéon), 01 46 33 22 57
■ Those who know this little Portuguese near the Odéon have kind words for its "honest" and sometimes "delicious" food, which it's been dishing up for over 20 years; the "aggressively lit" setting may not amount to much, but the "friendly" staff creates a "pleasant" ambiance in which to savor the likes of shellfish cooked in a *cataplana* (copper casserole) with one of the appealing Portuguese wines.

Alcazar ◐Ⓢ
10 | 17 | 12 | fr294

62, rue Mazarine, 6ᵉ (Odéon), 01 53 10 19 99; fax 01 53 10 23 23

■ Most agree that Sir Terence Conran's big, "noisy", "trendy" brasserie on the site of the old Alcazar nightclub near the Odéon is "visually appealing", with sleek decor and a skylit atrium, but opinions on the modern cooking range from "disappointing" to "excellent" (brunch and fish and chips are strengths); "wear something chic – Prada or Calvin Klein", and if seeking a "good bar scene", head upstairs.

Al Dar ◐Ⓢ
16 | 9 | 14 | fr242

8, rue Frédéric Sauton, 5ᵉ (Maubert-Mutualité),
01 43 25 17 15; fax 01 45 01 61 67
93, av. Raymond-Poincaré, 16ᵉ (Victor Hugo), 01 45 00 96 64

■ "Very good" Lebanese fare is served at this well-liked duo with a more stylish branch near the Place Victor Hugo and a laid-back Latin Quarter site near the Place Maubert; the decor is rather innocuous and some claim that quality depends on "the chef's mood", but reasonable prices, a "pleasant welcome" and "good" service help make up for any shortcomings; "great" takeaway is also a crowd-pleaser.

Al Diwan ◐Ⓢ
18 | 13 | 16 | fr282

30, av. George V, 8ᵉ (Alma-Marceau/George V),
01 47 23 45 45; fax 01 47 23 60 98

■ "This old-world Lebanese" off the Champs-Elysées earns nods for its "mouthwatering appetizers", "excellent chicken schwarma" and other "healthy", if rather "expensive", fare; it's "a bit noisy and smoky" and "you either love or hate the 1920s airport decor" (which some say could use an "overhaul"), but the "atmosphere created by the crowd and the music" on weekends makes some declare "it's Beirut."

Alivi (L') Ⓢ
▽ 18 | 13 | 13 | fr244

27, rue du Roi de Sicile, 4ᵉ (Hôtel-de-Ville/St-Paul),
01 48 87 90 20; fax 01 48 87 20 60

■ A "modern and creative approach to Corsican cooking, rarely found in Corsica itself", can be found in the Marais at this cozy restaurant where the food is enhanced by "good wines"; the "young" staff offers a "friendly welcome", and if a few suggest that service might improve if "someone woke the waiters up", perhaps that easygoing approach is part of the charm of the atmosphere.

Allard ◐
16 | 16 | 15 | fr342

41, rue St-André-des-Arts, 6ᵉ (Odéon), 01 43 26 48 23;
fax 01 46 33 04 02

■ "Old Parisian charm" and "duck with olives to die for" are the big lures at this sepia-tinted Left Bank bistro; while fans insist "you can always count on the cooking", a few find it "uneven" and "without much inspiration", also grumbling about "disinterested service and a clientele that's 80 percent American"; still, it's "an institution" and a "great place to bring sophisticated out-of-towners."

Allobroges (Les)
20 | 13 | 17 | fr246

71, rue des Grands-Champs, 20ᵉ (Maraîchers/Nation), 01 43 73 40 00

■ "It's worth the trip to this out-of-the-way" eatery in the 20th, a snug bistro that rewards the trip with "delicious" food and "very friendly" service in an "intimate" setting with wallpaper designed to mimic wood paneling; "good value" is another reason why supporters call it "an oasis of quality in a gastronomic desert."

Al Mounia
18 | 19 | 16 | fr308

16, rue de Magdebourg, 16ᵉ (Trocadéro), 01 47 27 57 28

■ A "transporting experience is guaranteed" at this "very good Moroccan" near the Trocadéro where "authentic" couscous, pastries and other specialties are enjoyed in a "calm, luxurious" setting (complete with leather pouf chairs that some find uncomfortable); despite a few grumbles about service and the "somewhat formal" ambiance, this is one invitation to the Casbah that most surveyors are happy to accept.

Alsace (L') ●S
14 | 13 | 12 | fr280

39, av. des Champs-Elysées, 8ᵉ (Franklin D. Roosevelt), 01 53 93 97 00; fax 01 53 93 97 09

■ "Lively" Alsatian brasserie that draws an eclectic crowd thanks to its prominent location and 24/7 operating policy (particularly "handy at 5 AM"); devotees dub it "one of the few worthwhile places on the Champs-Elysées" and can't get enough of the "excellent fish choucroute", but more delicate types find it too "noisy" and "busy" for their tastes.

Alsaco (L')
16 | 9 | 14 | fr226

10, rue Condorcet, 9ᵉ (Anvers/Poissonnière), 01 45 26 44 31; fax 01 42 85 11 05

■ What may be "Paris' best choucroute", "a terrific onion tart" and "very good Alsatian wines" make up for a room that's "too small, noisy", "smoky" and "far from the Métro" ("wish they'd move!") at this well-respected Alsatian *winstub* in the 9th; "the owner is a real character" who "fosters a congenial ambiance", and if not everyone digs his "discourse", the combo of "excellent" food and wines plus fair prices is a winner.

Altitude 95 S
9 | 22 | 11 | fr241

Tour Eiffel, Champ de Mars, 1er étage, 7ᵉ (Champ de Mars), 01 45 55 20 04; fax 01 47 05 94 40

◪ "The skies of Paris deserve better cooking" say surveyors smitten by the "superb views" but "disappointed" by the French food at this "touristy" restaurant on the first level of the Eiffel Tower; still, it's a good place to bring "visitors to Paris" or "celebrate a child's birthday", and better yet, it's "affordable."

Amadéo
▽ | 11 | 14 | 17 | fr190

19, rue François Miron, 4ᵉ (St-Paul), 01 48 87 01 02; fax 01 42 76 08 38

■ "Wonderful musical soirees", "nice decor" and a "warm welcome" seduce surveyors at this "classy" Marais bistro where meals are often accompanied by classical music; the "inventive" cooking with "nouvelle" tendencies can be "uneven", but "lyric dinners" (which include a recital) are an "excellent concept" and the "charming" staff is "friendly"; while popular with gay couples, everyone is welcome.

Amazigh
▽ | 18 | 15 | 18 | fr274

2, rue La Pérouse, 16ᵉ (Boissière/Kléber), 01 47 20 90 38; fax 01 47 20 44 08

■ "Tiny and hidden" with "simple decor" and a "calm" atmosphere, this Moroccan near Kléber in the 16th offers "well-prepared", "traditional" food and gets at least one vote for "the best couscous in Paris"; prices seem "high" to some, while others aver that it's "good value for the money."

Ambassade d'Auvergne S
| 17 | 13 | 16 | fr283

22, rue du Grenier St-Lazare, 3ᵉ (Rambuteau), 01 42 72 31 22; fax 01 42 78 85 47

■ "Country charm", a "warm welcome" and "hearty" Auvergnat fare win fans for this tavern not far from the Pompidou Center; the "*aligot* (a potato-cheese dish) is worth the trip" say partisans who also praise the likes of andouillette and blood sausage from a kitchen that "cares about authenticity"; some find the food a bit "heavy", the decor in need of "refreshing" and prices "a bit expensive", but overall "very pleasant" is the verdict.

Ambassade du Sud-Ouest S
| 17 | 11 | 14 | fr226

46, av. de La Bourdonnais, 7ᵉ (Ecole-Militaire), 01 45 55 59 59

◪ Most diners recommend this "rustic" Regional French near the Ecole Militaire for "very good, copious Southwestern fare", including foie gras eaten with bread you toast yourself, yet there are a few who report "uneven" cooking and say the decor could use a boost; an "amiable" staff and generally "affordable" tabs help tilt the balance in its favor.

AMBASSADEURS (LES) S
| 24 | 26 | 25 | fr696

Hôtel de Crillon, 10, place de la Concorde, 8ᵉ (Concorde), 01 44 71 16 16; fax 01 44 71 15 02

■ The "timeless decor" of this "sumptuous" dining room with marble floors, frescoes and chandeliers is as "magnificent" as its setting in the Hôtel Crillon overlooking the Place de la Concorde; it's "a pleasure for the palate" too thanks to Dominique Bouchet's "superb" French haute cuisine, with further kudos for the "brilliant sommelier", "incomparable wine list" and "attentive, respectful" service that makes diners feel like royalty – which may explain why few balk at the royal prices.

AMBROISIE (L')
27 | 25 | 25 | fr796

9, place des Vosges, 4ᵉ (Bastille/St-Paul), 01 42 78 51 45
■ Admirers use words such as "inspirational", "ambrosial" and "perfection" to describe Bernard Pacaud's French haute cuisine, which is served in a set of "elegant" if somewhat "somber" dining rooms with decor by François-Joseph Graf on the Places des Vosges in the Marais; on the downside, prices are "crazy", service can be "cold" and some say "beware the tiny back room" (could it be they "send all the English-speaking people" there?), but high ratings and the "impossibility of getting reservations" speak for themselves.

Ami Jean (Chez L')
13 | 12 | 14 | fr219

27, rue Malar, 7ᵉ (Invalides/La Tour-Maubourg), 01 47 05 86 89
■ "Good Southwestern French cuisine", including "rustic, savory Basque specialties", plus a "warm welcome", "good wines, convivial" atmosphere and "very reasonable prices" score points for this tiny spot near Les Invalides decked out with "sports decor" (and maybe some "TV sports commentators" at the tables); it's perfect "for rugby fans, with the food the game requires."

AMI LOUIS (CHEZ L') ❶ⓢ
22 | 13 | 16 | fr594

32, rue du Vertbois, 3ᵉ (Arts-et-Métiers), 01 48 87 77 48
☑ "One often sees stars" and "VIPs" (it "survived Clinton's visit") mixed in with the American "tourists" and others who adore this "very French" little bistro near the Place de la République, where "nothing's changed in 50 years"; famous for its foie gras and roast chicken, it serves "ridiculously copious" portions of solid eats ("take a pacemaker"), and if some find it "elitist" and "much too expensive", most are seduced by its "good food and old-fashioned atmosphere."

Ami Pierre (A l') ❶
– | – | – | I

5, rue de la Main d'Or, 11ᵉ (Bastille/Ledru-Rollin), 01 47 00 17 35
The few surveyors who know this old-fashioned bistro à vins behind the Bastille say it "makes you happy to be alive" with its good wines, homey cooking and atmosphere that's so Parisian it could have come "from a film about France made by Americans" (right down to the owner and his wife); low prices round out the pleasure of this "timeless" spot that's "perfect after the theater."

Amognes (Les)
21 | 8 | 13 | fr250

243, rue du Faubourg-St-Antoine, 11ᵉ (Faidherbe-Chaligny), 01 43 72 73 05; fax 01 43 28 77 23
☑ "Inventive cooking" from "a gifted chef" (Thierry Coué) is the reason to discover this modern French bistro in the 11th behind the Bastille – and a reason to overlook decor that, though recently redone, still underwhelms surveyors; service gets mixed marks, but given "gentle prices" and "very good quality", most feel it's an "excellent value."

Ampère (L')
12 | 12 | 12 | fr218

1, rue Ampère, 17ᵉ (Wagram), 01 47 63 72 05; fax 01 47 63 37 33
◪ The cooking of David Schiebold, who trained at nearby Apicius, gets mixed comments from patrons of this dressy bistro in the 17th, with some saying it gets "better and better" and others demurring that it's "insipid"; still, the location near the Place Péreire is convenient, the ambiance is "friendly" (you may "end up talking to people at the next table") and prices are easygoing.

Amphyclès
21 | 16 | 19 | fr598

78, av. des Ternes, 17ᵉ (Porte Maillot), 01 40 68 01 01; fax 01 40 68 91 88
◪ Philippe Groult's "remarkable" French cuisine impresses most diners at this upscale French in the 17th near the Porte Maillot, and it's enhanced by a "very good wine list" and "charming" reception by his wife; there are quibbles – some say the decor "lacks imagination", service isn't always up to snuff and the "nouvelle cuisine–style" fare features some "odd combos" – but the majority salutes "high quality" on all levels.

Amuse Bouche (L')
▽ 18 | 10 | 16 | fr232

186, rue du Château, 14ᵉ (Gaîté/Mouton-Duvernet), 01 43 35 31 61; fax 01 45 38 96 60
■ The decor may be "indifferent", but this "little bistro" in the 14th "compensates" with "good-buy" prix fixe menus featuring "original dishes" from young chef Gilles Lambert (ex Jacques Cagna); most consider it an "excellent address" in a "somewhat lost" part of town.

Anacréon
17 | 7 | 14 | fr232

53, bd St-Marcel, 13ᵉ (Les Gobelins), 01 43 31 71 18; fax 01 43 31 94 94
■ "Excellent food" (including an "exceptional *canard au sang*") in a "noisy", "sad-looking" setting sums up this small French in the 13th run by a former Tour d'Argent chef; "reasonable prices and a very warm welcome" boost its appeal, and while many wish they'd cheer the place up, one pragmatist notes that the decor is probably the only reason it's "still possible to get a table."

Anahï ●S
17 | 15 | 14 | fr281

49, rue Volta, 3ᵉ (Arts-et-Métiers/Temple), 01 48 87 88 24; fax 01 42 77 41 65
■ The Spanish owners, sisters Carmen and Pilar, "are always adorable and amusing" at this hip little South American bistro in a tiled former butcher's shop not far from the Place de la République; besides "excellent meat from the pampas" of Argentina and first-rate Spanish and South American wines, it has "good ambiance" and a "trendy, entertaining crowd", including the occasional celeb; some might go more often if it were less "expensive."

Anahuacalli [S] ▽ 15 9 19 fr190

30, rue des Bernardins, 5e (Maubert-Mutualité), 01 43 26 10 20; fax 01 42 53 06 82

■ The "best authentic Mexican in Paris" and it's "cheap, too" proclaim those partial to this little beamed-ceiling Latin Quarter spot decked out with Mexican glasses, pottery and the odd cactus; while most find it "friendly" and appreciate the "charming" hostess, others detect "little Latin warmth", but maybe they're talking about the "supermild salsa."

André (Chez) ◐ [S] 14 12 15 fr270

12, rue Marbeuf, 8e (Franklin D. Roosevelt), 01 47 20 59 57; fax 01 47 20 18 82

◪ This venerable bistro off the Champs-Elysées may have "lost its media" and fashion crowd, but "you can't get more Parisian" than this place and loyalists love its timelessness, "friendly" service from veteran waitresses and "solid", "reliable" fare; while a few grouse that's it's become "too expensive", others find "good value" here and say this "classic still plays well", especially for lunch or "after the movies."

Androuët 17 13 15 fr327

6, rue Arsène-Houssaye, 8e (Charles de Gaulle-Etoile), 01 42 89 95 00; fax 01 42 89 95 00

■ An "unforgettable voyage to the land of cheese" awaits at this "unique" boutique/restaurant near the Arc de Triomphe, a "mecca" for *fromage* "fanatics" where "everything's made with cheese, even the ice cream"; a few faultfinders feel it's "a little expensive" and knock "dreary" decor and a "menu that doesn't change much", but "if you love cheese, it's a must" – just "don't count on doing much work after lunch" here.

Angelina [S] 12 17 9 fr194

226, rue de Rivoli, 1er (Concorde/Tuileries), 01 42 60 82 00; fax 01 42 86 98 97

◪ This "elegant" tea salon with "red velvet", "Napoleon III decor" across from the Tuileries gardens draws "grannies in pearls" and other fans of its "killer hot chocolate" and "delicious", if pricey, desserts ("ah, the mont blanc!"); the rest of the light menu is deemed "average" and service fares even worse ("dictatorial", "slow as a snail"), but it's handy "for a break from the Louvre" or as a place "to take your cousin from the provinces."

Annapurna ◐ 15 14 13 fr299

32, rue de Berri, 8e (George V), 01 45 63 91 56

◪ Supporters of this Indian just off the Champs-Elysées call it "delicious and transporting", with "chic decor and a sitar player" at night, plus a "calm" ambiance that makes it good "for a business lunch"; others claim it's "not what it once was", but the fact that it's been around for over 30 years must mean it satisfies most.

Antiquaires (Les) S ▽ | 14 | 16 | 17 | ff317

Hôtel Pont Royal, 5-7, rue Montalembert, 7ᵉ (Rue du Bac), 01 42 84 70 11; fax 01 42 84 70 00

■ Few surveyors know this French in the recently reopened Hôtel Pont Royal off the rue du Bac on the Left Bank, perhaps because it's only open for breakfast and lunch, but the glassed-in sidewalk dining room is "tasteful" and the fare is "honorable, if nothing more"; since it's not cheap (though there is a prix fixe), it may have to work to draw the antique dealers (hence the name), editors and politicians who once made this their canteen.

APICIUS | 24 | 16 | 20 | ff602

122, av. de Villiers, 17ᵉ (Péreire), 01 43 80 19 66; fax 01 44 40 09 57

■ A study in "fine quality beautifully executed" is how admirers describe the haute cuisine of Jean-Pierre Vigato, chef-owner of this pricey "grand classic" near the Place Péreire; while few fault his "original, thoughtful" cooking, some feel it's let down by the setting ("dull" decor, "tightly spaced tables") and occasional service lapses, but overall it's a "delight" and perfect for a calm business meal.

Appart' (L') ◑S | 11 | 17 | 12 | ff257

9, rue du Colisée, 8ᵉ (Franklin D. Roosevelt), 01 53 75 16 34; fax 01 53 76 15 39

◩ Decorated to resemble an apartment, this French off the Champs-Elysées elicits better response for its "warm", "cozy" ambiance than for its sometimes "mediocre" "classic" cuisine; scene-watchers also claim that this one-time trendsters' haunt now draws an "older" crowd ("you won't catch anyone under 25 here"), though defenders insist it's still "fashionable" and "a good buy."

A Priori Thé S | 13 | 16 | 11 | ff146

35, Galerie Vivienne, 2ᵉ (Bourse/Palais Royal-Musée du Louvre), 01 42 97 48 75; fax 01 42 97 46 31

■ A "lovely tearoom" in the Galerie Vivienne near the Palais Royal that's an "excellent" choice for "delicious cakes and desserts" and "good salads" in a "calm, relaxing" setting; its "stylish feminine clientele" finds it "perfect for a light meal", even if a few critics carp about "appallingly slow" service and wonder "what's the point of paying these prices?"

Arbre à Cannelle (L') ▽ | 9 | 16 | 10 | ff152

57, passage des Panoramas, 2ᵉ (Bourse), 01 45 08 55 87
14, rue Linné, 5ᵉ (Jussieu), 01 43 31 68 31 S

■ "Talk about ambiance!" rave those smitten by the "charm and character" of this "warm" tearoom in a "historic setting" – "an old-fashioned *chocolaterie*" in a "beautiful" Napoleon III arcade near the Bourse (there's also a branch in the 5th); despite its modest food rating, it's deemed an "excellent buy" and a good choice "for lunch" in "pretty surroundings" with "pleasant service"; the "original and always fresh sweet and savory tarts are recommended."

Arbuci (L') ☾ [S] 11 | 11 | 12 | fr215

25, rue de Buci, 6e (Odéon/St-Germain-des-Prés), 01 44 32 16 00; fax 01 44 32 16 09

◪ Though tougher critics say it has "really fallen off", most agree this "decent brasserie in Saint-Germain" "can be appreciated for its oysters" and rotisserie-grilled meats and fowl; regular live jazz in the downstairs dining room also wins fans, as does the fact that "it's a pretty good buy."

Ardoise (L') ☾ [S] 19 | 6 | 14 | fr237

28, rue du Mont-Thabor, 1er (Concorde/Tuileries), 01 42 96 28 18

■ "Unimaginative decor belies the superior quality of the food" at this "smoky, noisy", "small" and "crowded" Contemporary French bistro not far from the Place de la Concorde and the Tuileries; while many find the service "not great", the welcome is warm and the real appeal is the "excellent cuisine" of young chef Pierre Jay; "one of the best values in Paris."

Argenteuil (L') [S] – | – | – | M

9, rue d'Argenteuil, 1er (Pyramides), 01 42 60 56 22

Not many voters know chef Bruno Schaeffer's Contemporary French bistro between the Avenue de l'Opéra and the Place Vendôme, but those who do say "the tasting menu is actually rather good", which is not surprising since this modern cook surfs between the best of nouvelle cuisine, classic bistro and various foreign influences; prices are moderate, and sidewalk tables are a pleasant option.

Aristide – | – | – | M

121, rue de Rome, 17^e^ (Rome), 01 47 63 17 83; fax 01 47 54 97 55

"Very serious" cooking is offered at this intimate bistro in the 17th near Rome, which may explain why it boasts over a century in business (founded in 1893); though its age may be showing ("a coat of white would be desirable"), most judge it a reliable, solid old-timer.

Aristippe (L') ▽ 17 | 13 | 16 | fr320

8, rue Jean-Jacques Rousseau, 1er (Palais Royal-Musée du Louvre), 01 42 60 08 80; fax 01 42 60 11 13

◪ "Innovative seafood", "friendly" staff and "rustic country decor" of white-painted beams and flowers are winning a following for this spot near the Louvre des Antiquaires; a few holdouts, however, think "service needs to be improved."

Armand au Palais Royal 17 | 17 | 18 | fr313

6, rue du Beaujolais, 1er (Bourse/Palais Royal-Musée du Louvre), 01 42 60 05 11; fax 01 42 96 16 24

■ Though it's been around for years, this French on the northern flank of the Palais Royal hasn't lost its allure as a "classic that's worth the money" for "good cooking" and a "warm welcome" in a vaulted 17th-century room where "you can speak confidentially"; serious and semiformal, it represents a vanishing breed of Parisian restaurants.

ARPÈGE (L') 27 | 20 | 25 | fr789

84, rue de Varenne, 7e (Varenne), 01 45 51 47 33; fax 01 44 18 98 39

◪ No. 2 for Popularity, chef Alain Passard's haute cuisine standout near Les Invalides in the 7th draws superlatives for his "divine", "very creative" fare (rated No. 3 for Food), with fans singling out the "innovative" wild duck, chicken cooked with hay and "great tomato dessert"; service is more controversial ("haughty" vs. "attentive") and the "modern" room with Lalique glass and pearwood strikes some as "stark" and "crowded"; nonetheless, most regard this "gourmet's galaxy" as "expensive but worth it" for a "memorable experience" that's "just about perfect."

Asian ◐ S 11 | 20 | 10 | fr278

30, av. George V, 8e (Alma-Marceau/George V), 01 56 89 11 00; fax 01 56 89 11 01

◪ The "superb", "sophisticated" modern decor draws the most applause at this "huge", "trendy" (some say "pretentious") Asian operating at a "frenetic pace" on two levels just off the Champs-Elysées; despite a few nods for the "charming hostesses", critics pan "disappointing" service and dismiss the "middling" fusion fare as "good for people who don't know anything about Asian food"; then again, no one really seems to come here just for the cooking.

Assassins (Aux) ◐ S ⊅ 7 | 11 | 9 | fr177

40, rue Jacob, 6e (St-Germain-des-Prés), no phone

◪ "Amusing with friends" say revelers who enjoy this rowdy bistro in Saint-Germain that's better known for its saucy sing-alongs and non-PC jokes than its "mediocre" food; while it's "not for the easily offended" (and master fanny pinchers may be lurking in the crowd), those ready to let their hair down say it makes for a "jolly night out."

Assiette (L') S 19 | 8 | 12 | fr433

181, rue du Château, 14e (Gaîté/Mouton-Duvernet), 01 43 22 64 86; fax 01 45 20 54 66

◪ "Pretty good, but expensive" is one take on this plain but plummy little French on the outskirts of Montparnasse, where an upscale crowd, including many politicians, puts a chic spin on the former butcher shop digs; many enjoy the hearty, good-quality eats, but some claim it comes with a dose of attitude: "you may feel undesirable here, but they don't forget you when it's time to bring the check."

Assiette Lyonnaise ◐ S 13 | 10 | 13 | fr201

21, rue Marbeuf, 8e (Alma-Marceau/Franklin D. Roosevelt), 01 47 20 94 80; fax 01 47 23 53 94

14, rue Coquillière, 1er (Les Halles), 01 42 36 51 60; fax 01 40 26 30 20

■ "Simple, but the ingredients are of very good quality" and service is "speedy" at these "no-frills" traditional bistros offering "classic" Lyonnaise cooking "with no surprises" in Les Halles and near the Champs-Elysées; supporters consider them "totally reliable" "havens of good value."

Astier
18 | 10 | 15 | fr208

44, rue J.P. Timbaud, 11ᵉ (Oberkampf/Parmentier), 01 43 57 16 35

■ "It's a tight squeeze, but how well you eat!" at this well-regarded bistro in the slowly gentrifying 11th near République; there's little by way of decor (especially upstairs) and some report "cold service", but its "very Parisian ambiance", "superb cheese tray" and "great wine list" make it "ideal with friends from the provinces or abroad"; best of all, it's a "good buy."

ASTOR (L')
23 | 17 | 20 | fr568

Hôtel Astor, 11, rue d'Astorg, 8ᵉ (Madeleine/St-Augustin), 01 53 05 05 20; fax 01 53 05 05 30

■ Chef Eric Lecerf, a protégé of Joël Robuchon, "has real talent" and turns out "excellent" cuisine ("on its way to three stars" opines one fan) at this Contemporary French in the Hôtel Astor in the 8th; though hardly cheap, it's deemed a "bargain" given the quality and "attentive" service, and while there's less unanimity about the Frédéric Mechiche decor ("elegant" vs. "heavy", "you have to like '50s style"), it's a well-liked "up-and-comer."

Atelier Berger (L')
– | – | – | M

49, rue Berger, 1ᵉʳ (Les Halles/Louvre-Rivoli), 01 40 28 00 00; fax 01 40 28 10 65

Only a handful of voters have visited this new duplex French with minimalist modern decor on the edge of Les Halles, and they'd probably be happy to keep it to themselves given "serious gourmet cooking" from an "enticing menu" by Norwegian chef Jean Christiansen, who trained with Michel Rostang; "motivated service" and "reasonable prices" add to its allure.

Atelier Gourmand
– | – | – | M

20, rue de Tocqueville, 17ᵉ (Villiers), 01 42 27 03 71; fax 01 42 27 03 71

With ocher-and-green decor meant to recall a painter's atelier, this French near Villiers pleases admirers with its "charming welcome and fair prices for carefully executed cooking", though quibblers say service can be "a bit fussy" and "the setting is not as good as the cuisine"; overall, though, it registers as a pleasant option should you find yourself in this part of town.

Atelier Maître Albert
13 | 19 | 14 | fr284

1, rue Maître Albert, 5ᵉ (Maubert-Mutualité), 01 46 33 13 78; fax 01 44 07 01 86

■ This Left Bank Traditional French "two minutes from Notre Dame and the bookstalls" along the Seine is lovely for a "tête-à-tête" thanks to its "romantic" setting with 15th-century charm and generally "honest, authentic cooking" at "good-value" prices; "warm and intimate" with a "superb fireplace", it makes "you feel you're in a country inn", but a fastidious sort asks "why not give it a good dusting?"

Atlas (L') S
18 | 15 | 16 | fr234

12, bd St-Germain, 5ᵉ (Maubert-Mutualité), 01 46 33 86 98; fax 01 40 46 06 56

■ "You must taste the tagine with raisins and almonds", not to mention the "yummy" couscous, urge habitués of this Left Bank Moroccan near the Institute of the Arab World; besides "excellent" food, there's a "welcoming ambiance" and "always smiling" service in a "good-looking" (or is it "kitsch"?) setting; all told, boosters rate it one of Paris' "best" Moroccans.

Auberge Aveyronnaise S
▽ 15 | 11 | 13 | fr199

40, rue Gabriel Lamé, 12ᵉ (Bercy), 01 43 40 12 24; fax 01 43 40 12 15

◪ The hearty cooking of the south-central Aveyron region is the specialty at this French near the Bercy sports arena in the 12th; fans salute its "consistent cuisine" and find the ambiance good "for group meals", and though contrarians carp about "cold decor" that "lacks charm" and a menu that's "too regional", fair prices and service that's "pleasant", if sometimes "slow", work in its favor.

Auberge Bressane (L') S
16 | 14 | 15 | fr254

16, av. de La Motte-Picquet, 7ᵉ (La Tour-Maubourg), 01 47 05 98 37; fax 01 47 05 92 21

■ A stylish crowd – "politicians, preppy young locals" – heads to this "good neighborhood bistro" in the 7th to enjoy "classic" "bourgeois cooking the way we like it" ("delicious chicken with morels", a "magnificent chocolate soufflé"); the "warm, rustic" setting, "friendly owner" and "charming service" also help make it "a sure bet", if a sometimes "noisy, smoky" one.

Auberge Dab (L') ●S
13 | 13 | 13 | fr286

161, av. de Malakoff, 16ᵉ (Porte Maillot), 01 45 00 32 22; fax 01 45 00 58 50

■ There's a "lively, noisy" atmosphere at this "classic brasserie" near the Porte Maillot, and though it strikes some as an "impersonal" "factory", most approve of its "honest", "reasonably priced" cooking, with special mention for the "good" shellfish and tartare; "speedy service" ("too speedy" at times) makes it "good for a business lunch."

Auberge des Dolomites
▽ 18 | 12 | 16 | fr267

38, rue Poncelet, 17ᵉ (Charles de Gaulle-Etoile/Ternes), 01 42 27 94 56; fax 01 47 66 38 54

◪ Admirers say this "charming" French in a quiet part of the 17th is "a good bourgeois neighborhood place where you always eat well" (fish is a specialty), outvoting dissenters who find it rather "precious" and "not what it once was"; "a convivial atmosphere" and "reasonable prices" help tilt the balance in its favor, though some wish they'd add a "room for nonsmokers."

Auberge du Champ de Mars
12 | 12 | 13 | fr219

18, rue de l'Exposition, 7^e (Ecole-Militaire), 01 45 51 78 08

◪ This French near the Eiffel Tower doesn't bowl everyone over ("a neighborhood bistro, nothing more"), but fans call it an "adorable little" place that "makes you feel you're in the country with its warm ambiance"; a "good-value" 100-franc prix fixe menu keeps it "always crowded", even if "a bit of renewal in the kitchen would be welcome."

Auberge du Clou (L') ◐
– | – | – | M

30, av Trudaine, 9 e (Pigalle), 01 48 78 22 48; fax 01 48 78 30 08

A team of young restaurateurs took over what had been a somewhat tired traditional French in the 9th and gave it a good dusting off, refreshing the 'old inn' decor upstairs (the ground floor still sports an old-fashioned look) and offering a modern Eclectic menu with accents from around the world; gently priced prix fixe menus offer a low-risk introduction.

Auberge Etchégorry ⬛
▽ 18 | 15 | 16 | fr234

41, rue Croulebarbe, 13e (Corvisart/Les Gobelins), 01 44 08 83 51; fax 01 44 08 83 69

◪ A venerable old-timer in the 13th near Gobelins, this Basque may "need a paint job", but regulars enjoy its "provincial ambiance" and "generous", "hearty" regional cooking, plus the fact that it's "a good buy"; still, the welcome exhibits temperature swings ("warm" or "rather cold") and some feel the kitchen has gotten "a bit tired."

Auberge Landaise
▽ 18 | 13 | 16 | fr300

23, rue Clauzel, 9^e (St-Georges), 01 48 78 74 40; fax 01 48 78 20 96

◪ Most agree that this Regional French near the Place Saint-Georges serves "good, flavorful" Southwestern cuisine, but surveyors fail to see eye to eye on the cost ("expensive" vs. "a good value") or the ambiance ("convivial" vs. "a bit sad at night"); in any case, the food seems to be what counts.

Auberge Nicolas Flamel ◐
▽ 13 | 20 | 18 | fr237

51, rue de Montmorency, 3^e (Etienne-Marcel/Rambuteau), 01 42 71 77 78; fax 01 42 71 78 79

◪ Traditional French that's "worth a detour for the history" of the 15th-century Marais building in which it's housed (reputed to be the oldest in Paris), even if opinions on the cuisine vary from "good" to "disappointing"; besides the "mythic" setting, it also earns compliments for "very good wines" "chosen by the owner" and "excellent value."

Auberge Pyrénées Cévennes (L') ◐▽
13 | 15 | 15 | fr254

106, rue de la Folie Mericourt, 11e (République), 01 43 57 33 78

◪ The rustic setting, complete with salamis dangling from the ceiling, creates an aura of bonhomie at this Regional French in the 11th, and the hearty Southwestern fare (think cassoulet) is a good match; though some feel it's become "less reliable" since a change of owners a few years ago, prices are easygoing, especially via the prix fixe menus.

Augusta ▽ 18 | 13 | 14 | fr484
98, rue de Tocqueville, 17ᵉ (Malesherbes/Villiers),
01 47 63 39 97; fax 01 47 63 33 97
■ An "elegant", "classic" fish house near Villiers that wins followers with "fine cuisine" showcasing "excellent ingredients" from "the kingdom of the sea"; "thoughtful" service is another compensation for prices that some find "too expensive."

Avant Goût (L') 22 | 10 | 16 | fr230
26, rue Bobillot, 13ᵉ (Place d'Italie), 01 53 80 24 00;
fax 01 53 80 00 77
■ Christophe Beaufront, a young chef with "a lot of potential", is drawing growing numbers of fans to this "noisy" bistro in "a lost corner of Paris" (the 13th), where he offers "delicious", "inventive" contemporary fare via prix fixe menus that are "a super buy"; the recently redecorated setting is "pretty", but the "small" tables are "closely spaced" and you'd better "reserve a week in advance" to get in on weekends.

Avenue (L') ◗ S 11 | 15 | 10 | fr313
41, av. Montaigne, 8ᵉ (Franklin D. Roosevelt),
01 40 70 14 91; fax 01 49 52 13 00
◪ "Great for people-watching" ("see John Galliano and other fashion stars"), this chic French near the Avenue Montaigne is now run by the Costes brothers and has some "typically Costes" attributes, i.e. "simple" food, a "trendy" crowd and "pretty" decor (by Jacques Garcia); critics say it also has poor service and more than a soupçon of attitude – "who you are and what you look like mean more than anything else here, except maybe what bag you carry", but even so some find it "amusing."

Ay!! Caramba!! ◗ S 11 | 17 | 13 | fr162
59, rue de Mouzaïa, 19ᵉ (Pré St-Gervais), 01 42 41 23 80;
fax 01 42 41 50 34
◪ While the "animated", "very noisy" atmosphere at this "loft-like" Mexican in the 19th may not work "for a lovers' supper", it's just right for a "night out with friends"; some find the food "vaguely industrial", others rate it "good", but live music and "easy" prices keep most happy here, as do "tasty margaritas that quickly boost the tab."

Baan-Boran ◗ – | – | – | M
43, rue de Montpensier, 1ᵉʳ (Palais Royal-Musée du Louvre),
01 40 15 90 45; fax 01 40 15 90 45
Not many surveyors have found their way to this tiny new Thai with two pretty dining rooms just across from the Palais Royal, but since it's a "good value", serves late and is handy after the theater, it's worth noting; the extensive menu spans that country's regions (with a few diet dishes), and service is "attentive."

Babylone (Au) ⌐ ▽ 14 | 12 | 11 | fr159
13, rue de Babylone, 7ᵉ (Sèvres-Babylone), 01 45 48 72 13

◼ They only serve lunch at this "very simple" little "family-run" bistro near the Bon Marché department store at Sèvres-Babylone, and if it's not worth crossing town for, the food is "wholesome" and "decent", not to mention cheap; service can be "arrogant if they don't know you", since it draws a solid crowd of regulars, but it's likable enough to have been around for over 50 years.

Bacchantes (Les) ◑ 14 | 12 | 10 | fr183
21, rue de Caumartin, 9ᵉ (Auber/Madeleine/Opéra),
01 42 65 25 35; fax 01 47 42 65 87

◼ "The owner personally selects the wines" at this bistro à vins near the Opéra, but while admirers say it goes down well with "good-quality" "traditional" fare served by a "smiling" staff, detractors find it "disappointing" and say service can be poor; still, prices are easily digestible and it comes in handy "in an area where it's hard to find" a "decent place" to eat.

Baie d'Ha Long (La) ▽ 19 | 13 | 14 | fr270
164, av. de Versailles, 16ᵉ (Porte de St-Cloud), 01 45 24 60 62;
fax 01 42 30 58 98

◼ "Candles everywhere create a romantic atmosphere" at this well-regarded, "refined" Vietnamese in the 16th near the Porte de Saint-Cloud, where an "attentive" (some say "slow") staff serves "fine, aromatic" fare; while "not cheap", that doesn't bother fans who consider it "among the best in this category."

Bains (Les) ◑ 7 | 12 | 7 | fr319
7, rue du Bourg l'Abbé, 3ᵉ (Etienne-Marcel/Réaumur Sébastopol),
01 48 87 01 80; fax 01 48 87 13 70

◼ "Go for a drink and dancing", since this famed nightspot in the 3rd is considered a "better disco" (downstairs) than restaurant (up); while critics find its "overpriced", "mediocre" Franco-Thai menu all wet and dis "waitresses who need training on polite service", another faction thinks it's "decent for such a trendy spot" and "worth the trip for the clientele" and ambiance.

Ballon des Ternes (Le) ◑ⓈS 14 | 12 | 14 | fr258
103, av. des Ternes, 17ᵉ (Porte Maillot), 01 45 74 17 98;
fax 01 45 72 18 84

◼ This "decent" brasserie near the Porte Maillot with "turn-of-the-century" decor and "a very Parisian ambiance" earns nods for its "good shellfish" and tartare, "thick, tasty steaks" and "excellent Gamay"; some cite "noise", "dusty decor" ("expecially upstairs") and prices that are "a bit high for the quality", but most give a thumbs-up to this "traditional, welcoming" spot.

Bamboche (Le) 18 | 14 | 14 | fr350

15, rue de Babylone, 7e (Sèvres-Babylone), 01 45 49 14 40; fax 01 45 49 14 44

■ Though founding chef David Van Laer has moved on to Le Maxence, the new kitchen crew continues to please most patrons of this "lovely, small" Contemporary French near the Bon Marché department store; "bravo to the new chef" (Claude Colliot) say those who cite "imaginative" food served in a stylish room decked out in "warm colors"; book ahead since "tables are limited."

Baracane ◐ ▽ 16 | 9 | 13 | fr226

38, rue des Tournelles, 4e (Bastille), 01 42 71 43 33

■ "Tiny and terrific" sums up this vest-pocket bistro on the edge of the Marais, where diners put up with drab decor in order to enjoy "brilliant cassoulet, confit de canard" and other Southwestern French fare washed down with "good country wines"; service is "pleasant" and it's "an excellent buy" to boot – now if they'd just hire a decorator.

Bar à Huîtres (Le) ◐ [S] 13 | 11 | 12 | fr266

112, bd du Montparnasse, 14e (Raspail/Vavin), 01 43 20 71 01; fax 01 43 20 52 04

33, rue St-Jacques, 5e (Cluny-La Sorbonne/Maubert-Mutualité), 01 44 07 27 37; fax 01 43 26 71 62

33, bd Beaumarchais, 3e (Bastille), 01 48 87 98 92; fax 01 48 87 04 42

◪ "Handy if you have a sudden urge for seafood" or need a bite "after the theater", these oyster bars earn points for their "excellent" bivalves and "good-value seafood platters", but critics shuck off the rest of the fare (and the service) as "just ok" and find the ambiance "noisy"; the new "maritime decor" by Jacques Garcia pleases some, while others mumble "mussels are better on your plate than on the wall."

Bar au Sel (Le) [S] 15 | 15 | 14 | fr314

49, quai d'Orsay, 7e (Invalides), 01 45 51 58 58; fax 01 40 62 97 30

■ The namesake dish, sea bass cooked in a salt crust, is "a delight" at this stylish yet "relaxed" seafooder on the banks of the Seine near Les Invalides, and most find the rest of the fare "well-prepared" and a "good value"; "cheerful", "neo-maritime" decor adds to the enjoyment, but the same can't always be said of service that's sometimes "slow."

Bar des Théâtres ◐ [S] 11 | 11 | 13 | fr239

6, av. Montaigne, 8e (Alma-Marceau), 01 47 23 34 63; fax 01 47 50 72 23

◪ "Excellent steak tartare", a "strategic" location on the superchic Avenue Montaigne and a "beautiful-people" crowd are the big appeals of this "noisy", "lively" Parisian "classic", though most agree the real "show is in the dining room", not on the Traditional French menu ("the priciest fast food in Paris" sniffs a critic); if "not what it used to be", it's still a place "to be seen" and "perfect after the theater."

Barfly ◕ 🅂   7 | 15 | 7 | fr284
49, av. George V, 8ᵉ (George V), 01 53 67 84 60; fax 01 53 67 84 67
☑ Its "see and be seen" phase may have peaked and it was never revered for its food, but this "noisy", "smoky" singles bar/restaurant off the Champs-Elysées is still hanging in there, drawing "wanna-be models" and others who nibble on Eclectic eats (sushi and brunch earn nods) amid modern decor; critics swat "mediocre" fare and "neophyte service."

Baron Rouge (Le) 🅂   ▽ 9 | 14 | 12 | fr146
1, rue Théophile Roussel, 12ᵉ (Ledru-Rollin), 01 43 43 14 32
☑ "My fondest memories of Paris always include the day I first pulled up here" muses one fan of this wine bar near the Marché d'Aligre; you go "for the wine and ambiance", not the food (charcuterie, fromage), though it is fun "to eat oysters on Sunday while standing at barrel tables with the regulars"; P.S. "the uninitiated" may face a cool welcome.

Barramundi ◕   ▽ 10 | 19 | 10 | fr241
3, rue Taitbout, 9ᵉ (Richelieu-Drouot), 01 47 70 21 21; fax 01 47 70 21 20
☑ "The elegant, stylish setting" at this fashionable new restaurant in the 9th draws compliments, but while some find the Eclectic menu "rather good", others think it "would be better if it were simplified"; service can leave something to be desired but there's a "good bar" for consolation.

Barrio Latino ◕🅂   8 | 21 | 8 | fr245
46-48, rue Faubourg St-Antoine, 12ᵉ (Bastille), 01 55 78 84 75; fax 01 55 78 84 76
☑ With its "exceptional" multilevel setting – a former furniture showroom near the Bastille with "sumptuous" neo-Latino decor – and "torrid ambiance" complete with a "superhot DJ" and stylish crowd, this newcomer has "lots to look at", so maybe it doesn't matter if critics carp about "ordinary" Latino fare and "badly organized service"; one party pooper sighs "it's too much, or maybe I'm too old."

Bartolo ◕🅂⊭   17 | 6 | 9 | fr231
7, rue des Canettes, 6ᵉ (St-Germain-des-Prés), 01 43 26 27 08
☑ Though the wood-burning pizza oven is pretty much the decor at this snug Saint-Germain Italian, all agree the pizzas are "excellent" and the pastas and other dishes "sublime"; some lament "high" prices and "forced smiles from the waiters if you're not a regular", but "one eats so well here."

Bar Vendôme 🅂   16 | 18 | 17 | fr380
Hôtel Ritz, 15, place Vendôme, 1ᵉʳ (Concorde/Madeleine), 01 43 16 33 63; fax 01 43 16 33 75
■ Almost everyone enjoys the "luxurious" elegance of this bar at the Hôtel Ritz that's "excellent for lunch, tea and drinks"; while perhaps a tad "pretentious" and more than a tad pricey, it's "lovely" for a "classy snack" or cocktail, with smart service, "good people-watching" and a plush terrace.

Bascou (Au)
18 | 11 | 14 | fr258

*38, rue Réaumur, 3ᵉ (Arts-et-Métiers), 01 42 72 69 25;
fax 01 42 72 69 25*

■ "Great regional dining", specifically "savory", "true Basque cooking", is featured at this "remarkable" bistro near the Place de la République; "ah, the wines" sighs one fan who, like many, praises the "warm setting", "friendly welcome" and "extraordinarily nice" owner; regulars might appreciate a few "innovations" once in a while, but that's a quibble.

Basilic (Le) 🅂
11 | 14 | 11 | fr260

*2, rue Casimir Périer, 7ᵉ (Invalides/Solférino), 01 44 18 94 64;
fax 01 47 53 77 96*

▨ The "tranquil" terrace "with a view of Sainte-Clothilde" church makes this "chic" French in the 7th an "oasis" come summer, even if enthusiasm is more measured for the "decent bourgeois-style" food ("leaves no real memory"); service sometimes falters and the interior can be "smoky and noisy", but overall it's not without "charm."

Bastide Odéon (La)
20 | 13 | 15 | fr264

7, rue Corneille, 6ᵉ (Odéon), 01 43 26 03 65; fax 01 44 07 28 93

■ Chef Gilles Ajuelos turns out "generous", "well-prepared" fare that captures the "perfume of Provence" at this "friendly" bistro near the Odéon theater and the Luxembourg garden; if the "rather somber" decor "isn't at the level of the cooking" and some say service "needs rethinking", it's hard to argue with such "creativity and flavor" for such "reasonable prices."

Bath's
19 | 16 | 15 | fr352

*9, rue de La Trémoille, 8ᵉ (Alma-Marceau), 01 40 70 01 09;
fax 01 40 70 01 22*

■ "Promising" newcomer helmed by Jean-Yves Bath, formerly of Clermont-Ferrand, now dishing up "delicious" "modernized cuisine from the Auvergne" near the Champs-Elysées; the decor (complete with a painting on velvet) "isn't very original", but the ambiance is "pleasant" and service (directed by Bath's son) is "adorable", if not always up to speed; lunch is an "affordable" way to try it.

Baumann Ternes ◖🅂
14 | 12 | 13 | fr285

*64, av. des Ternes, 17ᵉ (Charles de Gaulle-Etoile/Ternes),
01 45 74 16 66; fax 14 57 21 44 32*

■ Fans say this "classic" brasserie near the Place des Ternes is a "shade better" than most, touting its "choucroute with fish – a dream", and its "very original tartares"; despite grumbles about "expensive" prices, "kind of dull" decor and service that's not always up to snuff, it's considered reliable for a "well-prepared" meal.

Bauta (La)
17 | 12 | 14 | fr303

129, bd du Montparnasse, 6ᵉ (Vavin), 01 43 22 52 35;
fax 01 43 22 10 99

◪ According to one faction, this Venetian near Vavin is a place to enjoy "authentic" cuisine served by a "serious but warm" staff in a setting adorned with "Venetian pictures and masks"; yet even some fans think it's pricey for "rather skimpy" portions, and critics, while outvoted, see it differently ("becoming banal", "arrogant service").

Béatilles (Les)
19 | 13 | 17 | fr307

11 bis, rue Villebois-Mareuil, 17ᵉ (Charles de Gaulle-Etoile/
Ternes), 01 45 74 43 80; fax 01 45 74 43 81

■ This intimate, "serene" French off the Avenue des Ternes offers a "warm welcome" and "original menu" of "excellent" nouvelle-style cuisine; most complaints are mild ("always good but lacks something", "prices perhaps too high"), with the main debate centered around the decor: "relaxing" and "kind of Zen" to some, it's "sterile" and "cold" to others.

Beato
15 | 12 | 13 | fr344

8, rue Malar, 7ᵉ (Invalides), 01 47 05 94 27; fax 01 45 55 64 41

◪ "Chic but costly" Italian in the smart 7th offering "very good, no-surprises" cooking accompanied by Italian wines; it strikes some as "a bit stiff", but the fashionable clientele says you can enjoy "a great Italian moment" here.

Beaujolais d'Auteuil (Le) 🆂
13 | 11 | 13 | fr202

99, bd de Montmorency, 16ᵉ (Porte d'Auteuil), 01 47 43 03 56;
fax 01 46 51 27 81

■ A "bistro the way Parisians like them, with checked tablecloths", "family-style cooking", a "convivial" ambiance and, last but not least, "very good value" sums up this local haunt near Roland Garros Stadium; most find it "honest" and "pleasant", even if it "could use a little rejuvenating."

Beauvilliers (A.)
22 | 24 | 19 | fr578

52, rue Lamarck, 18ᵉ (Lamarck-Caulaincourt), 01 42 54 54 42;
fax 01 42 62 70 30

■ The "superb Napoleon III" decor ("even the rest rooms are refined"), "sumptuous flowers" and pretty terrace are the big draws at this "mythic" Montmartre French, and if some say the cooking is "declining", most still rate it "excellent"; in any case, the place is "so charming you think it's better than it is", at least until you get the hefty check.

Bec Rouge (Le)
▽ 14 | 9 | 13 | fr218

33, rue de Constantinople, 8ᵉ (Villiers), 01 45 22 15 02;
fax 01 45 22 35 03

■ "It's Alsace", or so it seems at this bistro near Villiers, appreciated for its "excellent meat" and "authentic Alsatian specialties" from Maurice Bitsch, who trained with Gérard Vié and Marc Meneau; the "value" factor also pleases, as does the "appealing" atmosphere – "modern without airs."

Bellecour (Le) ◐ 19 | 13 | 17 | fr375

22, rue Surcouf, 7e (Invalides/La Tour-Maubourg), 01 45 51 46 93; fax 01 45 50 30 11

■ This little "gem" near Les Invalides is a virtual "embassy" of Lyonnaise cuisine, earning goodwill with its "fine" food and "very complete wine list"; "attentive" service and a "good-value prix fixe" add to the pleasure, which is why few mind the "old-fashioned" decor and "crowded" tables.

Bellini ▽ 15 | 13 | 16 | fr287

28, rue Le Sueur, 16e (Argentine), 01 45 00 54 20; fax 01 45 00 11 74

■ "Good Italian cuisine" can be found at this "intimate" spot with "plush" (or is it "tacky"?) decor between the Porte Maillot and the Etoile; prices are considered "reasonable" by the well-heeled crowd it attracts.

Benkay [S] 20 | 17 | 18 | fr502

Hôtel Nikko, 61, quai de Grenelle, 15e (Bir-Hakeim/ Charles Michels), 01 40 58 21 26; fax 01 40 58 21 30

■ "If you like Japanese food there's no better place in Paris" and "what a view!" enthuse fans of this "grand classic" in the Hôtel Nikko overlooking the Seine in the 15th; tabs are as lofty as the quality, but that doesn't seem to deter devotees (including many Japanese) who lavish praise on its "very good" food and "attentive service."

Benoît [S] 21 | 18 | 19 | fr466

20, rue St-Martin, 4e (Châtelet), 01 42 72 25 76; fax 01 42 72 45 68

◪ "Horribly expensive" it may be, but this "Rolls-Royce of Paris bistros" near the Pompidou Center rolls on, inspiring patrons ("80 percent Americans" some claim) to dig deeper into their pockets to enjoy "wonderful classic recipes" in a "beautiful" old bistro setting; though not everyone is charmed ("pretentious", "cold reception", "lives on its rep"), many "would go more often if prices were lower."

Bermuda Onion ◐ [S] 9 | 16 | 11 | fr273

16, rue Linois, 15e (Charles Michels), 01 45 75 11 11; fax 01 40 59 92 94

◪ "Memorable view, memorable waitresses, forgettable food" is a fairly typical take on this "trendy" New French overlooking the river in Beaugrenelle; but even if brunch seems to be the culinary apex and many find it a bit "pricey" for what it is, the "amusing" trompe l'oeil decor, "pretty terrace" and "cute" servers still have drawing power.

Bernardaud 13 | 16 | 12 | fr219

9, rue Royale, 8e (Concorde), 01 42 66 22 55; fax 01 47 42 60 06

■ "So convenient for darlings of both sexes who are tired out after shopping" nearby, this tea salon run by Bernardaud in an arcade off the rue Royale lets patrons select the cups (Bernardaud, *bien sûr*) from which they'd like to sip at teatime; the food's pretty "good" and it's "an ideal place to invite a preppy friend", since it's "elegant" and "relaxing."

Berry's (Le) ◐ ▽ 14 | 12 | 14 | fr217

46, rue de Naples, 8e (Villiers), 01 40 75 01 56; fax 01 45 61 24 76

◪ This bistro near Villiers with "slightly tired rugby decor" is the little brother of Le Grenadin and features cuisine from the Berry region; while some say "it's an excellent buy", others contend the food "lacks imagination", but "smiling service" and old-fashioned ambiance please regulars.

Berthoud (Le) ◐ 16 | 13 | 14 | fr260

1, rue Valette, 5e (Maubert-Mutualité), 01 43 54 38 81; fax 01 43 54 98 38

◪ Tucked away in a side street near the Panthéon is this little French bistro known for its egg dishes, soups, vegetable purees and desserts; supporters say it's "always true to form", with "agreeable" food and a "warm" atmosphere, but dissenters claim it's just "not what it used to be."

Bertie's [S] 16 | 16 | 17 | fr340

Hôtel Baltimore, 1, rue Léo Delibes, 16e (Boissière), 01 44 34 54 34; fax 01 44 34 54 44

■ "Veddy British" Anglo restaurant in the Hôtel Baltimore, with "good-quality cuisine", "well-chosen wines" and the "ambiance of an English club"; "don't miss game in season" or the excellent array of whiskeys advise fans, solidly outvoting doubters who claim it "doesn't do justice to the quality of what you can find on the other side of the Channel."

Beudant (Le) ▽ 16 | 14 | 16 | fr269

97, rue des Dames, 17e (Rome/Villiers), 01 43 87 11 20; fax 01 43 87 27 35

■ There's a "young chef" turning out "serious" food at this low-profile (maybe even "forgotten") French near Villiers, and "excellent value" is a reason to remember it; besides some of the "best foie gras in Paris", it's cited for its "chic" ambiance, "discreet service" and "perfect welcome."

Biche au Bois (A la) 21 | 10 | 17 | fr214

45, av. Ledru-Rollin, 12e (Gare de Lyon), 01 43 43 34 38

■ The fan who'd like to keep this bistro near the Gare de Lyon "secret" must not have noticed that it's often "crowded" with people enjoying "excellent" fare (including "remarkable" game) at "best-buy" prices; there's a "warm welcome" and "agreeable service", and if the decor could use a "redo", your "taste buds won't care because they're in for a treat."

Bistro 121 ◐[S] 17 | 13 | 16 | fr312

121, rue de la Convention, 15e (Boucicaut/Convention), 01 45 57 52 90; fax 01 45 57 14 69

◪ Devotees of this bistro in the 15th don't mind if it's a bit "outdated", calling it "a classic one is always happy to visit" for "huge portions" of "good" food in an "old-fashioned" setting; critics knock "uninteresting cuisine" and service that "favors regulars", and though you may "feel you're in the provinces" here, prices are solidly Parisian.

Bistro de Gala (Le) ☽

| – | – | – | M |

45, rue du Faubourg-Montmartre, 9ᵉ (Grands Boulevards/Le Peletier), 01 40 22 90 50; fax 01 40 22 98 30

The few surveyors who know this bistro in the Faubourg Montmartre think it's an "excellent" option in an area where pickings are slim; expect "simple but pleasant" theater-poster decor and good-buy prix fixe menus from a chef who follows the seasons and offers an unusual cheese tray with choices from northern France; for trivia buffs: it's named for the wife of a former owner.

Bistro de la Grille ☽ S

| 13 | 14 | 13 | fr206 |

14, rue Mabillon, 6ᵉ (Mabillon), 01 43 54 16 87; fax 01 43 54 16 87

■ This "inexpensive" bistro in the heart of Saint-Germain may be "nothing extraordinary", but it's appreciated for its "warm decor", "attentive service" and "solid", "traditional" fare; what's more, "you can see stars here", though they're not at the tables but rather on the walls, which sport photos of French film celebs; nonstop service is a plus.

Bistro de l'Olivier

| ▽ | 18 | 16 | 16 | fr277 |

13, rue Quentin Bauchart, 8ᵉ (George V), 01 47 20 17 00; fax 01 47 20 17 04

■ Though just off the Avenue George V, this little bistro transports diners to Provence with its "savory" cuisine, regional wines and "cozy" decor; "calm" and "pleasant", it's "ideal for a business lunch" or "evening tête-à-tête", and some deem it "the best buy around the Champs-Elysées."

Bistro des Deux Théâtres (Le) ☽ S

| 12 | 11 | 12 | fr228 |

18, rue Blanche, 9ᵉ (Trinité), 01 45 26 41 43; fax 01 48 74 08 92

☑ "The prix fixe is a good deal" and the cooking is "decent and unpretentious" at this "bustling", "well-established" bistro near Trinity church that's "convenient" pre- or post-theater; however, some complain that it's "overcrowded (you'd think you were in the métro)" and say "too many busloads of tourists" can cause service to "fall off."

Bistro d'Hubert (Le) S

| 17 | 16 | 17 | fr268 |

41, bd Pasteur, 15ᵉ (Pasteur), 01 47 34 15 50; fax 01 45 67 03 09

☑ With "pretty" decor worthy of a magazine, this stylish contemporary bistro in the 15th makes diners feel they're in a chic "country kitchen", and most find the "copious, fairly creative" food and "nice service" equally appealing; a few judge it "uneven" and what's "good value" to some is "overpriced" to others, but overall it's "recommendable."

Bistro du 17ème (Le) ☽ S

| 13 | 10 | 12 | fr205 |

108, av. de Villiers, 17ᵉ (Péreire), 01 47 63 32 77; fax 01 42 27 67 66

■ Calling all bargain hunters for "an excellent buy" at this "one-menu-fits-all" bistro near the Place Péreire in the 17th; its "all-inclusive" prix fixe formula means "no surprises", which is fine with locals just seeking a "decent" meal; P.S. you'd "better reserve" and brace for "noise" at peak hours.

Bistro Melrose ◐ 🆂
∇ 13 | 12 | 11 | fr212

*5, place de Clichy, 17ᵉ (Place de Clichy), 01 42 93 61 34;
fax 01 42 93 76 45*

■ Snobs may judge it "marvelously ordinary", but those who approach this "efficient" bistro on the Place de Clichy with the right expectations praise its "good food and decor" and call its set-price menu an "unbeatable value"; it's fine "for a simple business meal" too, though some report an "unsatisfying reception."

Bistrot d'à Côté
15 | 13 | 14 | fr263

*10, rue Gustave Flaubert, 17ᵉ (Péreire/Ternes), 01 42 67 05 81;
fax 01 47 63 82 75* 🆂
*16, av. de Villiers, 17ᵉ (Villiers), 01 47 63 25 61; fax 01 47 64 35 84
4, rue Boutard, Neuilly-sur-Seine (Pont-de-Neuilly),
01 47 45 34 55; fax 01 47 45 15 08*

Bistrot...Côté Mer 🆂

*16, bd St-Germain, 5ᵉ (Cardinal Lemoine/Maubert-Mutualité),
01 43 54 59 10; fax 01 43 29 02 08*

▰ "Rich and savory" bistro fare served at "decent" prices in a "simple, pretty" setting is what you can expect at these upscale bistros created by Michel Rostang; they're crowd-pleasers, even if some find them "nothing special" and a bit "precious", with "service that could be improved"; N.B. Rostang's daughter has revamped the Latin Quarter site and added a seafood focus to the menu.

Bistrot d'Albert
∇ 21 | 18 | 21 | fr179

*150, bd Péreire, 17ᵉ (Péreire/Porte Champerret), 01 48 88 93 68;
fax 01 48 88 93 68*

■ According to the mostly happy handful of surveyors who know this easygoing bistro in the 17th near the Place Péreire, it's a "sweet" place offering "honest food" and a "very nice welcome", though some find the decor a bit "dull"; economical prix fixe menus are a plus.

Bistrot d'Alex
∇ 16 | 13 | 17 | fr277

*2, rue Clément, 6ᵉ (Mabillon/Odéon), 01 43 54 09 53;
fax 01 43 25 77 66*

▰ This longstanding bistro near the Odéon draws book editors, politicians and others who appreciate its "very good" Lyonnaise and Provençal cuisine, "nice local atmosphere" and "friendly owner" who is "maintaining the family tradition"; still, it's not immune to criticism: "lacks invention", decor "dated", service "slow when crowded."

Bistrot d'André (Le)
∇ 13 | 11 | 11 | fr165

232, rue St-Charles, 15ᵉ (Balard), 01 45 57 89 14; fax 01 45 57 97 15

■ While it once fed workers from the original Citroën car factory that stood nearby (the name refers to André Citroën), this vintage 1909 bistro in the 15th today pulls bargain-hunters who call it an "astonishing value"; it's adorned with Citroën memorabilia, and those who aren't crazy about the car say "happily, the food is better than the auto brand."

Bistrot de Breteuil (Le) 🅂   14 | 13 | 15 | fr219
*3, place de Breteuil, 7ᵉ (Duroc/Sèvres-Lecourbe),
01 45 67 07 27; fax 01 42 73 11 08*

■ The major draws of this bistro in the quiet, affluent 7th are its "terrace overlooking Les Invalides" and the fact that its all-inclusive prix fixe menus are "a very good value"; even if there's "no surprise" here, the cooking is pretty "good" and service is "attentive"; it can get "noisy" though.

Bistrot de l'Etoile Lauriston ◑   19 | 13 | 16 | fr290
*19, rue Lauriston, 16ᵉ (Charles de Gaulle-Etoile/Kléber),
01 40 67 11 16; fax 01 45 00 99 87*

■ "The taste of a grand restaurant on a reasonable budget" explains the appeal of this "chic" Guy Savoy bistro not far from the Etoile; an "attractive" crowd enjoys its "inventive cooking" and "friendly service", and if the "minimalist decor with strong lighting" doesn't suit everyone ("atmosphere of a hospital"), most still give the place a "big bravo."

Bistrot de l'Etoile Niel ◑   16 | 12 | 13 | fr271
75, av. Niel, 17ᵉ (Péreire), 01 42 27 88 44; fax 01 42 27 32 12

■ Another member of Guy Savoy's bistro trio near the Etoile, offering a "wisely inventive" menu with a "good quality/price ratio"; fans call it "a good place to feel cozy and cosseted", but service can be "slow" and one hungry patron complains that "portions are basically symbolic."

Bistrot de l'Etoile Troyon ◑   17 | 11 | 16 | fr261
*13, rue Troyon, 17ᵉ (Charles de Gaulle-Etoile), 01 42 67 25 95;
fax 01 46 22 43 09*

■ "Bravo Guy Savoy!" cheer patrons of the chef's original bistro offshoot, across from his eponymous flagship in the 17th; drawing a business crowd at noon and well-dressed couples at night, it provides "excellent" food and "good value", and if "it would be harder to be more squeezed in" than in this "minuscule" room, it's "good for a tête-à-tête."

Bistrot de l'Université   ▽ 14 | 12 | 12 | fr224
*40, rue de l'Université, 7ᵉ (Rue du Bac), 01 42 61 26 64;
fax 01 42 61 26 64*

■ A "very pleasant neighborhood bistro" in the stylish 7th frequented by publishing types, antiques dealers and other "Left Bank regulars" who like its "low prices", "good" food and "nice staff", even if service can be slow ("if you want to lunch in a reasonable time, forget it" says one); some find the decor "plain", but it has pretty vintage stucco moldings.

Bistrot de Marius (Le) ◑🅂   14 | 11 | 12 | fr290
6, av. George V, 8ᵉ (Alma-Marceau), 01 40 70 11 76

◪ This bistro annex to next-door Marius et Janette near the Place de l'Alma reels in "an Avenue Montaigne" crowd for "good seafood", even though comments suggest that service isn't always shipshape ("slow", "inefficient"); while not cheap, fans find the prices "honest."

Bistrot de Paris (Le) 🇸 14 | 13 | 13 | fr283
33, rue de Lille, 7e (Rue du Bac), 01 42 61 16 83; fax 01 49 27 06 09
◧ "Coming back up" say fans of this traditional bistro near the Musée d'Orsay, and if it still has a ways to go before regaining the prestige it enjoyed under founding chef Michel Oliver, it offers a "good compromise between quality and price" in "an expensive part of town"; it can be "noisy", though, and outvoted dissenters find it "disappointing."

Bistrot d'Henri (Le) ◕ ▽ 16 | 15 | 17 | fr233
16, rue Princesse, 6e (Mabillon/St-Germain-des-Prés), 01 46 33 51 12
◧ Vest-pocket bistro in Saint-Germain with old-fashioned moleskin banquettes, souvenir-adorned walls and "decent" eats; despite a "lack of space", admirers say it's a "pleasant place for convivial meals", but doubters say "slipping."

Bistrot du Dôme (Le) 🇸 17 | 13 | 15 | fr268
2, rue de la Bastille, 4^e (Bastille), 01 48 04 88 44; fax 01 48 04 00 59 ◕
1, rue Delambre, 14^e (Vavin), 01 43 35 32 00; fax 01 48 04 00 59
■ Seafood lovers salute these bistro spawn of the grand Le Dôme, one near the parent in Montparnasse and the other at the Bastille; they offer "very good fish for very small prices" in "cute" settings with "lamps shaped like grape clusters"; but "they could renew the menu from time to time."

Bistrot du Louvre ▽ 15 | 13 | 14 | fr275
48, rue d'Argout, 2^e (Sentier), 01 45 08 47 46
■ "Undeservedly unknown" say those who call this bistro in the garment district not far from the stock exchange a "rare good address in a neighborhood increasingly full of industrial-style eateries"; though not cheap, it offers sturdy fare and something of a "journalistic ambiance", perhaps because the offices of Le Figaro aren't too far away.

Bistrot du Peintre (Le) ◕🇸 ▽ 12 | 14 | 12 | fr152
116, av. Ledru-Rollin, 11^e (Ledru-Rollin), 01 47 00 34 39; fax 01 47 00 34 39
■ "Pretty" art nouveau decor and "honest cooking" add up to a "super bistro" according to fans of this hangout for Bastille hipsters in the 11th; "excellent steak tartare" is a hit, and the "very cheap" prices don't hurt a bit.

Bistrot du Sommelier 17 | 12 | 17 | fr397
97, bd Haussmann, 8^e (St-Augustin), 01 42 65 24 85; fax 01 53 75 23 23
■ Calling all vinophiles to this French in the 8th, where master sommelier/owner Philippe Faure-Brac offers a "voyage through the vineyards" via his "remarkable cellar" and "interesting" prix fixe menus pairing food with wines; if some feel the "cooking isn't up to" the drink, more rate it "very good" overall, so "go test your wine knowledge", having been forewarned that it's "a bit expensive."

Bistrot Papillon (Le) ▽ | 19 | 17 | 19 | fr295
6, rue Papillon, 9ᵉ (Cadet), 01 47 70 90 03;
fax 01 48 24 05 59

■ Surveyors who know this Traditional French near the Square de Montholon in the 9th have nothing but good words for its "excellent" food, "friendly service" and "pleasant" setting with circa 1900 decor; it's also judged a "good deal", with very reasonable prix fixe menus.

Bistrot St. Ferdinand ◑Ⓢ | 14 | 14 | 13 | fr194
275, bd Péreire, 17ᵉ (Porte Maillot), 01 45 74 33 32;
fax 01 45 74 33 12

■ "Value" is key to the appeal of this bistro near the Porte Maillot offering an all-inclusive prix fixe menu that's "good" and "consistent", if "not surprising", in an appealing setting with trompe l'oeil bookcases and a winter garden–style salon; maybe service can be "slow" and the locals it attracts can be noisy, but most leave satisfied and solvent.

Bistrot St. James ▽ | 14 | 13 | 16 | fr262
2, rue Général Henrion-Berthier, Neuilly-sur-Seine
(Pont-de-Neuilly), 01 46 24 21 06

■ "A bit hidden but worth looking for" say patrons of this "calm" bistro in Neuilly where the cooking is well executed if a bit "heavy", the wines are "excellent" and the service "warm"; it's the kind of place where you can just "order a little dish" without encountering "any pretension", and if some feel regulars get the best treatment, that's not such a bad thing.

BLUE ELEPHANT ◑Ⓢ | 20 | 24 | 15 | fr329
43-45, rue de la Roquette, 11ᵉ (Bastille/Voltaire),
01 47 00 42 00; fax 01 47 00 45 44

■ Paris' "best Thai" may be this beauty near the Bastille with "superb" food, a "sumptuous" plant-filled, teak-floored setting and generally "good service" ("because they're not French" opines one snide foreigner); a few call it a case of "much ado about nothing", but to most it offers instant "exoticism" albeit at "elephantine prices" – which may be why it draws a more mature media crowd despite being in a hip young area.

Bœuf Couronné (Au) ◑ | 17 | 14 | 15 | fr324
188, av. Jean Jaurès, 19ᵉ (Porte de Pantin), 01 42 39 44 44;
fax 01 42 39 17 30

■ "One of the last good meat-eater restaurants in the Villette area" (former site of the Paris slaughterhouses) is this vintage brasserie with "old-fashioned decor and divine steak tartare"; it's a "nostalgic" favorite of the old-boys' set, with "excellent meat" and "adorable service" that are good enough to justify "substantial prices" in an out-of-the-way part of town.

Bœuf sur le Toit (Le) ●🅂
13 | 17 | 13 | f286

34, rue du Colisée, 8ᵉ (St-Philippe-du-Roule),
01 53 93 65 55; fax 01 45 63 45 40

☑ Partisans of this art deco brasserie off the Champs-Elysées say "you have to go from time to time" for its "handsome 1930s decor", "amusing", "very French" ambiance and "decent", if somewhat "chain"-like, food (it's owned by the Flo group); critics call it a "factory" that's "much too noisy" ("loud guests? – bring them here, no one will notice"), but service is "pleasant" and there are some good prix fixe deals.

Bofinger ●🅂
15 | 21 | 15 | f301

5, rue de la Bastille, 4ᵉ (Bastille), 01 42 72 87 82; fax 01 42 72 97 68

☑ With "very pretty" decor including a "beautiful" glass cupola in the main room, this 19th-century brasserie near the Bastille is a hit with "tourists" and "handy after the opera" nearby; while the food doesn't bring the house down, it's generally "well prepared" and nods go to the "good choucroute and shellfish"; still, some sigh "like a lot of Paris institutions it's become just that, institutional."

Bon ●🅂
– | – | – | M

25, rue de la Pompe, 16ᵉ (La Muette), 01 40 72 70 00;
fax 01 40 72 68 30

Paris is all abuzz over this newcomer in the 16th from designer Philippe Starck and Laurent Taïeb (Lô Sushi); as you'd expect from Starck, the multiroom setting is eye-popping, complete with a conveyor-belt sushi bar, oversized sofas and a communal table, and the menu has a healthy slant (notes detail the supposed benefits of each dish), offering organic goods, sushi and other fare that won't do much damage to the waistlines of the fashionable clientele.

Bon Accueil (Au)
18 | 11 | 13 | f274

14, rue de Monttessuy, 7ᵉ (Alma-Marceau), 01 47 05 46 11

☑ "Fine, inventive" cuisine and "exceptional value" explain the popularity of this "neighborhood bistro" near the Champ de Mars in the 7th; in fact, it may be too popular, given reports that it can be "overcrowded" and "noisy", with "overwhelmed" service and a reception that's "the opposite of the name" (which means "good welcome"); on the whole, though, it's a crowd-pleaser.

Bonne Table (A la)
– | – | – | M

42, rue Friant, 14ᵉ (Porte d'Orléans), 01 45 39 74 91;
fax 01 45 43 66 92

This inventive French in the 14th wins praise from the few voters who know it for "good cooking" from a Japanese chef-owner (Yasunara Kawamoto) adept at "linking Asian flavors" with French cuisine, as in dishes such as a salad of shrimp with fresh herbs and salmon sashimi; decor that's "pretty" to some is "sad" to others, but most would agree it's "a good buy", with a 146-franc prix fixe menu.

Bon Saint Pourçain (Le) [S] ⊄ ▽ 15 | 12 | 15 | fr213
10 bis, rue Servandoni, 6e (Odéon/St-Sulpice), 01 43 54 93 63
■ Ideal on "cold evenings" and "pleasant" just about any time, this simple bistro behind the church of Saint-Sulpice in Saint-Germain has been "unchanged" for years, offering "good" food and "smiling" service at "gentle" prices; "if I didn't hold myself back, I'd eat there every day" sighs a fan.

Bons Crus (Aux) – | – | – | I
7, rue des Petits Champs, 1er (Bourse), 01 42 60 06 45; fax 01 42 60 09 66
It "really needs a coat of paint, but it's a pleasant place" says one patron of this long-running bistro à vins not far from the Place des Victoires with a mostly Lyonnaise menu that's "simple and good" and wines that are "better than honest"; bargain prices are welcome in this trendy area.

Bookinistes (Les) ◑ [S] 18 | 15 | 15 | fr284
53, quai des Grands-Augustins, 6e (St-Michel), 01 43 25 45 94; fax 01 43 25 23 07
◪ "Style and substance" is what most diners find at Guy Savoy's "trendy" Left Bank bistro overlooking the Seine in the 6th, where "creative" food is served in a "spirited" postmodern setting with colorful glass sconces, mirrors and distressed walls; some see it differently ("cold", "snobby"), but that doesn't bother the chic, "noisy" crowd it attracts.

Boucholeurs (Les) 17 | 13 | 16 | fr276
34, rue de Richelieu, 1er (Palais Royal-Musée du Louvre/ Pyramides), 01 42 96 06 86
■ Considered "a must for mussel lovers", this seafooder near the Palais Royal gets good marks for its food and service, and one swept-away diner goes so far as to call it "the most romantic restaurant I know – Brittany as it should have been"; regulars say "the simplest dishes are best" and also appreciate owners who are "almost like friends."

BOUCHONS DE FRANÇOIS CLERC (LES) 15 | 13 | 13 | fr293
12, rue de l'Hôtel Colbert, 5e (Maubert-Mutualité), 01 43 54 15 34; fax 01 46 34 68 07
7, rue du Boccador, 8e (Alma-Marceau), 01 47 23 57 80; fax 01 47 23 74 54
32, bd du Montparnasse, 15e (Duroc/Falguière), 01 45 48 52 03; fax 01 45 48 52 17
79, av. Kléber, 16e (Trocadéro), 01 47 27 87 58; fax 01 47 04 60 97 [S]
22, rue de la Terrasse, 17e (Villiers), 01 42 27 31 51; fax 01 42 27 45 76
◪ "Great-value" prices (just above cost) for "good-quality wines" is the winning concept behind chef François Clerc's bistros; opinions vary on the food, but dining here is really a "pretext" for "tasting premier crus" without busting the budget; the Latin Quarter original has a beamed-ceiling ground-floor room and "old stone walls" in the cellar.

Bouclard (Le) ◐   ▽ 20 | 15 | 15 | fr222
1, rue Cavallotti, 18ᵉ (Place de Clichy), 01 45 22 60 01; fax 01 45 22 60 01
■ The few surveyors who've discovered this bistro "hidden on a small street" in the 18th call it a "warm" place with "typical" bistro decor and "hearty", "authentic" eats; add in "generous" portions and "gentle prices" and it's no wonder some rank it as a personal favorite.

Bouillon Racine ◐ S   13 | 21 | 14 | fr221
3, rue Racine, 6ᵉ (Cluny-La Sorbonne/Odéon), 01 44 32 15 60; fax 01 44 32 15 61
◪ This "beautiful" Belgian near the Odéon impresses with its "superb" turn-of-the-century decor (the building is classified as a French historical monument) and most also enjoy its "sometimes surprising" beer-based cooking, not to mention its "remarkable choice of beers"; critics cite "uneven" fare and "slow" service, but the "copious" portions and "economical prices" are hard to argue with.

Boulangerie (La) S   – | – | – | I
15, rue des Panoyaux, 20ᵉ (Ménilmontant), 01 43 58 45 45; fax 01 43 58 45 46
"Good home cooking" is what you'd think you were eating at this traditional bistro in a former bakery shop in the increasingly trendy Ménilmontant area; aside from a mosaic floor made by local artists, the decor is "simple", but an aura of conviviality reigns and the mood isn't spoiled when the check arrives since most find it an "excellent value."

Bourdonnais (Le)/Cantine des Gourmets (La) S   20 | 14 | 18 | fr473
Hôtel de La Bourdonnais, 113, av. de La Bourdonnais, 7ᵉ (Ecole-Militaire), 01 47 05 16 54; fax 01 45 51 09 29
■ Considered a "sanctuary" by contented regulars, this "provincial-style" hotel restaurant in the 7th earns high praise for its "excellent" French cuisine, "great service" and "elegant", "sunny" yellow-toned decor that's a nice backdrop for "a family meal"; dissenters label it "snobbish", "uneven" and "terribly expensive", but the majority view is "attractive" and "solid."

Bourguignon du Marais (Au)   ▽ 17 | 14 | 13 | fr287
52, rue François Miron, 4ᵉ (Pont-Marie/St-Paul), 01 48 87 15 40; fax 01 48 87 17 49
■ "Superb Burgundies" at "reasonable prices" are the main attraction at this "delightful" bar à vins in the Marais, but it also boasts "very good, carefully prepared" regional cuisine; run by a "charming husband-and-wife team", it's a "clean, unfussy" space with blond-wood decor and a "calm" yet "convivial" ambiance; N.B. the owner is a fount of information on wines – ask to see his cellar.

Braisière (La)

| 20 | 13 | 18 | fr364 |

54, rue Cardinet, 17ᵉ (Malesherbes), 01 47 63 40 37; fax 01 47 63 04 76

■ "Charm, quality and originality combine with a warm welcome" to win admirers for this Traditional French near Malesherbes; besides "beautifully prepared food" by a "real artisan of cooking", it offers "excellent service" and "very good value", but "too bad the decor is so dreary."

Brasserie Balzar ●S

| 12 | 16 | 15 | fr243 |

49, rue des Ecoles, 5ᵉ (Cluny-La Sorbonne), 01 43 54 13 67; fax 01 44 07 14 91

■ Though this Latin Quarter brasserie next to the Sorbonne earns better grades for its "super ambiance" and "jovial service" than for its food, the latter is judged "solid and honest", if "nothing special"; that it's now owned by the Flo group may be why some feel it's "lost its soul", but it still draws everyone from academics and fashion folk to tourists, and thus can be "very noisy."

Brasserie de la Poste ●S

| 12 | 11 | 13 | fr228 |

54, rue de Longchamp, 16ᵉ (Trocadéro), 01 47 55 01 31; fax 01 44 11 03 79

◪ Opinion is split on this brasserie near Trocadéro; one side finds a "warm welcome" followed by "good" food, service and "value", while another calls it "average" and "uninteresting", claiming that it "lost its fashionable clientele" and "hasn't refound the formula that once made it a success"; gently priced prix fixe deals make it easy to check it out for yourself.

Brasserie de l'Ile St. Louis ●S

| 12 | 13 | 14 | fr213 |

55, quai de Bourbon, 4ᵉ (Cité/Pont-Marie), 01 43 54 02 59; fax 01 46 33 18 47

■ "A great location" on the Ile Saint-Louis across from Notre Dame and a summer terrace that's "people-watching central" make this brasserie a "star on the Seine" and an almost "obligatory stop" on the island; "dependable, hearty food", "joking servers" ("adorable when they know you", perhaps less so if they don't) and low prices boost its appeal, but some wonder "when are brasseries going to become more creative?"

Brasserie du Louvre ●S

| 10 | 12 | 12 | fr243 |

Hôtel du Louvre, Place du Palais Royal, 1ᵉʳ (Palais Royal-Musée du Louvre), 01 42 96 27 98; fax 01 44 58 38 01

◪ This brasserie tucked inside the Hôtel du Louvre is handy "after visiting the museum" or taking in "a show" nearby, but beyond that it divides diners, with some citing "decent food at an affordable price" and others finding "no interest except for the location"; it's popular enough that it can be "loud and bustling", and some gripe that the nonsmoking section tends to "disappear."

Brasserie Flo ●◐Ⓢ 13 | 17 | 14 | fr269
7, cour des Petites Ecuries, 10ᵉ (Château d'Eau),
01 47 70 13 59; fax 01 42 47 00 80

■ "Tough to find" in an alley near the Porte Saint-Denis in
the 10th, this "classic" brasserie "fits like an old slipper" for
fans of its "picturesque" art nouveau decor (complete with
stained glass windows), "appealing tavern-like ambiance"
and "good" eats, including a "sumptuous shellfish platter";
it's a natural "after the theater", and though critics knock
"pre-cooked food" and "too many tourists", they're outvoted.

Brasserie Lipp ●Ⓢ 14 | 18 | 14 | fr293
151, bd St-Germain, 6ᵉ (St-Germain-des-Prés), 01 45 48 53 91;
fax 01 45 44 33 20

◪ For better or worse, "Lipp holds back the hands of
time", remaining a Left Bank "monument" even if it's more
revered for its "superb atmosphere" than its brasserie
fare; "don't get shunted off upstairs" or you won't get a
good look at the "gorgeous" art nouveau tilework or the
"political and literary celebs" in the crowd; the service
and welcome can leave something to be desired, but
nonetheless, you "gotta go at least once."

Brasserie Lorraine ●◐Ⓢ 12 | 13 | 12 | fr317
2-4, place des Ternes, 8ᵉ (Ternes), 01 56 21 22 00; fax 01 56 21 22 09

◪ "The frères Blanc strike again", but whether their
ownership has improved this brasserie on the Place des
Ternes depends upon whom you ask; boosters say "bravo"
for "fresh seafood" and other good eats served in a "large,
airy", even "elegant", setting, while foes blast it as "banal",
"outdated" and "pricey"; either way, it's "well located"
and handy "after a show" nearby.

Brasserie Lutétia Ⓢ 14 | 13 | 14 | fr278
Hôtel Lutétia, 23, rue de Sèvres, 6ᵉ (Sèvres-Babylone),
01 49 54 46 76; fax 01 49 54 46 00

◪ Though it's perhaps "not very imaginative or special",
this "classic" brasserie in the Hotel Lutétia at Sèvres-
Babylone is appreciated for its "spacious, comfortable"
layout ("rare in Paris") and dependable food, including
"good seafood"; some find the ambiance "a bit cold" and
prices "a bit high", but it's generally a "sure" bet and
there are affordable prix fixe deals.

Brasserie Mollard ●Ⓢ 13 | 18 | 11 | fr295
115, rue St-Lazare, 8ᵉ (St-Lazare), 01 43 87 50 22;
fax 01 43 87 84 17

◪ "Splendiferous" turn-of-the-century decor with beautiful
art nouveau tiles is reason enough to visit this landmarked
brasserie across from the Gare Saint-Lazare, which is just
as well since beyond the "dreamy oysters" and seafood
platters, the food doesn't inspire much excitement; in the
complaint column, surveyors list service that's "not always
pleasant" and prices that seem high for the quality.

Brasserie Munichoise ◐ ▽ 19 | 18 | 16 | fr186

5, rue Danielle Casanova, 1er (Opéra/Pyramides), 01 42 61 47 16; fax 01 42 86 93 61

■ Try this German-style pub for "sausages after a night" at the nearby Opéra Garnier, or for "excellent oysters" and choucroute that some judge "the best in Paris"; a "convivial" ambiance, "exotic" (Teutonic) decor, "fast service" and very fair prices are more arguments in its favor.

Brasserie Stella ◐ [S] 12 | 8 | 11 | fr257

133, av. Victor Hugo, 16e (Victor Hugo), 01 47 27 60 54; fax 01 47 27 34 19

◪ This "noisy", "animated" brasserie in the 16th is such a magnet for chic locals that "if you're not from the area, you may feel you're bothering them"; opinions on the food range from "solid" to "not great" and some wish they'd "redo" the decor, but habitués "always return" because it's "practical", "efficient" and familiar; P.S. if "you're allergic to smoke, stay away."

Brézolles (Les) 19 | 15 | 16 | fr277

5, rue Mabillon, 6e (St-Sulpice), 01 53 10 16 10; fax 01 56 24 98 59

◪ In a "calm" setting across from the Marché Saint-Germain in the 6th, this contemporary bistro directed by Jean-Paul Duquesnoy offers "inventive" fare at "good-value" prices; a few deem it "overrated" and not everyone likes the modern beige-toned decor ("handsome" vs. "like an operating room"), but service is "attentive" and overall it's "very well done."

BRISTOL (LE) [S] 25 | 25 | 24 | fr673

Bristol Hôtel, 112, rue du Faubourg-St-Honoré, 8e (Miromesnil), 01 53 43 43 40; fax 01 53 43 43 01

■ The arrival of chef Eric Fréchon has sparked new excitement at the luxe Hôtel Bristol in the 8th: "best meal of my life", "perfect from A to Z" coo admirers; replacing Michel del Burgo (now at Taillevent), Fréchon turns out "sublime" haute cuisine that's expertly served in two "lovely" settings: an elegant oak-paneled oval room in winter and a pretty patio in summer; it's "as pricey as it is good", but that's what you'd expect from "a great restaurant in a great hotel."

Bûcherie (La) ◐ [S] 13 | 17 | 13 | fr336

41, rue de la Bûcherie, 5e (St-Michel), 01 43 54 24 52; fax 01 46 34 54 02

■ It's "romantic" to dine by the fireplace and enjoy the "view of Notre Dame" from this Classic French in the 5th, and if there are "no surprises" on the menu, that means you can fully focus on your date; most seem happy enough with its "warm" ambiance and "competently done" cuisine, even if it is "a bit expensive."

Buddha Bar ☾ [S] 10 | 22 | 9 | fr329
8, rue Boissy d'Anglas, 8e (Concorde), 01 53 05 90 00; fax 01 53 05 90 09
◪ This "trendy" Asian-themed restaurant/bar near the Place de la Concorde boasts an "amazing" bi-level setting with a giant Buddha, and while the Asian fusion fare isn't divine, there's distraction in the form of "pretty" people and "loud music"; it's "a must for a drink", if you don't mind stiff prices and a staff that might treat you "like old fish."

Buffalo Grill [S] 7 | 7 | 9 | fr147
15, place de la République, 3e (République), 01 40 29 94 98; fax 01 49 96 43 48 ☾
1, bd St-Germain, 5e (Jussieu), 01 56 24 34 49; fax 01 53 10 85 94
3, place Blanche, 9e (Blanche), 01 40 16 42 51; fax 01 44 91 81 24 ☾
36, bd des Italiens, 9e (Opéra), 01 47 70 90 45; fax 01 53 24 19 16 ☾
9, bd Denain, 10e (Gare du Nord), 01 40 16 47 81; fax 01 44 91 81 27
2, rue Raymond Aron, 13e (quai de la Gare), 01 45 86 76 71; fax 01 44 06 90 31 ☾
117, av. du Général-Leclerc, 14e (Porte d'Orléans), 01 45 40 09 72; fax 01 56 53 70 16
154, rue St-Charles, 15e (Charles Michels), 01 40 60 97 48; fax 01 40 60 17 46
6, place du Maréchal-Juin, 17e (Péreire), 01 40 54 73 75; fax 01 48 01 13 64 ☾
29, av. Corentin-Cariou, 19e (Porte de la Villette), 01 40 36 21 41; fax 01 53 26 88 17
◪ Though this Wild West–themed steakhouse chain is hardly a gourmet experience, "kids adore it" and their parents say it serves "decent" meat that's "not bad for this type of restaurant", or for these prices; but it takes some arrows for "tacky" decor and sometimes "indifferent" service from waiters dressed like sheriffs ("ridiculous").

Butte Chaillot (La) ☾ [S] 17 | 13 | 15 | fr291
110 bis, av. Kléber, 16e (Trocadéro), 01 47 27 88 88; fax 01 47 04 85 70
■ "Excellent" modern bistro fare, "attractive" decor and "competent" service please a "mix of 16th-arrondissement locals and international types" at this split-level Guy Savoy satellite; the "roast chicken and mashed potatoes are the best I've ever tasted!" exclaims one fan who isn't alone in admiring the house specialty; prices are reasonable too.

Byblos Café [S] ▽ 16 | 14 | 18 | fr235
6, rue Guichard, 16e (La Muette), 01 42 30 99 99; fax 01 42 30 54 54
■ According to fans, this Lebanese in the 16th serves some of "the best" food of its kind in Paris, a claim that would seem to be backed up by its large following among the local Middle Eastern population; friendly service and moderate prices boost its appeal, and its intimate atmosphere makes it "perfect for a dinner *à deux*."

Ca d'Oro

– | – | – | M

54, rue de l'Arbre Sec, 1er (Louvre-Rivoli), 01 40 20 97 79
"Not perfect" but very "authentic" is one take on this Italian near the Louvre with decor inspired by traditional Venetian wine bars and a crowd comprised of tourists and arty locals; despite a few critics who report "mediocre" food and "absent" service, most consider it a "good value" for "genuine" cooking in a transporting, if "noisy", ambiance.

Café Beaubourg ● S

10 | 18 | 11 | fr169

100, rue St-Martin, 4e (Châtelet-Les Halles/Hôtel-de-Ville), 01 48 87 63 96; fax 01 48 87 81 25
◪ With its slick split-level setting by architect Christian de Portzamparc and "great location" across from the newly renovated Pompidou Center, this perennially "trendy" Costes brothers cafe is a "zoo of fashionable types" out to "see and be seen" (best vantage point: the terrace in summer); most find it "decent" for a light bite or brunch, even if service is "not very smiling."

Café Bleu (Le)

9 | 14 | 13 | fr206

Lavin, 15, rue du Faubourg-St-Honoré, 8e (Concorde), 01 44 71 32 32; fax 01 44 71 31 17
◪ The "ideal place to invite a preppy friend who's dieting" say patrons of this "chic" cafe in the basement of the flagship Lanvin boutique on the gilded Faubourg-Saint-Honoré; the light French fare is "honest" to some, "ordinary" to others, but the ambiance is "elegant and discreet" (perhaps a bit "cold" and noisy) and the food is certainly cheaper than the clothes; no dinner.

Café Charbon ● S

8 | 17 | 10 | fr153

109, rue Oberkampf, 11e (Ménilmontant/Parmentier), 01 43 57 55 13
◪ This "trendy but still nice" cafe in the increasingly hip Ménilmontant area is, to borrow a famous line from French cinema, all about "atmosphere, atmosphere", with a gorgeous old setting complete with gas lamps and moleskin booths; as for the "simple, traditional" bistro cooking, they "could do better", but it's a "great place to hang out, people-watch, write, play cards", etc.

Café d'Angel (Le)

16 | 12 | 16 | fr241

16, rue Brey, 17e (Charles de Gaulle-Etoile), 01 47 54 03 33; fax 01 47 54 03 33
◼ Angelic indeed according to those who say this modern bistro near the Etoile serves "very creative, light" fare in "a cheery, homey atmosphere with very friendly service"; it's a "good value" for the area, too, though it can be "a bit noisy" and some feel it's best for a casual meal or "quick stop while shopping."

Café de Flore ◐Ⓢ
10 | 18 | 11 | fr220

172, bd St-Germain, 6ᵉ (St-Germain-des-Prés),
01 45 48 55 26; fax 01 45 44 33 39

◪ "After all these years", this Saint-Germain cafe with a prime people-watching terrace is "still delightful, still too expensive and still worth it"; once the haunt of existentialists, it draws "the Left Bank crowd", plus loads of tourists, who come to bask in "nostalgia" over coffee and snacks; breakfast is also popular, especially on Sundays when "politicos and journalists" abound.

Café de la Musique ◐Ⓢ
10 | 17 | 11 | fr216

213, av. Jean Jaurès, 19ᵉ (Porte de Pantin), 01 48 03 15 91;
fax 01 48 03 15 18

◪ Most agree that this sleek Costes brothers French cafe/ restaurant is "welcome in a lost corner of Paris", near the Cité de la Musique and La Villette, even if some say it "has the same drawbacks" as other Costes eateries: "noisy", "too pricey for the quality", servers who make "an art of being unpleasant"; still, it's "ideal" post-concert and liked for its "relaxing brunch" and terrace.

Café de la Paix ◐Ⓢ
12 | 18 | 12 | fr291

Grand Hôtel Inter-Continental, 12, bd des Capucines, 9ᵉ
(Auber/Opéra), 01 40 07 30 20; fax 01 40 07 33 86

◪ This brasserie "institution" near the Opéra Garnier in the heart of town doesn't set gourmets' pulses racing, but it's a "pleasant oasis" and "fine for late dining" or "a snack", with "handsome" vintage decor and a big terrace for people-watching; given the location, it's no surprise if it's "touristy."

Café de l'Esplanade (Le) ◐Ⓢ
– | – | – | M

52, rue Fabert, 7ᵉ (Invalides/La Tour-Maubourg),
01 47 05 38 80; fax 01 45 51 52 73

This brand-new entry in the ever-expanding Costes galaxy (Café Marly, Georges, etc.) has all the makings of a typical Costes hit: a stylish setting in the 7th with Empire-style decor by Jacques Garcia, sexy servers and casual French fare (gazpacho, club sandwiches, tartare); since *le tout Paris* has been flocking since day one, it looks like they have another hit on their trendy hands.

Café de l'Industrie ◐Ⓢ
9 | 16 | 10 | fr170

16, rue St-Sabin, 11ᵉ (Bastille/Bréguet-Sabin),
01 47 00 13 53; fax 01 47 00 92 33

■ "Leftish intellectuals, hippie types, artists" and "pretty little trendies" "come to show off" at this stylish hipsters' hangout near the Bastille with "grandmotherly" bistro cooking and a colonial-style "retro" ambiance; though no one raves about the food or service, it's a "cheap and cheerful" way to get into a "Bastille state of mind."

Café de Mars ◑🅂   11 | 13 | 12 | fr206
11, rue Augereau, 7ᵉ (Ecole-Militaire), 01 47 05 05 91;
fax 01 47 05 05 91

◪ Surveyors square off over this cafe/bistro near the Champ de Mars: defenders say it's a "nice, inexpensive little restaurant with good, varied dishes", while critics shrug "ordinary", "overrated"; but it has a "pleasant" (maybe even "romantic") ambiance, and the fact that you're advised to "reserve since it's often full" says something.

Café des Lettres 🅂   9 | 14 | 13 | fr215
53, rue de Verneuil, 7ᵉ (Rue du Bac/Solférino), 01 42 22 52 17;
fax 01 45 44 70 02

◪ The "tranquil" cobblestoned courtyard is "very pleasant on a summer evening", and the "super gravlax" and "excellent brunch" also earn nods at this Scandinavian cafe/tearoom in a calm corner of the 7th; but dissenters claim "quality has slipped" and complain of "amateur" service and reception.

Café de Vendôme 🅂   ▽ 16 | 15 | 17 | fr229
Hôtel de Vendôme, 1, place Vendôme, 1ᵉʳ (Concorde),
01 55 04 55 55; fax 01 55 04 55 64

◼ Voters who have visited the lavish marble and velvet dining room of the Hôtel de Vendôme on the famed Place of the same name send back mostly positive reports on the "succulent, varied and refined" French fare of Gérard Sallé (ex Plaza-Athénée) as well as the "excellent service"; prices are relatively "gentle" and if it can be empty at night, it's "perfect for a tranquil business meal."

Café du Commerce (Le) ◑🅂   10 | 14 | 10 | fr167
51, rue du Commerce, 15ᵉ (Emile Zola/La Motte-Picquet-
Grenelle), 01 45 75 03 27; fax 01 45 75 27 40

◪ "When you don't want to go broke", this circa 1922 brasserie in the 15th can supply "cheap", "simple" eats in an "amusing" setting – three floors built around a central atrium with a retracting roof; the ambiance is "young and noisy" and the place "so big there's always a seat", but critics who knock "slapdash cooking" and service say "only the bill saves it."

Café du Passage (Le) ◑🅂   ▽ 20 | 14 | 15 | fr285
12, rue de Charonne, 11ᵉ (Bastille), 01 49 29 97 64;
fax 01 47 00 14 00

◼ "A good address among the new generation of wine bars" say fans of this "snug", congenial spot tucked away near the Bastille; along with a "staggering wine list" it has "rich", "tasty" dishes, including a selection of first-rate *andouillette* (tripe sausage), and while prices aren't cheap, it's considered an "excellent value."

Café Faubourg S
▽ 16 | 17 | 12 | fr348

Sofitel Le Faubourg, 11 bis, rue Boissy d'Anglas, 8ᵉ
(Concorde), 01 44 94 14 14; fax 01 44 94 14 28
■ Steps from the Place de la Concorde is this "delightful surprise", a hotel dining room offering "budget-priced" (relatively speaking) Alain Dutournier cuisine – the Carré des Feuillants chef consults here and a former second turns out "very good" contemporary French Southwestern fare; service can "slip" and some find the decor "impersonal", but the setting is "restful", with a view of a small courtyard.

Café Flo
10 | 18 | 11 | fr182

Printemps, 64, bd Haussmann, 9ᵉ
(Auber/Havre-Caumartin), 01 42 82 58 84; fax 01 42 82 51 88
■ It's "lovely" to sit under the "magnificent" stained-glass cupola that dominates this Groupe Flo offshoot on the top floor of the Printemps department store, and while the French fare isn't as remarkable, it's "decent", making this "the right stop" for a "recharge" between purchases.

Café Indigo ●S
11 | 15 | 11 | fr237

12, av. George V, 8ᵉ (Alma-Marceau), 01 47 20 89 56;
fax 01 47 20 76 16
■ "Very stylish" French on the Avenue George V that buzzes with a trendy business crowd at noon but quiets down at night when it draws locals and guests from nearby hotels; its bistro menu is in step with the current vogue for light eating, and if some find it "too pricey for the quality", others deem it "enjoyable" and also laud the "charming welcome" and "lack of pretense."

Café la Jatte S
12 | 16 | 12 | fr263

60, bd Vital Bouhot, Neuilly-sur-Seine (Pont-de-Levallois),
01 47 45 04 20; fax 01 47 45 19 32
☑ This "huge", airy French on the Ile de la Jatte is popular for its "unique" setting that's "worthy of Steven Spielberg", with a "magnificent" dinosaur skeleton hovering over the room; critics grouse that "funky decor and a trendy crowd do not compensate for limp cuisine", but the "noisy" "ad types" who hang out here obviously disagree and it's "good for alfresco dining" in summer.

Café Les Deux Magots ●S
11 | 17 | 11 | fr225

6, place St-Germain-des-Prés, 6ᵉ (St-Germain-des-Prés),
01 45 48 55 25; fax 07 45 49 31 29
☑ Everyone makes at least one "pilgrimage" to this famed Saint-Germain cafe where Sartre and de Beauvoir once lingered; today, tourists outnumber intellectuals and "ouch, the price hurts for what you get" since you "pay for the setting", but it's "ideal" for a coffee or snack ("best at off-hours" say some) and a "hot spot for ogling", especially on the terrace.

Café Louis Philippe ◐ [S] ▽ 13 | 14 | 9 | fr199
66, quai de l'Hôtel-de-Ville, 4e (Pont-Marie), 01 42 72 29 42
■ It's not the standard-issue cooking so much as it is the "calm, classic" setting on the banks of the Seine in the Marais that draws people to this long-standing bistro; its "lovely, sheltered terrace gives you an impression of seclusion in the heart of the city", and gentle prices add to the good vibes.

Café M [S] 18 | 17 | 14 | fr322
Hôtel Hyatt, 24, bd Malesherbes, 8e (Madeleine/St-Augustin), 01 55 27 12 34; fax 01 55 27 12 35
■ In the Hyatt hotel not far from the Madeleine, this New French has stylish modern decor and "delicious", "light and inventive" cooking; popular with a business crowd at noon, it's much quieter (maybe "too calm") at night, and though "uneven" service and "expensive" prices cause a bit of grousing, most think "the young chef will go far."

CAFÉ MARLY ◐ [S] 12 | 23 | 11 | fr245
93, rue de Rivoli, 1er (Palais Royal-Musée du Louvre), 01 49 26 06 60; fax 01 49 26 07 06
◪ The "one-in-a-million setting" in a wing of the Louvre facing I.M. Pei's pyramid means it doesn't matter if the brasserie fare is "unremarkable" and service can be "snooty" at this Costes brothers hit – "the view" and "people-watching" are "worth the suffering", whether inside amid Napoleon III decor or on the "superb" terrace; since prices are deemed high for the quality, some prefer it for breakfast, "light snacks" or drinks.

Café Max ⊭ ▽ 13 | 17 | 21 | fr210
7, av. de La Motte-Picquet, 7e (Ecole Militaire/ La Tour-Maubourg), 01 47 05 57 66
■ Only a few surveyors comment on this snug little bistro near Les Invalides, and they focus more on the "original" and "amusing" chef-owner, Max, than on the hearty family-style eats; cozy, rummage-shop decor, friendly service and low prices make it easy to overlook kitchen ups and downs.

Café Ruc ◐ [S] 10 | 12 | 9 | fr231
159, rue St-Honoré, 1er (Louvre-Rivoli), 01 42 60 97 54; fax 01 42 61 36 33
◪ Across from the Louvre, this Jacques Garcia–designed brasserie from the Costes brothers takes whacks from critics for its food ("vacuum-packed", "not extraordinary", "expensive") and service ("deliberately unpleasant", "they're bored and let us know it"); that said, it's a "trendy" place and defenders like the "pleasant" modern decor, calling it ok "for a quick bite."

Café Runtz ◐ | 15 | 14 | 15 | fr237

16, rue Favart, 2e (Richelieu-Drouot), 01 42 96 69 86; fax 01 40 20 92 95

■ A "sure value" for "robust" Alsatian fare in a "slightly kitsch" setting in the 2nd near the Opéra Comique ("good" after a show); besides its "exceptionally light choucroute" and maybe "the best potatoes with Muenster cheese in Paris", this place pleases with its "warm ambiance", friendly welcome and reasonable prices, plus the effort it makes to "update traditional dishes."

Café Terminus [S] ▽ 17 | 15 | 17 | fr239

Concorde St-Lazare, 108, rue St-Lazare, 8e (St-Lazare), 01 40 08 43 30; fax 01 40 08 44 60

■ Next to the Saint-Lazare train station in the Hôtel Concorde Saint-Lazare (part of the Taittinger chain), this French is well regarded by the few voters who know it for its "inventiveness", "attentive, efficient" service and "excellent value"; though the decor's a bit drab, "the whole package is good" and the wine list has some nice "surprises" at nice prices.

Cafetière (La) 16 | 14 | 15 | fr283

21, rue Mazarine, 6e (Odéon), 01 46 33 76 90; fax 01 43 25 76 90

■ "Cute" vest-pocket Saint-Germain Italian adorned with old-fashioned metal coffeepots (inspiration for the name); those who label the cuisine "banal" may have preferred it back when it served French bistro fare, but admirers find the food "very good", ditto the service, and say the "atmosphere and decor are among the most pleasant in the 6th."

Café Véry [S] 8 | 20 | 11 | fr143

Jardin des Tuileries, 1er (Concorde/Tuileries), 01 47 03 94 84; fax 01 47 03 94 84

◪ The "mediocre" French cuisine "isn't up to the Tuileries Gardens" setting, but this kiosk restaurant's sandwiches, salads and other "light bites" come at "low prices" and are "good for kids"; even if service can be "slow and unpleasant" and there may be "long waits", the surroundings are so "marvelous in summer" you may not mind.

Caffé Toscano [S] – | – | – | M

34, rue des Saints-Pères, 7e (St-Germain-des-Prés), 01 42 84 28 95; fax 01 42 84 26 36

More cafe than restaurant, this "cozy" storefront Italian behind Saint-Germain-des-Prés is "good for a bite on the run" according to fans of its "fresh, original" fare; a few foes call it a "faux Italian", suggesting that a change of owners "wasn't beneficial" (formerly Caffé Bini, it belonged to Anna Bini of Casa Bini), but it's popular enough to "fill up fast", which can lead to "overwhelmed" service.

Cagouille (La) S

19 11 14 f320

10, place Constantin Brancusi, 14ᵉ (Gaîté), 01 43 22 09 01; fax 01 45 38 57 29

■ "Excellent seafood" "cooked with exemplary simplicity" nets this Montparnasse fish house a catch of compliments, despite modern decor that several call "sad" and "glacial" – happily, there's a "pleasant terrace" in summer on which to enjoy its "really, really" "good-quality" fare; if some find prices a bit high, more consider it a "best value" for seafood.

Cailloux (Les)

– – – l

58, rue des Cinq Diamants, 13ᵉ (Corvisart), 01 45 80 15 08; fax 01 45 65 67 09

This Italian newcomer in the 13th is making a name for itself because all the basics are in place: the well-executed menu is driven by the market, the setting has a pleasing neo-bistro look and, last but hardly least, prices are gentle.

Caméléon (Le)

∇ 17 10 18 f249

6, rue de Chevreuse, 6ᵉ (Vavin), 01 43 20 63 43; fax 01 43 27 97 91

■ "An excellent buy where one eats well and simply" say boosters of this Montparnasse bistro with retro decor, including a cracked tile floor and floral wallpaper ("tacky" to some); a few claim it's "less good since a change in ownership" two years ago, but for the majority it's a "sure bet" for a pleasant meal with "smiling, attentive service."

Camélia (Le) S

∇ 16 16 17 f342

7, quai Georges Clémenceau, Bougival (La Défense RER), 01 39 18 36 06; fax 01 39 18 00 25

■ This well-established Classic French in Bougival offers "good cooking in a bourgeois setting without pretension"; though nitpickers note that the decor is "aging" and say "there's not much of interest on the wine list", service is "attentive", prices are deemed reasonable for the quality and it's pleasant for a Sunday lunch "with friends."

C'Amelot (Le) ◖S

18 8 15 f217

50, rue Amelot, 11ᵉ (Chemin Vert), 01 43 55 54 04; fax 01 43 14 77 05

■ "You don't go for the setting" (small, simple, crowded), but rather for "inventive" food that's a "best bet for the money" say fans of this popular bistro between the Bastille and République; it offers a single prix fixe menu that changes daily, and if a few think it's not what it was under its founding chef, more feel "it's a pleasure to dine" at this homey spot.

Camille ◖S

∇ 13 13 14 f213

24, rue des Francs-Bourgeois, 3ᵉ (St-Paul), 01 42 72 20 50; fax 01 40 27 07 99

◪ According to supporters, this cozy Marais bistro is "a good address" for a "simple" meal "if you live nearby", but a lack of enthusiastic comments suggests that's not a universal view; still, it draws an interesting, diverse crowd and benefits from low prices and a nice terrace in summer.

Campagne et Provence

18 | 11 | 12 | fr286

25, quai de la Tournelle, 5ᵉ (Maubert-Mutualité), 01 43 54 05 17;
fax 01 43 29 74 93

■ "Full-flavored, authentic Provençal food" is the draw at
this patch of Provence on the quais of the Seine across from
Notre Dame; despite a few carps about "a cold welcome"
and "rather tacky" decor, fans find the cooking "superbly
good" (especially the "unforgettable lamb stew") as well
as "a good buy."

Cap Seguin (Le)

12 | 17 | 12 | fr252

face au 27, quai le Gallo, Boulogne-Billancourt
(Pont-de-Sèvres), 01 46 05 06 07; fax 01 46 05 06 88

■ This "pleasant restaurant on the banks of the Seine"
opposite Mont Valérien in Boulogne-Billancourt is a
summer favorite, especially "at sunset"; diners like the
"original setting" on an old barge and "magnificent view
of the river and Saint-Cloud park", and if the "decent" food
lists toward "pricey" and service can be "inattentive",
few mind since you feel "you're on a cruise" here.

Cap Vernet (Le) ●🅂

15 | 13 | 14 | fr297

82, av. Marceau, 8ᵉ (Charles de Gaulle-Etoile),
01 47 20 20 40; fax 01 47 20 95 36

■ Oysters and other "marvelous shellfish" plus fine fish
equal smooth sailing at this Guy Savoy seafooder near the
Etoile; besides "intelligent" cooking, it has an "amusing"
split-level setting with modern maritime-themed decor and
"well-spaced tables" that are "good for a business lunch";
despite a few grumbles ("bit of a factory", "irregular"
service), most feel it delivers "quality" at "affordable prices."

Caroubier (Le) 🅂

– | – | – | M

82, bd Lefebvre, 15ᵉ (Porte de Vanves),
01 40 43 16 12

Formerly in Montparnasse, this North African now has a
spacious new home in the 15th not far from the Porte de
Vanves, with decor featuring nostalgic photos of Algeria;
the few surveyors who know it say it offers "very good
couscous and tagines" (e.g. chicken tagine with preserved
lemons and olives) at "reasonable prices."

Carpe Diem

16 | 11 | 17 | fr308

10, rue de l'Eglise, Neuilly-sur-Seine (Pont-de-Neuilly),
01 46 24 95 01; fax 01 46 40 15 61

◪ "The tranquil charm of bourgeois Neuilly" is part of the
appeal of this smart little French that keeps locals satisfied
with "carefully prepared cooking" ("don't miss the desserts")
and good service; however, ratings suggest that the decor
could use a boost, and depending on your budget, it's
either "expensive for what it is" or "a pretty good buy."

CARRÉ DES FEUILLANTS   25 | 20 | 23 | fr656
14, rue de Castiglione, 1er (Concorde/Opéra),
01 42 86 82 82; fax 01 42 86 07 71

▧ "Both traditional and inventive" and always very "tasty" describes the "exceptional" haute cuisine of Alain Dutournier, who elevates "authentic food from the French Southwest to gastronomic heights" at his restaurant between the Tuileries and the Place Vendôme; the modern decor (with large paintings of fruits) is "chic" to some, "not up to the cooking" for others, and there are carps about "ridiculous" portions and "prohibitive prices", but overall it's judged one of the "tops."

Carr's 🅂   ▽ 10 | 12 | 13 | fr196
1, rue du Mont Thabor, 1er (Tuileries), 01 42 60 60 26;
fax 01 42 60 33 32

▧ This "warm and cozy" Irish pub near the Tuileries and the Place de la Concorde is "a great place to meet for a pint, but not a top choice for dining unless you've had one too many" according to cynics; still, defenders tout "tasty bread and succulent salmon" at what they call the "classiest Irish pub in Paris"; occasional Celtic music is a plus.

Cartes Postales (Les)   ▽ 19 | 9 | 14 | fr298
7, rue Gomboust, 1er (Opéra/Pyramides), 01 42 61 02 93;
fax 01 42 61 02 93

▧ "The food is the best feature by far at this modest" Contemporary French near the Place du Marché Saint-Honoré, where a Japanese chef who trained with Alain Dutournier offers "a very interesting menu" in a "crowded, narrow" setting with "minimalist decor"; some feel the menu "doesn't change enough", but the cooking is "flavorful" and it's deemed one of the better bets in the area.

Cartet Restaurant ⌀   – | – | – | E
62, rue de Malte, 11e (République), 01 48 05 17 65

Not many surveyors frequent this tiny, venerable Lyonnaise bistro behind the Place de la République, perhaps because prices seem high for such rustic but good dishes as roast lamb and lemon tart served in a retro ambiance; it closes early, service can be a bit stiff for nonregulars and the area isn't much fun at night, but it appeals to real bistro buffs with fat wallets.

Casa Alcalde 🅂   17 | 13 | 15 | fr253
117, bd de Grenelle, 15e (La Motte-Picquet-Grenelle),
01 47 83 39 71

■ "Great paella and a fun atmosphere" are why this Spanish-Basque in the 15th is "always packed" ("book" to be sure of a table); if a few doubters call it "expensive for the quality and portions" with "lukewarm" service, that doesn't bother fans who come for the likes of "good *pibales*" (baby eels) and grilled shrimp served in a "convivial", if "kind of cramped", room.

Casa Bini [S] 15 | 11 | 13 | fr264

36, rue Grégoire de Tours, 6e (Odéon), 01 46 34 05 60; fax 01 40 46 09 71

◪ Near the Odéon is what some call "Paris' most authentic Tuscan", serving "homemade pasta" and other tasty but "pricey" fare plus "excellent Italian wines" in a "stripped-down, high-design" setting that one diner likens to "a clinic waiting room"; there are also gripes about "minuscule portions", but to fans it's "the Italian you dream about – unpretentious and very good."

Casa Corsa ◐ ▽ 13 | 9 | 11 | fr240

25, rue Mazarine, 6e (Odéon), 01 44 07 38 98; fax 01 43 54 14 79

◪ Surveyors who've discovered this new Corsican bistro near the Odéon say "it should be encouraged" since it serves "very good" food (e.g. Corsican charcuterie, goat cheese–filled ravioli) in a setting with old-fashioned pictures and bric-a-brac from the island; outvoted complainers find prices "high" and the cooking and service "lacking finesse."

Casa del Habano (La) 12 | 12 | 12 | fr264

169, bd St-Germain, 6e (St-Germain-des-Prés), 01 45 49 24 30; fax 01 45 44 65 64

■ "The cigar is king" at this stogie-oriented Saint-Germain bistro with a walk-in humidor on the mezzanine; besides cigars, diners come "for good red meat, a nice Bordeaux" and the owner's warm welcome, but smoke phobes say ventilation isn't great and some rate the cooking just "ok"; still, it's "a nice bit of Havana" for a well-heeled blazers-and-jeans crowd of editors and politicians.

Casa Olympe 20 | 11 | 15 | fr298

48, rue St-Georges, 9e (St-Georges), 01 42 85 26 01; fax 01 45 26 49 33

■ "What a cook and what a character": well-known female chef Olympe Versini downshifted when she moved from her glamorous original venue in the 15th three years ago to this "simple bistro" in the 9th, but fans still adore her "inventive" fare, including Provençal dishes and a "roast leg of lamb that's a monument"; a few quibblers note "a slight decline in quality", but to most it's a "delicious" buy.

Casa Tina ◐ [S] 13 | 13 | 12 | fr212

18, rue Lauriston, 16e (Charles de Gaulle-Etoile/Kléber), 01 40 67 19 24; fax 01 40 67 18 48

◪ "This little corner of Spain" near the Etoile serves "nice tapas" and other tasty fare, including the famous 'Pata Negra' ham, to a trendy, well-heeled young crowd that comes here to relive their Iberian vacations; "it's a bit noisy, but service is friendly", if not always terribly efficient.

Catalogne (La) ◗ 🄢 — — — M

*4-6-8, Cour-du-Commerce-St-André, 6ᵉ (Odéon),
01 55 42 16 19; fax 01 55 42 16 33*

"Finally, good tapas!" exclaim fans of this "calm, well-designed" split-level Spaniard (bistro on the main floor, restaurant upstairs) in a cobbled lane in the 6th near Odéon; it's considered an "excellent value" for "very good" Catalonian fare (with wine suggestions for each course), and if service can be slow, no problem – "you have the whole night" to linger here.

Catherine (Chez) ▽ 19 13 18 fr308

*65, rue de Provence, 9ᵉ (Chaussée d'Antin-Lafayette),
01 45 26 72 88; fax 01 42 80 96 88*

■ Diners who know this "excellent bistro" tucked away in the 9th behind the big department stores "would rather not share it", since it serves "remarkable" food by chef-owner Catherine Guerraz in a small but "lovely" vintage setting with a copper bar and cracked-tile mosaic floor; since it's also an "excellent value", some wish they could "eat here every day."

Catounière (La) ▽ 13 8 12 fr216

*4, rue des Poissonniers, Neuilly-sur-Seine (Pont-de-Neuilly),
01 47 47 14 33; fax 01 55 24 93 72*

◪ "Pleasantly average" is one take on this Traditional French in Neuilly that caters to well-heeled locals; though not cheap, its prix fixe menus offer "good value", and if some find the setting "a bit cold" and "poorly laid-out", it's "agreeable" enough for a casual meal in a relaxing atmosphere with decent service.

Caveau du Palais (Le) ▽ 15 16 15 fr263

*17-19, place Dauphine, 1ᵉʳ (Cité/Pont-Neuf), 01 43 26 04 28;
fax 01 43 26 81 84*

■ "The charm of the Place Dauphine" near the main Paris courthouse, plus a lovely terrace and "delicious, well-presented" food add up to a positive verdict for this bistro; "efficient service" and "good value" also help make its case; popular with lawyers at noon, it's a fine spot for hand-holding in the evening, especially in summer.

Cave de l'Os à Moelle 🄢 — — — I

*181, rue de Lourmel, 15ᵉ (Lourmel), 01 45 57 28 28;
fax 01 45 57 40 10*

Bistros are imitating the big boys and starting to spin off simpler offshoots; this one, from the popular l'Os à Moelle nearby in the 15th, follows a table d'hôte format, with communal tables (seating a total of 15 – 20) and a multicourse set menu for just 130 francs (coffee included); there are also some bargains on the wine list.

Cave Drouot (La)   ▽ 14 | 7 | 13 | fr212
8, rue Drouot, 9ᵉ (Richelieu-Drouot), 01 47 70 83 38
■ This family-style bistro near the Drouot auction house
in central Paris is "good for lunch" (or breakfast – no
dinner served) in a very "Drouot ambiance", since it's
filled with antiques dealers and auctioneers; though it can
be "noisy" and ratings suggest the decor could use help,
the overall package is "pleasant, good and not expensive",
boosted by nice wines and a friendly welcome.

Cave Gourmande (La)   – | – | – | M
(fka Restaurant d'Eric Fréchon)
*10, rue du Général Brunet, 19ᵉ (Botzaris), 01 40 40 03 30;
fax 01 40 40 03 30*
Formerly known as the Restaurant d'Eric Fréchon, this
"best buy" in the 19th ("it's so far away!") is now run by
Fréchon's wife (he moved on to the Bristol hotel); most
still find the French fare "exceptional", but "it's too bad"
about the rather homely, "crowded" setting, and some
feel the wine list and welcome need work too; still, "one
feels well here" – let's "hope they don't raise prices."

Caves Pétrissans   15 | 11 | 12 | fr311
*30 bis, av. Niel, 17ᵉ (Péreire/Ternes), 01 42 27 52 03;
fax 01 40 54 87 56*
■ "Wine is king but the cooking is honest" at this old-
fashioned, "unpretentious" bistro near the Place des Ternes,
"a sure bet" for "hearty" fare such as "terrine with onion
jam" accompanied by a pick from the "very good cellar"
("ask the owners to suggest a bottle – they always have
an idea"); still, some grumble that it's "too expensive."

Caviar Kaspia ●   19 | 17 | 18 | fr554
*17, place de la Madeleine, 8ᵉ (Madeleine), 01 42 65 33 32;
fax 01 42 65 03 41*
■ An "oasis of luxury" overlooking the Madeleine ("sit
next to the windows" for the view), with a "romantic"
setting and "seductive food", i.e. "caviar, smoked salmon,
blini and chilled vodka"; though a few feel this "grand
classic" is "slipping" and "overpriced", the vast majority
says it's still "sublime" and perfect for "a celebratory meal."

Cazaudehore La Forestière 🄂   18 | 22 | 16 | fr487
*1, av. Kennedy, Saint-Germain-en-Laye (St-Germain-en-Laye
RER), 01 30 61 64 64; fax 01 39 73 73 88*
■ "What a magnificent dinosaur" says one surveyor
about this "chic, refined" hotel French west of Paris in
Saint-Germain-en-Laye; set on "beautiful country grounds",
it's "ideal for dinner with a new lover", especially on the
terrace, offering "excellent" food in a "restful" ambiance
with "attentive service"; prices are steep and a few find it
"banally old bourgeois", but most are quite content.

Céladon (Le) S

19 | 18 | 19 | fr469

Hôtel Westminster, 15, rue Daunou, 2ᵉ (Auber/Opéra), 01 47 03 40 42; fax 01 42 60 30 66

■ For "business at noon, romance at night", the dining room of the Hôtel Westminster steps from the Place Vendôme is generally viewed as "excellent all-around", from the French cuisine to the "very good service" and "lovely", "plush" setting (a bit "cold" to some); there's a "good-value lunch prix fixe", and though otherwise "expensive", it's judged "worth it."

Célébrités (Les) S

19 | 16 | 19 | fr463

Hôtel Nikko, 61, quai de Grenelle, 15ᵉ (Bir-Hakeim/ Charles Michels), 01 40 58 21 29; fax 01 40 58 21 50

◪ There's a "splendid view of the Seine" from this French with "relaxing modern decor" in the Hôtel Nikko in the 15th (where Joël Robuchon once reigned), and most also applaud its "flavorful", if "unsurprising", fare; the main complaint: "too expensive" (some add "pretentious"), though the "very pleasant, efficient" staff, plus the scenery, help atone.

Cercle Ledoyen (Le)

16 | 18 | 17 | fr391

1, av. Dutuit, 8ᵉ (Champs-Elysées-Clémenceau), 01 53 05 10 02; fax 01 47 42 55 01

◪ Less costly than big brother Ledoyen upstairs, this "clubby" space near the Champs-Elysées is ideal "for a business lunch" and super on the "marvelous terrace" with its "screen of greenery"; Christian Le Squer (who replaced Ghislaine Arabian two years ago) continues to provide "very good" French fare at "excellent-value" prices, and the crowd is "as interesting" as the food, a good thing since some find the tables "tightly spaced."

Cévennes (Les)

– | – | – | M

55, rue des Cévennes, 15ᵉ (Javel), 01 45 54 33 76; fax 01 44 26 46 95

This French "lost on the edge of the 15th" near Javel is "very good, but it's too bad it's not more animated", a point underlined by the fact that few surveyors have been there; with a market-based menu by Daniel Vien (ex Lasserre) and a reasonable prix fixe, it's a local favorite and a "good buy."

Chalet des Iles (Le) S

9 | 20 | 12 | fr304

Lac du Bois de Boulogne, 16ᵉ (Av. Henri Martin/Rue de la Pompe), 01 42 88 04 69; fax 01 45 25 41 57

◪ "What a wonderful sensation it is to take the boat" (the only means of access) to this restaurant on an island in the Bois de Boulogne, but critics moan "what a sinking sensation to get out one's wallet to pay for such an ordinary meal"; still, the "magical setting" and lovely terrace make it worth it, at least "for tea."

Champ de Mars (Le) [S] 13 12 14 fr241

17, av. de La Motte-Picquet, 7e (Ecole-Militaire/La Tour-Maubourg), 01 47 05 57 99; fax 01 44 18 94 69

■ Most have no complaints about this "good" neighborhood bistro near the Ecole Militaire, praising its "consistent" quality, "reasonable prices" and "agreeable setting", but opinions do diverge when the check comes ("good value" vs. "a bit expensive"); a few outnumbered carpers find it "undistinguished" with "grumpy service."

Chantairelle [S] – – – M

17, rue Laplace, 5e (Maubert-Mutualité), 01 46 33 18 59; fax 01 46 33 18 59

With a reconstructed village well, tapes of bird sounds and vials of local scents on sale in a tiny boutique, this Latin Quarter Regional French makes a real effort to bring the Auvergne to Paris; while fans laud its "good cooking and country ambiance", other find the food "heavy and fatty", but easygoing prices make it popular with a mix of students, tourists and academics.

Chardenoux ▽ 18 19 16 fr266

1, rue Jules Vallès, 11e (Charonne/Faidherbe-Chaligny), 01 43 71 49 52; fax 01 45 62 04 07

■ Atmospheric early-1900s decor (stucco moldings, a big zinc bar, etched-glass windows) distinguishes this bistro on a quiet street in the 11th near Charonne; most also give high marks to its "fine", "copious" fare and "pleasant welcome", though some feel prices are "a bit high" and the place is in "too many tourist guides."

Charlot - Roi des Coquillages ◐ [S] 14 12 12 fr329

12, place de Clichy, 9e (Place de Clichy), 01 53 20 48 00; fax 01 53 20 48 09

◪ This self-titled 'king of shellfish' on the Place de Clichy with "kitschy" "1970s decor" strikes fans as "a great place to go with friends" for a "can't-go-wrong" seafood platter, but critics claim the emperor has no clothes, citing high prices, "overcooked fish" and quality that's "fallen off"; still, it can satisfy an urge for oysters if you're in the area.

Charpentiers (Aux) [S] 12 13 13 fr243

10, rue Mabillon, 6e (Mabillon/St-Germain-des-Prés), 01 43 26 30 05; fax 01 46 33 07 98

◪ Veteran bistro near the Marché Saint-Germain appreciated by admirers for its "unpretentious" ambiance, "tasty, traditional" fare and "gruff yet warm welcome"; naysayers claim it's "a shadow of its former self" and has become "touristy", but they're outvoted by those for whom it remains "solid and durable", "a good place to take visitors who want to experience" the Left Bank.

Chartier [S] 9 | 21 | 13 | fr151

7, rue Faubourg-Montmartre, 9^e (Cadet/Grands Boulevards), 01 47 70 86 29; fax 01 48 24 14 68

◪ "A period hash house" sums up this lively classic for "students and tourists" on the Rue Montmartre, known for its "cheap" prices ("the tab is tallied on the paper tablecloth"), "authentic turn-of-the-century" decor and "ultrafast" (if a bit "cold") service; maybe the Traditional French fare is "totally forgettable", but here's your chance to "eat canned peas in a Belle Epoque" ambiance and have a "real cultural experience."

Chat Grippé (Le) [S] ▽ 16 | 11 | 18 | fr311

87, rue d'Assas, 6e (Port Royal), 01 43 54 70 00; fax 01 43 26 42 05

◪ "Calm" and "intimate" "candy-box" of a French near the Port Royal that earns decent marks for its food as well as its "courteous welcome" ("too rare" these days say manners mavens); if some find the cooking "variable" (and "a bit too expensive") and the '70s decor "sad", its "discreet bourgeois charm" and "pleasant service" win most over.

Chen 21 | 12 | 13 | fr480

15, rue du Théâtre, 15e (Charles-Michels), 01 45 79 34 34; fax 01 45 79 07 53

◪ Forget its dreary location in the underpass of a high-rise in the 15th and the "lugubrious" decor ("Mao is dead!" shouts one aesthete) – this "fabulous" Chinese provides "outstanding", "stunningly original" fare (e.g. "unbelievable zucchini flowers" stuffed with crab); service is "uneven" and it's "outrageously pricey" (one cynic blames its Michelin star), but that doesn't stop fans from coming back for more.

Cherche Midi (Le) ◐ [S] 15 | 11 | 13 | fr248

22, rue du Cherche-Midi, 6e (Sèvres-Babylone/St-Sulpice), 01 45 48 27 44

◪ "Noisy" and "smoke-filled" but not without "charm", this Saint-Germain Italian pleases most with its "good food", sought-after terrace and the buzz created by its "fashionable" crowd; doubters find it "snobby" and say it's "for those who like to eat on their neighbors' knees", but they're outvoted by admirers who insist it's "easygoing and easy to enjoy."

Chez Eux (D') 18 | 13 | 17 | fr366

2, av. Lowendal, 7^e (Ecole-Militaire), 01 47 05 52 55; fax 01 45 55 87 79

■ The "perfect place to feed a rugby team" is this bistro near the Ecole Militaire serving "gargantuan" portions of "excellent Southwestern French" fare in a red-and-white-checked–tablecloth setting that "offers a postcard-perfect take on France"; if some say it's best "for those with a big wallet as well as a big appetite", the hungry horde howls back "rustic, abundant and not to be missed."

Chiberta 19 | 15 | 18 | fr536

3, rue Arsène Houssaye, 8e (Charles de Gaulle-Etoile/George V), 01 53 53 42 00; fax 01 45 62 85 08

◩ Chef Eric Coisel (ex Lucas Carton and the Negresco in Nice) is giving "new energy" to this "elegant" French off the Champs-Elysées, offering such dishes as lamb with anise-scented béarnaise sauce; though the "hopelessly '80s" black-lacquer decor doesn't thrill everyone and some find the ambiance "not much fun", the cooking is "very good" (if "pricey"), service is "pleasant" and "it's great for a business lunch."

Chicago Meatpackers ☾ [S] 7 | 11 | 10 | fr173

8, rue Coquillière, 1er (Châtelet-Les Halles/Louvre-Rivoli), 01 40 28 02 33; fax 01 40 41 95 84

◩ While doubters are "not sure why anyone would want to go here, except for the occasional burger" or rib craving, others supply two good reasons to frequent this American in Les Halles: it's "fantastic for kids", complete with "a little train running around the ceiling", and "inexpensive"; service that's "pleasant" but not always swift means there can be "long waits."

Chicago Pizza Pie Factory ☾ [S] 6 | 10 | 9 | fr151

5, rue de Berri, 8e (George V), 01 45 62 50 23; fax 05 45 63 87 56

◩ This "noisy", "giant factory for pizza eaters and beer drinkers" off the Champs-Elysées won't win any culinary awards ("gives Chicago a bad name" says one critic), but it's handy "after a movie, amusing later at night" and "good for kids" or "if you need to gain weight"; "cheap" prices and "good cocktails" don't hurt either.

Chieng Mai ☾ [S] ▽ 19 | 10 | 12 | fr215

12, rue Frédéric Sauton, 5e (Maubert-Mutualité), 01 43 25 45 45

◩ "It's not pretty but you eat well" at this Thai near Maubert-Mutualité – try the "very good soup" before sampling its other "fine and savory" fare; service can veer from "too fast" to "slow", but prices are "excellent" and the interesting crowd includes Latin Quarter trendies plus the occasional celeb.

Chien qui Fume (Au) ☾ [S] 14 | 15 | 15 | fr225

33, rue du Pont-Neuf, 1er (Châtelet/Les Halles), 01 42 36 07 42; fax 01 42 36 36 85

■ "Classic Parisian brasserie in the heart of Les Halles" that's a "handy" option in a difficult neighborhood, offering a "warm welcome", "pretty fine" fare (including "excellent shellfish platters") and a "convivial ambiance" amid dog-themed decor; "decent prices" and "late" hours also work in its favor.

China Club ◐ S
12 | 24 | 13 | fr256

*50, rue de Charenton, 12ᵉ (Bastille/Ledru-Rollin), 01 43 43 82 02;
fax 01 43 43 79 85*

◪ "Rare in Paris", this Franco-Chinese behind the Opéra Bastille boasts a "superb" setting (with a "magnificent" upstairs smoking lounge and downstairs cabaret), "excellent cocktails" and "plush" decor that recalls "'30s Shanghai"; though many feel the bar outshines the restaurant, it's ideal "for a chic and cozy dinner."

China Town Belleville ◐ S
▽ 14 | 10 | 14 | fr214

*27-29, rue du Buisson St-Louis, 10ᵉ (Belleville),
01 42 39 34 18; fax 01 42 39 48 88*

◪ For "dinner with a gang of friends in Belleville", some tout this big Chinese with a "diverse" menu – "order lots of dishes so you can taste as many as possible"; others find the cooking "mediocre" and "only go for the karaoke."

China Town Olympiades ◐ S
13 | 7 | 11 | fr186

44, av. d'Ivry, 13ᵉ (Porte d'Ivry), 01 45 84 72 21; fax 01 45 84 74 52

◪ While no one thinks much of the "rather kitschy" decor at this sprawling eatery in the city's modern Chinatown in the 13th, fans say it serves "real Chinese" food to a largely Asian clientele; but even "inexpensive" prices fail to convince doubters who call it a "factory."

Chope d'Alsace (La) ◐ S
▽ 10 | 10 | 11 | fr229

*4, carrefour de l'Odéon, 6ᵉ (Odéon), 01 43 26 67 76;
fax 01 46 34 58 30*

◪ "Copious" portions of "unsurprising" but generally "dependable" Alsatian fare are served at this "noisy" brasserie at the Odéon; it takes some knocks for "bland" dishes and "tacky" decor, but there's "a warm welcome" to kick off the meal and a "moderate" bill to end it.

Christine (Le)
– | – | – | M

*1, rue Christine, 6ᵉ (Odeon/St-Michel), 01 40 51 71 64;
fax 01 42 18 04 39*

On a side street in Saint-Germain, this cozy French with stone walls and a view of a courtyard garden is a "charming" setting for "delicious" cooking at "reasonable prices"; "lovely waitresses" help make it a good place "to eat with children", and it's "perfect after a movie" nearby; another plus: moderate prices for top-flight Bordeaux wines.

Churrasco ◐ S
10 | 6 | 9 | fr186

*277, bd Péreire, 17ᵉ (Porte Maillot), 01 40 55 92 00;
fax 01 44 09 80 13*

◪ Boosters of this Argentine steakhouse near the Porte Maillot say the "meat's a dream and there are some good South American wines", plus "dishes you won't find elsewhere"; foes rate it "mediocre" and few are impressed by the decor ("sad"), but portions are "big", prices are reasonable and it's decent enough for "a quick lunch."

Cigale (La)

▽ 17 10 14 fr216

11 bis, rue Chomel, 7ᵉ (Sèvres-Babylone), 01 45 48 87 87;
fax 01 45 48 87 87

▪ "The best for soufflés in Paris, and so in the world" crows one fan of this bistro near Sèvres-Babylone, where a former Ledoyen chef offers both sweet and savory versions plus other "simple but good" fare; the decor has been spiffed up (ratings notwithstanding) and the crowd includes book editors and shoppers at noon, well-heeled locals at night.

Cinq (Le) ◑Ⓢ⒮

▽ 21 23 22 fr784

Four Seasons George V, 31, av. George V, 8ᵉ (George V),
01 49 52 71 54; fax 01 49 52 71 81

▪ Philippe Legendre, ex Taillevent, is now in the kitchen of this marble-and-gilt French in the recently reopened Four Seasons George V hotel off the Champs-Elysées; fans find "perfection and motivation" in his cuisine, and though a few doubters cite "robotic service" and high prices, it's a place to "watch closely" – could be a future "great."

Clément (Chez) ◑Ⓢ

10 15 11 fr196

17, bd des Capucines, 2ᵉ (Opéra), 01 53 43 82 00; fax 01 53 43 82 09
21, bd Beaumarchais, 4ᵉ (Bastille), 01 40 29 17 00; fax 01 40 29 17 09
123, av. des Champs-Elysées, 8ᵉ (Charles de Gaulle-Étoile/
George V), 01 40 73 87 00; fax 01 40 73 87 09
19, rue Marbeuf, 8ᵉ (Franklin D. Roosevelt), 01 53 23 90 00;
fax 01 53 23 90 09
106, bd du Montparnasse, 14ᵉ (Vavin), 01 44 10 54 00;
fax 01 44 10 54 09
407, rue de Vaugirard, 15ᵉ (Porte de Versailles),
01 53 68 94 00; fax 01 53 68 94 09
99, bd Gouvion-St-Cyr, 17ᵉ (Porte Maillot), 01 45 72 93 00;
fax 01 45 72 93 09
47, av. de Wagram, 17ᵉ (Ternes/Wagram), 01 53 81 97 00;
fax 01 53 81 97 09
15 bis, quai Rennequin Sualem, Bougival, 01 30 78 20 00;
fax 01 80 48 20 00
98, av. Edouard Vaillant, Boulogne-Billancourt
(Marcel Sembat), 01 41 28 90 00; fax 01 41 22 90 09

▪ Opinions are all over the map when it comes to this bistro chain, but the fact that so many people have been there is telling; most find them ok if "nothing special", with "amusing" faux-farmhouse decor (complete with copper pots and pans), "passable" food and "good-value" prices; however, some say "it all depends on the branch" you visit.

Clémentine

– – – M

5, rue St-Marc, 2ᵉ (Bourse/Grands Boulevards),
01 40 41 05 65; fax 01 45 08 08 77

"Disappointments are rare" at this bistro near the stock exchange, offering cooking that's "at once classic and original" at "decent" prices, plus "smiling" service and a wine list with some "nice surprises"; since it's busy (and "a little noisy") at lunch, book ahead or go in the evening.

Cloche des Halles (La) ⊟   ▽ 17 | 11 | 13 | fr163
28, rue Coquillière, 1ᵉʳ (Les Halles/Louvre-Rivoli), 01 42 36 93 89

■ "A vintage welcome" awaits at this old-fashioned wine bar near Les Halles, named for the bell that signaled the opening of Paris' main food market, once located in the area; it's a "high-quality" spot beloved for its "generous plates of charcuterie, well-chosen wines by the glass" and good prices – "perfect for eating on the run", since "it's not a real restaurant."

Cloche d'Or (La) ◑🅂   ▽ 16 | 15 | 18 | fr353
3, rue Mansart, 9ᵉ (Blanche/Pigalle), 01 48 74 48 88;
fax 01 40 16 40 99

🔲 Though the few voters who comment on this venerable Pigalle night-owl haunt (last orders at 4 AM) disagree about its Traditional French fare ("reliable" vs. "slipping"), a rise in ratings is an encouraging sign; good service and an old-fashioned setting (white tablecloths, waiters in dinner jackets) help keep it popular with journalists and the theater crowd, even if prices are going up.

Clos des Gourmets (Le)   21 | 13 | 19 | fr274
16, av. Rapp, 7ᵉ (Alma-Marceau/Ecole-Militaire),
01 45 51 75 61; fax 01 47 05 74 20

■ Surveyors rave about this "excellent" French run by an "energetic young couple" in the 7th not far from the Eiffel Tower, saluting "innovative food that works", "reasonable prices", "nice service" and a "pleasant terrace"; the "pretty", yellow-and-blue Louis XVI dining room is "a bit snug" and the crowd of local preppies can be "very noisy", but overall it's a "favorite."

Closerie des Lilas (La) ◑🅂   15 | 19 | 15 | fr358
171, bd du Montparnasse, 6ᵉ (Raspail/Vavin),
01 40 51 34 50; fax 01 43 29 99 94

🔲 "After years of hibernation", this "chic" landmark near the Port Royal that once drew Verlaine and Hemingway, among others, "has woken up" say those who feel it "benefited" from a change in owners and chef; while not everyone is won over by its French fare, most love its "charm" and "history", whether on the terrace or in the piano bar, restaurant or less-costly (and thus preferred) brasserie, where "all of Paris eats steak tartare."

Clos Morillons (Le)   22 | 13 | 18 | fr341
50, rue des Morillons, 15ᵉ (Porte de Vanves),
01 48 28 04 37; fax 01 48 28 70 77

■ "A beacon" in a remote part of the 15th is how fans view this French known for the chef's "interesting use of spices" – "what flavors and originality!"; the colonial decor isn't as piquant and a doubter or two wishes they'd get off the spice route now and then, but most relish the cooking's "savors and scents", even if it comes at a price; P.S. "the chocolate desserts are voluptuous enough to make you faint."

Clovis ◐ – | – | – | M

33, rue Berger, 1er (Châtelet-Les Halles), 01 42 33 97 07; fax 01 42 33 97 07

If one modernist asks "don't they know the days of the old Les Halles are over?", admirers hope this veteran never finds out so it will keep on serving "traditional old Parisian bistro fare" in a charming classic setting with "good service"; expect dishes such as chicken-liver terrine and blanquette de veau at relatively moderate prices.

Clovis (Le) ▽ 19 | 16 | 19 | fr503

Sofitel Arc de Triomphe, 2, av. Bertie Albrecht, 8e (Charles de Gaulle-Etoile/George V), 01 53 89 50 53; fax 01 53 89 50 51

■ The place "where bankers invite you" is one take on this French in the Sofitel Arc de Triomphe near the Etoile, a feeling that might be inspired by its hefty prices and rather nondescript modern decor, but there's no reason why the pleasure of Bruno Turbot's "very good cooking" should be reserved for financial types; service is equally commendable.

Clown Bar ◐ [S] ≠ ▽ 18 | 22 | 18 | fr177

114, rue Amelot, 11e (Filles-du-Calvaire), 01 43 55 87 35

■ "The circus decor is magic" at this tiny wine bar near the Cirque d'Hiver in the 11th adorned with landmarked art nouveau clown-themed tiles; besides a "fun, festive" ambiance, it boasts "great old-fashioned bistro fare at reasonable prices" and a wine list with "lots of interesting and little-known bottles"; service is friendly but can be "quickly overwhelmed" when busy.

Club Matignon (Le) [S] ▽ 14 | 12 | 12 | fr336

1, av. Matignon, 8e (Franklin D. Roosevelt), 01 43 59 38 70; fax 01 45 61 90 66

◪ Former pub near the Rond-Point of the Champs-Elysées that's now a seafood-focused eatery with "nautical" decor and, according to the few surveyors who know it, "good cooking"; some cite "snobby", "uneven" service and think the "wine list needs work", but most are happy enough to put into port for a meal here, even if prices are a bit high.

Coco de Mer ◐ ▽ 16 | 17 | 13 | fr221

34, bd St-Marcel, 5e (Les Gobelins/St-Marcel), 01 47 07 06 64; fax 01 47 07 41 88

◪ An "amusing" "trip to an Indian Ocean beach", complete with a patch of sand at the entrance, can be enjoyed via this Latin Quarter spot serving "good fish" and other dishes from the Seychelles islands; most find it "original" and "perfect for taste buds needing a little exoticism", but a few cynics grumble "overrated", "authentic right down to the same bad service we received in the Seychelles."

Coco et sa Maison
14 | 13 | 15 | fr287

*18, rue Bayen, 17ᵉ (Charles de Gaulle-Etoile/Ternes),
01 45 74 73 73; fax 01 45 74 73 52*

■ Enduringly trendy, media-crowd bistro in the 17th run by the affable Coco and sister Virginie (wife of singer Julien Clerc); though a bit "pricey", just about everyone likes its "refined", "inventive" Mediterranean-accented cuisine, "good service" and "gracious welcome", all of which have won it "a lot of regulars"; P.S. one figure-watcher says you can get low-cal fare "if you ask for it."

Coconnas S
11 | 16 | 12 | fr280

*2 bis, place des Vosges, 4ᵉ (Bastille/St-Paul), 01 42 78 58 16;
fax 01 42 78 16 28*

◪ Everyone loves the great location under the arcade framing the Place des Vosges, but this French run by Claude Terrail (of La Tour d'Argent) sparks quarrels over its food, with some citing "amusing peasant cuisine" and others fuming "it's a disgrace to profit from the site" by serving such disappointing fare; still, some would come just for the setting, especially to dine alfresco in summer.

Coffee Parisien ◖S
12 | 11 | 10 | fr176

*4, rue Princesse, 6ᵉ (Mabillon), 01 43 54 18 18; fax 01 43 54 94 96
7, rue Gustave-Courbet, 16ᵉ (Trocadéro), 01 45 53 17 17;
fax 01 43 54 94 96*

◪ There's Americana on the walls and on the menu of these eateries that pull a "young, hip" crowd with the likes of "excellent burgers", cheesecake and "incredible eggs Benedict" at brunch ("get there very early"); "noisy", "crammed" and "smoky", they're a tad "expensive" for what they serve and how it's served ("you wait hours"), but most find them "pleasant" anyway.

Coin des Gourmets (Au) S
▽ 19 | 9 | 15 | fr240

5, rue Dante, 5ᵉ (Maubert-Mutualité), 01 43 26 12 92

■ This tiny Indochinese near the Place Maubert has some "big" hits on its menu; it comes highly recommended for "the welcome, the service and especially the authentic cuisine, with many Cambodian dishes", and "in summer, the small terrace lets you avoid the uninteresting decor"; N.B. book ahead, since it's popular with a Latin Quarter crowd plus a sprinkling of film and fashion stars.

Colette
9 | 14 | 10 | fr193

213, rue St-Honoré, 1ᵉʳ (Tuileries), 01 55 35 33 93; fax 01 55 35 33 99

◪ "Dress in black" since you "can't get hipper than this in Paris" is the word on this "Zen-like", lunch-only light eats cafe in the basement of Colette, the minimalist chic store near the Tuileries; "I know I'm a fashion victim, but I admit it, and this place is great" confesses one of the stylish types who perch here for "simple, light" food and a "terrific" choice of mineral waters; the unimpressed say "snobby", "for anorexic hipsters."

Comédiens (Les) ◐ ▽ 12 | 12 | 14 | fr246

7, rue Blanche, 9e (Trinité), 01 40 82 95 95; fax 01 40 82 96 95

◪ The few surveyors who know this new bistro in the 9th find the cooking "good and copious" and say the place has "atmosphere", thanks to a sensitive restoration of an old-fashioned room; drawing a lively crowd, it can be "too noisy" with "tightly spaced" tables, but prices are modest, there are "nice wines" and it's "pleasant after the theater."

Communautés (Les) 17 | 12 | 16 | fr376

CNIT, 2, place de la Défense, Puteaux (La Défense Grande Arche), 01 46 92 10 30; fax 01 46 92 28 16

■ Admirers say "the only high-level restaurant in La Défense" (the business district just west of Paris) is this well-mannered French with "delicious" food and "well-spaced tables" that make it "ideal for inviting clients"; while some might agree that "it lacks a certain something", its good service, "nice wine cellar" and "quality cooking" satisfy most, even if it is "expensive."

Comptoir des Sports (Le) – | – | – | I

3, rue Hautefeuille, 6e (Odéon/St-Michel), 01 43 54 35 46; fax 01 43 54 35 46

Sort of a Gallic take on a sports bar, this cozy bistro near the Odéon has photos of athletes on the walls and the kind of hearty meat-and-potatoes fare an athlete could use; figure in low prices and a convivial ambiance fostered by the owner, a former rugby player, and it scores with some as "best place in the neighborhood."

Comptoir du Saumon 13 | 9 | 13 | fr209

60, rue François Miron, 4e (St-Paul), 01 42 77 23 08; fax 01 42 77 44 75

61, rue Pierre Charron, 8e (George V/Franklin D. Roosevelt), 01 45 61 25 14; fax 01 45 63 47 04

116, rue de la Convention, 15e (Boucicaut), 01 45 54 31 16; fax 01 45 54 49 68

3, av. de Villiers, 17e (Villiers), 01 40 53 89 00; fax 01 40 53 89 89

◪ Opinions vary on these salmon and caviar specialists: admirers laud their "good smoked salmon" and other "fresh and sometimes rare" offerings, while foes carp about high prices and "impersonal" decor ("as convivial as a frozen food store"); still, they're "practical for a fast business meal" and "good for vegetarians" who eat fish.

Comptoir Paris-Marrakech ◐[S] – | – | – | I

37, rue Berger, 1er (Les Halles/Louvre-Rivoli), 01 40 26 26 66; fax 01 42 21 44 24

Formerly Le Comptoir, this trendy spot on the edge of Les Halles now has warm new decor and a revamped Moroccan-accented menu; though a few judge it "less good than before" ("better for a drink"), it's not expensive and its young clientele calls it a nice "change from the usual", plus there's a great terrace in summer.

COMTE DE GASCOGNE (AU) 23 | 20 | 20 | fr558

89, av. Jean-Baptiste Clément, Boulogne-Billancourt (Pont-de-St-Cloud), 01 46 03 47 27; fax 01 46 04 55 70

■ This "palace of foie gras" in Boulogne-Billancourt may be "very expensive", but it's highly touted not only for the foie gras (perhaps "best in Paris"), but also for the tasting menu, proof that "the chef has mastered" a full range of Southwestern French fare; "attractive" decor, "attentive" service and "interesting" wines round out the experience.

Congrès (Le) ◐ [S] 13 | 11 | 12 | fr295

80, av. de la Grande Armée, 17e (Porte Maillot), 01 45 74 17 24; fax 01 45 72 39 80

◪ "Well-located" and open 24/7, this "classic brasserie" at the Porte Maillot comes in "handy at any hour" for a "good seafood platter", perhaps washed down with "champagne by the carafe", but it's "crowded and noisy", and both the menu and decor could use "refreshing"; critics call it a "tourist factory" that's "becoming banal."

Conti 20 | 14 | 17 | fr421

72, rue Lauriston, 16e (Boissière), 01 47 27 74 67; fax 01 47 27 37 66

■ "The best on the Rue Lauriston, and there's lots of competition" is an opinion most would second when it comes to this veteran in the 16th, where Michel Ranvier (former chef on the Orient Express) brings a French touch to Italian cuisine, producing "a savory and exceptional melange" enhanced by "very good wines" and service; it's pricey and a few find the room a bit "confined", but even so a meal here is "always a delight."

Contre-Allée (La) 14 | 14 | 14 | fr255

83, av. Denfert-Rochereau, 14e (Denfert-Rochereau), 01 43 54 99 86; fax 01 43 25 05 28

■ A fairly "swank setting" in the 14th and "creative food" make this French "a step up" from a standard neighborhood spot; "sort of trendy but not too much so", it's pleasant "for an evening with friends", offering good "value" and a terrace in summer.

Copenhague 18 | 14 | 16 | fr386

142, av. des Champs-Elysées, 8e (Charles de Gaulle-Etoile/ George V), 01 44 13 86 26; fax 01 42 25 83 10

■ Featuring some of "the best salmon in Paris" plus other "excellent" Scandinavian fare, this long-running Champs-Elysées "classic" would be a Nordic nirvana for fans if only they'd update the "boring" decor; the "menu doesn't have a lot of variety" and a doubter or two says "it's slipping", but most find it "very pleasant", especially for a "business meal loosened up by aquavit."

Coq de la Maison Blanche (Le) ▽ 19 | 13 | 18 | fr353
37, bd Jean Jaurès, St-Ouen (Mairie de St-Ouen),
01 40 11 01 23; fax 00 40 11 67 68
■ "Quality bourgeois cooking" makes the majority happy at this "worthwhile" "auberge" in suburban Saint-Ouen; even if prices are "a bit high" and some find the decor "depressing", its "excellent cuisine" and "exceptional" welcome help keep it "filled with actors" and other bon vivants, which may explain why some complain of "cigaret smoke"; there's a pretty terrace in summer.

Cosi ●⓿S⊄ 16 | 10 | 12 | fr134
54, rue de Seine, 6ᵉ (Odéon/St-Germain-des-Prés),
01 46 33 35 36; fax 01 46 33 48 40
■ "The owner's passion is opera and good wine", which is why this "original" little sandwich shop near the Odéon has background opera music and a small choice of wines to accompany the main event: "excellent" sandwiches and panini made on "delicious" bread; it's ideal "for a snack", even if some claim "prices have risen" and the "smiling" staff can be "inefficient."

Costes ●⓿S 13 | 23 | 11 | fr365
Hôtel Costes, 239, rue St-Honoré, 1ᵉʳ (Concorde),
01 42 44 50 25; fax 01 42 44 50 01
☑ Everyone loves the "sumptuous" decor – an "amusing" "rococo" take on Napoleon III style – at this super "trendy" French in the equally trendy Hôtel Costes near the Place Vendôme, so it doesn't matter if critics say the food is "mediocre" and service can be "snobby" and "cold" (unless you're "Bruce Willis") – the "atmosphere makes you forget the faults", if not the high check; the terrace is a scene in summer.

Côte de Bœuf (La) ▽ 19 | 12 | 14 | fr261
4, rue Saussier-Leroy, 17ᵉ (Ternes), 01 42 27 73 50
■ This convivial bistro off the Avenue des Ternes pleases regulars with its "superb prime rib" (the house specialty) as well as the likes of a "super *bourride*" (fish soup), served in a "vaguely provincial" ambiance; prices are moderate and the friendly owner likes to help clients navigate the impressive wine list.

Côté 7ème (Du) S 12 | 12 | 14 | fr204
29, rue Surcouf, 7ᵉ (Invalides/La Tour-Maubourg),
01 47 05 81 65; fax 01 47 05 80 03
■ Partisans say this "unpretentious" bistro near Les Invalides is a "reliable standby" for a "good-value" meal (the prix fixe includes an apéritif, three courses, wine and coffee), outvoting naysayers who shrug that it's "not very interesting"; after a change in owner in '99, the new team is said to be "successfully maintaining the formula" and maybe even "adding some subtlety to the cooking."

Côté Soleil – | – | – | M

1-3, rue St-Hyacinthe, 1er (Tuileries), 01 55 35 30 25; fax 01 55 35 30 27

Beams and "old stone walls" form the backdrop for "delicate Provençal cooking" at this casual spot with a Southern French accent near the Tuileries; if one cynic grouses that it's "like all the others, but with more tourists", others point to its tasty dishes, "warm welcome and nice small check."

Cottage Marcadet (Le) – | – | – | M

151 bis, rue Marcadet, 18e (Lamarck-Caulaincourt), 01 42 57 71 22

"Lovers of good food" will be happy here according to admirers of this "cozy little" Classic French with "pretty" decor in the 18th; it's not well known among surveyors and doubters feel it's "lost a bit of spirit", but good-value prix fixe menus help win it a solid local following.

Coude Fou (Le) ◐ [S] ▽ 11 | 9 | 13 | fr190

12, rue du Bourg Tibourg, 4e (Hôtel-de-Ville), 01 42 77 15 16; fax 01 48 04 08 98

◪ Though opinions on the cooking are mixed ("good bread, excellent steaks" vs. "irregular"), most agree "you can have a good time" at this simple bistro in the Marais thanks to its nice ambiance, "appealing decor" (with old stone walls) and "varied wine list"; decent prices add appeal.

Cou de la Girafe (Le) ◐ 11 | 11 | 10 | fr232

7, rue Paul Baudry, 8e (Franklin D. Roosevelt/ St-Philippe-du-Roule), 01 43 59 47 28; fax 01 42 25 06 62

◪ This trendy Eclectic behind the Champs-Elysées takes hits from critics ("nothing original but the name"), yet it's popular enough to be "very noisy"; some are attracted by "the ambiance" and "pretty waitresses", even if service is "too relaxed" and the bill "too expensive."

Coupe-Chou (Le) ◐ [S] 14 | 23 | 14 | fr288

9, rue de Lanneau, 5e (Maubert-Mutualité), 01 46 33 68 69; fax 01 43 25 94 15

■ "Full of charm for lovers", who can "dine by candlelight" or cozy up to the fireplace at this "calm" Classic French in a "picturesque" old mansion near the Panthéon; maybe the "food doesn't always live up to" the setting, but the place has "undeniable cachet", despite the "tourists" in the crowd.

Coupole (La) ◐ [S] 13 | 19 | 13 | fr284

102, bd du Montparnasse, 14e (Vavin), 01 43 20 14 20; fax 01 43 35 46 14

◪ This Montparnasse legend "looks like your dream of a Parisian brasserie", and if it doesn't taste that way, the "atmosphere and decor make you forget" the food; now part of the Flo group, it's long past its glory years when it drew the likes of Sartre, de Beauvoir and the artists who painted the columns in the sprawling art deco room, but nostalgists say it's still "a must", despite the "noise" and "tourists."

Cour de Rohan (La) **S**

▽ | 14 | 20 | 15 | fr158 |

59-61, rue St-André-des-Arts, 6ᵉ (Odéon),
01 43 25 79 67

■ "Intimate, comfortable little tearoom on the edge of a noisy neighborhood" near the Odéon that's "perfect for a snack", especially "on a rainy afternoon"; if one or two feel it's "letting itself go", most are won over by its "coquettish decor" and "exquisite hot chocolate"; P.S. "the welcome can be a bit stiff, but everything goes well afterwards."

Crêperie de Josselin (La) ●**S**⊅

| 17 | 7 | 13 | fr122 |

67, rue du Montparnasse, 14ᵉ (Edgar Quinet/Montparnasse-Bienvenüe), 01 43 20 93 50

■ Everyone loves this "outstanding crêperie" tucked away in Montparnasse, thus it's always "packed", which means that diners are "on top of each other" and get the "impression they shouldn't linger" ("forget Saturday night, it's much too crowded and smoky" says a regular); still, this form of "supergood" French fast food would make José Bové (the anti-McDonald's crusader) proud.

Crus de Bourgogne (Aux)

| 15 | 13 | 14 | fr232 |

3, rue Bachaumont, 2ᵉ (Les Halles/Sentier), 01 42 33 48 24; fax 01 48 26 66 41

■ With its tile floors and "red-and-white tablecloths", this old-time bistro near Les Halles is "authentic and very pleasant", drawing crowds with "excellent lobster" (a specialty) and other classics at "moderate prices"; though a few feel the cooking has "fallen off", the majority delights in "very good traditional" fare in a "picturesque" area.

Cuisinier François (Le)

| 18 | 12 | 17 | fr276 |

19, rue le Marois, 16ᵉ (Porte de St-Cloud), 01 45 27 83 74; fax 01 45 27 83 74

■ "Beautifully prepared, well-conceived" "traditional and contemporary French cooking" by Thierry Conte, who worked with Joël Robuchon, Marc Meneau and Gérard Boyer, is the draw at this small, "tranquil" spot with "friendly service" in the 16th near the Porte de Saint-Cloud; given the "quality of the dishes" and the "attractive prices", it hardly matters if the "decor doesn't have much character."

Dagorno **S**

| 15 | 14 | 13 | fr298 |

190, av. Jean Jaurès, 19ᵉ (Porte de Pantin), 01 40 40 09 39; fax 01 48 03 17 23

■ A "temple of good meat" that recalls the days when slaughterhouses were located nearby, this 19th-century brasserie at the Villette also does a good job with "very fresh shellfish"; despite "long waits, noise and smoke", it's deemed a "sure bet" for the basics; N.B. prices were recently lowered and there's a good-value prix fixe menu.

Dalloyau S
16 14 13 fr239

2, place Edmond Rostand, 6ᵉ (Luxembourg), 01 43 29 31 10;
fax 01 43 26 25 72
101, rue du Faubourg-St-Honoré, 8ᵉ (Miromesnil/
St-Philippe-du-Roule), 01 42 99 90 00; fax 01 45 63 82 92
69, rue de la Convention, 15ᵉ (Javel), 01 45 77 84 27;
fax 01 45 75 27 99

■ Polite, old-fashioned tearooms that are "superb for tea and pastries", less remarkable for their "limited lunch menu" (no dinner); a dissenter or two finds them "overrated" with "inattentive" service, but "yum-yum" is the predominant reaction to the "fabulous dessert selection"; "note that the friendly welcome isn't just reserved for old ladies."

Dame Jeanne
▽ 18 10 14 fr225

60, rue de Charonne, 11ᵉ (Ledru-Rollin), 01 47 00 37 40;
fax 01 47 00 37 45

■ On the trendy Rue de Charonne near the Bastille, this modern bistro offers "good value" in the form of "truly inventive fare from a real cook" working with "excellent ingredients"; "depressing" decor aside, fans call it "one of the best in eastern Paris" and "worth discovering."

Dame Tartine ●S
9 9 9 fr123

2, rue Brisemiche, 4ᵉ (Hotel de Ville), 01 42 77 32 22;
fax 01 42 77 32 22
59, rue de Lyon, 12ᵉ (Bastille), 01 44 68 96 95; fax 01 44 68 95 50

◪ These French-style *tartine* (open sandwich) shops strike some as "good for a snack", especially the branch next to the Pompidou Center with its "view of the fountain by Niki de Saint Phalle", but as ratings attest, not everyone is a fan ("I didn't think it was possible to make bad sandwiches"); still, budget-watchers find them "satisfying" enough.

Da Mimmo ●
▽ 14 5 12 fr241

39, bd de Magenta, 10ᵉ (Jacques Bonsergent), 01 42 06 44 47

◪ While this Neapolitan near the Gare de l'Est draws a "fashion" crowd that never takes its sunglasses off, those not on a "see-and-be-seen" trip claim it "profits from its clientele" to charge high prices for "boring pizza" and other "overrated" fare; defenders call it "pleasant", but concede that you may have to "know the owner" to appreciate it.

Daru (Le)
▽ 14 11 16 fr328

19, rue Daru, 8ᵉ (Courcelles), 01 42 27 23 60; fax 01 47 54 08 14

◪ "Discreet, romantic little Russian" in the shadow of the Russian Orthodox Church near the Place des Ternes that generally pleases with its "good salmon", "pleasant setting" and "excellent vodka"; if a few nyetsayers are unimpressed and note that it can be "expensive", the fact that it's one of the oldest Russians in Paris means it's doing something right.

Dauphin (Le) S
16 | 10 | 15 | fr254

*167, rue St-Honoré, 1er (Palais Royal-Musée du Louvre),
01 42 60 40 11; fax 01 42 60 01 18*

■ Chefs Didier Oudill and Edgar Duhr, of the well-regarded Café de Paris in Biarritz, took over this venerable bistro across from the Comédie Française in late '99, offering modern Southwestern French fare that's "excellent and original" as well as a "good value"; despite a mix of 19th-century fixtures and art deco touches, the room is rather spare and can be noisy, yet it makes for a "satisfying" meal.

Davé
▽ 14 | 11 | 15 | fr254

*39, rue St-Roch, 1er (Pyramides/Tuileries), 01 42 61 49 48;
fax 01 42 61 49 48*

◪ "Charming" owner Davé "knows how to conquer his clients", which is why "showbiz" and fashion stars frequent this "very 'in'" Chinese on a side street near the Tuileries; while fans find it "captivating", its popularity is a "mystery" to critics who say the "decent" cooking "hardly justifies the prices" and isn't helped by "pitiful decor."

Débarcadère (Le) ◗ S
10 | 14 | 10 | fr272

*11, rue du Débarcadère, 17e (Porte Maillot), 01 53 81 95 95;
fax 01 53 81 95 96*

◪ "You'd think you were in New York" at this loft-like French near the Porte Maillot; debate over the food ("mediocre" vs. "pretty good" for a "trendy" spot) doesn't concern the "young" "see-and-be-seen" types who gather here, not minding if the "music is loud" or "portions are too small" and "a bit pricey"; service can seem like "the slowest in Paris."

Délices d'Aphrodite (Les) ◗
▽ 19 | 14 | 16 | fr226

*4, rue de Candolle, 5e (Censier-Daubenton), 01 43 31 40 39;
fax 01 43 36 13 08*

■ Set in the Latin Quarter just off the Rue Mouffetard, the sister to Mavrommatis offers "lovely food at more affordable prices" in a "vacation-like" setting "nicely decorated with photos and plants"; a "warm welcome" and "shrewd wine list" are more reasons why some consider it the "best Greek" around.

Délices de Szechuen S
17 | 12 | 14 | fr252

*40, av. Duquesne, 7e (St-François-Xavier),
01 43 06 22 55*

■ "Consistently delicious" Chinese fare, a "courteous welcome" and "reasonable" prices draw an "elegant crowd" to this "well-located" spot with a relatively "plush" ambiance (and a lovely terrace) near Saint-François-Xavier in the 7th; "Peking duck served in three courses" is a highlight on a menu that's especially appealing "if you like spicy cooking."

Denise (Chez) ◐ 19 | 18 | 17 | fr270
5, rue des Prouvaires, 1er (Châtelet-Les Halles/Louvre-Rivoli), 01 42 36 21 82; fax 01 45 08 81 99
■ This "wonderful" "old Les Halles rendezvous" near the former site of Paris' wholesale food market still serves big portions of "good, hearty" French fare and "quality" beef to everyone from macho meat eaters to dating couples to night owls (it's open till 7 AM), all chowing down cheek-by-jowl at tables with red-checked tablecloths; it's so popular that "reservations are necessary even at midnight" and beyond (closed weekends).

Dessirier [S] 16 | 13 | 15 | fr398
9, place du Maréchal Juin, 17e (Péreire), 01 42 27 82 14; fax 01 47 66 82 07
◪ Supporters say there's been "lots of progress" since Michel Rostang took over this seafooder near the Place Péreire a few years ago, saluting "creative, flavorful" fare and a "warm welcome"; detractors deem it "middling and expensive", also knocking the "'70s decor"; on balance, it gets mostly ayes for its "good fish and oysters", even if some claim the latter are "priced like gold."

Detourbe Duret 16 | 11 | 14 | fr292
23, rue Duret, 16e (Argentine), 01 45 00 10 26; fax 01 45 00 10 16
◪ Though the "rather modern decor" of Philippe Detourbe's contemporary bistro near the Etoile doesn't please everyone ("a bit too cafeteria"-like), the "delicious" prix fixe menu compensates, since it's a fine "value" for "inventive cooking"; "friendly, courteous" service also helps make it popular with business types at noon, affluent yuppies at night.

Deux Abeilles (Les) 13 | 11 | 10 | fr218
189, rue de l'Université, 7e (Alma-Marceau), 01 45 55 64 04
■ This "charming", "chintz"-bedecked tearoom in the 7th near the Pont de l'Alma is "ideal for a ladies' lunch" or light snack, if you don't mind being "squeezed in like sardines"; some report an "excellent welcome", others find the ambiance a bit "snobby", but overall it's an "agreeable" place to savor tasty "homemade goodies."

Deux Canards (Aux) ▽ 15 | 15 | 15 | fr273
8, rue du Faubourg-Poissonnière, 10e (Bonne Nouvelle), 01 47 70 03 23; fax 01 47 70 18 85
■ Rustic, auberge-style Traditional French on the Grands Boulevards near the Rex cinema, known for its house specialty, duck à l'orange, as well as the showy personality of its owner; devotees quack about its "good little dishes", and if the owner's chatter isn't everyone's cup of tea ("make him be quiet!"), most feel the place is "worth discovering."

Diable des Lombards (Le) S ▽ 9 | 13 | 11 | fr178
64, rue des Lombards, 1ᵉʳ (Châtelet-Les Halles), 01 42 33 81 84; fax 01 42 33 28 22
■ "The best place for a late brunch on Sunday", this "friendly", long-running Les Halles French with a large gay clientele isn't likely to win any awards for its menu of burgers, grills, salads and other light eats, but easygoing prices and an "unpretentious" ambiance help explain why "it's always full and never goes out of style."

Diamantaires (Les) S ▽ 13 | 9 | 16 | fr215
60, rue La Fayette, 9ᵉ (Cadet/Le Peletier), 01 47 70 78 14; fax 01 44 83 02 73
◪ It's not the Middle Eastern–style decor that draws diners to this Greek-Armenian near the Square Montholon in the 9th, but rather the authentic, "very good" food and lively, convivial ambiance (with live music most nights); in business for decades, it's popular with Paris' Armenian community, with prices that are almost as appetizing as the stuffed grape leaves and souvlaki.

Diane (Chez) ◗ ▽ 10 | 15 | 14 | fr233
25, rue Servandoni, 6ᵉ (Luxembourg/St-Sulpice), 01 46 33 12 06; fax 01 43 25 96 55
◪ Cozy, romantic little Left Bank bistro across from the Luxembourg Garden; the few voters who know it approve of its setting (with candlelight and a big bouquet of flowers) as well as the "charming welcome" from owners Diane and Didier, but while fans call it a "good value", critics knock "assembly-line food at real-cuisine prices."

Diep (Chez) ◗S 18 | 14 | 15 | fr321
55, rue Pierre Charron, 8ᵉ (Franklin D. Roosevelt), 01 45 63 52 76; fax 01 42 56 46 56
◪ "If you want to see and be seen" while also enjoying "outstanding Peking duck" and other "excellent" fare, this elegant Chinese off the Champs-Elysées is the place, but some wish portions were "bigger" and prices smaller ("the most expensive spring rolls in Paris"); service is "quick" and efficient to the point that cynics suspect they're trying to "turn over the table" – "bill arrived before the first dish."

Dînée (La) 20 | 14 | 17 | fr356
85, rue Leblanc, 15ᵉ (Balard), 01 45 54 20 49; fax 07 40 60 73 76
■ Good news for diners who find Christophe Chabanel's "wonderful food" too pricey – there's now an "excellent-value" prix fixe menu at this well-regarded but slightly secret Contemporary French deep in the 15th near the Porte de Versailles; the decor is a bit grandmotherly and the "attentive" service can be stiff, but few mind given cooking from "one of the best" young chefs in town.

Divellec (Le) 22 | 17 | 19 | fr664

107, rue de l'Université, 7e (Invalides), 01 45 51 91 96; fax 01 45 51 31 75

◪ On the esplanade of the Invalides in the 7th, this "very classic" luxury fish house serves "exceptional" fare to a "select" crowd unfazed by "scandalously expensive" prices; nitpickers find the ambiance "rather cold" and the decor a bit "sad", while outright critics bemoan "disappointing" food that "lacks originality", but they're swimming against a tide of praise that pronounces it one of "the best" for seafood.

Dix Vins (Le) ◐ ≠ ▽ 16 | 8 | 14 | fr156

57, rue Falguière, 15e (Pasteur), 01 43 20 91 77

■ "A divine surprise" awaits those who venture to this little wine bar in the Falguière district of the 15th, since it offers "an unbeatable 100-franc" prix fixe menu at lunch and dinner plus "a good choice of wines" in a simple "bistro ambiance"; it's "always full to bursting", thus "a little too cramped", but "what a value" – "hope they can keep it up."

Dôme (Le) ◐ [S] 19 | 17 | 17 | fr444

108, bd du Montparnasse, 14e (Vavin), 01 43 35 25 81; fax 01 42 79 01 19

■ "Unforgettable sole", "turbot that's a true reference", "superb shellfish" – this venerable Montparnasse seafooder rides a high tide of praise for its food, though it hits some choppy waters with service that can "leave something to be desired" and a bill that's "very costly"; otherwise, it's smooth sailing at this "chic" place that's ideal for "special occasions."

Dominique ◐ 15 | 14 | 15 | fr348

19, rue Bréa, 6e (Vavin), 01 43 27 08 80; fax 01 43 26 88 35

◪ "The new owner deserves encouragement for trying to wake up" this veteran Montparnasse Russian; if doubters feel it "isn't typically Russian enough", supporters cite "promising progress" at a place that "never goes out of style", praising the likes of caviar and some of the "best blini in Paris"; just beware vodka by the carafe, since it can boost the bill as well as your spirits.

Doobie's [S] 9 | 13 | 10 | fr223

2, rue Robert Estienne, 8e (Franklin D. Roosevelt), 01 53 76 10 76; fax 01 42 25 21 71

◪ Make your way to this still-"trendy" place off the Champs-Elysées for "a Sunday brunch that's one of the best" or "to have a drink and show off" at the bar, perhaps "after having dined elsewhere", since its Eclectic menu doesn't generate much enthusiasm; some find the ambiance "a little too showbiz", but most like its "warm decor", "festive" feel and "varied" clientele.

Dos de la Baleine (Le) [S] 15 | 12 | 14 | fr215

40, rue des Blancs Manteaux, 4e (Hôtel-de-Ville/Rambuteau), 01 42 72 38 98; fax 01 42 71 40 59

■ "Cheap and chic", this "lively" bistro between the Marais and the Pompidou Center is "an unbeatable buy in the heart of Paris"; it can be "noisy" with "slow" service, but it's "good for a dinner with friends" given its appealing decor and gentle prices; popular with a "gay clientele", it welcomes everyone, so "be sure to reserve" in advance.

Driver's ◐ ▽ 9 | 11 | 12 | fr232

6, rue Georges Bizet, 16e (Alma-Marceau), 01 47 23 61 15; fax 01 47 23 80 17

◪ Surveyors don't get too revved up over this bistro with racing-themed decor in the 16th; some call it "good and pleasant", others point to "conventional" food and claim "you have to know the chef to be served correctly"; still, "if you like auto racing", you'll at least like the ambiance.

Drouant 21 | 19 | 19 | fr517

18, rue Gaillon, 2e (Opéra/Quatre-Septembre), 01 42 65 15 16; fax 01 49 24 02 15

◪ This "very classic" French near the Opéra is where the Goncourt jury decides the winner of France's top literary prize, and by most accounts, every diner walks out a winner thanks to "excellent" food, "magnificent service" and a "quiet", "handsome" setting with a famed art deco banister by Ruhlmann; though a few find it "too traditional" and "stiff", most feel it works for "business" or "celebration" and is "worth" the cost; P.S. there's a less formal grill next door.

Drugstore Champs-Elysées ◐[S] 6 | 7 | 8 | fr198

133, av. des Champs-Elysées, 8e (Charles de Gaulle-Etoile), 01 44 43 79 00; fax 01 47 23 00 96

◪ In a "mini shopping mall" near the Etoile, this Gallic version of a coffee shop takes lots of knocks ("weird", "avoid"), but it's "ok for a quick meal" and "good to know about" late at night (open till 2 AM); prices are decent and the '60s decor with "red moleskin" banquettes is so "kitsch" it even has a few fans (maybe they're *Wallpaper* subscribers).

DUC (LE) 24 | 14 | 18 | fr566

243, bd Raspail, 14e (Raspail), 01 43 20 96 30; fax 01 43 20 46 73

■ "Chic, good, pretty and expensive" is the majority opinion on this seafooder near Raspail serving "remarkable fish" to a Left Bank power crowd in a setting recalling a "luxury liner" (mutineers label the decor "dull" with "not much room between tables"); if some feel they "take themselves too seriously", more salute "superb" quality that "almost justifies" the "hefty bill"; P.S. it can be a "nonsmoker's hell."

Durand Dupont ◐ S
10 | 12 | 9 | fr231

*14, place du Marché, Neuilly-sur-Seine (Les Sablons),
01 41 92 93 00; fax 01 46 37 56 79*

◪ Young, affluent Neuilly types consider this stylish bistro "ideal" for a "gigantic" (if "noisy") Sunday brunch and "pleasant" for "a drink" at the bar or alfresco dining out front or in the rear garden, where "you sometimes run into celebs"; yet few rate the food much more than "good", while service is scolded for being "amateurish."

Ebauchoir (L')
15 | 10 | 11 | fr202

*43-45, rue de Cîteaux, 12ᵉ (Faidherbe-Chaligny), 01 43 42 49 31;
fax 01 43 42 43 80*

■ "What a bistro should be", this "convivial" spot between the Bastille and Nation offers "simple, excellent" food at "good prices" in a "friendly, bustling" setting, which is why it's a hit with local hipsters and also draws followers from all over town; "noise" notwithstanding, "you're in for a treat."

Ecaille et Plume
21 | 9 | 16 | fr371

*25, rue Duvivier, 7ᵉ (Ecole-Militaire), 01 45 55 06 72;
fax 01 45 51 38 35*

■ Fish and game specialist near the Ecole Militaire that earns high marks for its "exceptional" cuisine and "themed menus"; run by a "whimsical" host (whose welcome may "take some time to warm up"), it pleases most with its "superb" food, even if prices are steep and many find the setting "a bit tired" with "tightly spaced" tables.

Ecluse (L') ◐ S
11 | 12 | 11 | fr223

*15, quai des Grands-Augustins, 6ᵉ (St-Michel), 01 46 33 58 74;
fax 01 44 07 18 76*
64, rue François 1er, 8ᵉ (George V), 01 47 20 77 09; fax 01 40 70 03 33
*15, place de la Madeleine, 8ᵉ (Madeleine), 01 42 65 34 69;
fax 01 44 71 01 26*
*13, rue de la Roquette, 11ᵉ (Bastille), 01 48 05 19 12;
fax 01 48 05 04 88*
*1, rue d'Armaillé, 17ᵉ (Charles de Gaulle-Etoile), 01 47 63 88 29;
fax 01 44 40 41 91*

◪ Fans find these "lively" wine bars "enjoyable" thanks to "simple", "honest cooking", a "big choice" of vintages and carefully concocted old-fashioned decor (bare wood floors, wine barrels), outvoting doubters who call them "touristy", "uneven" and "pricey for what they are"; they're undeniably handy for "snacking" and sipping in a casual mode.

El Mansour
▽ 20 | 19 | 18 | fr365

*7, rue de La Trémoille, 8ᵉ (Alma-Marceau), 01 47 23 88 18;
fax 01 47 66 11 93*

■ "Everything here is tops, including the prices" say admirers of this "excellent classic Moroccan" in the 8th that keeps regulars happy with delicious tagines and b'steeya, plus "good service" and elegant decor; it's popular with locals and dating couples at night, business diners at noon.

El Picador **S**
– | – | – | M

80, bd des Batignolles, 17ᵉ (Villiers), 01 43 87 28 87; fax 01 43 87 67 17
"*Olé*" shout fans of the "good Spanish cooking" at this veteran in the 17th offering the "best paella", "excellent sangria" and tasty tapas; style mavens aren't mad about the "ridiculous decor with plastic dolls", but since everyone likes the "satisfying" eats, "friendly" service and modest prices, "alas, it's always full."

ELYSÉES DU VERNET (LES) **S**
24 | 23 | 21 | fr666

Hôtel Vernet, 25, rue Vernet, 8ᵉ (Charles de Gaulle-Etoile/George V), 01 44 31 98 98; fax 01 44 31 85 69
■ "Excellent food", "fabulous" decor and "wonderful service" add up to "grand" haute cuisine dining in the Hôtel Vernet off the Champs-Elysées; Alain Solivérès "never ceases to amaze" with his Provençal-accented menu, and the same could be said of the "remarkable sommelier" and glass cupola by Gustave Eiffel; in short, "one of the best restaurants in Paris", and priced accordingly.

Emporio Armani Caffé
13 | 16 | 11 | fr253

149, bd St-Germain, 6ᵉ (St-Germain-des-Prés), 01 45 48 62 15; fax 01 45 48 53 17
◪ A "trendy clientele" refuels on "good-quality" Italian fare at this "chic", "always crowded" cafe on the mezzanine of the Armani boutique in Saint-Germain; the "minimalist" Milanese decor makes some ask "where's the Italian warmth?", but the staff "goes to a lot of trouble" (when they aren't "swamped") and some would "return more often if prices weren't so prohibitive" and the wait so "long."

Enfants Gâtés (Les) **S**
– | – | – | I

43, rue des Francs-Bourgeois, 4ᵉ (St-Paul), 01 42 77 07 63
Marais tearoom that's "ideal" for a light meal, especially on "a tranquil weekend"; its low prices and healthy slant help draw an arty young crowd, and while the jury is still out on the effect of new ownership, it's a pleasant place to stop for some quiche or a salad while shopping at nearby boutiques.

Enoteca (L') ◖ **S**
15 | 13 | 15 | fr264

25, rue Charles V, 4ᵉ (St-Paul), 01 42 78 91 44; fax 01 44 59 31 72
◪ Most agree that this "rustic" Marais bistro à vins has "one of the best Italian wine lists in Paris" plus lots of "bohemian" "charm", with Murano lamps, an ancient beamed ceiling and "warm" service, but there's a bit of debate on the Italian food: "real and refined", "excellent ingredients" vs. "the wine is better", "how can you cook pasta badly?"; fans carry the vote, though, hence it can be "too crowded and noisy."

Entoto

▽ | 16 | 8 | 14 | fr192 |

143-145, rue L.M. Nordmann, 13ᵉ (Glacière), 01 45 87 08 51

■ "What a trip!" say those who know this little dinner-only Ethiopian in the 13th where "you eat with your fingers", using bread to scoop up spicy stew-like dishes; it's a "unique" experience and "worth" discovering for the "originality" of the cooking as well as the modesty of the tab.

Entracte (L') (Chez Sonia et Carlos) S

| – | – | – | M |

44, rue d'Orsel, 18ᵉ (Abbesses/Anvers), 01 46 06 93 41

Something of "a secret", this Traditional French near Sacré Cœur hasn't been discovered by many surveyors, which is fine with fans who say its "greatness is in its modesty"; expect "simple" food made from "excellent ingredients", a "warm" setting and friendly service, all at gentle prices.

Entrecôte (L') – Dédicace

| 14 | 10 | 11 | fr204 |

33, rue de Verneuil, 7ᵉ (Rue du Bac), 01 42 61 13 94;
fax 01 42 61 11 28

■ As the name suggests, "good meat" is the raison d'être of this standby in the 7th with a prix fixe menu offering steak topped with a "magic sauce" plus french fries and dessert; some may deem it "banal", but it does the trick for habitués who find it "amusing" for a bargain beef fix.

Entrepôt (L') S

▽ | 11 | 16 | 11 | fr197 |

7, rue Francis de Pressensé, 14ᵉ (Pernety), 01 45 40 60 70;
fax 01 45 45 49 94

■ "The decor and ambiance" are the big draws at this French set in a Montparnasse art movie house, but the food also gets some applause and the "warm welcome", pleasant terrace and occasional music add appeal; penny-pinchers say it's "maybe a little pricey" for what it is, though.

En Ville

| – | – | – | M |

6, rue du Sabot, 6ᵉ (St-Germain-des-Prés), 01 42 22 21 56;
fax 01 42 22 26 21

Replacing Le Sybarite, this smart new bistro with a good-value prix fixe menu is proving to be a success in the heart of Saint-Germain, drawing casual yet stylish young locals who come to enjoy well-prepared traditional fare in a setting with old stone walls, beams and candles; the cheese course is also a hit, featuring selections from Quatrehommes, the excellent fromagerie in the Rue de Sèvres.

Epicure 108

| – | – | – | M |

108, rue Cardinet, 17ᵉ (Malesherbes), 01 47 63 50 91

"Alsatian inspiration and Japanese techniques" yield "very good" cooking at this original French near the Square des Batignolles; chef Tetsu Goya trained at some of the top restaurants in Alsace and displays an impressive mastery of the region's cuisine; the narrow room isn't much to look at, but the food is not only satisfying, it's a "good value."

Epi d'Or (L') ∇ 18 | 14 | 18 | fr267

25, rue Jean-Jacques Rousseau, 1er (Louvre-Rivoli), 01 42 36 38 12; fax 01 42 36 46 25

■ This venerable bistro between Palais Royal and Les Halles serves "very good traditional cuisine" in an "intimate", old-fashioned setting with moleskin banquettes and faience on the walls; "elegant but relaxed", it's a "consistent" local standby that has stood up to the test of time, and while not cheap, it delivers quality for the money.

EPI DUPIN (L') 22 | 13 | 17 | fr256

11, rue Dupin, 6e (Sèvres-Babylone), 01 42 22 64 56; fax 01 42 22 30 42

■ "Excellent in all respects", this little bistro at Sèvres-Babylone is a big hit not only because of François Pasteau's "delicious", "inventive" cooking, but also because it's a "fantastic" prix fixe value; service is "pleasant" and "relaxed" (if sometimes "slow") and though the setting is "cramped" it has "charm", with "stone walls" and beams, leaving "just one regret": "having to book so far in advance."

Erawan 18 | 12 | 15 | fr247

76, rue de la Fédération, 15e (La Motte-Picquet-Grenelle), 01 47 83 55 67; fax 01 47 34 85 98

■ "Almost the real thing" say admirers of this "lively" Thai in the 15th with "surprising", "piquant" flavors and "rapid, efficient service"; a warm welcome and simple yet "chic" decor are more reasons why boosters consider it "one of the best" of its kind in Paris.

Escale (L') [S] 💳̸ – | – | – | M

1, rue des Deux Ponts, 4e (Pont-Marie), 01 43 54 94 23

The warm hospitality of the Auvergnat owners makes this snug wine bar on the Ile Saint-Louis feel like "a friend's" place; regulars find it easy to while away the afternoon here, enjoying the "pleasure of a good glass of wine" plus simple homey fare such as *andouillette* (sausage) and veal stew at easy prices; no dinner.

Escargot Montorgueil (L') [S] 16 | 18 | 15 | fr330

38, rue Montorgueil, 1er (Les Halles), 01 42 36 83 51; fax 01 42 36 35 05

◪ Everyone admires the "beautiful" Napoleon III decor of this venerable bistro in Les Halles run by the sister of La Tour d'Argent's Claude Terrail, but while supporters say it remains a "temple of snails", others claim the escargots "have no taste" and come at "rather elevated" prices, like the rest of the menu; still, out-of-towners "adore" it.

Espace Sud-Ouest/Chez Papa ◐ [S] 12 | 6 | 9 | fr164

29, rue de L'Arcade, 8e (St-Lazard), 01 42 65 43 68
206, rue La Fayette, 10e (Louis Blanc), 01 42 09 53 87; fax 01 42 09 53 87

(Continues)

Espace Sud-Ouest/Chez Papa (Cont.)
*6, rue Gassendi, 14^e (Denfert-Rochereau), 01 43 22 41 19;
fax 01 43 22 41 19*
101, rue de la Croix Nivert, 15^e (Commerce), 01 48 28 31 88
■ These specialists in Southwestern French fare dish up
"huge portions of tasty country food" for "small prices",
which is why they're a hit with "students" and other "under-
30" types ("who don't yet know good cooking" snipes an
outvoted critic); though diners are "piled in like sardines" and
the wines and service "leave something to be desired",
that doesn't stop the "noisy" crowds from streaming in.

ESPADON (L') S   22 | 24 | 22 | fr684
*Hôtel Ritz, 15, place Vendôme, 1er (Concorde/Opéra),
01 43 16 30 80; fax 01 43 16 33 75*
■ "Ritzy" indeed, this haute cuisine dining room in the
famed hotel on the Place Vendôme has a new chef, Maurice
Guilloüet, a Robuchon student, and while there's a bit of
debate about the cooking, ratings back those who find
it "excellent", with further praise for the "luxury, calm and
voluptuousness" of the setting and the "courtesy and
competence" of the staff; it all comes at a price, of course.

Espadon Bleu (L')   15 | 14 | 15 | fr315
*25, rue des Grands-Augustins, 6e (Odéon/St. Michel),
01 46 33 00 85; fax 01 43 54 54 48*
◪ Jacques Cagna's casual seafooder across from his
eponymous flagship in Saint-Germain has "pretty" decor
(white-painted beams and mosaic-topped tables) and
"very pleasant service", but while the food gets decent
ratings, disappointed diners feel "Cagna should do better",
perhaps influenced by prices that seem high for simply
prepared fare; a new chef may improve things, since
some call it "a real revelation" since his arrival.

Etoile (L') ◐S   15 | 19 | 13 | fr393
*12, rue de Presbourg, 8^e (Charles de Gaulle-Etoile),
01 45 00 78 70; fax 01 45 00 78 71*
◪ "Considering that you go" for the "magnificent view" of
the Arc de Triomphe and the "trendy" scene (you may find
yourself "sitting next to" a celeb), the "food is surprisingly
good" at this stylish French that's "ideal for business meals"
or dining with "friends from the provinces"; service could
be improved and it's "expensive", but there's "a real cook
in the kitchen" and you "can't beat that view."

Etoile Marocaine (L') S   ▽ 19 | 15 | 17 | fr280
56, rue Galilée, 8e (George V), 01 47 20 44 43; fax 01 47 20 69 85
◪ Come to this Moroccan in the 8th near the Champs-
Elysées for "good couscous" in a "tranquil" ambiance
advise fans of this "slightly pricey" spot with "attractive
decor" that's warmer than the usual tiled North African look;
if not everyone agrees ("mediocre"), ratings suggest that
most enjoy the cooking as well as the professional service.

Etrier (L')
— — — I

154, rue Lamarck, 18ᵉ (Guy Môquet), 01 42 29 14 01
"Intimate" bistro in Montmartre offering "a warm welcome" and "well-thought-out" market-inspired fare prepared by two chefs who once cooked for François Mitterrand; though known by few surveyors, it's popular with regulars (booking advised) since it's one of the rare places in the area where you can eat well for a decent price.

Excuse (L')
▽ 15 14 15 fr278

14, rue Charles V, 4ᵉ (St-Paul), 01 42 77 98 97; fax 01 42 77 88 55
■ This low-profile French with "plush" decor near Saint-Paul in the Marais "deserves to be better known" say admirers of Anthony Laboubé (ex Lucas Carton and Yvan), who turns out an inventive menu that includes dishes such as ravioli stuffed with crab and bean sprouts; it's a bit pricey, but service is good and the ambiance is one of quiet chic.

Fabrice (Chez)
— — — I

38, rue Croix des Petits Champs, 1ᵉʳ (Palais Royal-Musée du Louvre), 01 40 20 06 46
"Holding well to its course", chef-owner Fabrice Wolff's little dining room near the Place des Victoires serves "good, original" French fare at "remarkably low prices" via a choice of prix fixe menus; "to be encouraged" say fans.

Fabrique (La) ◗ⓢ
▽ 10 12 12 fr170

53, rue du Faubourg-St-Antoine, 11ᵉ (Bastille), 01 43 07 67 07; fax 01 43 07 69 00
■ "Not the place for a romantic dinner" or quiet chats, this Alsatian-style bistro/'beer bar' near the Bastille draws a "young" crowd with "excellent" DJ music, "good" eats like tarte flambé and flowing beer served amid retro-"futuristic" decor; "cheap" prices make it all the more "amusing."

Fakhr el Dine ◗ⓢ
19 14 17 fr306

3, rue Quentin Bauchart, 8ᵉ (Charles de Gaulle-Etoile), 01 47 23 44 42; fax 01 53 70 01 81
30, rue de Longchamp, 16ᵉ (Trocadéro), 01 47 27 90 00; fax 01 53 70 01 81
■ For admirers, the "best Lebanese" fare in Paris is served at this duo in the 8th and the 16th; besides "high-quality" fare, assets include "good service" and "luxurious" decor, which help justify prices that some find a bit "expensive."

Faucher
22 15 19 fr464

123, av. de Wagram, 17ᵉ (Ternes/Wagram), 01 42 27 61 50; fax 01 46 22 25 72
■ "Serious" French cuisine sparked by occasional touches of "daring" wins high marks for Gérard Faucher's well-regarded restaurant in the 17th; "attentive" service, "original" wines and an ambiance that's "chic" yet "familial" are more reasons why it's considered a "good value" despite high prices; the terrace is appreciated in summer.

FAUGERON

24 | 17 | 22 | fr651

*52, rue de Longchamp, 16ᵉ (Trocadéro), 01 47 04 24 53;
fax 01 47 55 62 90*

◪ "A grand classic" is how admirers view Henri and Gerlindé Faugeron's haute cuisine standout in the 16th; "maybe it's not too modern, but all the better", it "never disappoints" with its "excellent" food, "nonpompous service" and "well-spaced tables"; dissenters demur, finding both the food and decor in need of "a face-lift", but as ratings show, they're solidly outvoted; P.S. there's "marvelous game" in season.

Fellini

17 | 13 | 16 | fr303

*47, rue de l'Arbre Sec, 1ᵉʳ (Louvre-Rivoli), 01 42 60 90 66 Ⓢ
58, rue de la Croix Nivert, 15ᵉ (Commerce/Emile Zola),
01 45 77 40 77; fax 01 45 77 22 54*

◪ For an Italian meal "without chichi", fans laud this duo in the 1st and the 15th; not only is the food of "good quality", but the welcome is "warm" and service is "efficient and pleasant", like "in Italy"; still, a few spoilers feel the cooking has "slipped a bit" and note that it's "kind of expensive"; N.B. aesthetes may prefer the branch in the 1st, which has a warm setting with exposed stone walls.

Ferme de Boulogne (La)

▽ 18 | 16 | 18 | fr279

*1, rue de Billancourt, Boulogne-Billancourt (Pont-de-St-Cloud),
01 46 03 61 69; fax 01 46 04 55 70*

■ "Cozy" French near the Saint-Cloud bridge that reaps praise for its "excellent" cooking and "attentive reception" and service; since it can be "a bit crowded at lunch", dinner might be an easier option, especially since there are well-priced prix fixe menus; expect a business crowd at noon, a local bourgeois crowd in the evening.

Ferme des Mathurins (La)

▽ 16 | 12 | 11 | fr237

*17, rue Vignon, 8ᵉ (Havre-Caumartin/Madeleine),
01 42 66 46 39; fax 01 42 66 00 27*

■ "Lovers of old-fashioned food who aren't on a diet" will be in heaven at this Traditional French with a Burgundian accent near the Madeleine, serving "heaping plates" of "stick-to-your-ribs" food in a setting that "transports you back" a few decades; the quality/price ratio is "satisfying" and it would be "hard to get more down-home" than this.

Ferme (La) ⌀

– | – | – | ⌐

*55-57, rue St-Roch, 1ᵉʳ (Pyramides), 01 40 20 12 12;
fax 01 40 20 06 06*

"In step with the times", since Parisians are suddenly interested in all-natural eating, this "original concept" in the 1st offers "excellent sandwiches" and other quick eats made from "exceptional", mostly organic ingredients and served at low prices in a "relaxing, minimalist" setting; converts consider it "a must for lunch" (no dinner).

Ferme St-Hubert (La) 16 | 10 | 12 | fr221

21, rue Vignon, 8e (Madeleine), 01 47 42 79 20; fax 01 47 42 46 97

■ "A must" for fromage fanciers, this respected cheese shop near the Madeleine also serves a menu of "very good dishes based on cheese"; while there are no complaints about the food, service gets mixed responses: "friendly and professional" vs. "too long and too few smiles."

Ferme St-Simon (La) 20 | 16 | 18 | fr377

6, rue de St-Simon, 7e (Rue du Bac/Solférino), 01 45 48 35 74; fax 01 40 49 07 31

◪ "Always delicious" is how one satisfied customer sums up this rustic Traditional French frequented by politicians, editors and locals from the 7th; if a fractious faction suggests "it's napping – wake up!" and note that diners are "on top of each other", more appreciate its "very good quality and service", even if it comes at a rather high price.

Fermette du Sud-Ouest (La) – | – | – | M

31, rue Coquillière, 1er (Les Halles/Palais Royal-Musée du Louvre), 01 42 36 73 55

"Very good, basic" Southwestern French cuisine is served at this cozy spot near Les Halles; the few surveyors who know it appreciate its "traditional, flavorful" fare (cassoulet is the house specialty), if not service that can be "too quick"; the old-fashioned rustic setting, with stone walls and pine paneling, can seem charming or a bit worn.

Fermette Marbeuf 1900 (La) ◐ [S] 13 | 22 | 14 | fr311

5, rue Marbeuf, 8e (Alma-Marceau), 01 53 23 08 00; fax 01 53 23 08 09

◪ "If only the food would catch up with the cost" and "superb" Belle Epoque decor, this Traditional French near the Champs-Elysées (now part of the Blanc brothers chain) would be an unqualified hit; but even as it is, many people find the cuisine and service "good" and the ambiance "enjoyable", recommending it "for business dining."

Fernandises (Les) ◐ ▽ 16 | 10 | 16 | fr269

19, rue de la Fontaine-au-Roi, 11e (République), 01 48 06 16 96

■ "Too bad this kind of place is becoming so rare, because it *is* France" say fans of this rustic spot near the Place de la République offering "hearty" cuisine from Normandy in a setting that's homey if a little "dull"; "good wines" enhance the pleasure, as do well-priced prix fixe menus.

Filoche (Le) ▽ 17 | 11 | 17 | fr238

34, rue du Laos, 15e (Cambronne/La Motte-Picquet-Grenelle), 01 45 66 44 60

■ "Traditional" bistro fare is served in "generous portions" at this "nice neighborhood" place near Cambronne; fish is a specialty, and while the cooking may be "unsurprising", the flavors are "perfect" and diners are welcomed "like family"; moderate prices and a relaxed ambiance also please locals.

Findi ◐ 🅂
13 | 14 | 13 | fr240

24, av. George V, 8ᵉ (Alma-Marceau/George V), 01 47 20 14 78;
fax 01 47 20 10 08

■ According to admirers (the majority), "*la dolce vita*" can be experienced at this "chic" Italian near the Champs-Elysées that sports a "warmer" new 'palazzo'-like look in the wake of its takeover by the Blanc brothers; both the food (especially the pasta) and service earn praise, and while it remains popular with stylish young yuppies at night, "space between tables" makes it good "for a business lunch."

Fins Gourmets (Aux) ⊟
11 | 13 | 14 | fr221

213, bd St-Germain, 7ᵉ (Rue du Bac), 01 42 22 06 57;
fax 01 42 22 06 57

■ This "unpretentious traditionalist" on the Boulevard Saint-Germain near Solférino is "an oasis" for those seeking "typical" Southwestern French fare at moderate prices in an "authentic", "old-fashioned" bistro setting; even those who feel the cooking "is less pleasant than the rest" are charmed by its ambiance, service and "crowd of habitués" – let's hope "nothing changes" here.

Finzi ◐ 🅂
14 | 10 | 11 | fr264

182, bd Haussmann, 8ᵉ (St-Philippe-du-Roule), 01 42 25 48 04;
fax 01 45 61 41 05

▨ It "feels like Milan" in this "animated" Italian on the Boulevard Haussmann where diners dig into "delicious" pastas while putting up with "noise", "cramped" tables and service that can be "vague" ("are we disturbing them?"); critics consider it "uninteresting" and "overpriced."

Flambée (La)
– | – | – | I

4, rue Taine, 12ᵉ (Daumesnil/Dugommier), 01 43 43 21 80;
fax 01 43 47 32 04

"Very good cassoulet" is a standout on the Southwestern French menu, which is mostly cooked before your eyes on a wooden fire in the middle of this bistro in the 12th near Daumesnil; some feel the "rustic" decor is verging on "tacky" and say that apart from the owner, the staff could stand to polish its service skills, but it's hard to argue with the "good-value" prices.

Flamboyant (Le) 🅂
– | – | – | M

11, rue Boyer-Barret, 14ᵉ (Pernety), 01 45 41 00 22

Dining at this little Caribbean in the Pernety quarter of the 14th is "like being invited to someone's home in the French West Indies" – the food is "excellent" and so is the welcome: "even after a long absence, I was recognized and fussed over"; moderate prices and live music on some nights are more reasons to check it out.

Flandrin (Le) ◐ [S] — 11 | 10 | 11 | fr306

80, av. Henri Martin, 16^e (Rue de la Pompe), 01 45 04 34 69; fax 01 45 04 67 41

◪ Seated on the terrace of this brasserie in a former train station in the 16th, "you'd think you were on the Croisette in Cannes" given the "showy" crowd and "symphony of cell phones"; critics find the service "even snobbier" than the patrons and also bash costly, "uninteresting food", but defenders point to "quality" cooking and a "strategic" location that's "very practical" if you live nearby.

Flora Danica [S] — 17 | 15 | 15 | fr331

142, av. des Champs-Elysées, 8e (Charles de Gaulle-Etoile/ George V), 01 44 13 86 26; fax 01 42 25 83 10

■ "To try it is to like it" say fans of this Scandinavian downstairs from big brother Copenhague on the Champs-Elysées; offering "very good herring", "excellent salmon" and "fresh beer", it's a little "pricey" but perfect for a "quick" lunch or bite "before a movie", and its indoor patio is a "calm" haven in a busy area.

Flore en l'Ile (Le) ◐ [S] — ▽ 13 | 15 | 10 | fr221

42, quai d'Orléans, 4e (Hôtel-de-Ville), 01 43 29 88 27; fax 01 43 29 73 54

◪ The food doesn't arouse much enthusiasm and service can be "impersonal", but this brasserie on the Ile Saint-Louis boasts a "top terrace" with an "unbeatable view of Notre Dame", hence it can be "overcrowded" with locals and tourists in summer.

Floridita (Le) — ▽ 9 | 13 | 11 | fr298

19, rue de Presbourg, 16e (Charles de Gaulle-Etoile), 01 45 00 84 84; fax 01 45 00 60 63

◪ Stogie aficionados are happy to puff away at this Latin-accented cigar bar/French restaurant with "elegant" decor on the Champs-Elysées, but even they would probably admit that the house specialty is "Havanas, not cuisine"; fuming critics say "it has nothing in common with the mythic" Hemingway hangout in Havana for which it's named, and ratings suggest that the overall verdict is middling.

Florimond — 17 | 14 | 18 | fr276

19, av de La Motte-Picquet, 7^e (Ecole-Militaire), 01 45 55 40 38; fax 01 45 55 40 38

■ Though few surveyors know this "small" but stylish French in the 7th, it's "often full" of well-heeled locals who come here to unwind in the evening and enjoy its "very good food" (including stuffed cabbage, the house specialty) and "very friendly" demeanor; moderately priced prix fixe menus are a bonus.

FocLy S
17 | 11 | 16 | fr253
79, av. Charles de Gaulle, Neuilly-sur-Seine (Les Sablons), 01 46 24 43 36; fax 01 46 24 48 46

■ A "sure bet" for "high-quality Chinese" (plus other Asian dishes) say patrons of this Neuilly fixture; if some find it "on the pricey side", well-heeled locals don't mind, especially since the ambiance is "calm" and service "discreet."

Fogón Saint Julien ●S
19 | 14 | 14 | fr253
10, rue St-Julien-le-Pauvre, 5ᵉ (Maubert-Mutualité/ St-Michel), 01 43 56 31 33; fax 01 43 54 07 00

■ "Prodigious paella" served on "tables hardly bigger than your plate" is a standout at this Latin Quarter Spaniard that also earns olés for its "superb tapas", charcuterie and "interesting" Spanish wines; the intimate setting is "full of charm", and though one or two complainers find it "overrated", fans have just one regret: "the calories."

Fontaine d'Auteuil (La)
▽ 20 | 13 | 19 | fr378
35 bis, rue La Fontaine, 16ᵉ (Jasmin), 01 42 88 04 47; fax 01 42 88 95 12

■ "Intelligent, high-quality cuisine" backed up by "attentive service" wins approval for this French in the Auteuil district of the 16th; though not cheap, it delivers "very good value", especially via the prix fixe; one quibble: the decor's a bit "sad."

Fontaine de Mars (La) S
16 | 16 | 17 | fr268
129, rue St-Dominique, 7ᵉ (Ecole-Militaire), 01 47 05 46 44; fax 01 47 05 11 13

■ Besides a "fine sampling of Southwestern French cuisine", this "authentic", "old-style" bistro near the Ecole Militaire has lots of "charm" thanks to its "picturesque", "checkered-tablecloth" setting, "jovial service" and "good crowd"; the terrace makes it all the better in summer.

Fontaines (Les) S
18 | 4 | 13 | fr225
9, rue Soufflot, 5ᵉ (Maubert-Mutualité), 01 43 26 42 80; fax 01 44 07 03 49

■ "A little effort with the decor" is sorely needed and "there isn't much room to maneuver", yet fans are willing to "stand and wait" if necessary to dig into the "robust, copious" Traditional French fare served at this bistro near the Panthéon; service is "quick and courteous", and the bill that follows makes it all the more "worthwhile."

Fontanarosa S
▽ 18 | 13 | 15 | fr252
28, bd Garibaldi, 15ᵉ (Cambronne), 01 45 66 97 84; fax 01 47 83 96 30

■ Though few surveyors know it, this Italian with terra-cotta-toned walls and a garden-like look in the 15th is "often crowded", in which case the reception can "leave something to be desired", but the "food and decor are worth the detour" according to admirers; a moderately priced lunch prix fixe and summer terrace also argue in its favor.

Foujita ▽ 17 | 6 | 8 | fr193
41, rue St-Roch, 1er (Pyramides), 01 42 61 42 93
■ "Excellent sushi" and "excellent value" are keys to the appeal of this little Japanese near the Tuileries Gardens in the heart of town; service is "quick", and though there's not much by way of decor, the "ambiance really recalls Tokyo."

Fouquet's (Le) ◐ [S] 13 | 17 | 15 | fr409
99, av. des Champs-Elysées, 8e (George V), 01 47 23 50 00; fax 01 47 23 50 55
◪ The Lucien Barrière group's makeover of this "chic" Champs-Elysées institution gets mixed reviews: fans say it's been "resuscitated in fine form", with spiffed-up showbiz-oriented decor and "more inventive" French fare, but foes find "no interest, apart from the history", citing "acceptable" eats at stiff prices; still, it's a "lively" scene, especially on the terrace, and a popular "rendezvous" in a busy part of town.

Fous d'en Face (Les) ◐ [S] ▽ 12 | 8 | 12 | fr202
3, rue du Bourg Tibourg, 4e (Hôtel-de-Ville), 01 48 87 03 75; fax 01 42 78 38 03
■ Maybe it's "nothing spectacular" and the decor is "a bit dull", but this "nice, cheap" bistro near the Hôtel de Ville boasts "classic dishes prepared with the right amount of originality", an owner with a sense of "humor" and "some excellent wines to discover"; the terrace is a plus.

Francis (Chez) ◐ [S] 11 | 13 | 11 | fr328
7, place de l'Alma, 8e (Alma-Marceau), 01 47 20 86 83; fax 01 47 20 43 26
◪ A "prime location" at the Place de l'Alma with a view of "the Eiffel Tower glittering" across the river, "good seafood" and sidewalk tables are this brasserie's drawing cards, and they're strong enough to keep "habitués" coming despite grumbles about service and "ridiculously high prices."

Françoise (Chez) ◐ [S] 14 | 12 | 15 | fr292
Aérogare Invalides, face 2, rue Fabert, 7e (Invalides), 01 47 05 49 03; fax 01 45 51 96 20
■ To rub elbows with politicos, head to this Classic French that's perfect for dining with your "favorite deputy" from the nearby Assemblée Nationale; set in the *aérogare* of the Invalides, it's considered a "good value" for "consistent" cooking and "professional" service, but there's a split vote on the decor: "pleasant" vs. "sad."

Fred (Chez) ▽ 15 | 9 | 12 | fr245
190 bis, bd Péreire, 17e (Porte Maillot), 01 45 74 20 48; fax 01 45 74 20 48
■ "Traditional and reassuring" describes this bistro overlooking the gardens of the Boulevard Péreire; there are a few grumbles about the welcome and some find it a bit "worn", but even they concede it's "authentic", offering Lyonnaise cuisine augmented by some "nice little wines."

Frégate (La)   – – – M

30, av. Ledru Rollin, 12ᵉ (Gare de Lyon), 01 43 43 90 32
Though not widely known to surveyors, this veteran fish house in the 12th is said to be a "very good seafood value", with a prix fixe menu offering such dishes as salmon with scallops; besides "quality" cooking at moderate prices, it boasts a "nice nautical setting" and "friendly service."

Fumoir (Le) ◐S   10 18 10 fr237

6, rue de l'Amiral-de-Coligny, 1ᵉʳ (Louvre-Rivoli), 01 42 92 00 24; fax 01 42 92 05 05
◪ It's not the French food ("decent") that makes this cafe/restaurant a "hot" scene, but rather its "fabulous" ambiance and "superb location" across from the Louvre; "ideal for a cocktail", it draws a "trendy" crowd with its "seductive" decor (with a 'library' room in back), but on some nights "it really lives up to its name" (The Smoking Room).

Gallopin ◐   12 17 13 fr256

40, rue Notre-Dame-des-Victoires, 2ᵉ (Bourse), 01 42 36 45 38; fax 00 42 36 10 32
■ "Time-pressed businessmen" at lunch and theatergoers at night are among the many who appreciate this circa 1876 brasserie near the stock exchange, with "food and service that go the distance" and "beautiful" old-fashioned decor; it can be "very noisy" at noontime – listen carefully and you might pick up "some tips" from the brokers who fill the room.

Galoche d'Aurillac (La) ◐   ▽ 16 12 10 fr220

41, rue de Lappe, 11ᵉ (Bastille), 01 47 00 77 15
■ Not only does this Traditional French near the Opéra Bastille provide "authentic" Auvergnat fare, including fine charcuterie and sausage with *aligot* (potatoes with cheese and garlic), it also sells *galoches* (clogs) for those really in a "country" mood; the decor could stand "redoing" but it's a "pleasant" old-fashioned outpost in a trendy part of town.

Gamin de Paris (Au) ◐S   15 11 12 fr193

51, rue Vieille du Temple, 4ᵉ (Hôtel-de-Ville/St-Paul), 01 42 78 97 24
■ The "wait can be too long" and you may "have to beg to be served", but that doesn't deter fans of this Marais French with an "original", greenery-filled setting and "copious" portions of "good", traditional fare; if some feel "success has spoiled it", more consider it a "best buy."

Gare (La) ◐S   10 18 10 fr239

19, chaussée de la Muette, 16ᵉ (La Muette), 01 42 15 15 31; fax 01 42 15 15 23
◪ Packed with "preppies" from the 16th, this big, "noisy", "trendy" French boasts a "clever" setting in the former Passy–La Muette train station, with a "magnificent terrace"; the rotisserie-focused fare "doesn't leave a lasting memory", but "slow" service might: "we're still waiting for our apéritif."

Gastroquet (Le)
▽ | 19 | 12 | 18 | fr275

10, rue Desnouettes, 15ᵉ (Convention), 01 48 28 60 91; fax 01 45 33 23 70

■ The "freshness" of a menu "updated according to the market" "assures the success" of this "excellent neighborhood" French in the 15th behind the Porte de Versailles, and "on top of that", diners are warmly received by the owners; moderate prix fixe menus are another bonus.

Gaudriole (La) S
▽ | 14 | 19 | 15 | fr294

30, rue Montpensier, 1ᵉʳ (Palais Royal-Musée du Louvre), 01 42 97 55 49; fax 14 29 75 50 46

■ To best enjoy this Classic French, visit in summer, when its "remarkable setting" in the gardens of the Palais Royal is at its loveliest and dining on the terrace is "unbeatable", making the "reasonably good" food seem all the better; some find the indoor decor a little "sad" by comparison.

Gauloise (La) S
13 | 13 | 13 | fr290

59, av. de La Motte-Picquet, 15ᵉ (La Motte-Picquet-Grenelle), 01 47 34 11 64; fax 01 40 61 09 70

■ This one-time Mitterrand haunt in the 15th near the Motte-Picquet "has found a way to carry on" in his absence, serving "no-unpleasant-surprises" brasserie fare in a "convivial" setting adorned with "photos of celebs"; its popularity is such that "you'd better reserve."

Gavroche (Le) ◑
▽ | 17 | 10 | 15 | fr220

19, rue St-Marc, 2ᵉ (Bourse/Richelieu-Drouot), 01 42 96 89 70

■ "Please, don't bring any tourists here" plead patrons of this "real old-style bistro" near the stock exchange; it's "noisy" and diners are "squeezed in like sardines", but the food is "very savory" ("best beef rib ever!"), service is "acrobatic and efficient" and the ambiance is "warm" and homey; oh yes, it's also "inexpensive."

Gaya, L'Estaminet
17 | 14 | 16 | fr338

17, rue Duphot, 1ᵉʳ (Madeleine), 01 42 60 43 03; fax 01 42 60 69 35

■ "Deserves a bigger following" say admirers of this upscale seafooder behind the Place de la Madeleine ("ideal for a business lunch in this area"); while the cooking is "not innovative", the fish is of "excellent quality" ("the meat too"), service is "good" and the setting, adorned with ceramic tiles, is appealing.

Gaya Rive Gauche
22 | 15 | 17 | fr412

44, rue du Bac, 7ᵉ (Rue du Bac), 01 45 44 73 73; fax 01 45 44 73 73

■ "First-class fish" "cooked with talent" and occasional "flashes of brilliance" draws a "very 7th arrondissement" crowd (literary and political types) to this "quiet and nicely small" Left Bank seafooder; a "good wine list", "friendly welcome" and "pretty" decor are further assets, but "prices are really getting up there."

Gazelle (La)
— — — M

9, rue Rennequin, 17ᵉ (Ternes), 01 42 67 64 18; fax 01 42 67 82 77

"Africa in Paris" can be experienced at this change of pace in the 17th, popular with Paris' West African population; it offers mostly Cameroonian, plus other West African, dishes, including shrimp and manioc beignets and chicken with lemon and onions; there are some good prix fixe deals too.

Gégène (Chez) S
▽ 7 17 10 fr187

162 bis, quai de Polangis, Joinville-le-Pont (Joinville-le-Pont), 01 48 83 29 43; fax 01 48 83 72 62

◪ "Everyone knows that you don't go" to this old *guinguette* (restaurant/dance hall) just outside Paris in Joinville for the brasserie fare, but rather to "dance" and bask in "nostalgia" while enjoying the "exceptional setting on the banks of the Marne", complete with terrace; critics who apparently aren't in a dancing mood simply shout "help!"

Georges ●S
— — — M

Centre Georges Pompidou, pl. Beaubourg, 4ᵉ (Rambuteau), 01 44 78 47 99; fax 01 44 78 16 80

Atop the newly renovated Pompidou Center is one of the latest Costes brothers creations: a loft-like space with sleek, arty decor, a magnificent panoramic view (ask for a window table) and a mixed crowd of trendsters and tourists here to check out the scene and nibble on contemporary Franco-Italian-Asian fare; DJ music and wanna-be models as servers give it a nightclub attitude and ambiance.

Georges (Chez)
18 14 18 fr329

1, rue du Mail, 2ᵉ (Bourse), 01 42 60 07 11

■ "May Georges always be Georges" is a typical reaction to this "very French", "very traditional" bistro behind the Place des Victoires, where "friendly waitresses" serve "solid", "grandmotherly" food in an "old-fashioned" setting; it draws a mix of chic Parisians, as well as tourists, and if it's a bit "pricey", that makes it feel "more like a celebration."

Georges Porte Maillot (Chez) ●S
15 12 14 fr289

273, bd Péreire, 17ᵉ (Porte Maillot), 01 45 74 31 00; fax 01 45 74 02 56

◪ Some argue that "it's no longer what it used to be", but devotees consider this circa 1926 bistro near the Porte Maillot "a sure bet" for "top-notch leg of lamb" and other "good", "classic" fare served in a "provincial" ambiance; budget-watchers say "it would be perfect" if it cost less.

Gérard (Chez) S
▽ 15 13 15 fr209

10, rue Montrosier, Neuilly-sur-Seine (Les Sablons/ Porte Maillot), 01 46 24 86 37; fax 01 46 37 21 72

■ Nothing more, and nothing less, than "a very good neighborhood bistro", and since that's fairly "rare" in this area of Neuilly, this one is all the more appreciated for its "varied" menu, "pleasant welcome" and moderate prices.

GÉRARD BESSON
25 | 17 | 21 | fr641

5, rue Coq Héron, 1er (Louvre-Rivoli/Palais Royal-Musée du Louvre), 01 42 33 14 74; fax 01 42 33 85 71

■ "Excellent in all areas" is the verdict on this intimate haute French between Les Halles and the Place des Victoires; Gérard Besson is "a real pro" whose "superb" cuisine is "by turns classic and inventive", and it's well backed up by careful service and impressive wines; if some label the setting a bit "boring", more find it "cozy and refined" and hope this place "continues on" just as it is; P.S. it's a must "for game lovers."

Germaine (Chez) ⊅
▽ 15 | 11 | 17 | fr136

30, rue Pierre Leroux, 7e (Duroc/Vaneau), 01 42 73 28 34

■ "Unique in its category", this "little canteen" in the 7th is something of a cheap eats "institution", offering "good, simple" traditional fare at "mini prices" in a "friendly, family-style" atmosphere; such is its popularity (and small size) that diners have been known to "line up and wait" for a seat.

Gildo (Chez)
17 | 12 | 14 | fr377

153, rue de Grenelle, 7e (La Tour-Maubourg), 01 45 51 54 12; fax 01 45 51 54 12

◪ "Calm, high-end Italian" at the Tour Maubourg that pleases admirers with its "authentic", "sophisticated" cuisine and "nice seasonal menus" featuring the likes of white truffles; critics complain of high prices and find it rather "old-fashioned – not what's happening."

Gitane (La)
15 | 11 | 15 | fr222

53 bis, av. de La Motte-Picquet, 15e (La Motte-Picquet-Grenelle), 01 47 34 62 92; fax 01 40 65 94 01

■ "Always crowded" French near the Champ de Mars that owes its popularity to "solid cooking", "excellent prices" and a "nice terrace"; service is "energetic" and though the decor is simple, the ambiance is pleasantly "cosmopolitan"; P.S. "try the cassoulet" advises a regular.

Giulio Rebellato ⬓
18 | 12 | 16 | fr357

136, rue de la Pompe, 16e (Victor Hugo), 01 47 27 50 26

◪ Most agree that this Italian near the Place Victor Hugo does a fine job in the kitchen, turning out "very good" to "excellent" cuisine, but prices are "rather exaggerated", especially when you factor in a "small" setting and decor that some find just "passable"; it's very popular with a preppy crowd of regulars, which lends it a clubby feel.

Glénan (Les)
▽ 17 | 13 | 15 | fr296

54, rue de Bourgogne, 7e (Varenne), 01 47 05 96 65; fax 01 45 51 27 34

■ "Small but good" seafooder in the 7th; not everyone agrees that it's a "value" and some find the decor "cold", but most have no complaints about the food, and the "tranquil" ambiance makes it easy to have "a conversation" here.

GOUMARD
23 | 18 | 20 | fr562

9, rue Duphot, 1er (Madeleine), 01 42 60 36 07; fax 01 42 60 04 54

■ The "seafood meal of your dreams" can become a reality at this "fish lover's heaven" behind the Madeleine, with modern decor that belies the fact that it's been around since 1872; some find the ambiance a bit "solemn" and service "sometimes long", but that doesn't faze those who focus on the "always excellent" food and "good wines"; if prices give you the bends, try the "splendid" lunch prix fixe.

Gourmet de l'Isle S
▽ 11 | 11 | 10 | fr235

42, rue St-Louis-en-l'Ile, 4e (Pont-Marie), 01 43 26 79 27

■ Locals and visitors alike say it's "a pleasure" to dine on the Ile Saint-Louis, and if this Traditional French "doesn't leave a grand memory", it does offer "decent food" at fair prices in an exposed-beam cellar room; it's "nice for a meal with friends" in an area where good options are rare.

Gourmets des Ternes (Les)
18 | 10 | 12 | fr273

87, bd de Courcelles, 8e (Ternes), 01 42 27 43 04

■ Carnivores converge at this "lively" bistro near the Place des Ternes for "magnificent" meat "cooked to perfection", plus other solid fare topped off by a baba au rhum that's "worth the trip"; the owner is said to favor "regulars", but that doesn't bother those who focus on the good food and "value"; P.S. the terrace is "superb on a spring day."

Graindorge
20 | 13 | 18 | fr334

15, rue de l'Arc-de-Triomphe, 17e (Charles de Gaulle-Etoile), 01 47 54 00 28; fax 01 47 54 00 28

■ Something of a "secret", this "relaxed" eatery near the Etoile offers "original, subtly flavored" Flemish fare served by an "attentive" staff in an art deco–style setting; "intelligently chosen wine and beer menus" and "affordable" (for the locale) prices are more reasons why a meal here can "add some Northern [European] sunshine to your day."

Grand Café des Capucines (Le) ●S
12 | 16 | 13 | fr289

4, bd des Capucines, 9e (Opéra), 01 43 12 19 00; fax 01 43 12 19 09

◪ Though this big, 24-hour brasserie strikes some as a "factory" with "ordinary" food and service, its location near the Opéra Garnier makes it "ideal" post-curtain and it's handy for "night owls in search of tartare at 4 AM"; "successfully restored", "rococo" Belle Epoque decor is another reason why fans feel this old-timer "still works well."

Grand Colbert (Le) ●S
13 | 20 | 15 | fr270

2, rue Vivienne, 2e (Bourse), 01 42 86 87 88; fax 01 42 86 82 65

◪ Everyone loves the "remarkable" period decor at this brasserie in the 18th-century Passage Vivienne near the Place des Victoires, but while fans say it provides a "fine meal" with "efficient" service from "dashing waiters", others report "industrial" eats and "too many tourists"; still, it's a popular "after-theater" stop with a "lively", "showbiz" buzz.

Grande Armée (La) ◗ 🅂   11 | 17 | 10 | fr256

3, av. de la Grande-Armeé, 16ᵉ (Charles de Gaulle-Etoile),
01 45 00 24 77; fax 01 45 00 95 50
◩ A "good-looking" crowd and Jacques Garcia's nouveau Napoleon III decor ensure that this "hip" Costes brothers creation near the Etoile is "stylish all day long" (it serves from 7 AM–2 AM); those not conquered by its "unimaginative" French fare and sometimes AWOL service dismiss it as just another "exercise in decoration", but that doesn't stop the "chic" armies of the night from rolling in.

GRANDE CASCADE (LA) 🅂   21 | 26 | 21 | fr589

Bois de Boulogne, allée de Longchamp, 16ᵉ (Porte Maillot),
01 45 27 33 51; fax 01 42 88 99 06
■ This "peaceful haven" set in a Napoleon III pavilion in the Bois de Boulogne boasts "well-prepared, attractively presented" French fare, "magnificent" decor and service that's "graceful under pressure"; though it's "pricey" and a few feel the food is "not up to" the "remarkable" setting, all agree it's "magic in summmer" (especially on the terrace) and a "superb place to take a visitor – or a lover."

Grandes Marches (Les) ◗🅂   12 | 15 | 13 | fr288

6, place de la Bastille, 12ᵉ (Bastille), 01 43 42 90 32;
fax 01 43 44 80 02
◩ Expected to reopen in September after a makeover by new owner the Flo group, this "classic" brasserie has long been regarded as a "good" choice before or after a show at the Opéra Bastille next door; while boosters hope they "won't change a thing" about its food or service, the redo might win over doubters who found it "pretty pricey for little originality."

Grand Louvre (Le) 🅂   ▽ 13 | 18 | 15 | fr360

Musée du Louvre, sous la Pyramide, 1ᵉʳ (Palais Royal-
Musée du Louvre), 01 40 20 53 41; fax 01 42 86 04 63
◩ Few surveyors seem to know about this restaurant under the Louvre's pyramid, which serves hearty Southwestern French cuisine in a modern setting by Jean-Michel Wilmotte; fans pronounce it "charming and good."

GRAND VÉFOUR (LE)   27 | 29 | 26 | fr750

17, rue de Beaujolais, 1ᵉʳ (Palais Royal-Musée du Louvre),
01 42 96 56 27; fax 01 42 86 80 71
■ To experience "heaven on earth", surveyors say look no further than this "historic" restaurant under the arches of the Palais Royal; "out-of-this-world" Directoire decor (rated No. 1), Guy Martin's "memorable" haute cuisine and service that "blends professionalism with real kindness" explain why it just snagged its third Michelin star; "alas, the check" is on an equally high plane, but diners sigh "there's nothing to say except 'bravo'."

Grand Venise (Le)
20 | 13 | 18 | fr487

171, rue de la Convention, 15ᵉ (Convention), 01 45 32 49 71; fax 01 45 32 07 49

■ "Copious" portions of "savory" Italian fare earn high marks for this vet in the 15th, and while the bill is nearly as big as the servings, "what a festival" exclaim fans, some of whom can't get "past the antipasti" before crying 'uncle'; the "warm" reception adds to the pleasure.

Grange Batelière (A la) S
▽ 18 | 13 | 17 | fr372

16, rue de la Grange-Batelière, 9ᵉ (Richelieu-Drouot), 01 47 70 85 15; fax 01 47 70 85 15

■ Its location near the Drouot Auction House in central Paris may explain why this French can be "noisy and packed" at lunch, a bit "sad" at night, but either way it offers "high-quality" fare (and moderate prix fixe menus) in a "familial" ambiance with vintage bistro decor; P.S. some say there's been a "marked improvement" under a new chef.

Grenadin (Le)
▽ 22 | 13 | 18 | fr370

44, rue de Naples, 8ᵉ (Villiers), 01 45 63 28 92; fax 01 45 61 24 76

■ There's "imagination and surprise" in the "carefully prepared" fare turned out by Patrick Cirotte at this small but well-regarded French between Villiers and the Parc Monceau; a few feel the food can border on "pretentious", but the "serene" ambiance, "attentive service" and "good wine cellar" help keep most diners happy.

Grenier de Notre Dame (Le) S
– | – | – | M

18, rue de la Bûcherie, 5ᵉ (Maubert-Mutualité/St-Michel), 01 43 29 98 29

For a "respite from the rich sauces" so prevalent around town, try this pint-sized, plant-festooned Saint-Michel Vegetarian featuring a "good choice" of "well-prepared, healthy food"; even carnivores might appreciate its cheap prix fixe deals and "delicious" fruit juice cocktails.

Griffonnier (Le) ◐
– | – | – | I

8, rue des Saussaies, 8ᵉ (Champs-Elysées), 01 42 65 17 17

"Simple, robust cuisine" accompanies the "remarkable selection of wines" at this "authentic" bistro à vins near the Elysée Palace in the heart of the 8th; its "noisy", "jovial" ambiance, "friendly" staff and easy prices are more reasons why it's "very likable."

Grille (La)
– | – | – | M

80, rue du Faubourg Poissonnière, 10ᵉ (Poissonnière), 01 47 70 89 73

Fans appreciate this little bistro in the 10th for its "jovial welcome" as well as its hearty familial fare, including the highly touted house specialty, "delicious, plentiful" grilled turbot with beurre blanc; the "inimitable owner" ("like a character out of a novel") adds to the charm of a room adorned with old-fashioned wrought ironwork.

Grille Montorgueil (La) ●S
▽ 17 | 19 | 20 | fr316

50, rue Montorgueil, 2ᵉ (Etienne Marcel), 01 42 33 21 21;
fax 01 42 33 21 21

■ "What atmosphere!" say admirers of this "true bistro" that provides a nostalgic trip back to the days of the old Les Halles market district; a stylish crowd comes to enjoy "good-quality" food and "excellent wines by the glass" amid "pretty" "pre-war" decor with a "sublime" zinc bar.

Grille St-Honoré (A la)
▽ 12 | 9 | 12 | fr274

15, place du Marché-St-Honoré, 1ᵉʳ (Tuileries), 01 42 61 00 93;
fax 01 47 03 31 64

◪ "Good" fish and other traditional fare, "thoughtful" service and a "pleasant" terrace near the Saint-Honoré market are what fans find at this bistro; critics claim the "only interest" is the location, but that does make it "perfect for lunch."

Grizzli (Le)
14 | 12 | 15 | fr226

7, rue St-Martin, 4ᵉ (Châtelet-Les Halles/Hôtel-de-Ville),
01 48 87 77 56

◪ A "little charmer" featuring "real Southwestern French" bistro fare that's a happy "surprise" in a "touristy area" near the Pompidou Center; if a few perceive "a decline in quality", more praise its "hearty" eats, including "Auvergne ham that will bring you to your knees"; there's a terrace too.

Guinguette de Neuilly (La) S
11 | 14 | 12 | fr235

12, bd Georges Seurat, Neuilly-sur-Seine (Porte de Champerret),
01 46 24 25 04; fax 01 46 24 39 82

■ This "charming" French boasts a "unique setting" by the Seine on the Ile de la Jatte in Neuilly; the cooking is "decent", and if not everyone thinks it's a "value", most would agree it's worth it for a table outside "on a lovely day."

Guirlande de Julie (La) S
▽ 12 | 13 | 13 | fr236

25, place des Vosges, 3ᵉ (Chemin Vert/St-Paul),
01 48 87 94 07; fax 01 48 87 01 22

■ Given its "beautiful" location on the Place des Vosges, this French is a bit "touristy", but it also draws locals with its "good", if not rave-worthy, food, including the specialty, pot-au-feu; run by Claude Terrail of La Tour d'Argent, it has a nice ambiance, "especially outdoors" in summer.

GUY SAVOY
26 | 19 | 24 | fr708

18, rue Troyon, 17ᵉ (Charles de Gaulle-Etoile/Ternes),
01 43 80 40 61; fax 01 46 22 43 09

■ Mixing "invention", "passion" and "culinary intelligence", Guy Savoy produces a "festival of flavors" at his haute cuisine flagship near the Etoile – even "the simplest dishes" "reach new heights", and meals are enhanced by "beautiful presentations" and "efficient" service; the main complaint, "unexceptional decor", should be addressed by a redo by Jean-Michel Wilmotte set for summer 2000, improving upon one of Paris' "most enjoyable dining experiences."

Hangar (Le) ◐ ⊄ — 18 | 9 | 14 | fr211

12, impasse Berthaud, 3e (Rambuteau), 01 42 74 55 44

■ "Creative", "refined" cuisine, made on-site from "quality ingredients", is offered at "good-value" prices at this bistro in an "original" location, hidden in a dead end behind the Pompidou Center; it's a "nice lunch spot" and the moist chocolate cake "is to die for", but a few big eaters say servings are "insufficient", and ratings suggest the same might be said of the decor.

Hédiard — 14 | 14 | 13 | fr298

21, place de la Madeleine, 8e (Madeleine), 01 43 12 88 99; fax 01 43 12 88 98

◪ "Good smells coming from" the namesake gourmet foods shop downstairs and a "calming", "beautiful" setting "work up your appetite" at this French on the Place de la Madeleine; while most appreciate the "imaginative menu", recommending it especially "for chic lunches", some are let down by small portions ("nothing much in the plate"), "slow" service and a check they claim is "not justified."

Hélène Darroze — 21 | 14 | 13 | fr463

4, rue d'Assas, 6e (Sèvres-Babylone), 01 42 22 00 11; fax 00 14 22 25 40

◪ Hélène Darroze, a student of Alain Ducasse and member of a respected restaurant family, has made a "stunning start" in Paris, offering "mountains of foie gras" and other Southwestern French fare of "rare quality" in a "Zen" setting (wood floors, plum and tomato-red walls) near Sèvres-Babylone; while critics cite "uneven" food and "amateurish" service, most see a bright future for this "promising" arrival; N.B. the casual ground-floor bistro has a brief menu of daily specials at gentler prices.

Higuma [S] — ▽ 14 | 5 | 10 | fr168

32 bis, rue Ste-Anne, 1er (Pyramides), 01 47 03 38 59

■ The decor could induce "depression", but even so this "canteen"-like Japanese not far from the Opéra Garnier is recommended for its "excellent" noodles, "savory ravioli and soups" and "healthy selection of rice-based goodies"; "cheap, fun and good" sums it up.

Hippopotamus ◐ [S] — 9 | 7 | 9 | fr172

29, rue Berger, 1er (Les Halles), 01 45 08 00 29; fax 01 40 41 98 63
1, bd des Capucines, 2e (Opéra), 01 47 42 75 70; fax 01 42 65 23 08
1, bd Beaumarchais, 4e (Bastille), 01 44 61 90 40; fax 01 48 87 84 67
9, rue Lagrange, 5e (Maubert-Mutualité), 01 43 54 13 99; fax 01 44 07 18 20
119, bd du Montparnasse, 6e (Vavin), 01 43 20 37 04; fax 01 43 22 68 95
5, bd Batignolles, 8e (Place de Clichy), 01 43 87 85 15; fax 01 47 20 95 31
42, av. des Champs-Elyseés, 8e (Franklin D. Roosevelt), 01 53 83 94 50; fax 01 53 83 94 51

Hippopotamus (Cont.)
20, rue Quentin-Bauchart, 8e (George V), 01 47 20 30 14; fax 01 47 20 95 31
68, bd du Montparnasse, 14e (Montparnasse), 01 40 64 14 94; fax 01 43 21 46 10
CNIT, 2, place de la Défense, Puteaux (La Défense Grande Arche), 01 46 92 13 75; fax 01 46 92 13 69
Plus other locations throughout Paris.
◪ Supporters say this "efficient" steak-frites chain provides "good meat" at "reasonable prices" and is a "sure bet" for a "quick" family meal; but it can feel like a "factory" with "overwhelmed" service and "excessive waits"; its severest critics accuse it of "lowering French culinary standards."

Homero | 10 | 19 | 11 | fr332
37, av. de Friedland, 8^e^ (Charles de Gaulle-Etoile), 01 42 89 99 60; fax 01 42 25 11 76
◪ Run by well-known party planner Homero Machry, this French off the Place de l'Etoile is a candidate for "hip restaurant" of the year award; it has "unique" colonial decor and "beautiful people" at the tables, but while some say you can eat well here, others knock "ordinary" food, "cold service" and a "pretentious" ambiance, concluding that the high prices "aren't justified"; P.S. there's a "nice bar."

Huitrier (L') [S] | 19 | 10 | 15 | fr294
16, rue Saussier Leroy, 17^e^ (Ternes), 01 40 54 83 44; fax 01 40 54 83 86
■ "First-rate" oysters "throughout the year", "served with a little sausage like in Arcachon" (a seaside resort) please bivalve buffs at this "find" near the Place des Ternes; the decor's a bit sparse and though a meal here can be "a little light, the check isn't", but "high quality" doesn't come cheap.

I Golosi ☾ | 20 | 10 | 16 | fr244
6, rue de la Grange-Batelière, 9e (Richelieu-Drouot), 01 48 24 18 63; fax 01 45 23 18 96
■ Given "cold decor", the "excellent" food comes as a "nice surprise" at this "authentic" Italian behind the Drouot auction house; its weekly changing menu offers some "extraordinary dishes" (e.g. "tagliatelle with truffles that will make you cry") and there's a "nice wine list" (over 500 bottles) plus "desserts to die for", but some grumble that prices are "out of line for a plate of pasta."

Il Baccello | ▽ 20 | 12 | 15 | fr272
33, rue Cardinet, 17^e^ (Wagram), 01 43 80 63 60; fax 01 43 80 63 65
■ Raphaël Bembaron, who did stints at Florence's Enoteca Pinchiorri, Joia (the gourmet vegetarian in Milan) and at Lucas Carton with Alain Senderens, offers "inspired" Franco-Med fare, made mostly from organic products, at this "original" newcomer near the Parc Monceau; "pleasant" Milan-meets-Tokyo decor is another reason it's "crowded" despite rather high prices.

Il Barone ◐ [S] 16 | 9 | 13 | fr232

5, rue Léopold-Robert, 14e (Raspail/Vavin), 01 43 20 87 14; fax 01 69 48 70 49

■ On a small street off Boulevard Montparnasse, this "good neighborhood Italian" offers a "warm welcome", "tasty, varied pastas" and antipasti that "smell of Italy"; while few fault the "authentic but simple dishes" and "delicate wines", some grumble that the space is "a bit crowded" and "smoky."

Il Carpaccio [S] ▽ 20 | 15 | 19 | fr443

Hôtel Royal Monceau, 37, av. Hoche, 8e (Charles de Gaulle-Etoile), 01 42 99 98 90; fax 01 42 99 89 94

■ Admirers give solid marks to this tony Italian in the Hôtel Royal Monceau near the Arc de Triomphe, calling it a "good representative" of that country's cuisine, with "superb food, wine and service"; however, even they admit that the bill can "soar" and outvoted critics claim that "everything is average except the prices."

Il Cortile 19 | 17 | 16 | fr414

Hôtel Castille, 37, rue Cambon, 1er (Concorde/Madeleine), 01 44 58 45 67; fax 01 44 58 45 69

■ In the "charming" interior courtyard of the Hôtel Castille behind the Place Vendôme is what partisans call one of Paris' "best Italians", praised for its "inventive" (if pricey) Italo-Med fare and "attentive service"; it's "a dream" in summer, when one dines with "the soft murmur of the fountain" as backdrop, but a few dissenters hear only the din of "too many cell phones" and feel the food "doesn't deserve its reputation."

Ile (L') ◐ [S] 14 | 21 | 12 | fr267

170, quai de Stalingrad, Parc de l'Ile St-Germain, Issy-les-Moulineaux (Issy Val de Seine RER), 01 41 09 99 99; fax 01 41 09 99 19

◪ All agree that this "fashionable" French in a Paris suburb is "beautiful inside or out" thanks to its "marvelous" park setting, "pretty decor" and "perfect terrace"; views on the food and service are less unanimous, but even if it can be "uneven", "all can be forgiven" for a meal outdoors.

Iles Marquises (Aux) ◐ ▽ 18 | 10 | 15 | fr262

15, rue de la Gaîté, 14e (Montparnasse-Bienvenüe), 01 43 20 93 58

■ Amid the cluster of theaters (and sex shops) on the Rue de la Gaîté in Montparnasse, this "authentic" seafooder is "worth a stop" for "very good" (maybe even "superb") fish, with extra praise for daily specials that are "perfectly adapted to the seasons"; if some find the "old-fashioned" decor "sad", others say the crowd of habitués gives it a "good ambiance."

Il était une Oie dans le Sud-Ouest ▽ 16 | 6 | 11 | fr234

8, rue Gustave-Flaubert, 17e (Ternes/Villiers), 01 43 80 18 30; fax 01 43 80 99 50

■ "Be hungry" if you're coming to this Southwestern French specialist near the Place des Ternes, where the "heavy but good" offerings include housemade foie gras and "confit that's worth a detour", with "more-than-honorable wines" to wash it all down with; the decor may be "uninteresting", but the ambiance is "calm" and most think the "simple" cuisine "always pleases."

Il Ristorante 16 | 11 | 13 | fr359

22, rue Fourcroy, 17e (Courcelles), 01 47 54 91 48; fax 01 47 63 34 00

■ "Excellent", "classic" Italian cuisine, a "warm" ambiance and "attentive service" guarantee a "successful evening" according to admirers of this eatery behind the Place des Ternes; though diners feel "very crowded together" in the "small" room and a few find the cooking "good but boring" (and "pricey"), the overall reaction is positive.

Il Sardo ▽ 21 | 5 | 16 | fr184

46, bis rue de Clichy, 9e (Liège), 01 48 78 25 38; fax 01 48 78 25 38

■ Near the Eglise de la Trinité in the 9th, this "unpretentious" little trattoria has less than divine decor, but that doesn't detract from "the joy of a wonderfully perfumed plate of pasta" and other "quality" Italian fare at modest prices; regulars say it's "ideal for lunch if you don't mind noise" and "aren't in a hurry", since the friendly service can be slow.

Impala Lounge ◐ [S] – | – | – | M

2, rue de Berri, 8e (George V), 01 43 59 12 66; fax 01 45 61 25 38

The space near the Champs-Elysées that once housed the Alpine-style Val d'Isère has undergone a continental shift and is now home to this à la mode African; expect a Franco-African menu and a crowd that's as stylish as the African-accented decor, done in warm tones with high-back chairs and leopard-print banquettes.

Impatient (L') 20 | 12 | 16 | fr226

14, passage Geffroy-Diderot, 17e (Rome/Villiers), 01 43 87 28 10; fax 01 43 87 28 10

■ "What a find!", "can't wait to go back" exclaim admirers of this "calm" French "hidden" in a passageway in the 17th, where "inventive dishes" are prepared by a "passionate chef" who "loves to innovate"; there's some debate as to whether it's an "excellent value" or "slightly pricey", but most think it's "worth it" for a "memorable" meal.

Improviste (A l') ▽ 16 | 12 | 15 | fr255

21, rue Médéric, 17e (Courcelles/Monceau), 01 42 27 86 67

■ Although this Traditional French in the 17th doesn't inspire much surveyor comment, fans consider it a good "neighborhood bistro" that exhibits "great class"; moderately priced prix fixe menus for lunch and dinner offer an easy introduction.

Inagiku ▽ 17 | 10 | 18 | fr290

14, rue de Pontoise, 5e (Maubert-Mutualité), 01 43 54 70 07; fax 01 40 51 74 44

■ Who would have thought one could find "a sushi bar just like in Tokyo" near the banks of the Seine in the 5th?; not only do reviewers love this "authentic" Japanese for its teppanyaki, sushi and other "refined", "impressive" cuisine "prepared in front of you", they also applaud its "pleasant welcome" and consider it an "excellent value."

Indiana Café ◐ [S] 7 | 9 | 8 | fr165

7, bd des Capucines, 2e (Opéra), 01 42 68 02 22
1, place de la République, 3e (République), 01 48 87 82 35
130, bd St-Germain, 6e (Odéon), 01 46 34 66 31
235-237, rue du Faubourg-St-Honoré, 8e (Ternes), 01 44 09 80 00
79, bd de Clichy, 9e (Place de Clichy), 01 48 74 42 61
14, place de la Bastille, 11e (Bastille), 01 44 75 79 80
72, bd du Montparnasse, 14e (Montparnasse-Bienvenüe), 01 43 35 02 34; fax 01 43 35 07 25

◪ Handy "in a pinch" for a "quick bite", this Tex-Mex chain draws a "young crowd" with its "good cocktails" and "fun" atmosphere ("especially during happy hour"), and if the food "isn't that great", it's "acceptable" and cheap (burgers are a good bet); just be advised that it can be "loud and smoky" with "overwhelmed" service.

Indra ◐ 17 | 16 | 14 | fr340

10, rue du Commandant Rivière, 8e (St-Philippe-du-Roule), 01 43 59 46 40; fax 01 44 07 31 19

◪ "Delicious" food, "well-spaced tables" and a "calm" ambiance have admirers calling this "delight" in the 8th "one of the best Indians"; however, a few feel it's "nothing special" and there are grumbles that it's "a bit pricey" with service that can seem like "the slowest in Paris."

Isami [S] ▽ 24 | 9 | 15 | fr389

4, quai d'Orléans, 4e (Pont-Marie), 01 40 46 06 97

■ Sushi and sashimi lovers say this "refined" Japanese on the Ile Saint-Louis serves "very good quality" fare (some even deem it "magnificent") in a simple but appealing setting; even if service can be "slow" and prices aren't cheap, it's a "real treat" and "rare in Paris", so "you need to reserve", especially since it's small.

Isse
▽ 20 | 14 | 15 | fr426

*56, rue Ste-Anne, 2ᵉ (Pyramides/Quatre-Septembre),
01 42 96 67 76; fax 01 42 96 82 63*
■ Between the Place de la Bourse and the Opéra, this traditional Japanese with a fashion-crowd following serves "excellent sashimi" and "irreproachable" sushi ("best in Paris" claims an enthusiast) in a "typically Japanese setting"; prices are high but so is the quality, thus fans say it's worth "treating yourself from time to time."

Jacky (Chez)
– | – | – | E

109, rue du Dessous-des-Berges, 13ᵉ (Bibliothèque F. Mitterrand/Nationale), 01 45 83 71 55; fax 01 45 86 57 73
It may be a "typical bistro", but that's rare in this mostly Asian part of the 13th, so the few surveyors who know this veteran appreciate its "quality" and sense of "tradition"; if it looks a little "sad" and is "perhaps a bit expensive", that doesn't bother fans who say "be quiet and enjoy."

Jacques Cagna
22 | 21 | 20 | fr622

*14, rue des Grands-Augustins, 6ᵉ (Odéon/St-Michel),
01 43 26 49 39; fax 01 43 54 54 48*
◪ A "great name in French gastronomy", Jacques Cagna's eponymous flagship between the Seine and the Odéon is lauded for its "excellent" cuisine, "extraordinary wine list" and "superb" setting – an old townhouse with exposed beams and banquettes into which one can "sink and drift back to the 17th century"; prices are strictly 21st century and dissenters feel the cooking "lacks a certain spark", but on the whole it leaves diners with "very good memories."

Jacques Mélac
13 | 12 | 15 | fr216

*42, rue Léon Frot, 11ᵉ (Charonne), 01 43 70 59 27;
fax 01 43 70 73 10*
■ It's "always a pleasure" to visit this "warm" bistro à vins "off the beaten track" in the 11th, where generations of fans have sat at "old wooden tables" and downed "excellent" wines amid rustic "wine-cellar decor"; the food (mostly specialties from Aveyron) earns a few nods, but it's the liquid assets that matter most here.

Jacquot de Bayonne
– | – | – | I

*151, rue de Charenton, 12ᵉ (Gare de Lyon/Reuilly Diderot),
01 44 74 68 90; fax 01 44 74 68 90*
"Encourage it – it deserves it!" urges a fan of this "good new place" with a "short but well-conceived menu" of affordable Southwestern French fare, including some "well-done Basque" items; being in a part of the 12th that's "poor in restaurants" also helps it win approval from the few voters who know it, as does the "wonderful welcome" from "very amicable owners."

JAMIN 25 | 20 | 24 | fr611

32, rue de Longchamp, 16e (Trocadéro), 01 45 53 00 07; fax 01 45 53 00 15

■ Diners detect "no weaknesses" at this "elegant" French near the Trocadéro, originally opened by Joël Robuchon and run for the past few years by his "brilliant" pupil, Benoît Guichard; besides "flawless", "original" cuisine, assets include a "calm", "comfortable" ambiance and "very professional" service, making it "a real pleasure" whether for "business or personal" dining; steep prices go with the territory, but few seem to mind.

Janou (Chez) ◐ [S] ≠ ▽ 14 | 13 | 13 | fr204

2, rue Roger-Verlomme, 3e (Chemin Vert), 01 42 72 28 41

◪ The "Mediterranean feel" of this Provençal bistro near the Place des Vosges is enhanced by its "pleasant terrace" on a "charming little square", so even if surveyors debate the merits of the cooking ("good", "simple" fare vs. "you wait a long time for nothing much"), it's "worth it" to sit outside in summer.

Jarasse [S] 18 | 11 | 14 | fr401

4, av. de Madrid, Neuilly-sur-Seine (Pont-de-Neuilly), 01 46 24 07 56; fax 01 40 88 35 60

■ While this "classic" Neuilly seafooder earns near unanimous praise for its "very good" aquatic fare, it also induces a bit of queasiness with its "high prices"; the "old-fashioned" decor isn't to everyone's taste and service can bob between "adorable" and "indifferent", but if you go "exclusively for the fish", odds are you won't be disappointed.

Jardin (Le) [S] ▽ 18 | 22 | 22 | fr594

Hôtel Royal Monceau, 37, av. Hoche, 8e (Charles de Gaulle-Etoile), 01 42 99 98 70; fax 01 42 99 89 91

■ In the garden courtyard of the Hôtel Royal Monceau in the 8th, this glass-walled French with a "beautiful" terrace is a "dream" in summer, and there's "also pleasure on the plate and in the glass" thanks to "very good–quality" food and an "excellent sommelier"; though "prices can soar", it makes for a "refined and sunny" meal; N.B. the post-*Survey* departure of chef Bruno Cirino, who has been succeeded by his second in command, may bring changes.

Jardin des Cygnes [S] – | – | – | E

Hôtel Prince de Galles, 33 av. George V, 8e (George V), 01 53 23 78 50; fax 01 53 23 78 78

"Surprising for a hotel restaurant" say admirers who find "delicious cuisine" in a "divine" setting at this French in the Prince de Galles hotel just off the Champs-Elysées; "discreet" and elegant, with "careful service" and a lovely patio, it's "ideal for business meals" or a "romantic rendezvous", offering the kind of quality "you would expect for the price."

Jardins de Bagatelle (Les) [S] 14 | 22 | 13 | fr346

Route de Sèvres à Neuilly, 16e (Pont-de-Neuilly),
01 40 67 98 29; fax 01 40 67 93 04

◪ Its location in the famous Bagatelle gardens makes this Classic French an "ideal place to detox from the city"; while most admit they come "essentially for the setting", not the "uninteresting" though "honorable" fare (including dishes from the Jura), all agree it's "one of the most pleasant places in Paris" and is definitely "worth a visit in summer."

Jean (Chez) ▽ 14 | 12 | 11 | fr245

8, rue St-Lazare, 9e (Cadet/Notre-Dame-de-Lorette),
01 48 78 62 73; fax 01 48 78 35 30

◪ "The sort of much-better-than-expected neighborhood restaurant that was once the pride of Paris" is how fans describe this French near the Eglise de la Trinité in the 9th, and though critics find it "overrated", it's worth a stop "if you're already" in the area; the vintage '50s decor and relaxed ambiance are pleasant, but ratings suggest that both the setting and the service could use a boost.

Jenny (Chez) ☾ [S] 13 | 18 | 14 | fr260

39, bd du Temple, 3e (Filles-du-Calvaire/République),
01 42 74 75 75; fax 01 42 74 38 69

◪ "What a pleasure for the eyes and the palate" exclaim fans of this veteran "temple of choucroute", a "warm", "traditional" brasserie near the Place de la République serving "good" food in a "splendid" setting where you can "marvel at the marquetry" by famed Alsatian artist Spindler; even those who find the fare "so-so" say "go once" for the decor; N.B. it's now part of the Frères Blanc chain.

Je Thé...Me ▽ 18 | 18 | 18 | fr212

4, rue d'Alleray, 15e (Convention/Vaugirard), 01 48 42 48 30;
fax 01 48 42 70 66

■ "Excellent family-style cooking" and "desserts like grandma's" are made even more appealing by the "sense of welcome" that pervades this little bistro/tearoom set in a 19th-century grocery shop (now listed as a historical monument) in the 15th; old-fashioned prices and "warm" owners are more reasons why patrons "feel good" here.

Joe Allen ☾ [S] 11 | 14 | 13 | fr238

30, rue Pierre Lescot, 1er (Etienne-Marcel), 01 42 36 70 13;
fax 01 42 36 90 80

◪ "New York in Paris" (or more precisely, near Les Halles) can be experienced at this relaxed American serving "casual food", i.e. "generous salads", "good burgers" and brunch; detractors say "if this is American food, I'm staying in France", but prices are reasonable and it beats a "transatlantic trip to find coleslaw or cheesecake."

Jo Goldenberg ●S   13 | 11 | 11 | fr225
7, rue des Rosiers, 4ᵉ (St-Paul), 01 48 87 20 16; fax 01 42 78 15 29
🔲 The Jewish–Eastern European eats are "heavy, but
sometimes you want that" and in any case this "institution"
is almost "a required stop" in the Marais; though critics
find it "overpriced and unremarkable", claiming "you must
rely on faith to appreciate it", believers say it's a good
place to "relive the past" in a setting that's so "chaotic"
and poorly decorated it "ends up being sweet."

Joséphine "Chez Dumonet"   19 | 13 | 15 | fr378
*117, rue du Cherche-Midi, 6ᵉ (Duroc/Falguière),
01 45 48 52 40; fax 01 42 84 06 83*
■ "A reason to be happy to be French" crows one fan of
this "typical" traditional bistro with Belle Epoque decor
near Montparnasse; "if you want a good leg of lamb, it's
here", as are the likes of a "super truffle omelet" and
"delicious Grand Marnier soufflé"; some find the setting
"depressing" and prices a bit high, but most have "no
complaints" – just "bring cards or Scrabble" since
service can be slow.

JULES VERNE S   22 | 27 | 20 | fr638
*Tour Eiffel, 2ème étage, 7ᵉ (Bir-Hakeim), 01 45 55 61 44;
fax 01 47 05 29 41*
■ "The top, from all points of view", this Classic French
perched on the second level of the Eiffel Tower is a
"magical experience" thanks to its "heavenly setting" and
"unparalleled" views that make you "forget the tourists"
all around; if a handful are let down by the food, more rate
it "excellent", complaining only about "dizzying" prices
and the need to book "two months ahead" to dine with
"Paris at your feet."

Julien (Brasserie) ●S   15 | 21 | 14 | fr284
*16, rue du Faubourg St-Denis, 10ᵉ (Strasbourg-St-Denis),
01 47 70 12 06; fax 01 42 47 00 65*
🔲 "One of the most beautiful" Belle Epoque decors in
Paris lends "irresistible charm" to this "classic", "noisy"
brasserie in the 10th, part of the Flo group; high praise
ends with the setting, though, as food comments range
from "very good" to "disappointing" and service can be
"overstretched", but it's a "fabulous place to take visitors"
and fairly "reasonable" to boot.

Jumeaux (Les)   ▽ 18 | 10 | 19 | fr225
73, rue Amelot, 11ᵉ (Chemin Vert), 01 43 14 27 00
■ "A nice discovery" that will make you "want to come
back" say fans of this Contemporary French near the
Cirque d'Hiver in the 11th; run by twin brothers (hence the
name, which means 'twins'), it offers a regularly changing
menu that's generally "successful" and "not expensive",
and though some find the ambiance "dreary", solicitous
service helps compensate.

Juvenile's
14 | 9 | 14 | fr201

47, rue de Richelieu, 1ᵉʳ (Bourse/Palais Royal-Musée du Louvre), 01 42 97 46 49; fax 01 42 60 31 52

■ "Enjoyable" bar à vins near the former Bibliothèque Nationale in the 1st and run by a Scotsman who is "mad about wine", offering "delicious" choices on a list with "some discoveries"; the food, an "original" mix of Spanish, Portuguese and British fare, also gets mostly positive reviews and if service can be "slow", it's still a good "standby."

Kambodgia
17 | 19 | 14 | fr279

15, rue de Bassano, 16ᵉ (George V), 01 47 23 31 80; fax 01 47 23 31 80

◪ "The interior is magnificent" at this Asian in the 16th that draws celebs and "lovers" with its "romantic" ambiance (carved wood, "soft lighting"), "ultradiscreet service" and "good" cooking; a few foes say romance "counts more than food", citing "stingy portions" and "slipping" quality.

Khun Akorn S
▽ 19 | 13 | 15 | fr224

8, av. de Taillebourg, 11ᵉ (Nation), 01 43 56 20 03; fax 01 40 09 18 44

■ An "excellent Thai that doesn't get talked about enough" say supporters of this spot near the Place de la Nation; "very affordable prices" and the "terrace in summer" are other good reasons to pass the word around, even if the staff can sometimes appear to be "absent."

Kim Anh S
▽ 23 | 14 | 20 | fr340

15, rue de l'Eglise, 15ᵉ (Charles Michels/Félix-Faure), 01 45 79 40 96; fax 01 40 59 49 78

■ What some call Paris' "best Vietnamese" is this "tiny room" in the 15th that looms large in the minds of those impressed by the "beauty of each plate" – "what marvelous cuisine and what a welcome" exclaims one fan who clearly doesn't mind if it can be "expensive"; given its size and the fact that it only serves dinner, you should reserve.

Kim Lien
▽ 17 | 12 | 10 | fr223

33, place Maubert, 5ᵉ (Maubert-Mutualité), 01 43 54 68 13

◪ As ratings show, this Vietnamese on the Place Maubert wins mostly approval for its "good", "refined" cooking, but some feel it's "spoiled" by poor service; nevertheless, prices are reasonable and "it's pleasant on the terrace."

Kinugawa
22 | 14 | 19 | fr405

9, rue du Mont Thabor, 1ᵉʳ (Tuileries), 01 42 60 65 07; fax 01 42 60 45 21
4, rue St-Philippe-du-Roule, 8ᵉ (St-Philippe-du-Roule), 01 45 63 08 07

■ "A little pricey but worth it" is the word on this Japanese duo; admirers praise "first-class" cooking of "irreproachable quality", and though the decor fails to make much of an impression, they're considered "havens of peace"; still, big eaters gripe you "leave hungry and with lots less money."

Kiosque (Le) [S] 13 | 14 | 13 | fr234

1, place de Mexico, 16e (Trocadéro), 01 47 27 96 98; fax 01 45 53 89 79

■ Featuring food from a different French region each week, served along with "the local newspapers", this "original" concept behind the Trocadéro pleases most diners with its "good food" and value, "witty decor" and "welcoming" attitude; even those who find the fare "uneven" admit that it "doesn't lack charm", and the changing menu keeps things interesting.

Kitty O'Sheas [S] 7 | 13 | 9 | fr185

10, rue des Capucines, 2e (Madeleine/Opéra), 01 40 15 00 30; fax 01 42 56 49 54

◪ "For a pint, yes!", but this Irish pub/restaurant on a street off the Place Vendôme arouses less enthusiasm for its food, though it does serve the likes of Irish stew and is popular for Sunday brunch; in any case, the "atmosphere and the beers" are the real appeal here.

Lac-Hong [S] ▽ 24 | 10 | 14 | fr314

67, rue Lauriston, 16e (Boissière/Victor Hugo), 01 47 55 87 17

◪ Most surveyors appreciate this Vietnamese in the 16th for its "very delicate", "good" cooking, but decor that's "beautiful" to some is "kitschy" to others and critics find the tab "too expensive" (though there is a reasonable lunch prix fixe); regulars advise "let yourself be guided by the chef's suggestions."

Ladurée 15 | 21 | 12 | fr255

75, av. des Champs-Elysées, 8e (Franklin D. Roosevelt), 01 40 75 08 75; fax 01 40 75 06 75 ◐ [S]

16, rue Royale, 8e (Concorde/Madeleine), 01 42 60 21 79; fax 01 49 27 01 95 ◐ [S]

Printemps, 62, bd Haussmann, 9e (Havre-Caumartin), 01 42 82 40 10; fax 01 42 82 62 00

◪ "Exquisite desserts", including macaroons that are "a must", and "superb" decor (especially at the vintage 1862 Rue Royale original and flashy Champs-Elysées branch) are the big draws at these tearooms; the rest of the fare gets little mention and the mood turns sour when it comes to "high prices" and "unacceptable service", but most complaints cease at the sight of "those pastries!"

Lalqila ◐ [S] – | – | – | M

88, av. Emile Zola, 15e (Charles Michels), 01 45 75 68 40; fax 01 45 79 68 61

The few surveyors who know this Indian in the 15th send back very encouraging reports, praising its "delicious", "savory" fare and "picturesque" palatial decor that's both "kitschy and transporting"; if service can be "slow", at least there are clips of Indian films to keep diners amused.

Languedoc (Le) 🆂 ▽ 18 | 10 | 18 | fr181
64, bd de Port-Royal, 5ᵉ (Les Gobelins), 01 47 07 24 47
■ "Tasty" French fare of "excellent quality" wins fans for this "down-to-earth" bistro with "red-checkered tablecloths" near the Val-de-Grâce; the decor may be slightly faded but given the "good prices", "what more can you ask?"

Lao Siam 🆂 – | – | – | I
49, rue de Belleville, 19ᵉ (Belleville/Pyrénées), 01 40 40 09 68
"You only come here for the cuisine, but what cuisine!" say patrons of this Belleville Asian serving "authentic" Thai and Laotian fare in a "no-frills" setting; elemental prices are another reason why fans say it's "tough to beat."

Lao Tseu ◗🆂 – | – | – | M
209, bd St-Germain, 7ᵉ (Rue du Bac), 01 45 48 30 06; fax 01 45 50 36 38
This stylish duplex Chinese near the Rue du Bac satisfies well-heeled regulars with its "very obliging welcome and service" and reliable fare (dim sum, spring rolls, soups and seafood dishes are popular); the decor's a bit generic, but the ambiance is relaxing and so are prices.

Lapérouse 🆂 15 | 24 | 15 | fr504
51, quai des Grands-Augustins, 6ᵉ (Pont-Neuf/St-Michel), 01 43 26 90 14; fax 01 43 26 99 39
◪ With its "historic" decor and "intimate" private dining rooms, this circa 1766 Classic French on the banks of the Seine in the 6th is perfect for a "secret" meal or "special occasion"; but while fans say the cuisine is worthy of the "unique" setting, foes call it "disappointing" and find prices "out of line"; the arrival of a new owner and new chef from Chiberta, plus a decor and service tune-up, could help.

LASSERRE 23 | 24 | 24 | fr692
17, av. Franklin D. Roosevelt, 8ᵉ (Franklin D. Roosevelt), 01 43 59 02 13; fax 01 45 63 72 23
◪ The "view of the stars", courtesy of the retracting roof, and the "sumptuous" yet "intimate" interior awe just about everyone at this French vet near the Grand Palais; "vigilant" service also wins praise, yet while some gush over "culinary virtuosity", others find the cooking "too traditional" (perhaps they haven't noticed chef Michel Roth's attempts at modernization); in any case, it's worth it , "at least once."

LAURENT 22 | 24 | 23 | fr667
41, av. Gabriel, 8ᵉ (Champs-Elysées-Clémenceau), 01 42 25 00 39; fax 01 45 62 45 21
◪ Though this "great classic" is lauded for its "sublime" setting in the Champs-Elysées gardens and "beautiful terrace", the French haute cuisine gets a more mixed reaction: "excellent" to most, it's "disappointing" and pricey to some; still, service is "lovely" and if you're "on an expense account", it's easy to pronounce it "perfect."

Ledoyen
22 | 24 | 23 | fr642

1, av. Dutuit, 8ᵉ (Concorde), 01 53 05 10 01; fax 01 47 42 55 01
☑ "Each visit is an unforgettable experience" sigh fans of this French in the Champs-Elysées gardens; while a few miss former chef Ghislaine Arabian and feel the place is "not up to its reputation", others claim the cuisine is even "better" under Christian Le Squer, applauding "outstanding" food, "exceptional" service and elegant Napoleon III decor by Jacques Grange, all of which help justify the cost.

Léna et Mimile
▽ 10 | 17 | 9 | fr234

32, rue Tournefort, 5ᵉ (Censier-Daubenton), 01 47 07 72 47
■ Near the bustle of the lively Rue Mouffetard, this vintage 1937 French beckons diners with its "calm" setting, "nice terrace" ("the most beautiful in the Latin Quarter" according to one booster) and sturdy fare including Alsatian specialties; regulars think its appeal will "never wear out."

Léon (Chez)
10 | 8 | 10 | fr212

32, rue Legendre, 17ᵉ (Villiers), 01 42 27 06 82; fax 01 46 22 63 67
■ The "perfect neighborhood bistro" is how habitués view this simple spot in the 17th; around for decades, it's a "legend" to those who enjoy its "good" food, reasonable prix fixe menus and "rapid" service; one patron who claims it was better "20 or 30 years ago" keeps coming back anyway, which says something about the loyalty it inspires.

Léon de Bruxelles ●Ⓢ
7 | 6 | 8 | fr155

120, rue de Rambuteau, 1ᵉʳ (Les Halles), 01 42 36 18 50; fax 01 42 36 27 50
3, bd Beaumarchais, 4ᵉ (Bastille), 01 42 71 75 55; fax 01 42 71 75 56
131, bd St-Germain, 6ᵉ (Mabillon/Odéon), 01 43 26 45 95; fax 01 43 26 47 02
55, bd du Montparnasse, 6ᵉ (Montparnasse Bienvenüe), 01 45 44 78 05; fax 01 45 44 78 85 ☐
63, av. des Champs-Elysées, 8ᵉ (Franklin D. Roosevelt), 01 42 25 96 16
8, place Clichy, 9ᵉ (Place de Clichy), 01 48 74 00 43
1-3, place Pigalle, 9ᵉ (Pigalle), 01 42 80 28 33
30, bd des Italiens, 9ᵉ (Opéra), 01 42 46 36 15
8, place de la République, 11ᵉ (République), 01 43 38 28 69; fax 01 43 38 28 69
82 bis, bd du Montparnasse, 14ᵉ (Vavin/Montparnasse-Bienvenüe), 01 43 21 66 62; fax 01 43 21 66 76
349, rue de Vaugirard, 15ᵉ (Convention), 01 55 76 99 72
95, bd Gouvion-St-Cyr, 17ᵉ (Porte Maillot), 01 55 37 95 30; fax 01 55 37 95 35
☑ If you "don't expect gastronomic heights", you might agree with those who say this moules-frites chain is an ok "change from McDonald's" for a "quick" bite or "family" meal at "painless prices"; harsher critics think it costs a lot of clams for "industrial mussels", "dismal service" and "nonexistent decor", but in a pinch, it can come in handy.

Lescure 12 | 11 | 13 | fr193
7, rue de Mondovi, 1er (Concorde), 01 42 60 18 91
◪ "A tradition that's still alive" is one take on this vintage 1919 bistro near the Place de la Concorde that's been handed down for three generations and continues to provide "very decent" food at "very reasonable prices"; "tables are tight" and service can seem "gruff", but it has a "warm" ambiance and there's a little terrace in summer.

Lina's 10 | 9 | 7 | fr102
UGC Forum des Halles, 1er (Les Halles), 01 42 21 36 64 [S]
50, rue Etienne-Marcel, 2e (Etienne-Marcel/Sentier), 01 42 21 16 14; fax 01 42 33 78 03
22, rue des Saints-Pères, 6e (St-Germain-des-Prés), 01 40 20 42 78
8, rue Marbeuf, 8e (Alma-Marceau), 01 47 23 92 33
105, rue du Faubourg-St-Honoré, 8e (Miromesnil), 01 42 56 42 57
30, bd des Italiens, 9e (Opéra), 01 42 46 02 06 [S]
2, rue Henri Desgrange, 12e (Bercy), 01 43 40 42 42; fax 01 43 40 65 11 [S]
23, av. de Wagram, 17e (Charles de Gaulle-Etoile/Ternes), 01 45 74 76 76; fax 01 45 74 76 77
156, av. Charles de Gaulle, Neuilly-sur-Seine (Pont-de-Neuilly), 01 47 45 60 60
CNIT, 2, place de La Défense, Puteaux (La Défense Grande Arche), 01 46 92 28 47
Plus other locations throughout Paris.
◪ Most like this chain's "good sandwiches" made "on demand" from "tasty" ingredients, but some find prices "prohibitive" for what are, after all, just sandwiches; still, they're popular for a "lunch on the go" in modern settings complete with newspapers to read, which might come in handy given reports of "long" lines and "inefficient" service.

Livingstone ◐ [S] ▽ 13 | 20 | 13 | fr213
106, rue St-Honoré, 1er (Louvre-Rivoli), 01 53 40 80 50; fax 01 53 40 80 51
◪ The "very beautiful decor" mixing art deco and African touches with lots of "exotic bric-a-brac" is a crowd-pleaser at this new Thai between Les Halles and the Louvre; while some also salute "savory flavors from the Far East", others feel it doesn't cook as good as it looks, but the "calm" ambiance and "warm" service work in its favor.

Livio (Chez) [S] 12 | 12 | 13 | fr223
6, rue de Longchamp, Neuilly-sur-Seine (Pont-de-Neuilly), 01 46 24 81 32; fax 01 47 38 20 72
◪ For a "business lunch", "family" meal or get-together "with friends", this "institution" is where "all of Neuilly" meets to enjoy traditional Italian fare, including "good pizzas", in a "noisy", "good-natured atmosphere"; if some think it's "resting on its laurels" and knock shrinking portions ("in a few years, the pizzas will be as small as five-franc coins"), the fact that it's "always crowded" says a lot.

Loir dans la Théière (Le) [S] ▽ 13 | 16 | 10 | fr134
3, rue des Rosiers, 4e (St-Paul), 01 42 72 90 61; fax 01 40 86 72 74
◪ "All the spirit of the Marais without the 'too trendy' side" is how fans describe this French in the 4th that serves "good cakes" and other tearoom fare plus more substantial dishes in a laid-back setting with mismatched chairs and tables; though some feel the cooking has "become banal", others like its "cheap" prices and consider brunch "unmissable" (but "get there early").

Lô Sushi ◐[S] 12 | 18 | 9 | fr250
8, rue de Berri, 8e (George V), 01 45 62 01 00; fax 01 45 62 01 10
◪ "Original", "trendy" and "amusing" is how most view this "chic" sushi bar near the Champs-Elysées where food "goes by on a conveyor belt", allowing diners to choose "according to their inspiration" (if you get carried away, brace for an "expensive" tab); slick Andrée Putman decor is another reason to "go once", but critics claim it resembles an "East German factory canteen" and find it better for "people-watching" than dining.

Lozère (La) ▽ 17 | 9 | 15 | fr248
4, rue Hautefeuille, 6e (St-Michel), 01 43 54 26 64; fax 01 44 07 00 43
■ "Authentic" cooking from the Lozère region is featured at this "unpretentious" spot near the Place Saint-Michel in the Latin Quarter; despite "rudimentary" decor ("more like a tourism office than a restaurant"), it's appreciated for its "delicious *aligot*" (a potato-cheese dish) and "reasonable prices", but you'd better be hungry since portions are "gargantuan."

LUCAS CARTON 26 | 25 | 24 | fr750
9, place de la Madeleine, 8^e (Concorde/Madeleine), 01 42 65 22 90; fax 01 42 65 06 23
■ "Spectacular", "hats off to the chef", "paradise" are typical accolades for Alain Senderens' art nouveau bastion of haute cuisine on the Place de la Madeleine, where "everything is near perfect", except maybe the "delirious prices" (the lunch prix fixe offers some relief); if a few critics report "disappointing" meals and service, they're outnumbered by those who salute "awesome food and wine pairings" and an "extraordinary" tasting menu that makes this "one of the world's greatest – 'nuf said."

Luna (La) 21 | 13 | 15 | fr455
69, rue du Rocher, 8^e (Villiers), 01 42 93 77 61; fax 01 40 08 02 44
■ "Exceptional" fish and "great mashed potatoes" earn acclaim for this "sophisticated yet simple" seafooder near the Gare Saint-Lazare; nitpickers object to "high" prices and a "pretentious" welcome, and no one has much to say about the decor, but the "admirably prepared" food carries the vote.

Lyonnais (Aux) ◐
∇ 13 | 17 | 16 | fr226
32, rue St-Marc, 2ᵉ (Bourse/Richelieu-Drouot), 01 42 96 65 04;
fax 01 42 97 42 95

◪ This "typical" *bouchon*, or Lyonnaise bistro, near the Bourse is liked for its "true bourgeois cuisine" and pretty decor with art nouveau tiles; while some find the reception "adorable", others cite "snobby" attitude, but since it's been around for a century it obviously treats most diners right.

Ma Bourgogne ◐S⊞
16 | 16 | 14 | fr229
19, place des Vosges, 4ᵉ (Bastille/St-Paul), 01 42 78 44 64;
fax 01 42 56 33 71

■ Terrace dining with a "fab view" of the Place des Vosges sets this bistro apart; "good salads" and "excellent steak tartare" draw huzzahs, and though service can be "cool" it's "efficient", leaving most with no complaints.

Ma Bourgogne
15 | 10 | 13 | fr251
133, bd Haussmann, 8ᵉ (Miromesnil), 01 45 63 50 61;
fax 01 42 78 19 37

◪ Louis Prin presides over this homey wine bar near Saint-Augustin, where you can nibble on a sandwich at the bar or head downstairs for a home-cooked meal of coq au vin or kidneys à l'anglaise; though a few harrumph it's "living on its reputation", most appreciate this "timeless" spot for its old-fashioned feel and "charming welcome."

Macéo
15 | 17 | 15 | fr338
15, rue des Petits Champs, 1ᵉʳ (Bourse/Palais
Royal-Musée du Louvre), 01 42 97 53 85; fax 01 47 03 36 93

◪ Devotees of this striking New French near the Place des Victoires laud its "wide-ranging wine list" and "eclectic" dishes; run by Mark Williamson (Willi's Wine Bar), it also might be "the best restaurant for vegetarians" around, even if some say it's "not a big deal" and service can be "slow."

Maharajah (Le) ◐S
– | – | – | M
72, bd St-Germain, 5ᵉ (Maubert-Mutualité/St-Michel),
01 43 54 26 07; fax 01 40 46 08 18

This Latin Quarter curry palace draws a mix of academics, tourists and neighborhood types who enjoy its convenience and pointedly ignore the uninspiring decor; it's Paris' oldest Indian restaurant, and despite its "royal" moniker, penny-pinchers are pleased that it's "not too expensive."

Maison (La) ◐S
∇ 10 | 16 | 8 | fr259
1, rue de la Bûcherie, 5ᵉ (Maubert-Mutualité/St-Michel),
01 43 29 73 57; fax 01 42 78 97 30

◪ The "delightful" tree-shaded terrace is a bit of "paradise" for fans of this Latin Quarter French where a hip crowd eyes one another while sipping the house wine and feasting on the likes of "excellent roast chicken"; detractors yawn that the food is "mediocre" and insist that outdoor dining with a bird's-eye view of Notre Dame is "the only interest" here.

MAISON BLANCHE
20 | 24 | 18 | fr564

15, av. Montaigne, 8ᵉ (Alma-Marceau), 01 47 23 55 99; fax 01 47 20 09 56

◪ There's universal praise for the "sublime" panorama of the "roofs of Paris" offered at this posh and pricey New French atop the Théâtre des Champs-Elyseés on the Avenue Montaigne, but debate about everything else: "imaginative" vs. overly "complicated" food, "superb" vs. "very cold" modern decor and "unintrusive" vs. "amateurish" service; still, a strong chorus trills it's "underrated by guidebooks, adored by clients."

Maison Courtine (La)
– | – | – | M

157, av. de Maine, 14ᵉ (Alesia), 01 45 48 08 04; fax 01 45 45 91 35

In the former home of Lous Landès, this Traditional French near the Porte d'Orléans in Denfert-Rochereau proffers such Southwestern specialties as "excellent" cassoulet, duck and foie gras at "good-value" prices; cynics nix "slow" service and wonder "why cigars are forbidden when cigarets are not."

Maison de l'Amérique Latine
16 | 24 | 17 | fr374

217, bd St-Germain, 7ᵉ (Rue du Bac/Solférino), 01 45 49 33 23; fax 01 40 49 03 94

■ Everyone loves the "sumptuous" setting – an 18th-century mansion that's also home to the Latin American cultural center – of this New French in the heart of Saint-Germain with a "lovely garden" that's a summer "oasis"; the "refined" Japanese-tinged cuisine of Yasuo Nanaumi also pleases most, which helps justify the "expensive" tabs.

Maison du Caviar (La) ●S
17 | 12 | 16 | fr458

21, rue Quentin-Bauchart, 8ᵉ (George V), 01 47 23 53 43; fax 01 47 20 87 26

■ Conveniently located just off the Champs-Elysées, this veteran caviar house is perfect for a "deluxe snack" "after the movies"; besides some of Paris' "best caviar", the menu includes salmon, confit de canard and borscht (plus "good vodkas" to wash them down with), all predictably "expensive" – though the well-to-do deem it "affordable" for what it is.

Maison Prunier
21 | 21 | 19 | fr605

16, av. Victor Hugo, 16ᵉ (Charles de Gaulle-Etoile), 01 44 17 35 85; fax 01 44 17 90 10

■ "Very beautiful, very good, very expensive" sums up this swellegant seafooder near the Arc de Triomphe with an "exceptional" art deco setting and "always perfect" fish and oysters; while bon vivants prefer the posh upstairs dining room, plebes feel more at ease at the mosaic bar on the ground floor; N.B. rumor has it that YSL president Pierre Bergé is taking over the premises to create a caviarteria.

Maître Paul (Chez) S

| 17 | 12 | 16 | fr289 |

12, rue Monsieur-le-Prince, 6ᵉ (Odéon), 01 43 54 74 59; fax 01 46 34 58 33

■ "Never disappointing" French bistro in the Latin Quarter specializing in the robust cooking of the Jura region; despite so-so decor ("we'd welcome a coat of paint"), admirers laud the "large" servings and "pleasant service", which might account for the noise and bustle at this "wonderful find."

Mandarin (Au) ◐S

| – | – | – | M |

1, rue de Berri, 8ᵉ (George V), 01 43 59 48 48; fax 01 43 59 06 08

"Good value" draws a crowd of tourists, locals and suits to this long-established Chinese near the Champs-Elysées; expect "basic" yet authentic fare (including Peking duck and some dandy dim sum) in a "very pretty setting."

Mandarin de Neuilly

▽ | 15 | 6 | 12 | fr249 |

148, av. Charles de Gaulle, Neuilly-sur-Seine (Pont-de-Neuilly), 01 46 24 11 80

■ A "super welcome" kicks off meals at this Chinese in the chic suburb of Neuilly, considered "one of the best" of its kind in Paris by devotees; specialties like shrimp with caramelized walnuts lure crowds to this venerable venue in spite of its narrow dining room and drab decor.

Mandragore (La) S

| – | – | – | M |

74, rue Botzaris, 19ᵉ (Place des Fêtes), 01 42 39 86 18; fax 01 42 39 02 76

Near the lush Buttes-Chaumont park in the 19th, this bistro delivers "good" Traditional French cooking along the lines of foie gras and confit de canard; its cozy, "relaxing" ambiance has made it a favorite of a trendy young locals, and even nonlocals remark it's "worth the trip across town."

Man Ray ◐S

| 12 | 22 | 13 | fr321 |

34, rue Marbeuf, 8ᵉ (Franklin D. Roosevelt), 01 56 88 36 36; fax 01 42 25 36 36

☑ People-watchers hit pay dirt at this "enormous" Eclectic near the Champs-Elysées, created by restaurateur Thierry Klemeniuk (ex Arc, Les Bains and Barfly) with such celeb investors as Sean Penn and John Malkovich; while the "fantastic" decor and "hip" crowd are "beautiful", the Asian-accented menu doesn't fare as well ("uninteresting", "pricey"), leading some to shrug "worth one visit – only one."

Mansouria S

| 19 | 15 | 14 | fr264 |

11, rue Faidherbe, 11ᵉ (Faidherbe-Chaligny), 01 43 71 00 16; fax 01 40 26 21 97

☑ Admirers of this "excellent" Moroccan between the Bastille and the Place de la Nation praise its "sophisticated" takes on couscous and pigeon b'steeya, as well as its "nice" "Moorish" ambiance; foes fret that it's "overrated" and "overpriced", but as ratings attest, they're in the minority.

Manufacture (La) 17 | 17 | 15 | fr288

20, esplanade de la Manufacture, Issy-les-Moulineaux (Corentin-Celton), 01 40 93 08 98; fax 01 40 93 57 22

■ This airy Classic French in the southern suburb of Issy-les-Moulineaux was once the curing room of a state-run tobacco factory, and pleased patrons puff about its stylish decor, "pretty terrace" and "inventive" kitchen that delivers "excellent value"; however, a few critics carp about "slow service" and sniff it's "noisy, crowded and trendy – so what?"

Marais-Cage (Le) ▽ 17 | 14 | 19 | fr260

8, rue de Beauce, 3e (Arts-et-Métiers), 01 48 87 31 20; fax 01 48 87 49 19

■ "The French Antilles may change but the Marais-Cage doesn't", and fans of this venerable (since 1966) Caribbean hangout in the Marais are pleased that it's retained its "authentic" flavor over the years; the "warm welcome" and hot spices (especially the "very good *feroce*", a zesty casserole) turn on fire-eaters, but more "fragile" stomachs should choose carefully; N.B. reservations suggested.

Marcel (Chez) – | – | – | M

7, rue Stanislas, 6e (Notre-Dame-des-Champs), 01 45 48 29 94

Given Montparnasse's plethora of fast-food joints and pizza palaces, it's gratifying to stumble on this family-run bistro with retro decor that "takes you back to another time"; habitués who appreciate its Lyonnaise specialties and "nice service" say "they don't make them like this anymore."

MARÉE (LA) 23 | 15 | 20 | fr636

1, rue Daru, 8e (Ternes), 01 43 80 20 00; fax 01 48 88 04 04

■ Fin fanatics don't have enough superlatives for this seafooder in the 8th near the Salle Pleyel concert hall; "excellent" cuisine by former Lucas Carton chef Bernard Pinaud draws huzzahs (especially the "very special *mille-feuille*"), while the service and "top wines" are equally satisfying; sure, it's "pricey" and the decor strikes a few as "old-fashioned", but the overall word is "exceptional."

Marée de Versailles ▽ 18 | 15 | 15 | fr279

82, rue au Pain, Versailles (Versailles Rive Droite), 01 30 21 73 73; fax 01 39 50 55 87

◪ This Versailles seafooder gets mixed notices from surveyors, with admirers "warmly recommending it" for "extra-fresh" fish, "superb" wines and "professional" service, while a disgruntled minority pans the "dull" decor and "unchanging" menu; "good value for the money" works in its favor.

Mariage Frères [S] 16 | 19 | 15 | fr197

30, rue du Bourg Tibourg, 4e (Hôtel-de-Ville), 01 42 72 28 11; fax 01 42 74 51 68

13, rue des Grands-Augustins, 6e (St-Michel), 01 40 51 82 50; fax 01 44 07 07 52

Mariage Frères (Cont.)
260, rue du Faubourg-St-Honoré, 8e (Ternes), 01 46 22 18 54; fax 01 42 67 18 54
■ Parisian trio catering to tea lovers who consider them a "must"-stop, not only at teatime, but for "delicious" brunches and light lunches too (no dinner served); their "colonial" settings, "incredible selection" and "highly knowledgeable" (some say "condescending") staff keep the trade brisk, even if tightwads gripe that it all comes "at the price of caviar."

Marianne (Chez) ◐ [S] — 14 | 11 | 10 | fr146
2, rue des Hospitalières St-Gervais, 4e (St-Paul), 01 42 72 18 86; fax 01 42 78 75 26
■ "Nothing seems to have changed for 20 years" at this "small but warm" place "in the heart of the Marais" serving large portions of Eastern European and Jewish specialties to a diverse crowd; since it's "informal, tasty and inexpensive", it's usually mobbed, so reservations are recommended.

Marie et Fils — ▽ 12 | 13 | 12 | fr266
34, rue Mazarine, 6e (Odéon), 01 43 26 69 49; fax 01 43 26 11 99
◪ Owned by one of entertainer Eddie Barclay's many ex-wives and run by her son, this Left Bank bistro attracts the "chic" set (though a few fashionistas fume that it's drawing "too many tourists"); expect "fairly successful" fare in a "pretty setting" but possibly "inadequate service."

Marie-Louise — ▽ 12 | 6 | 11 | fr263
52, rue Championnet, 18e (Simplon), 01 46 06 86 55
■ Old-time bistro near the Porte de Clignancourt with fewer than 10 tables, the feel of a 1950s French film and a menu of traditional favorites such as house-made head cheese; loyalists like this "warm" place just the way it is and hope the new owners "don't change anything."

Marines (Les) — – | – | – | M
27, av Niel, 17e (Péreire/Ternes), 01 47 63 04 24
Its decor recalls a yacht, and this little Mediterranean bistro in the heart of the 17th lures fish fans with its marine cuisine, including a "marvelous specialty of *daurade*" (sea bream) with honey and spices; however, foes fret over a menu offering "little choice" and find prices a bit high for portions that can seem a bit small.

Marius — 19 | 13 | 17 | fr371
82, bd Murat, 16e (Porte de St-Cloud), 01 46 51 67 80; fax 01 47 43 10 24
■ Granted, it might be "a bit crowded" and "a bit pricey", but otherwise this "classic" fish house in the 16th garners praise for its "warm welcome" and "superb cuisine" (including "exquisite bouillabaisse"); regulars hint that "the best choices aren't on the menu, but rather on the daily specials list."

Marius et Janette [S] 19 | 16 | 16 | fr493

4, av. George V, 8e (Alma-Marceau), 01 47 23 84 36; fax 01 47 23 07 19

◪ "Straightforward seafood" "melts in your mouth" at this "classy" fish place near the Pont de l'Alma, and though it's "crowded", you might find Gérard Depardieu or a dancer from the nearby Crazy Horse at the next table; party poopers cite "mediocre service" and "absurd" prices ("ouch!").

Marlotte (La) 14 | 14 | 14 | fr315

55, rue du Cherche-Midi, 6e (Sèvres-Babylone/St-Placide), 01 45 48 86 79; fax 01 45 44 34 80

◪ Calling all editors and publishers: this homey, candlelit bistro near the Bon Marché department store attracts a bookish crowd with its "dependable" "bourgeois cooking" (don't miss the lentil salad); but some say the new owners will have to "work hard" to keep quality up and prices down.

Maroc (Le) ◐ [S] – | – | – | M

9, rue Danielle-Casanova, 1er (Pyramides), 01 42 61 38 83; fax 0142604933'

Despite its "wonderful fish", "good couscous" and other North African specialties, this Moroccan near the Opéra Garnier remains relatively unknown to surveyors; insiders savor its "warm welcome" and transporting setting, though there is some rumbling that it's becoming "unaffordable."

Marty [S] 15 | 15 | 17 | fr288

20, av. des Gobelins, 5e (Les Gobelins), 01 43 31 39 51; fax 01 43 37 63 70

◪ In business since 1913, this "real Parisian brasserie" in the Gobelins district of the 5th turns out "excellent cuisine" in "cozy" surroundings that have been "unchanged for decades"; a minority moans it's "too expensive for the quality", but note that the upstairs dining room is cheaper.

Mascotte (La) ▽ 13 | 6 | 14 | fr235

270, rue du Faubourg-St-Honoré, 8e (Ternes), 01 42 27 75 26; fax 01 40 31 15 06

■ Specialties from the Auvergne grace the menu of this Traditional French brasserie near the Place des Ternes; an "unpretentious" atmosphere, "very good meat" and "superb rice pudding" keep regulars regular, though a few wouldn't mind less smoke, less noise and lower prices.

Mathusalem (Le) 17 | 12 | 16 | fr190

5 bis, bd Exelmans, 16e (Exelmans), 01 42 88 10 73; fax 01 42 88 42 43

■ "Congenial", "noisy" bistro located out there in the 16th, where a "friendly but overworked staff" serves "generous portions" of tasty dishes like the "very good *croustillant de Camembert*"; it also pleases the parsimonious as it offers enough "value to take your breath away."

Maupertu ▽ 18 | 18 | 20 | fr261

94, bd de La Tour-Maubourg, 7e (La Tour-Maubourg), 01 45 51 37 96; fax 01 42 73 17 35

■ Popular with sight-seers who like to sit on the terrace and gaze upon the gilded dome of Les Invalides, this "tiny" Classic French also garners kudos for its "fabulous" food and "cozy" ambiance; even better, prices are "reasonable."

Mauzac (Le) ◐ ▽ 16 | 11 | 14 | fr193

7, rue de l'Abbé de l'Epée, 5e (Luxembourg), 01 46 33 75 22

■ Look for the "Sorbonne and École Normale Supérieure crowd" tucking into "excellent" lunches at this little wine bar near the Luxembourg Garden offering "rustic" fare and "good wines"; fans of this "delightful" bistro are pleased that it is now open for dinner Monday through Friday.

Mavrommatis [S] 19 | 15 | 15 | fr301

42, rue Daubenton, 5e (Censier-Daubenton), 01 43 31 17 17; fax 01 43 36 13 08

■ The dressier and more expensive big brother of nearby Les Délices d'Aphrodite, this Hellenic favorite in the Latin Quarter earns raves for its "authentic" food and "charming", old-fashioned setting; though some find it "a little pricey" and "a little overrated", more call it "the best Greek in Paris."

Maxence (Le) 19 | 14 | 15 | fr383

9 bis, bd du Montparnasse, 6e (Duroc), 01 45 67 24 88; fax 14 45 67 10 22

◪ Flemish chef David Van Laer (ex Le Bamboche, La Manufacture) offers an "inventive" northern take on Classic French cooking in a spare modern setting in the 6th; while supporters feel "this place could become a major" player, a handful gripes that it's "pretentious" and "expensive", with a "dreary" atmosphere to boot.

Maxim's 14 | 25 | 19 | fr669

3, rue Royale, 8e (Concorde/Madeleine), 01 42 65 27 94; fax 01 40 17 02 91

◪ Although chef Bruno Stril is trying to breathe new life into this mythic French off the Place de la Concorde, opinion remains split, with fans calling it "a magic place" that's "excellent in every way", especially the "over-the-top" Belle Epoque decor (now with a handsomely redone facade), and foes asking "how could the most celebrated restaurant in the world fall so low?"; all would agree prices are stratospheric.

Maxim's ▽ 14 | 12 | 16 | fr391

Aerogare Orly Ouest, Orly (Orly Ouest par liaison Orlyval), 01 49 75 16 78; fax 01 46 87 05 39

■ For "luxury where you wouldn't expect it", fly by this Orly satellite of the famed Rue Royale original; "good" French cooking, "efficient service" and an amusing, faux art nouveau setting lead partisans to concur it's "better than other airport" options, though it might be too "pricey."

Méditerranée (La) S
14 | 15 | 13 | fr336

2, place de l'Odéon, 6ᵉ (Odéon), 01 43 26 02 30;
fax 01 43 26 18 44

◪ Venerable Left Bank seafooder overlooking the Théâtre de l'Europe and the Place de l'Odéon, featuring "nicely prepared" fish served on plates designed by Jean Cocteau; though popular with celebs in the '50s and '60s, modernists say it has become a "factory" that's too "pricey for mediocre quality"; still, the "good" prix fixe deals have adherents.

Mère Agitée (La)
▽ 15 | 7 | 15 | fr189

21, rue Campagne Première, 14ᵉ (Raspail), 01 43 35 56 64;
fax 01 43 35 56 64

■ The menu at this petite Montparnasse bistro depends on what chef Valérie Delahaye has found at the market that day, but you can count on "flavorful" Traditional French dishes that "aren't expensive" (though the choices might be "limited"); the ambiance is so casual that the chef sometimes waits on tables and thus "other patrons become friends."

Meurice (Le) S
▽ 20 | 24 | 22 | fr647

Hôtel Meurice, 228, rue de Rivoli, 1ᵉʳ (Concorde/Tuileries),
01 44 58 10 55; fax 01 44 58 10 15

■ "Everything's perfect" at this "luxurious" hotel dining room near the Tuileries Gardens, recently reopened after a no-expense-spared renovation; it has retained the same chef who turns out French cuisine worthy of "a palace" (indeed, some say it's like "dining at Versailles"), and though the bill is steep, you can anticipate nothing less than "100 percent satisfaction."

Michel (Chez) ☾
20 | 9 | 15 | fr275

10, rue de Belzunce, 10ᵉ (Gare du Nord/Poissonnière),
01 44 53 06 20; fax 01 44 53 61 31

■ Brainchild of chef Thierry Breton, this popular "tucked-away" bistro near the Gare du Nord is like a "country restaurant in the city"; the decor may be "discouraging" but the "marvelous" Traditional French regional cooking (including many dishes from the chef's native Brittany) comes at what admirers consider to be "unbeatable" prices.

Michel Courtalhac
▽ 18 | 10 | 17 | fr284

47, rue de Bourgogne, 7ᵉ (Invalides/Varenne),
01 45 55 15 35; fax 01 53 59 94 73

■ Traditional French in the 7th near the Palais-Bourbon that's a "good value" thanks to "careful service" and dishes featuring "fresh seasonal products" that are "beautifully presented" with all the "flavors alive"; the menu might be "limited" and the decor a wee bit "rustic", but patrons (including members of the nearby Assemblée Nationale) mostly have a "delicious" time.

MICHEL ROSTANG 26 | 21 | 24 | fr697

20, rue Rennequin, 17ᵉ (Péreire/Ternes), 01 47 63 40 77; fax 01 47 63 82 75

■ "They have a way of making you feel at home" at this sophisticated temple of haute cuisine near the Place des Ternes in the 17th; chef Michel Rostang's "perfectly run establishment" is an "understated" marvel, earning plaudits for the "inventive" kitchen, "excellent service" and "elegant", newly renovated surroundings; it's "expensive", but then again, it's "one of the best, without a doubt."

Milonga (La) ◐ [S] – | – | – | M

18, rue Guisarde, 6ᵉ (Mabillon/St-Germain-des-Prés), 01 43 29 52 18; fax 01 39 08 03 70

"Everyone is a regular, even if it's their first time" at this Argentine oasis in the heart of the Latin Quarter presided over by a "friendly owner"; the food is "very typical" (i.e. lots of grilled meat), and if it strikes perfectionists as "a little disappointing", there's weekend tango and *milonga* music and seasonal courtyard dining to compensate.

Mirama [S] ▽ 19 | 3 | 9 | fr176

17, rue St-Jacques, 5ᵉ (Maubert-Mutualité/St-Michel), 01 43 54 71 77; fax 01 43 25 37 63

■ This "fairly priced" storefront Chinese in the 5th is lauded for its "excellent noodle soups" and "divine duck dishes"; despite dismal decor and service that's "almost as unfriendly as the cuisine is excellent", it has enough of a following for some to suggest you "go early to avoid the lines."

Moissonnier 17 | 11 | 15 | fr305

28, rue des Fossés-St-Bernard, 5ᵉ (Jussieu), 01 43 29 87 65

■ Friendly Lyonnaise bistro in the 5th whose timeworn banquettes and tile floor evoke a "cozy", "family" feel; the "heavy but well-prepared" food (think meat, tripe and quenelles) might not suit the calorie-conscious, but "large portions" at fair prices have made it a long-running favorite.

Monde des Chimères (Le) – | – | – | M

69, rue St-Louis-en-l'Ile, 4ᵉ (Pont-Marie), 01 43 54 45 27; fax 01 43 29 84 88

Cécile Ibane and her daughter run this tiny Traditional French on the historic Ile Saint-Louis that purveys "unique" fare at "reasonable prices"; still, a minority fusses that it's "more a place for famished tourists than Parisian gourmets."

Moniage Guillaume (Le) – | – | – | E

88, rue de la Tombe-Issoire, 14ᵉ (Alésia/St-Jacques), 01 43 22 96 15; fax 01 43 27 11 79

A warm, cozy fireplace in winter, cool patio in summer and a glass roof year-round make this French seafooder in the 14th a "good neighborhood" stop; but while afishionados report everything is "excellent", critics carp it's "too expensive" for only an "average" meal.

Monsieur Lapin S   ▽ 14 | 14 | 17 | fr297

11, rue Raymond Losserand, 14ᵉ (Gaîté), 01 43 20 21 39;
fax 01 43 21 84 86

■ For rabbit prepared in every possible way, hop over to this "kitschy" French in the 14th near the Montparnasse cemetery; enthusiasts say it's "worth a visit" for its "very good" cooking (which also includes nonhare fare) and "amusing" rabbit-themed decor, but a few turn tail, complaining of "uneven" food and "expensive" wines.

Montalembert (Le) S   ▽ 14 | 18 | 15 | fr305

Hôtel Montalembert, 3, rue de Montalembert, 7ᵉ (Rue du Bac),
01 45 49 68 03; fax 01 45 49 69 49

■ "Superb minimalist decor" by Christian Liaigre sets the stage for a "well-presented", if also rather "minimalist", French menu at this stylish hotel dining room in the 7th; though prices aren't quite as minimal, it draws tourists as well as business folk, art and antiques dealers and publishing types from nearby Gallimard.

MONTPARNASSE 25 (LE)   23 | 16 | 19 | fr484

Le Méridien-Montparnasse, 19, rue du Commandant René
Mouchotte, 14ᵉ (Montparnasse-Bienvenüe), 01 44 36 44 25;
fax 01 44 36 49 03

■ This French inside the Méridien hotel in Montparnasse wins raves for Christian Moine's "excellent gastronomic cuisine" as well as what some regard as Paris' "best cheese cart" – three trolleys-full babied to perfection by cheese wiz Gérard Poulard; the mock art deco is "depressing" to some, "classy" to others, but what counts is "high-quality" fare that's a "good buy."

Monttessuy (Le)   ▽ 14 | 13 | 15 | fr254

4, rue de Monttessuy, 7ᵉ (Alma-Marceau), 01 45 55 01 90;
fax 01 45 55 01 90

■ In winter, diners at this traditional bistro in the 7th near the Champ de Mars warm themselves with "good Lyonnaise food" served on red-and-white-checked tablecloths by a cozy stove; in summer, sidewalk seating offers a picture-postcard view of the Eiffel Tower, which offers distraction should service be "a bit slow."

Morot-Gaudry   19 | 19 | 18 | fr446

8, rue de la Cavalerie, 15ᵉ (La Motte-Picquet-Grenelle),
01 45 67 06 85; fax 01 45 67 55 72

◪ All agree that this 8th-floor French in the 15th has "one of the prettiest views of Paris", including the Eiffel Tower and the Invalides, from its terrace; most also enjoy its "very good traditional" fare, but foes find it "disappointing for the price" (maybe they missed the "good-value" prix fixe menus) and also knock "old-hat" decor; since it draws a dressy bourgeois crowd, "be careful what you wear."

Moulin à Vent "Chez Henri" (Au)   18 | 13 | 16 | fr352 |

20, rue Fossés-St-Bernard, 5ᵉ (Jussieu), 01 43 54 99 37;
fax 01 40 46 92 23

■ "A rare survivor" from the "disappearing" crop of "old Lyonnaise bistros", this Latin Quarter vet offers some of "the best meat in Paris" and other hearty eats in a setting that's "pleasant", even if diners are "crowded in like herrings in a barrel"; if some fret that it's "much too expensive for what it is", more hope it never changes.

Moulin/Galette Graziano ●🅂   14 | 20 | 15 | fr305 |

83, rue Lepic, 18ᵉ (Abbesses/Blanche), 01 46 06 84 77;
fax 01 47 58 11 91

■ The "shadow of Dalida", the singer who once patronized this Montmartre Italian near the former Moulin de la Galette cabaret, still floats above the tourists and showbiz folk who like its pastas and other traditional fare; the "flower-filled" setting earns high marks, and a 60-franc prix fixe deal makes it "ideal for a family lunch", but beyond the set menus prices are "rather high" and some find it "a bit pretentious."

Muniche (Le) 🅂   11 | 13 | 10 | fr276 |

7, rue St-Benoît, 6ᵉ (St-Germain-des-Prés), 01 42 61 12 70;
fax 01 42 61 22 04

■ This veteran wood-paneled, vaguely art deco Latin Quarter brasserie down the street from the Café de Flore pleases fans who say it serves "traditional" fare with "professionalism"; maybe it's "not super" and some "preferred it" back when it was on the Rue de Buci, but it "still works, and that's as it should be."

Muscade 🅂   ▽ 9 | 16 | 9 | fr233 |

36, rue Montpensier, 1ᵉʳ (Bourse/Palais Royal-Musée du Louvre), 01 42 97 51 36; fax 01 42 97 51 36

■ Surveyors agree that this "chic" tearoom/restaurant overlooking the gardens of the Palais Royal has a lovely setting and "exquisite", "varied", desserts, with special praise for the "marvelous chocolate macaroons"; otherwise the food is "nothing extraordinary", but it's "marvelous to dine in the evening on the terrace."

Muses (Les)   ▽ 22 | 14 | 22 | fr364 |

Hôtel Scribe, 1, rue Scribe, 9ᵉ (Opéra), 01 44 71 24 26;
fax 01 44 71 24 64

■ A "promising" new chef, Yannick Alleno, formerly of Drouant and silver medalist in the '99 Bocuse d'Or culinary competition, is "looking to surprise" diners at this "quiet" French in the Hôtel Scribe near the Opéra, and comments such as "discovery of the year" suggest he's succeeding; "good service" helps make it "a place to return to", even if some find the basement setting "not for claustrophobes."

Natacha ◕
12 | 12 | 9 | fr230

17 bis, rue Campagne Première, 14ᵉ (Raspail), 01 43 20 79 27

◰ Movie stars and high-profile media types head to this "hip" Montparnasse bistro "to be seen"; as for the food, comments range from "good" to "uneven" (or worse) and service also takes a few jabs ("zero", "disdainful"), but then few come to this clubby spot just to dine.

Nemrod (Le)
▽ 12 | 6 | 14 | fr173

51, rue du Cherche-Midi, 6ᵉ (Sèvres-Babylone/St-Placide), 01 45 48 17 05

■ This Left Bank bistro near the Bon Marché department store serves "country"-style Auvergnat fare, including "marvelous beef from Aubrac", in a setting that "deserves a bit more taste", which is why regulars tout the terrace; handy for "a drink after shopping", it offers a "good-natured" welcome and "value", especially via its bargain prix fixe.

Nénesse (Chez)
– | – | – | M

17, rue de Saintonge, 3ᵉ (Filles-du-Calvaire/République), 01 42 78 46 49; fax 01 42 78 46 49

The few surveyors who know this old-fashioned French in the Marais disagree on its merits; fans praise "succulent" fare from new chef-owner Roger Leplu, who trained at Prunier and Le Grand Véfour, while detractors say "quality has slipped and prices went up"; in any case, it draws fashion types and local regulars alike.

New Jawad ⬛
▽ 16 | 14 | 18 | fr196

12, av. Rapp, 7ᵉ (Alma-Marceau), 01 47 05 91 37; fax 01 45 50 31 27

◰ While supporters say this Indian in the former La Flamberge inn in the chic 7th turns out "very good" food, a few doubters shrug "trying hard, but the cuisine is mediocre"; still, it's conveniently located, prices are easy and the dining room is spacious and attractive, with kudos for the "excellent service" and "perfect welcome."

New Nioullaville ◕⬛
14 | 10 | 11 | fr179

32-34, rue de l'Orillon, 11ᵉ (Belleville), 01 40 21 96 18; fax 01 40 21 96 58

■ What may be "the most Chinese" of all Chinese eateries in Paris is this big, "noisy" place in Belleville that "makes you think you're in Hong Kong" with its lively ambiance and "delicious" food, including rolling carts of dim sum; "middling" decor and low prices are also typical of the genre.

Ngo (Chez) ◕⬛
18 | 16 | 13 | fr283

70, rue de Longchamp, 16ᵉ (Trocadéro), 01 47 04 53 20; fax 01 47 04 53 20

■ "Small", "chic" Chinese near Trocadéro that's appreciated for its "exotic" fare and "deluxe" ambiance, with a wood-paneled dining room, huge wall mural and private salons ("pleasant for little groups"); on the downside, service can be lacking and prices strike some as a little too deluxe.

Noces de Jeannette (Les) S ▽ | 11 | 12 | 14 | fr295
14, rue Favart, 2ᵉ (Richelieu-Drouot), 01 42 96 36 89; fax 01 47 03 97 31
■ Near the Salle Favart concert hall is a "neighborhood spot for the budget-conscious" serving "good, traditional" bistro fare in a setting with old-fashioned Parisian charm and "excellent service"; if some feel it's "for tourists", most don't seem to mind.

Noura ● S | 14 | 9 | 11 | fr236
121, bd du Montparnasse, 6ᵉ (Vavin), 01 43 20 19 19; fax 01 43 20 05 40

Noura Pavillon ● S | 16 | 12 | 15 | fr288
21, av. Marceau, 16ᵉ (Alma-Marceau), 01 47 20 33 33; fax 01 47 20 60 31
■ "No need to go to Lebanon" because eating at these "always crowded" siblings is "like being in Beirut"; the Pavillon is more elegant than its Montparnasse sib (which is liked for its "very good" garden), but all supply "excellent" food and "good value", with special praise for the maza (appetizers); there's a take-out annex at 27 Avenue Marceau.

Nouveau Village Tao-Tao ● S ▽ | 17 | 12 | 13 | fr188
159, bd Vincent Auriol, 13ᵉ (Nationale), 01 45 86 40 08; fax 01 45 86 46 21
■ Champions of this Chinese in the 13th say it serves "quality" cuisine, maybe even "the best" of its kind in Paris, recommending the "salt-and-pepper shrimp – a delight", and the "super" Peking duck; "alas, it's a little out-of-the-way" and the nonsmoking room isn't as "pretty" as the main room.

O à la Bouche (L') ● | 18 | 12 | 15 | fr269
124, bd du Montparnasse, 14ᵉ (Vavin), 01 56 54 01 55; fax 01 43 21 07 87
■ "Warm and enthusiastic", this Montparnasse bistro offers Frank Paquier's "clever" French fare at "merciful" prices; some find the decor "dull" and service "a bit rushed", claiming that "success has killed a bit of its charm and tranquility", but "lunch is more agreeable (less noisy)" and most feel the food "makes up for" any faults.

Obélisque (L') S | 18 | 16 | 18 | fr445
Hôtel de Crillon, 4, rue Boissy d'Anglas, 8ᵉ (Concorde), 01 44 71 15 15; fax 01 44 71 15 02
■ "Excellent" Classic French fare, "marvelous desserts" and "courteous service" – "what more could one ask?" wonder admirers of this "serious" little brother of Les Ambassadeurs in the famed Crillon hotel on the Place de la Concorde; one might ask for lower prices, but "the magic of the Crillon" doesn't come cheap.

Oeillade (L') 16 | 11 | 14 | fr267

10, rue de St-Simon, 7e (Rue du Bac/Solférino), 01 42 22 01 60

■ Well-heeled denizens of the 7th head to this bistro for a "large selection of classics" at "good-value" prices; even if the "room is a little dull" and service can swing from "laid-back" to "grumpy", it's judged "pleasant" overall.

Oenothèque (L') ▽ 14 | 14 | 12 | fr419

20, rue St-Lazare, 9e (Notre-Dame-de-Lorette), 01 48 78 08 76; fax 01 40 16 10 27

■ "Superb wines" ("let the owner choose them") enhance the "good" traditional fare at this "adorable" bistro à vins neighboring the Gare Saint-Lazare; it's "a bit pricey", but "consistency", along with some "impressive" libations, draws the besotted back "again and again"; P.S. make reservations.

Olé Bodéga! 🌙 11 | 20 | 14 | fr203

16-18, rue du Faubourg-St-Antoine, 12e (Bastille), 01 43 47 30 27; fax 01 43 47 24 79

■ "Resolutely young and trendy" describes the mood and the crowd at this "loud", "smoke"-filled Spaniard in a big bi-level space with bullfight-themed decor near the Bastille; while some praise "excellent" tapas and "quality" wines served by an "ultrarapid" (if slightly "novice") staff, ratings suggest that "the setting and ambiance" are the big draws.

Olivades (Les) 18 | 12 | 14 | fr286

41, av. de Ségur, 7e (Ségur), 01 47 83 70 09; fax 01 42 73 04 75

■ This "real taste of Provence" in the 7th may be "short on space" and decor, but the "full-flavored", modestly priced cooking of Flora Mikula, a former Alain Passard protégé, keeps the place "lively with locals" and also "swarming with Americans"; though a few report "uneven" quality and service, most consider it "delicious" and "charming", "so reserve early – it is tiny."

Omar (Chez) 🌙 [S] 🚫💳 16 | 11 | 15 | fr188

47, rue de Bretagne, 3e (Arts-et-Métiers/Temple), 01 42 72 36 26

■ The artists, fashion designers and other "pretty, young" things who frequent this "hip" couscous house in the Marais like its "mix of genres – North African cuisine and brasserie decor" – and "love" owner Omar, a "pro" who has "a smile" for everyone; you may have to "tolerate waits and smoke", but the payoff is "lots of good food" served by a "friendly" staff at "reasonable prices."

Opportun (L') – | – | – | M

64, bd Edgar Quinet, 14e (Edgar Quinet/Montparnasse-Bienvenüe), 01 43 20 26 89; fax 01 43 21 61 88

Specializing in excellent meat, this tiny bistro near Vavin is appreciated by the few surveyors who've visited for its "enormous portions" of "hearty food" as well as its "good wines" and "warm service", all at moderate prices.

Orangerie (L') ◐ S
19 │ 24 │ 21 │ fr458

28, rue St-Louis-en-L'Ile, 4ᵉ (Pont Marie), 01 46 33 93 98

■ "Bravo" for owner Jean-Claude Brialy, whose "ravishing" Ile Saint-Louis Classic French remains "one of Paris' most romantic restaurants" and an "elegant rendezvous for the jet set"; "what flowers!" exclaim admirers who also laud the "good" food, "warm" staff and prix fixe format that means a tab "without surprises"; if some claim it looks better than it cooks, more think it makes for an "excellent evening."

Orient-Extrême S
18 │ 12 │ 12 │ fr260

4, rue Bernard Palissy, 6ᵉ (St-Germain-des-Prés),
01 45 48 92 27; fax 01 45 48 20 94

■ "Delicious" sushi and sashimi lure a trendy crowd to this "smoky, noisy" Japanese in Saint-Germain; "cold" decor, service that could use fine-tuning and "expensive" tabs fail to deter fans, and if some find the place a bit "Europeanized", that makes it "a good intro for the noninitiated."

Ormes (Les)
▽ 19 │ 8 │ 16 │ fr287

8, rue Chapu, 16ᵉ (Exelmans), 01 46 47 83 98; fax 01 46 47 83 98

■ "Go before everyone finds out" about this "little secret" in the 16th that's "off to a good start", offering "fine" Classic French cuisine and "friendly service" in a "pretty setting"; the fact that it's "not expensive" is another reason why it's a welcome addition to this rather barren neighborhood.

Os à Moelle (L') ◐
22 │ 12 │ 17 │ fr275

3, rue Vasco-de-Gama, 15ᵉ (Lourmel), 01 45 57 27 27;
fax 01 45 57 27 27

■ At this "remarkable" little bistro with "retro" decor in the 15th, chef-owner Thierry Faucher offers an "extraordinary" daily changing set menu distinguished by "surprising flavors" and "uncommon value"; tables are "crammed in" and some cite "assembly-line service" on busy nights, but "if you can get a seat", the food is worth it; N.B. check out its bistro à vins, La Cave de l'Os à Moelle, across the street.

Ostéria (L')
21 │ 8 │ 12 │ fr270

10, rue de Sévigné, 4ᵉ (St-Paul), 01 42 71 37 08

■ "Perhaps Paris' best Italian" enthuse fans of the "sublime risotto", "cloud-like gnocchi" and other "classic" dishes at this "hidden treasure" in the Marais; though the railroad-car-like setting is "cramped", service is "courteous" and the ambiance "relaxing"; still, some find prices a bit high.

Ostréade (L') S
▽ 15 │ 12 │ 14 │ fr224

11, bd de Vaugirard, 15ᵉ (Montparnasse-Bienvenüe),
01 43 21 87 41; fax 01 43 21 55 09

■ A handy whistle-stop before boarding a train at the adjacent Gare Montparnasse, this fish restaurant provides "good eats" and "good value"; the "original" decor, with tile mosaics lending a Catalonian feel to the duplex space, is a welcome change from most station canteens.

Oulette (L') 20 | 14 | 18 | fr327

15, place Lachambeaudie, 12ᵉ (Cour St-Emilion/ Dugommier), 01 40 02 02 12; fax 01 40 02 04 77

■ It's "worth the trek to Bercy", the evolving neighborhood in eastern Paris, to enjoy Marcel Baudis' "inventive" Southwestern French fare according to patrons of this "treasure that's not too well known"; "lovely" service, an "intelligent wine list" and a "modern" setting that's roomy enough so "tables aren't on top of each other" add appeal.

Oum el Banine 19 | 13 | 17 | fr317

16 bis, rue Dufrenoy, 16ᵉ (Porte Dauphine/Rue de la Pompe), 01 45 04 91 22; fax 01 45 03 46 26

■ "Excellent Moroccan cuisine", including the "lightest couscous" around, earns fans for this "familial" North African in the 16th; though "a bit pricey", it's "to be recommended" for its "always good" food and "pleasant ambiance."

Pacific Eiffel ◐ [S] ▽ 8 | 12 | 10 | fr263

Hôtel Hilton, 18, av. de Suffren, 15ᵉ (Bir-Hakeim), 01 44 38 57 77; fax 01 44 38 56 10

◪ This bi-level hotel Californian near the Eiffel Tower may earn anemic ratings, but defenders say it's "improving on all levels", with an "interesting" menu and Malibu-style decor that make it worth a visit; pickier types call it a "poor excuse for California cuisine" and knock "slow" service.

Pactole (Au) ◐ ▽ 12 | 10 | 11 | fr390

44, bd St-Germain, 5ᵉ (Maubert-Mutualité), 01 46 33 31 31; fax 01 46 33 07 60

■ Not many surveyors have visited this traditional Latin Quarter French since it morphed into a more stylish spot with modern accents in its food and decor; the young female owner's background at Guy Savoy's bistros shows in such touches as colorful lamp shades and inventive dishes; the few who know it deem it "correct" and no doubt appreciate newly lowered prices (not yet reflected in our scores).

Palanquin (Le) – | – | – | I

12, rue Princesse, 6ᵉ (Mabillon/St-Germain-des-Prés), 01 43 29 77 66

"Original" describes the cooking at this Vietnamese as well as the setting: an old stone house with wood beams in the hopping bar district of Saint-Germain; though hearty eaters find portions just "barely enough", prices are also light.

Palenque (El) ◐ 🚫💳 ▽ 17 | 7 | 12 | fr210

5, rue de la Montagne-Ste-Geneviève, 5ᵉ (Maubert-Mutualité), 01 43 54 08 99; fax 01 64 38 09 84

■ "The only Argentine restaurant worthy of the name" declare fans of this "intimate" bit of Buenos Aires on the Left Bank; besides "excellent" meat straight "from the pampas", it has "friendly service" and "good South American wines", but gauchos in need of room to roam moan "cramped."

Pamphlet (Le) ◐ ▽ 19 | 11 | 18 | fr227
38, rue Debelleyme, 3e (Filles-du-Calvaire), 01 42 72 39 24; fax 01 42 72 12 53
■ "Homey decor hides creative, delicious" French cooking, including dishes from the Béarn and Basque country, at chef-owner Alain Carrère's "neighborhood joint" on the edge of the Marais; while most laud the food and service, those who find the rustic setting (with dark beams and carriage lamps) on the "dull" side advise "go with friends, not a date."

Paolo Petrini [S] 19 | 11 | 15 | fr350
6, rue du Débarcadère, 17e (Argentine/Porte Maillot), 01 45 74 25 95; fax 01 45 74 12 95
■ The decor "isn't great", prices are "quite expensive" and it's "difficult to park" on this little street in the 17th, yet even so surveyors are won over by this Italian's "excellent" food, "warm" ambiance and "pleasant welcome by the owner"; regulars consider it a must "in truffle season."

Paparazzi ◐ ▽ 16 | 9 | 12 | fr152
7 bis, rue Geoffroy-Marie, 9e (Grands Boulevards), 01 48 24 59 39; fax 01 42 74 54 68
■ "Excellent" pizzas so big they're best for "sharing" ("I defy anyone to eat two") make for "amusing" meals at this Montmartre Italian, and if "average service" and "crowding" don't provoke too many smiles, the modest bill does.

Paprika (Le) – | – | – | M
28, av. Trudaine, 9e (Anvers/Pigalle), 01 44 63 02 91; fax 01 44 63 09 62
"Good music" helps make this Hungarian in the 9th a "pleasant" experience at night, even if a few Magyar mavens maintain that "other than the name, it has nothing to do with authentic Hungarian cuisine"; still, they serve classics like duckling roasted with cabbage, and an appealing terrace and interesting crowd also keep local regulars happy.

Parc aux Cerfs (Le) [S] 16 | 13 | 14 | fr240
50, rue Vavin, 6e (Vavin), 01 43 54 87 83; fax 01 43 26 42 86
■ "Country cuisine and the spirit of Montparnasse" meet in this arty bistro that's become something of a local "institution"; though a few deem it "nothing special", admirers say that in light of its "good food", "agreeable setting" and "excellent value", it "should be better known."

Paris (Le) ▽ 18 | 16 | 18 | fr587
Hôtel Lutétia, 23, rue de Sèvres, 6e (Sèvres-Babylone), 01 49 54 46 90; fax 01 49 54 46 00
■ "Very good from all points of view" is the verdict on this Classic French in the Hotel Lutétia near the Bon Marché department store; a "great wine list" and "pretty" art deco decor by Sonia Rykiel earn special mention, and the "intimate" space is suitable for "business lunches" – which is fitting since prices are suitable for expense accounts.

Paris Main d'Or 20 | 6 | 15 | fr255

133, rue du Faubourg-St-Antoine, 11e (Ledru-Rollin), 01 44 68 04 68; fax 01 44 68 04 68

■ By day, it's a cafe serving cold dishes and drinks, but at night, this spot just beyond the Bastille serves Corsican fare that prompts admirers to say the island "seen from this angle really is beautiful" thanks to "good charcuterie" and other "delicious" food made even better by the staff's "welcoming" attitude; though a few quibblers cite "pricey" wines and "rather austere" decor, fans deem it an "unbeatable value."

Passage (Le) ◐ ▽ 19 | 15 | 16 | fr230

18, passage de la Bonne-Graine, 11e (Ledru-Rollin), 01 47 00 73 30; fax 01 47 00 14 00

■ "A discovery" for those who "love *andouillettes* [sausages] and good wines" by the glass or bottle sums up this rustic bistro à vins in a "calm" setting "off the beaten path" behind the Bastille; popular with trendy types who've invaded the area in recent years, it's a "friendly" place with friendly prices.

Passy Mandarin [S] 16 | 12 | 15 | fr268

6, rue d'Antin, 2e (Opéra), 01 42 61 25 52; fax 01 42 60 33 92 ◐

6, rue Bois le Vent, 16e (La Muette), 01 42 88 12 18; fax 01 45 24 58 54

■ "Delicious Peking duck" is a standout at these "upscale" Chinese siblings where the high-quality fare also includes an "excellent choice for vegetarians"; other pluses: an "inexpensive" lunch prix fixe, "Chinese fantasy decor" and service that "respects the client."

Patrick Goldenberg ◐ [S] 10 | 7 | 9 | fr226

69, av. de Wagram, 17e (Ternes), 01 42 27 34 79; fax 01 40 53 02 45

◪ According to fans, "you get what you're looking for", i.e. "good, traditional" Central European–Jewish fare, at this "unpretentious" spot near the Place des Ternes, though it apparently doesn't come with much by way of decor or service; dissenters say "grandma's cooking was much better", but at least you "can taste the memories here."

Paul (Chez) [S] ▽ 11 | 14 | 13 | fr245

15, place Dauphine, 1er (Pont-Neuf), 01 43 54 21 48; fax 01 56 24 94 09

■ Once much more popular, this venerable old-fashioned bistro on the Ile de la Cité doesn't draw much surveyor comment, but those who know it consider it a "good address" that's especially worth a visit "in summer", when sidewalk seating makes it easy to enjoy its setting on the pretty Place Dauphine near the Seine; expect a very traditional menu and a splendidly sepia setting.

Paul (Chez) ●⬛
15 | 14 | 12 | fr206

13, rue de Charonne, 11ᵉ (Bastille/Ledru-Rollin), 01 47 00 34 57; fax 01 48 07 02 00

▨ "Reservations are imperative", but odds are the "wait will be long" anyway at this "bustling" Bastille bistro that's always "swarming with people"; its "traditional" cuisine and "simple", "warm" ambiance please most, but a few label it "overrated" and say it can be overloaded with "smoke" and "tourists."

Paul (Chez) ●⬛
▽ 15 | 13 | 14 | fr221

22, rue Butte-aux-Cailles, 13ᵉ (Corvisart/Place d'Italie), 01 45 89 22 11; fax 01 45 80 26 53

■ This "pleasant" bistro in the pretty Butte-aux-Cailles area not far from the Place d'Italie earns mostly plaudits for its "good cooking" (featuring regional and Lyonnaise fare), and if some feel the "decor could be improved", that doesn't bother many since it can be "too crowded" and "noisy" with people enjoying hearty dishes such as suckling pig or blood sausage.

Paul Chêne
20 | 14 | 19 | fr429

123, rue Lauriston, 16ᵉ (Trocadéro/Victor Hugo), 01 47 27 63 17; fax 01 47 27 53 18

■ Expect "no surprises" but also "no disappointments" (and "no nonsense or chichi" either) at this "very solid" traditional French veteran between the Place Victor Hugo and the Trocadéro; some find it "too pricey for frequent visits" and feel the "old-fashioned" decor could use "freshening", but that doesn't detract from the "good bourgeois cooking" and "charming reception."

Pauline (Chez)
18 | 15 | 15 | fr433

5, rue Villedo, 1ᵉʳ (Palais Royal-Musée du Louvre/ Pyramides), 01 42 96 20 70; fax 01 49 27 99 89

▨ Partisans say this "deluxe" bistro near the Palais Royal is the kind of place "you dream of when you're hungry", offering "serious" food (including "good game") in a rather serious setting with mirrors, wood paneling and red banquettes; but it's far from cheap and a few cite "uneven" cooking ("is the chef asleep?").

Paul Minchelli
21 | 15 | 18 | fr652

54, bd de La Tour-Maubourg, 7ᵉ (La Tour-Maubourg), 01 47 05 89 86; fax 01 45 56 03 84

▨ Offering "first-class fish" prepared with a "Zen"-like aesthetic, this upscale spot near the Invalides leaves no one indifferent: fans call chef-owner Minchelli "the god of seafood" and say the "decor, food and service all show rare creativity", while foes blast "pretension at astronomic prices" – but maybe they just don't get the "humor" of a menu that lists gag dishes (e.g. a tin of sardines for more than 1,000 francs) alongside authentic ones.

Pavillon des Princes S
16 | 14 | 14 | fr389

*69, av. de la Porte d'Auteuil, 16ᵉ (Porte d'Auteuil),
01 47 43 15 15; fax 01 46 51 16 94*

■ "It's a bit of a ride" to this Classic French near the Porte d'Auteuil, "but the effort is worth it" according to those who cite "refined food and service" in a "handsome", "spacious" setting where it's "possible to talk"; prices are "reasonable" for the quality, and there's "pleasant" outdoor seating.

Pavillon Elysée ◑
17 | 20 | 17 | fr411

*10, av. des Champs-Elysées, 8ᵉ (Champs-Elysées-Clémenceau),
01 42 65 85 10; fax 01 42 65 76 23*

◪ Though there's some debate about the traditional French fare ("very good", "making progress" vs. "average"), most agree that you can pass "a pleasant moment in a very pleasant place" at this pretty 19th-century pavilion "in the heart of the Champs-Elysées gardens"; it's especially "appealing in summer", and the prix fixe lunch menu is a "wonderful value."

Pavillon Montsouris S
17 | 22 | 15 | fr382

*20, rue Gazan, 14ᵉ (Cité-Universitaire), 01 45 88 38 52;
fax 01 45 88 63 40*

◪ "To dine on the edge" of the Parc Montsouris in the 14th, "seated beneath the terrace umbrellas", is reason enough to visit this French in a "charming" 18th-century pavilion, and by most accounts the "rustic" food is also satisfying, if not exciting; service may "leave something to be desired", but "on a nice day in good company", few are complaining.

Pavillon Puebla
▽ 17 | 21 | 15 | fr357

*Parc des Buttes-Chaumont, 19ᵉ (Buttes-Chaumont/Pyrénées),
01 42 08 92 62; fax 01 42 39 83 16*

■ "Very good and original" is the word on this restaurant serving Catalonian-accented French fare in a "pretty" pavilion with a "calm" terrace in the Parc des Buttes-Chaumont in the 19th; if the cooking "isn't quite up to the level" of the "exceptional setting and decor", it's still a "treat" and a "good value" for what, and where, it is.

Pento (Chez)
▽ 11 | 12 | 13 | fr195

*9, rue Cujas, 5ᵉ (Cluny-La Sorbonne/Luxembourg),
01 43 26 81 54; fax 01 43 26 81 54*

■ Appealing to those watching their pennies or feeling "nostalgic" for student days, this narrow, rustic bistro behind the Sorbonne is "reliable, good, inexpensive and unpretentious", qualities not always easily found in this "rather touristy" area; even those who feel "the ambiance lacks warmth" concede it's an "excellent value."

Père Claude (Le) S

15 | 11 | 14 | fr271

51, av. de La Motte-Picquet, 15ᵉ (La Motte-Picquet-Grenelle), 01 47 34 03 05; fax 01 40 56 97 84

▪ Owner "Claude [Perraudin] is media-savvy" and draws a "well-heeled crowd" of aristos and power-brokers (including some politicians) to his bistro near the Ecole Militaire; the food is affordable and "good" ("notably the excellent rotisserie" items) and the place has ambiance, but a few find it "overrated" and claim the welcome isn't so warm "if you're not a friend of the owner."

Pergolèse (Le)

21 | 16 | 19 | fr466

40, rue Pergolèse, 16ᵉ (Porte Dauphine/Porte Maillot), 01 45 00 21 40; fax 01 45 00 81 31

▪ "A sure thing in a bourgeois neighborhood" is one take on this pricey French between the Porte Maillot and the Porte Dauphine in the 16th; though a few quibblers complain of a menu "without inventiveness" and feel the decor isn't "at the level of the cuisine", ratings side with those who are "never disappointed."

Perraudin ⊟

12 | 12 | 13 | fr156

157, rue St-Jacques, 5ᵉ (Luxembourg), 01 46 33 15 75

▪ This "unpretentious", circa 1903 bistro near the Panthéon in the 5th "conjures up decades past" and is usually "crowded" with "penniless profs" and others who appreciate its "simple, traditional food", vintage decor and, last but not least, "cheap" prices; it has a "good little wine cellar" and garden courtyard too.

Perron (Le) S

▽ 17 | 12 | 15 | fr290

6, rue Perronet, 7ᵉ (St-Germain-des-Prés), 01 45 44 71 51; fax 01 45 44 71 51

▪ The decor doesn't set pulses racing, but this "real Italian" in Saint-Germain "attracts interesting people because it's good" and moderately priced, with special praise for the pastas, risottos and wine list; though it's just five minutes from the Café de Flore and Café Les Deux Magots, it attracts a loyal crowd of local regulars and very few tourists.

Persiennes (Les) ◗

13 | 13 | 12 | fr277

23, rue Marbeuf, 8ᵉ (Franklin D. Roosevelt), 01 56 69 26 90; fax 01 53 75 39 89

▪ "Fresh", "inventive" Mediterranean and Middle Eastern cuisine from an "often-changing" menu makes for "very agreeable" dining at this spot in the 8th; advocates call it an outstanding "value" and say it's "one of the few serious restaurants in the neighborhood – to be encouraged"; P.S. don't miss some of the rare Iranian dishes.

Petit Bofinger ◐ [S] 12 | 10 | 12 | fr205

6, rue de la Bastille, 4e (Bastille), 01 42 72 05 23; fax 01 42 72 97 68
10, place de Clichy, 9e (Place de Clichy), 01 48 74 44 78; fax 01 42 72 97 68
10, place Maréchal Juin, 17e (Péreire), 01 56 79 56 20; fax 01 56 79 56 21
18, av. Charles de Gaulle, Neuilly-sur-Seine (Porte Maillot), 01 47 22 37 25; fax 01 46 24 95 35

◪ These little brothers of the venerable brasserie Bofinger (located across the street from the Bastille branch) may be "standard", but they're "practical, quick" options for a "good, no-fuss meal at a good price" in a "retro ambiance"; still, critics fault them for having "average food" and "no personality"; N.B. other branches will be opening soon.

Petit Coin de la Bourse (Le) ▽ 15 | 12 | 14 | fr310

16, rue Feydeau, 2e (Bourse/Grands Boulevards), 01 45 08 00 08; fax 01 45 08 47 99

■ "A good, traditional restaurant for business dining" describes this French veteran not far from the Bourse, popular with old-boy types who appreciate its sturdy fare and reasonable prix fixe options; regulars call it the kind of place you "like to go back to", which explains why it's been around for over a century.

Petit Colombier (Le) 21 | 16 | 19 | fr458

42, rue des Acacias, 17e (Argentine/Charles de Gaulle-Etoile), 01 43 80 28 54; fax 01 44 40 04 29

◪ Regulars have been going to this inn-like French near the Etoile "for a long time and always with the same pleasure", enjoying "excellent", albeit "pricey", cuisine (featuring truffles and game in season) served by a "pleasant" staff; but a few report "unsteady quality" and feel the "dusty" decor could use "redoing."

Petite Chaise (A La) [S] 11 | 13 | 12 | fr276

36, rue de Grenelle, 7e (Sèvres-Babylone/St-Germain-des-Prés), 01 42 22 13 35; fax 01 42 22 33 84

◪ "One of Paris' oldest restaurants", this circa 1680 bistro in Saint-Germain provides "honest" food at "reasonable" prices in a "quaint", "tranquil" ambiance; even if some say it "relies on its historic reputation" more than its present-day cooking, few can resist its "amiability"; N.B. a renovation is planned.

Petite Cour (La) ◐ [S] 16 | 19 | 15 | fr355

8, rue Mabillon, 6e (Mabillon/St-Germain-des-Prés), 01 43 26 52 26; fax 01 44 07 11 53

■ "Dining outdoors in Saint-Germain without being on the sidewalk" is the big appeal of this traditional French with an "exceptional" courtyard garden near the Place Saint-Sulpice; it also offers "good food" and "friendly service", but budget-watchers warn that "the bill can really add up."

Petite Sirène de Copenhague (La) ◐

▽ 17 | 12 | 21 | fr229

47, rue Notre Dame de Lorette, 9ᵉ (St-Georges), 01 45 26 66 66
■ For a "good" meal as well as a "change of scenery", surveyors recommend this Scandinavian in the 9th, praising its "pleasant", if "not very varied", cooking (think salmon) and "charming" chef-owner, Peter Thulstrup (ex Crillon and La Tour d'Argent); prix fixe menus are an affordable intro, as long as you don't get carried away with the aquavit.

Petites Sorcières (Les)

▽ 16 | 12 | 13 | fr247

12, rue Liancourt, 14ᵉ (Denfert-Rochereau), 01 43 21 95 68; fax 01 43 21 95 68
■ "A great neighborhood haunt with bewitching service" is how admirers view this bistro at Denfert-Rochereau; it boasts a "good performance/price ratio", yet some claim it "doesn't leave a lasting memory" – perhaps that's what happens when the spell wears off.

Petite Tour (La)

▽ 15 | 11 | 17 | fr384

11, rue de la Tour, 16ᵉ (Passy), 01 45 20 09 31; fax 01 45 20 09 31
◪ To regulars, this small, serious French in Passy is like an "excellent provincial restaurant", with "good", classic fare served by an "extremely kind" staff in an old-fashioned setting; a few find the bill a tad "expensive" and the cooking "too heavy", but even they concede it's "not bad", and many appreciate the place as a reminder of the kind of polite, traditional eatery that was once found all over town.

Petit Keller (Le)

– | – | – | ❘

13, rue Keller, 11ᵉ (Bastille/Voltaire), 01 47 00 12 97
Two words sum up this little Bastille bistro: "simple" and "inexpensive", which probably explains why it's been around for half a century; locals (including trendy types) consider it a lifesaver "when funds are low", and while it might not be worth a major detour, it's a reliable option if going to the Opéra Bastille or a local gallery opening.

Petit Laurent (Le)

▽ 14 | 13 | 16 | fr475

38, rue de Varenne, 7ᵉ (Rue du Bac), 01 45 48 79 64; fax 01 45 44 15 95
◪ While doubters say this elegant Classic French in the 7th arrondissement "has been better", supporters insist it still provides "very good" meals, albeit at "expensive" prices and in a rather "austere" ambiance; those qualities may not faze clients drawn from nearby embassies, however.

Petit Lutétia (Au) 🅂

16 | 17 | 14 | fr222

107, rue de Sèvres, 6ᵉ (Vaneau), 01 45 48 33 53; fax 01 45 48 74 59
■ "Charming" and "authentic", this little brasserie near Vaneau wins praise for its "sublime oysters", "good-value" prix fixe deals and "warm, turn-of-the-century" setting with dark wood, mosaic floors and mirrors; true to the genre, it can be "a little noisy" and "full of smoke."

Petit Mabillon (Le)   ▽ 13 | 10 | 11 | fr233

6, rue Mabillon, 6ᵉ (Mabillon), 01 43 54 08 41

■ A "crowd of regulars" has long frequented this "simple, small" Left Bank Italian near the busy bar district between Saint-Sulpice and Saint-Germain, drawn by "very good" fresh pasta and other "authentic", "inexpensive" fare; despite praise for the "nice welcome", there are a few grumbles about service, so "try to avoid arguing with your waiter" (good advice at any restaurant).

Petit Mâchon (Le)   ▽ 13 | 10 | 14 | fr198

158, rue St-Honoré, 1ᵉʳ (Louvre-Rivoli/Palais Royal-Musée du Louvre), 01 42 60 08 06; fax 01 42 60 08 06 S
123, rue de la Convention, 15ᵉ (Boucicaut/Palais Royal-Musée du Louvre), 01 45 54 08 62

■ "Good charcuterie, good carafe wine – what more could you ask?" wonder admirers of these affordable *mâchons* (or bistros) near the Palais Royal and in a remote corner of the 15th (the latter presided over by a "restaurateur with character"); specializing in traditional Lyonnaise cuisine, they're "pleasant" and "picturesque" places "to discover."

Petit Marguery (Le)   20 | 14 | 18 | fr334

9, bd de Port-Royal, 13ᵉ (Les Gobelins), 01 43 31 58 59; fax 01 43 36 73 34

■ Devotees of this bistro in the Gobelins district of the 13th consider it "a sure bet" for "very good traditional food", admitting that they "dream all year" of its seasonal specialties (notably "out-of-this-world" game and mushroom dishes); run by the Cousin brothers, it also earns praise for its "friendly" attitude and "best-value" prix fixe menus – in sum, "a true joy."

Petit Navire (Le)   ▽ 19 | 14 | 16 | fr341

14, rue des Fossés-St-Bernard, 5ᵉ (Jussieu), 01 43 54 22 52

■ This "unpretentious" seafooder in the Jussieu district "has been the same for 30 years", and that's just the way regulars like it; run by "charming owners", it offers "extra-fresh" aquatic fare in a "pleasant" setting with nautical decor, and those with an eye on the bottom line say it "may be the best-value fish restaurant in Paris."

Petit Niçois (Le) S   18 | 12 | 14 | fr241

10, rue Amélie, 7ᵉ (La Tour-Maubourg), 01 45 51 83 65; fax 01 44 18 07 84

■ "Seafood with character" and without complications has long been the stock-in-trade of this "consistently good" Provençal-accented "neighborhood restaurant" in the 7th; the bouillabaisse alone is "worth a detour", and "good value" is another reason to drop line here; N.B. a change of owners means some are taking a wait-and-see attitude.

Petit Plat (Le) ●
_ _ _ M

49, av. Emile Zola, 15ᵉ (Charles Michels), 01 45 78 24 20; fax 01 45 78 23 13

A "pretty terrace" and an affordable 135-franc prix fixe menu for lunch and dinner are two attributes of this storefront bistro deep in the 15th; if some claim it's "slipped" a bit, the kitchen is still capable of doing nice bistro dishes and for the price it's hard to complain too loudly; P.S. the wine list is chosen by food critic Henri Gault, whose daughter is married to one of the owners.

Petit Poucet (Le) ●S
12 | 18 | 13 | fr269

4, rd-pt Claude Monet, Levallois-Perret (Pont-de-Levallois), 01 47 38 61 85; fax 01 47 38 20 49

■ "Everything is pretty" at this Contemporary French, from its Seine-side setting on the Ile de la Jatte to the staff and "fashionable" "advertising"/"business" crowd; opinions on the food vary from "good" to "ordinary", but the trademark steak tartare is excellent and either way dining on the "lovely" terrace is "divine" in summer.

Petit Prince de Paris (Le) ●S
▽ 15 | 13 | 16 | fr212

12, rue de Lanneau, 5ᵉ (Maubert-Mutualité), 01 43 54 77 26; fax 01 43 54 36 77

■ Set on a cobbled lane on the slopes of the Panthéon, this bistro is well liked by a well-dressed, gay professional crowd (among others) for its "good and rather original" Classic French cuisine as well as for the "very pleasant ambiance" of its candlelit dining room in an old house; claims that "service is a bit sexist" could mean just about anything here.

Petit Rétro (Le)
▽ 13 | 14 | 15 | fr236

5, rue Mesnil, 16ᵉ (Victor Hugo), 01 44 05 06 05; fax 01 44 05 06 05

■ It may feel "stifling when crowded" (they "pack you in like sardines"), but this cozy traditional French a few steps from the Place Victor Hugo is worth the squeeze thanks to "good homestyle cuisine", a "warm welcome" and a "simple but authentic" setting with art nouveau tiles and a zinc bar; it's also considered a "good value" in this pricey nabe.

Petit Riche (Au) ●
15 | 19 | 15 | fr303

25, rue Le Peletier, 9ᵉ (Le Peletier/Richelieu-Drouot), 01 47 70 68 68; fax 01 48 24 10 79

◪ "Travel through time" via this bistro in the 9th with decor that "must not have changed since it opened" in 1880; gas lamps (now electric), etched glass and wood panels set the stage for "good" Loire-accented cuisine and wines, plus excellent oysters, and if a few feel the place is "living on its reputation", it still has "charm" and is a "business dining" standby for bankers and others in the area.

Petit St. Benoît (Le) ⌒

| 11 | 11 | 12 | fr195 |

4, rue St-Benoît, 6ᵉ (St-Germain-des-Prés), 01 42 60 27 92

◪ The staff dishes up "hearty" food and "amusing abuse" ("they're chosen for their repartee") at this "inexpensive, traditional" bistro down the street from the Café de Flore in Saint-Germain; sure, it draws "lots of tourists" and some claim it's "not what it used to be", but it has real "Paris ambiance" – "there aren't many left like this one."

Petit Victor Hugo (Le) ◖

| 11 | 11 | 11 | fr241 |

143, av. Victor Hugo, 16ᵉ (Rue de la Pompe/Victor Hugo), 01 45 53 02 68; fax 01 44 05 13 46

◪ "Perhaps the most 16th arrondissement–like restaurant in the 16th" (i.e. "preppy", "a little snobby"), this "classic" brasserie draws locals in search of "decent" if "unsurprising" meals at decent prices in a "pleasant" setting; though some say "it could do much better", it's almost "unavoidable" if in the area.

Petit Zinc (Le) ⬛

| 13 | 17 | 12 | fr279 |

11, rue St-Benoît, 6ᵉ (St-Germain-des-Prés), 01 42 61 20 60; fax 01 42 60 37 75

◪ If the food at this brasserie in the heart of Saint-Germain "isn't up to the level of the decor" – a "pretty pastiche" with art nouveau–style ceramics and wood paneling – it's "honorable" enough and even more satisfying when dining on the "nice terrace"; there's debate over cost, though: "good value" vs. "pricey for what it is"; more popular with tourists than locals, it's part of the Frères Blanc chain.

Petrossian

| 19 | 16 | 15 | fr418 |

18, bd. de La Tour-Maubourg, 7ᵉ (La Tour-Maubourg), 01 44 11 32 32; fax 01 44 11 32 35

◪ The famed caviar house is now supplying Parisians with "beautifully presented" Russian and Scandinavian-inspired luxury eats as well as smoked fish and caviar at the stylish new restaurant over its '20s-vintage shop near Les Invalides in the 7th; supporters find it "very promising", citing "fabulous fish and desserts", an "attentive" staff and a "more than pleasant setting", but doubters knock "amateur service", "onerous tabs" and "no soul"; no one complains about the icy vodka at 20 francs a shot, however.

Pétrus ⬛

| 18 | 15 | 15 | fr476 |

12, place du Maréchal Juin, 17ᵉ (Péreire Levallois), 01 43 80 15 95; fax 01 47 66 49 86

◼ Fish aficionados say "satisfaction is assured" at this upscale seafooder in the 17th that wins special notice for its "original" preparations and "very good oysters", among other shellfish; but it takes a few harpoons for "very expensive" prices.

Pharamond 🅂

_	_	_	M

*26, rue de la Grande Truanderie, 1ᵉʳ (Etienne Marcel),
01 40 28 03 00; fax 01 60 28 01 81*

This circa 1832 Les Halles brasserie with lovely landmarked decor (art nouveau tiles, a winding wooden staircase) seemed in danger of closing and becoming just another of the area's many clothing shops a few years ago, but new owners rode in to the rescue; it still offers earthy food with a normande accent, including its famous *tripes à la mode de Caen* (cooked in cider), but at welcome lower prices.

Philippe Detourbe

22	15	18	fr322

*8, rue Nicolas Charlet, 15ᵉ (Pasteur), 01 42 19 08 59;
fax 01 45 67 09 13*

■ Back in the kitchen of his original bistro in the 15th, chef-owner Philippe Detourbe "still surprises" diners with "refined, inventive" dishes offered via a daily changing, "gently priced" fixed menu; "attentive" service and "warm decor" add to the appeal, and though there are quibbles ("a little precious", "hell when crowded"), this is one young chef who keeps "rising and rising."

Philosophes (Les) ◗🅂

▽ 12	15	14	fr191

*28, rue Vieille du Temple, 4ᵉ (Hôtel-de-Ville/St-Paul),
01 48 87 49 64; fax 01 42 71 31 81*

■ "Despite the crowd at all hours, you can eat well and cheaply" at this "friendly" Marais bistro offering "simple", traditional French fare; serving all day, it's "handy for light, last-minute meals", and even if the street is "noisy" it has what some call the area's "best sidewalk cafe."

Pichet (Le)

17	10	15	fr379

*68, rue Pierre Charron, 8ᵉ (Franklin D. Roosevelt),
01 43 59 50 34; fax 01 42 89 68 91*

■ You can "see race-car drivers, politicians" and other notables while enjoying "simple food" made with "superior" ingredients at this brasserie off the Champs-Elysées; its "varied" fish and shellfish offerings earn special praise, and while "high prices" prompt grumbles, you get "consistent" quality and a "very Parisian ambiance" for your buck.

Pied de Chameau (Au) ◗🅂

▽ 13	18	10	fr246

*20, rue Quincampoix, 4ᵉ (Hôtel-de-Ville), 01 42 78 35 00;
fax 01 42 78 00 50*

◩ Supporters of this Marais Moroccan say it serves "delicious tagines" and other "very rich, authentic" fare in a "pretty" setting; detractors claim "you can get better couscous" and the like elsewhere, but with its "lively" ambiance and belly dancers on some nights, it's an instant "getaway" and "fun for groups."

Pied de Cochon (Au) ●⬛   13 | 15 | 13 | fr287
6, rue Coquillière, 1er (Châtelet-Les Halles), 01 40 13 77 00; fax 01 40 13 77 09

▣ Even "when the city is asleep", this 24-hour Les Halles "classic" remains "noisy and crowded" with "night owls" (and "tourists") dining on its pig's feet, onion soup and other brasserie fare; if some find it more "practical" than good, "nostalgists" don't mind since "the spirit of the [old] Les Halles is preserved" here; N.B. the decor has been redone, but regulars may wonder what happened to the colorful old bunch-of-grape sconces (now monotone) and regret the rising prices.

Pied de Fouet (Au) ⊄   ▽ 13 | 13 | 13 | fr147
45, rue de Babylone, 7e (St-François-Xavier), 01 47 05 12 27

■ "Move in the cameras and roll" to capture the look and feel of an old-fashioned bistro that "reeks of Paris"; though set in the chic 7th district, it's a homey place with "simple", "family-style" food, "low prices" and a "convivial" feel – "everyone seems to know each other", perhaps because it's so small it's hard not to rub elbows with fellow diners.

"Pierre" A la Fontaine Gaillon ●   17 | 16 | 17 | fr382
1, place Gaillon, 2e (Opéra), 01 42 65 87 04; fax 01 47 42 82 84

■ Its "plush" setting in a Mansart townhouse, "central" location "on a calm street not far from the Opéra" Garnier and "very good food and service" make this long-standing Classic French "ideal for business meals" and an honest "value" for what it is (especially the prix fixe menus); though it can seem "a tad stiff", most would "recommend it."

Pierre au Palais Royal ●   16 | 12 | 14 | fr350
10, rue Richelieu, 1er (Palais Royal-Musée du Louvre), 01 42 96 09 17; fax 01 47 96 09 62

▣ Since you enter this French next to the Palais Royal via its attached florist shop, meals start off on a "pleasant" note, and for most the mood continues thanks to "refined" cuisine and decor, a "stylish crowd" and a "very present" owner (Jean-Paul Arabian); outvoted critics report "variable" food and service, but a new chef is getting good reviews for his modern bistro cooking; the fact that it's handy "after the theater" is a plus.

Pierre (Chez)   ▽ 16 | 9 | 16 | fr306
117, rue de Vaugirard, 15e (Duroc/Falguière), 01 47 34 96 12; fax 01 47 34 96 12

▣ This little Burgundian bistro in the 15th not far from Montparnasse has been around for years, yet few surveyors seem to know it; despite a change in ownership a few years ago, we hear it's "still a good address", especially for its wines and bœuf bourguignon, though some find the service and decor "discouraging."

PIERRE GAGNAIRE
27 | 21 | 25 | fr800

Hôtel Balzac, 6, rue Balzac, 8ᵉ (Charles de Gaulle-Etoile/ George V), 01 44 35 18 25; fax 01 44 35 18 37

■ "An explosion of flavors and culinary surprises" makes for "not-to-be-missed" dining at "genius" chef Pierre Gagnaire's haute cuisine dazzler in the Hôtel Balzac; every dish "is a palette of color, texture and taste" "signed by a great artist" and served by pros, and if some find the decor "a bit severe", that hardly detracts from the "poetry on the plate"; such perfection comes at "a price", of course.

Pitchi Poï **S**
▽ 12 | 11 | 11 | fr207

7, rue Caron, 4ᵉ (St-Paul), 01 42 77 46 15; fax 01 42 77 75 49

■ "Friendly, informal" Marais restaurant serving Jewish–Eastern European fare (blini, corned beef, lots of vodkas) at "good prices"; the ambiance is "appealing", "especially on the terrace" for brunch.

Plage Parisienne (La) **S**
10 | 20 | 9 | fr250

Port de Javel Haut, 15ᵉ (Javel), 01 40 59 41 00

☑ The setting overlooking the Seine at the Port de Javel in the 15th is "delicious", and if the same can't be said of the French fare, dining here is still "appealing", especially in summer; service can be choppy and it's "a little pricey", but there's an "amazing view" and perhaps an "up-close look" at the TV folk who sometimes drop anchor here.

Plancha (La) ◗⇥
– | – | – | I

34, rue Keller, 11ᵉ (Bastille), 01 48 05 20 30

Though fans sigh "it's a shame the secret is out about this charming Basque" near the Bastille, not many surveyors seem to be clued in; those who are tout its "simple menu", "formidable sangria" and "festive ambiance"; "few tables" means you might have to wait before being seated.

Planet Hollywood ◗ **S**
5 | 12 | 8 | fr204

78, av. des Champs-Elysées, 8ᵉ (Franklin D. Roosevelt/ George V), 01 53 83 78 27; fax 01 45 63 02 84

☑ The Champs-Elysées outpost of this Hollywood-themed American chain arouses Gallic gall – "a bad caricature of the US and its food", "tourist rip-off", "is there a waiter for my table?" – but some find it "amusing", especially "with kids" or "after midnight" (better yet, "after a few beers"); bottom line: it's "exactly what one would expect."

Pluvinel (Le) **S**
– | – | – | M

Hôtel Regina, 2, place des Pyramides, 1ᵉʳ (Pyramides/Tuileries), 01 42 60 31 10; fax 01 40 15 95 16

Convenient to the Louvre and the Tuileries, this French in the Belle Epoque–vintage Hôtel Regina has "good" food, "affordable" wines and turn-of-the-century ambiance, complete with fireplace; it's fine for a quiet lunch before or after a museum visit, and the tiny terrace in an interior courtyard is a calm place for a midsummer's night meal.

Polidor ●🅂⊅   11 | 13 | 10 | fr151
41, rue Monsieur-le-Prince, 6ᵉ (Luxembourg/Odéon),
01 43 26 95 34; fax 01 43 26 95 34
■ This Latin Quarter bistro is a "cheap eats" "classic" that draws a "nice mix" of "students", "tourists and locals" seeking "good" food and "value" in a "warm, traditional" setting "right out of *Les Miz*"; around since the 1800s, it's demonstrated "astonishing continuity", so few mind if it can be "noisy" with service that varies from "hasty" to "slow."

Poquelin (Le)   ▽ 16 | 15 | 19 | fr303
17, rue Molière, 1ᵉʳ (Palais Royal-Musée du Louvre),
01 42 96 22 19; fax 01 42 96 05 72
■ Though "little" in size, this bistro between the Opéra and the Palais Royal makes a big impression on fans who salute "husband-and-wife owners who've maintained its quality for over 20 years"; designed as an homage to Molière, the setting strikes some as a bit "austere", but "very attentive" service warms it up.

Port Alma   20 | 14 | 19 | fr461
10, av. de New York, 16ᵉ (Alma-Marceau), 01 47 23 75 11;
fax 01 47 20 42 92
■ "Lots of professionalism" and "respect for natural flavors" distinguish this upscale seafooder in the 16th, where the fish is so "fresh" "you'd think you were on the Côte d'Azur", an impression heightened by the "soothing decor"; less soothing are prices as high as the quality.

Port du Salut (Le) 🅂   12 | 15 | 13 | fr136
163 bis, rue St-Jacques, 5ᵉ (Luxembourg), 01 46 33 63 21;
fax 01 46 33 63 21
■ "Economical" prix fixe menus please budget-watchers at this "unpretentious" Latin Quarter basement dining room; admirers consider it "a pearl in an area not well endowed" with sources of affordable "good" food.

Poste (La) ●   13 | 21 | 11 | fr309
22, rue de Douai, 9ᵉ (Blanche/Place de Clichy), 01 45 26 50 00;
fax 01 45 26 08 02
◪ "Magnificent decor" is the strong suit of this Indochinese set in a 19th-century Pigalle townhouse that once belonged to Georges Bizet; diners mostly enjoy the food (especially the "excellent fish"), but some find it "too expensive" and feel it "just doesn't pull it all together."

Potager du Roy (Le) 🅂   19 | 13 | 17 | fr343
1, rue du Maréchal-Joffre, Versailles (Versailles Rive Gauche),
01 39 50 35 34; fax 01 30 21 69 30
■ "Solid food and solid locals enjoying it" is what you can expect at this "calm and welcoming" French in Versailles; while opinions on the decor range from "chic" to "dated" and some feel the place "doesn't progress", most savor the "excellent cuisine" – "too bad it's not in Paris."

Pouilly Reuilly ▽ 21 12 17 fr358

68, rue André Joineau, Le Pré-St-Gervais (Hoche), 01 48 45 14 59; fax 01 48 45 93 93

■ "Generous" portions of "country-style" cuisine, "convivial service" and old-style decor make this bistro in Le Pré-Saint-Gervais "worth discovering"; devotees consider it a bastion of "authentic French good eats."

Poule au Pot (La) ◐ [S] ▽ 13 13 13 fr241

9, rue Vauvilliers, 1er (Châtelet-Les Halles/Louvre-Rivoli), 01 42 36 32 96; fax 01 40 91 90 64

■ For "a late-night dinner" in Les Halles, this bistro "institution" (open till 5 AM) is a natural choice; it's been around so long (since 1935) that some even find it kind of "hip", an impression reinforced by the many famous night owls (Rod Stewart, etc.) it's drawn through the years; P.S. regulars swear by the namesake dish, hen poached in broth with vegetables.

PRÉ CATELAN (LE) [S] 23 24 21 fr638

Bois de Boulogne, route de Suresnes, 16e (Porte Dauphine), 01 44 14 41 14; fax 01 45 24 43 25

■ "Enchanting in every regard" is the consensus on this "pretty" French that makes a fine first impression with its "magical" Bois de Boulogne setting and follows it up with "excellent" food by rising chef Frédéric Anton, a Robuchon protégé, that most find "equal to" the surroundings (and prices); add "lovely" wines, generally "attentive" service and an "irresistible terrace" and you have an experience that's "a dream" in summer and "memorable" year-round.

Président (Le) ◐ [S] ▽ 12 16 11 fr139

120, rue du Faubourg du Temple, 11e (Belleville), 01 47 00 17 18; fax 01 43 38 28 34

■ The "room seems to go on forever, just like the menu" at this giant Belleville Chinese with "incredible" decor complete with a cupola and monumental stairway; what's on the plate also appeals, i.e. "good-quality" food (including some Thai and Cambodian dishes) at "reasonable prices"; it's "worth a detour", especially since it stays open "late."

Pressoir (Au) ▽ 21 18 20 fr540

257, av. Daumesnil, 12e (Michel Bizot), 01 43 44 38 21; fax 01 43 43 81 77

■ Its "edge-of-Paris" location in the 12th may explain why this French is still somewhat "unrecognized" despite "excellent" cuisine from a chef, Henri Séguin, who strikes partisans as "much more creative" than some better-known names ("the tasting menu is marvelous"); a "warm welcome", "efficient service" and appealing decor also help justify a bill that's rather "heavy."

Procope (Le) ◖S
12 | 20 | 12 | fr279

13, rue de l'Ancienne Comédie, 6ᵉ (Odéon), 01 40 46 79 00; fax 01 40 46 79 09

☑ You can see "the tables where Voltaire and Diderot" held court at this circa 1686 cafe near the Odéon, but critics who denounce "boring" brasserie fare and too many "tourists" claim "Voltaire wouldn't go there today"; still, others find the food "satisifying" and most agree that its "voyage-back-in-time" decor makes it "a must", at least once.

Prune (Chez) S
▽ 12 | 21 | 18 | fr154

36, rue Beaurepaire, 10ᵉ (République), 01 42 41 30 47; fax 01 42 00 32 28

■ "Reasonable prices" and interesting "people-watching" are two assets at this contemporary bistro/cafe with a neo-boho ambiance in the Valmy area (the latest stomping ground for cutting-edge trendies); it's especially "good for lunch or brunch", with a "welcoming staff" and "excellent location" near the Canal Saint-Martin; N.B. light dishes are served after 9 PM.

P'tit Troquet (Le)
▽ 18 | 13 | 17 | fr220

28, rue de l'Exposition, 7ᵉ (Ecole-Militaire), 01 47 05 80 39; fax 01 47 05 80 39

■ "Very good, fresh food" from a market-driven menu is served at "value"-minded prices at this contemporary bistro with a Basque-Béarnais accent in the 7th; the wines and service also earn nods, but it seems that the ambiance can swing from "calm" to "noisy and bustling" depending on the night.

Quai Ouest ◖S
11 | 17 | 11 | fr255

1200, quai Marcel Dassault, St-Cloud (Pont-de-St-Cloud), 01 46 02 35 54; fax 01 46 02 33 02

☑ "Fun" for "summer dining, birthdays, large groups" or just "to be seen" amid "trendy" types, this "big, noisy", "stylish" riverside French in Saint-Cloud remains "as overbooked as an airline" despite simply "decent" food and service that can be "slower than the pancake syrup" at Sunday brunch, one of its busiest meals ("you'd better adore kids"); for best results, "reserve in advance" and "ask for a seat by the water."

404 (Le) ◖S
17 | 22 | 14 | fr251

69, rue des Gravilliers, 3ᵉ (Arts-et-Métiers), 01 42 74 57 81; fax 01 42 74 03 41

■ "You think you're in Marrakech" thanks to the "excellent couscous", "transporting decor" and "smiling service" at this Moroccan between Les Halles and the Marais, but "heavens, is it cramped!"; under the same ownership as London's ultratrendy restaurant Momo, it has such a "supernice ambiance" that it makes you "forget you're squeezed in and the music can be too loud."

Quercy (Le)
_ | _ | _ | M

36, rue Condorcet, 9ᵉ (Anvers/Cadet), 01 48 78 30 61;
fax 01 48 78 16 29

"Very good cassoulet" is a highlight at this longtime
purveyor of Southwestern French fare between Pigalle
and the Gare du Nord in a gentrifying part of the 9th; the
food is "authentic" as well as a "good value", but waist-
watchers add another adjective, "heavy", which some
would also apply to the hasn't-been-touched-in-years decor.

Quincy (Le) ⊅
▽ 21 | 13 | 21 | fr423

28, av. Ledru-Rollin, 12ᵉ (Gare de Lyon/Quai de la Rapée),
01 46 28 46 76; fax 01 46 28 46 76

■ It's a "joy" to dive into so much "cholesterol" exclaim
fans of this "excellent" bistro near the Bastille and the
Gare de Lyon, presided over by "colorful" owner Michel
Bosshard ("hail Bobosse!"); serving "generous" portions
of "good bourgeois cuisine" from the Berry and Ardèche
regions in a suitably "provincial ambiance", it's "worth
the trip", even if prices are on the high side.

Quinson (Le) 🄂
▽ 14 | 10 | 12 | fr254

5, place Etienne Pernet, 15ᵉ (Félix-Faure), 01 45 32 48 54;
fax 01 44 19 73 18

■ "Recommended for its bouillabaisse", this Provençal-
accented fish house in the 15th doesn't net much surveyor
comment, but it must have a following since it's been
around since 1945, dishing up the likes of mussels with
pistou sauce and *brandade de morue* (salt cod and mashed
potatoes); renovation work is planned for late summer
2000, but fans hope that the winsome '50s decor will
survive the freshening up.

Ravi
_ | _ | _ | E

50, rue de Verneuil, 7ᵉ (Rue du Bac), 01 42 61 17 28

The "excellent" cuisine at this intimate Indian near the
Musée d'Orsay keeps both the bar and the dining room
"crowded", even though house specialties like basmati
rice and the delicious cheese naan are priced as extras
and can result in Himalayan tabs.

Récamier (Le)
19 | 16 | 17 | fr452

4, rue Récamier, 7ᵉ (Sèvres-Babylone), 01 45 48 86 58;
fax 01 42 22 84 76

☑ "Publishers and editors" (and those who like to watch
them) gather on the terrace of this "chic" French in Saint-
Germain to compare notes over "excellent", "old-fashioned"
Burgundian cooking (including dishes featuring game or
wild mushrooms); but all agree that prices are "high"
and critics call it a "snobbish" scene that could stand to
"shake itself up" a bit.

Rech (Le) ●🅂
17 | 11 | 16 | fr365

62, av. des Ternes, 17ᵉ (Charles de Gaulle-Etoile/Ternes),
01 45 72 29 47; fax 01 45 72 41 60

■ Serving Classic French fare since 1925, this brasserie on the Place des Ternes is a well-established source of "excellent seafood" and quality Camembert; fans applaud the service and "very good value", and while the aging room is not without "charm", some feel it could use spiffing up.

Réconfort (Le)
▽ 15 | 18 | 15 | fr202

37, rue de Poitou, 3ᵉ (St-Sébastien-Froissart), 01 42 76 06 36;
fax 01 42 76 04 74

■ Admirers of this "cozy", bi-level Provençal bistro in the Marais say it "lives up to its name" (which means 'comfort'), praising its winning combination of "traditional" cuisine, "good service" and "great value"; its "provincial charm" secures it many supporters, so it's best to arrive early.

Régalade (La) 🅂
21 | 10 | 14 | fr281

49, av. Jean Moulin, 14ᵉ (Alésia), 01 45 45 68 58; fax 01 45 45 68 58

■ Mink coats mingle with backpacks at this out-of-the-way French near the Porte d'Orléans, where habitués praise the "excellent", "inventive" cuisine and "great value" even as they deplore the "cafeteria decor", noise level and "elbow-to-elbow" seating; but even in a "sardine-can" setting chef Yves Camdeborde remains a talent to watch.

Relais Beaujolais 🅂
– | – | – | M

3, rue Milton, 9ᵉ (Notre Dame-de-Lorrette), 01 48 78 77 91

This lively, "noisy", old-fashioned bistro in the 9th lives up to its name as a source of "good Beaujolais" and other wines, matched with some "excellent" takes on "standard bistro fare"; with an ex-butcher for an owner, it's also noteworthy for its choice cuts of meat.

Relais Chablisien
– | – | – | I

4, rue Bertin-Poirée, 1ᵉʳ (Châtelet-Les Halles/Pont Neuf),
01 45 08 53 73; fax 01 45 08 53 73

Fans admit to being "conquered" by this French in an old stone building a stone's throw from the Louvre, where both the food and the wines have a serious touch of Burgundy; foes who find it "disappointing" cite "few choices" and "mediocre quality", but they must be outvoted since you're advised to "reserve far ahead of time."

Relais d'Auteuil
22 | 17 | 20 | fr478

31, bd Murat, 16ᵉ (Michel-Ange Molitor/Porte d'Auteuil),
01 46 51 09 54; fax 01 40 71 05 03

■ Refined and flower-filled, this tony French in the chic 16th is home to "exceptional" French cuisine enhanced by "attentive service" and the "care put into each detail", from the china to the presentations; though some find the decor a bit "nouveau riche" and many chafe at the "high prices", the majority feels it exhibits "great class" on all levels.

Relais de l'Entrecôte (Le) ☾ [S] ▽ 19 | 9 | 16 | fr187

20 bis, rue St-Benoit, 6e (St-Germain-des-Prés), 01 45 49 16 00; fax 01 45 49 29 75

15, rue Marbeuf, 8e (Franklin D. Roosevelt), 01 49 52 07 17; fax 01 47 23 34 98

■ An "inexpensive" meat eater's paradise in Saint-Germain (and near the Champs-Elysées) known for its "very tender" steak accompanied by "inimitable" secret-recipe pepper sauce and possibly "the best french fries in Paris"; its set-price fixed-menu format means "no surprises" – and that goes for the dowdy decor too.

Relais de Sèvres (Le) ▽ 21 | 16 | 18 | fr470

Sofitel-Porte de Sèvres, 8-12, rue Louis Armand, 15e (Balard), 01 40 60 33 66; fax 01 45 57 04 22

■ Near the Parc des Expositions in the far reaches of the 15th, chef Pierre Miécaze offers innovative, "very good" French cuisine in the dining room of the Sofitel Porte de Sèvres hotel; contrarians cavil about the dull decor but concede "it's ok" if you're "in the neighborhood."

Relais de Venise (Le) ☾ [S] 18 | 10 | 14 | fr224

271, bd Péreire, 17e (Porte Maillot), 01 45 74 27 97

■ "Get there early" or face a "long line" at this popular, no-reserving meat-eaters' "monument" near the Porte Maillot that draws throngs with its set menu featuring "excellent" sirloin steak accompanied by its "famous sauce" ("I'd give a lot to know the recipe") and "light" frites; chocolate mousse and fruit tart finish up the feast and affordable house wines add to the value.

Relais du Parc (Le) [S] 18 | 17 | 16 | fr380

Le Parc Sofitel Demeure, 55-57, av. Raymond Poincaré, 16e (Trocadéro/Victor Hugo), 01 44 05 66 10; fax 01 44 05 66 49

■ "Not just a hotel dining room", this French in the 16th impresses with its "terrific cuisine", "attentive service", "pretty" Ralph Lauren–like decor and lovely interior garden that's "great for lunch in summer"; menu items can be prepared in either a traditional or updated style, and though a few cite "irregular" results, they're outvoted; N.B. the news that Alain Ducasse will no longer oversee the kitchen may put into question the above food rating.

Relais Louis XIII 22 | 21 | 18 | fr484

8, rue des Grands-Augustins, 6e (Odéon/St-Michel), 01 43 26 75 96; fax 01 44 07 07 80

■ "Inventive", "high-level" Traditional French fare from former Tour d'Argent chef Manuel Martinez is the highlight of the royal treatment at this "sublime" "oasis of good taste" near the Odéon; the "classy" service and "refined" air suit the resplendent room in a landmarked medieval house, though a dubious few find it "pricey" and "pretentious."

Relais Plaza (Le) ◐Ⓢ
⎯ 17 ⎯ 18 ⎯ 19 ⎯ fr436

*Hôtel Plaza-Athénée, 21, av. Montaigne, 8ᵉ (Alma-Marceau/
Franklin D. Roosevelt), 01 53 67 64 00; fax 01 53 67 66 66*

☑ This upscale brasserie in the Hôtel Plaza-Athénée is
deemed "agreeable" by its well-heeled (and sometimes
"illustrious") clientele, winning praise for its "very good"
French cuisine and a recently redone art deco room;
but some find it "pretentious" and say the decor isn't
the only thing "that had a face-lift" recently.

Réminet Ⓢ
▽ 18 ⎯ 9 ⎯ 15 ⎯ fr240

*3, rue des Grands-Degrés, 5ᵉ (Maubert-Mutualité),
01 44 07 04 24; fax 01 44 07 17 37*

■ Lit by crystal chandeliers, this tiny French just across the
Seine from Notre Dame may be "cramped" but foodies
consider it a "great find" thanks to "excellent cuisine"
at "good-value" prices prepared by a chef who has been
known to "come out and chat with the patrons."

Rendez-vous des Camionneurs (Au) ⌂
▽ 11 ⎯ 8 ⎯ 11 ⎯ fr162

34, rue des Plantes, 14ᵉ (Alésia/Plaisance), 01 45 40 43 36

■ Expect a hearty welcome from chef-owner Claude Huart
to complement his "simple", "traditional" French cooking
at this penny-wise old-style bistro near Montparnasse;
relaxed regulars ignore the drab decor and liken the
experience to a "pit stop" in a "small town."

Rendez-vous des Chauffeurs (Au) Ⓢ
▽ 12 ⎯ 10 ⎯ 15 ⎯ fr131

*11, rue des Portes-Blanches, 18ᵉ (Marcadet-Poissonniers),
01 42 64 04 17*

■ "Quick" and "very inexpensive" French bistro in the
depths of the 18th that serves as a convivial "canteen"
where the owner chats with regulars as they tuck into
pot-au-feu and other filling traditional fare; at these prices,
no one's complaining about the no-frills digs.

René (Chez)
19 ⎯ 12 ⎯ 18 ⎯ fr275

*14, bd St-Germain, 5ᵉ (Maubert-Mutualité), 01 43 54 30 23;
fax 01 43 26 43 92*

■ Tile floors, moleskin banquettes and white linens give this
vintage '50s spot in the Latin Quarter a "classic bistro" look,
and it backs it up with "excellent", "authentic" Lyonnaise
cooking; nostalgists reckon it a "rarity" with "welcoming,
pleasant" service that makes diners "feel at home."

Repaire de Cartouche (Le)
19 ⎯ 12 ⎯ 16 ⎯ fr261

99, rue Amelot, 11ᵉ (St-Sébastien-Froissart), 01 47 00 25 86

■ Enthusiasts endorse the "varied and inventive menu"
devised by Rodolphe Paquin, the "devoted chef" at this rustic
bi-level French near the Bastille; his up-to-date spins on
old-fashioned regional recipes come at "reasonable prices",
which is why most are willing to overlook the "sad" decor.

Restaurant (Le)
_ | _ | _ | M

32, rue Véron, 18ᵉ (Abbesses/Blanche), 01 42 23 06 22; fax 01 42 23 36 16

Once a fashionable insiders' hangout, this French bistro sandwiched between Pigalle and Montmartre is a very popular destination these days, hence tables are tightly spaced and service can be uneven; nonetheless, it's a convenient spot for cash-conscious tourists in search of classic, fresh-from-the-market cooking.

Restaurant de la Tour
19 | 15 | 19 | fr353

6, rue Desaix, 15ᵉ (Dupleix), 01 43 06 04 24; fax 01 47 83 79 63

■ In a quiet bourgeois corner of the 15th, not far from the Hilton Hotel, chef Roger Conticini offers "original", "very refined" French fare in a room adorned with paintings of varying styles; supporters salute the "real effort" that goes into the "unusual dishes" and say it's "always pleasant to come back again."

Restaurant des Beaux Arts S
11 | 12 | 12 | fr136

11, rue Bonaparte, 6ᵉ (St-Germain-des-Prés), 01 43 26 92 64; fax 01 43 29 70 44

■ A long-running "cheap and cheery" bistro standby for artists, tourists and other budget-watchers near the Latin Quarter's Ecole des Beaux Arts; most surveyors appreciate its "generous" "good eats" and "rather romantic" air, and even holdouts concede it's "still better than McDonald's."

Restaurant des Chauffeurs S
11 | 6 | 9 | fr177

8, chaussée de la Muette, 16ᵉ (La Muette), 01 42 88 50 05

◪ "There aren't many places like this left" say patrons of this veteran French bistro that offers "excellent value" in the chic 16th via its "simple", "honest" cooking; a few nix "banal fare" and say the welcome could be friendlier, but its regulars (including the likes of Joël Robuchon) consider it the "model" of a "neighborhood restaurant."

Restaurant du Marché
▽ 18 | 11 | 16 | fr372

59, rue de Dantzig, 15ᵉ (Porte de Versailles), 01 48 28 31 55; fax 01 48 28 18 31

■ Connoisseurs of Southwestern French cuisine say the recent advent of chef-owner Bruno Fava has sparked a "renaissance" in this kitchen near the Porte de Versailles; though some are less taken by the ordinary decor and "high prices", the majority says it's "to be encouraged."

Restaurant du Musée d'Orsay S
11 | 24 | 11 | fr244

1, rue de Bellechasse, 7ᵉ (Solférino), 01 45 49 47 03; fax 01 42 22 34 12

◪ With parquet floors and ormolu moldings "fit for a king", the Musée d'Orsay's restaurant elicits bravos for its "sumptuous" decor, if not for its "decent" Traditional French fare; still, it's "fine for a museum" break and as one booster notes "the setting makes it – who cares about the rest?"

Restaurant du Palais Royal 18 | 20 | 17 | fr345

110, Galerie de Valois, 1er (Bourse/Palais Royal-Musée du Louvre), 01 40 20 00 27; fax 01 40 20 00 82

■ "A midsummer night's dream", "magic", "heaven" are typical reactions to the "fabulous terrace" of this French oasis in the gardens of the Palais Royal, and most feel it offers "food and service to match"; however, a fastidious few fret that it's "too crowded" and can be "a bit uneven."

Restaurant Jean Bouin [S] ▽ 12 | 16 | 12 | fr225

26, rue du Général Sarrail, 16e (Porte d'Auteuil), 01 40 71 61 00; fax 01 40 71 61 63

■ This bistro near the Jean Bouin stadium at the Porte d'Auteuil has a certain "athletic" cachet along with French fare rated from "good" to "middling", but the real draw is "very pleasant" garden seating that offers the "rare" chance to linger "under the trees" and savor the "delicious sensation of being completely isolated from the world."

Restaurant La Zygothèque – | – | – | I

15 bis, rue de Tolbiac, 13e (Bibliothèque F. Mitterrand), 01 45 83 07 48; fax 01 44 73 46 63

Run by the same team that scored with Les Zygomates, this snug French bistro is a recent arrival in the evolving Left Bank neighborhood around the Bibliothèque nationale; serving a market-inspired menu in two small dining rooms, it wins praise for "friendly service" and some "surprisingly good wines", and the fact that it's "inexpensive" doesn't hurt a bit.

Restaurant Opéra 20 | 23 | 21 | fr517

Grand Hôtel Inter-Continental, 5, place de l'Opéra, 9e (Madeleine/Opéra), 01 40 07 30 10; fax 01 40 07 33 86

■ Insiders would prefer to keep this luxe French in the Grand Hôtel near the Opéra Garnier a secret, but it won't be easy now that chef François Rodolphe "has conquered Paris" with his "delicious" fare, which is enhanced by the "magnificent" Napoleon III setting and first-class service; those seeking a "reasonable" tab should try it for lunch.

Restaurant W [S] ▽ 19 | 13 | 11 | fr421

Hôtel Warwick, 5, rue de Berri, 8e (George V), 01 45 61 82 08; fax 01 45 63 75 81

◪ The restaurant in the Hôtel Warwick just off the Champs-Elysées now has a new chef: Jérôme Galidie, former second at Les Elysées du Vernet; while most give good marks to his sophisticated French fare with a Southeastern accent, some report "patronizing" attitude and find the rather minimalist setting "crowded" and "depressing."

Ribe (Chez) ▽ 12 | 12 | 14 | fr267

15, av. de Suffren, 7e (Bir-Hakeim/Champ de Mars), 01 45 66 53 79; fax 01 45 66 53 79

■ "Good food with no surprises" is what you can expect at this dependable French bistro with a Belle Epoque look and affordable prix fixe menus; it's so heavily frequented by tourists staying at the Hilton or visting the nearby Eiffel Tower that even Parisians get the sense they're "on vacation here."

River Café [S] 12 | 19 | 12 | fr279

146, quai de Stalingrad, Issy-les-Moulineaux (Issy Plaine RER), 01 40 93 50 20; fax 01 41 46 19 45

◪ Frequented by "showbiz" and "ad" types, this "trendy" *peniche* (barge) moored on the Seine in Issy-les-Moulineaux is more notable for "amusing" people-watching than for its French cooking; still, it's "pleasant in summer", kid-friendly year-round and the parking valet "will even wash your car."

Robe et le Palais (La) ▽ 16 | 13 | 15 | fr223

13, rue de Lavandières-Ste-Opportune, 1er (Châtelet-Les Halles), 01 45 08 07 41; fax 01 45 08 07 41

■ This centrally located French bistro near Châtelet serves as a roost for legal eagles from the nearby Palais de Justice and also pleases surveyors with its "wonderful marriage of wine and food" and daily chalkboard specials; it's "not too expensive" and has a "very good ambiance" thanks in no small part to the "convivial owner."

Robert et Louise ⊄ ▽ 16 | 11 | 13 | fr241

64, rue Vieille du Temple, 3e (Rambuteau), 01 42 78 55 89

■ Admirers appreciate the "folkloric", "picturesque" charms of this "country French" in the Marais, where lace curtains and red-checkered tablecloths are the perfect complement to "sublime red meat" cooked over an open fire in the hearth; fastidious types think it could use a spruce-up though.

Rocher Gourmand (Le) – | – | – | M

89, rue du Rocher, 8e (Villiers), 01 40 08 00 36; fax 01 40 08 05 29

The decor's nothing to write home about, but that allows this diminutive eatery in the 8th to put the focus on chef Sébastien Gilles' refined and savvy modern French cuisine; a choice of reasonably priced prix fixe menus means that a meal here won't break the bank, and the young team in the dining room is efficient and friendly.

Roi du Pot-au-Feu (Le) ▽ 15 | 12 | 13 | fr202

34, rue Vignon, 9e (Madeleine), 01 47 42 37 10

■ It's no secret that "excellent" pot-au-feu is the raison d'être of this "very Parisian bistro" with '30s decor near the Madeleine, though the menu does offer other rustic, home-cooked fare as well; a few tougher critics say it's "a bit overrated, but good" nonetheless.

Romantica (La)
20 | 15 | 16 | fr440

73, bd Jean-Jaurès, Clichy (Mairie-de-Clichy), 01 47 37 29 71; fax 01 47 37 76 32

■ Cognoscenti claim that this expensive Clichy Italian lives up to its name as a "romantic" destination ideal for a "tête-à-tête", with "imaginative" cuisine (pasta served from a hollowed-out round of Parmesan is a favorite), "soothing decor" and a "pleasant" garden; complainers ("pretentious", "Italian for tourists") are solidly outnumbered.

Rond de Serviette (Le)
▽ 19 | 15 | 17 | fr285

97, rue du Cherche-Midi, 6ᵉ (Vaneau), 01 45 44 01 02; fax 01 42 22 50 10

■ "English candy-box" decor, "a friendly welcome" and "inventive, refined" fare are a crowd-pleasing combination at this "calm and intimate" Latin Quarter French; what's more, it offers some of "the best value in the neighborhood."

Rosimar
▽ 19 | 9 | 19 | fr245

26, rue Poussin, 16ᵉ (Michel-Ange Auteuil/Porte d'Auteuil), 01 45 27 74 91; fax 01 45 27 34 10

■ To satisfy a passion for paella or an affection for anchovies, try this corner Catalonian near the Porte d'Auteuil; aside from the "excellent Spanish cuisine", amigos warm to its "good value" and "smiling welcome", though some feel the mirrored interior "is not up to the rest" of the production.

Rôtisserie (La)
16 | 9 | 13 | fr255

24, rue Anatole France, Levallois-Perret (Louise-Michel), 01 47 48 13 82

■ "Reliably good" rotisserie fare is the draw at this Levallois French set in a renovated warehouse, and if some feel that "neither the service nor the cuisine sufficiently warms up the atmosphere" when the room is empty, most deem it a "restaurant that works well", citing its "good value."

Rôtisserie d'Armaillé
15 | 13 | 14 | fr305

6, rue d'Armaillé, 17ᵉ (Charles de Gaulle-Etoile), 01 42 27 19 20; fax 01 40 55 00 93

■ One of Jacques Cagna's thriving trio of satellite eateries, this rustic French near the Etoile offers "well-prepared" rotisseried meats and fowl in a "calm", "pretty" setting; menus in English and Japanese offer a clue to its main clientele, but natives also find it "agreeable and original", though "perhaps a bit expensive."

Rôtisserie d'en Face (La)
18 | 14 | 17 | fr287

2, rue Christine, 6ᵉ (Odéon), 01 43 26 40 98; fax 01 43 54 22 71

■ Jacques Cagna's first rotisserie, across from his eponymous haute cuisine haunt in Saint-Germain, is a hit since it offers "creative" French fare from a "great chef" at "affordable prices"; welcome touches include "cheerful colors and flowers" and an "adorable" staff, though service can be "a bit rushed" and decibels high when busy.

Rôtisserie du Beaujolais (La) S
16 | 12 | 14 | fr266

19, quai de la Tournelle, 5ᵉ (Jussieu/Pont Marie),
01 43 54 17 47; fax 01 56 24 43 71

◪ "Quick, more duck and mashed potatoes!" plead fans of Claude (La Tour d'Argent) Terrail's Latin Quarter rotisserie on the banks of the Seine; champions call the "classic Lyonnaise cuisine" "food like mother made" and welcome the "attentive service" and "reasonable" tabs, and if a few cynics claim the "only authentic thing is the checkered tablecloths", most are "rarely disappointed."

Rôtisserie Monsigny (La) ◑
15 | 12 | 14 | fr276

1, rue Monsigny, 2ᵉ (Quatre-Septembre), 01 42 96 16 61;
fax 01 42 97 40 97

◼ Near the Bourse in the 2nd, this Jacques Cagna bistro/rotisserie serves "high-quality", "simply prepared" French fare in a "pleasant modern" setting; it's popular for business lunches and pre-theater outings, and though it can be "empty" later on, that's fine with those seeking a "calm" meal.

Rotonde ◑S
▽ 12 | 13 | 13 | fr266

105, bd du Montparnasse, 6ᵉ (Vavin), 01 43 26 48 26;
fax 01 46 34 52 40

◪ Venerable French brasserie in the heart of Montparnasse that strikes supporters as a "great place to linger with out-of-town guests" thanks to its "character" and "good food"; others find the eats "monotonous", but even they say "it works for a light bite if in the area."

Rouge Vif (Le)
▽ 13 | 9 | 15 | fr199

48, rue de Verneuil, 7ᵉ (Solférino), 01 42 86 81 87

◼ This lively, "charming bistro" near Solférino is favored by locals who appreciate the "warm welcome" from the "very nice owners" as well as the "good classic cuisine" at "great prices"; given its conviviality and value, few mind if the snug room "rapidly becomes noisy."

Rubis (Le) ⇎
13 | 10 | 12 | fr179

10, rue du Marché-St-Honoré, 1ᵉʳ (Tuileries), 01 42 61 03 34

◼ If hungry for a home-cooked meal near the gleaming Marché-Saint-Honoré, check out this "real" French bistro where hearty eats like *petit salé aux lentilles* (pork rib with lentils) are washed down with lots of Beaujolais; though "cramped", it has a warm, "homey" feel (especially "if the owner likes you") and is a "great happy-hour stop."

Rue Balzac ◑S
– | – | – | M

3-5, rue Balzac, 8ᵉ (George V); 01 53 89 90 91; fax 01 53 89 90 94

A very Parisian team – chef/restaurateur Michel Rostang and singer Johnny Hallyday – is behind this newcomer near the Etoile; expect good-looking modern decor and a menu that mixes modern and traditional, sophisticated and rustic elements, offering everything in full or half portions (the latter no doubt a nod to its figure-conscious clientele).

Rughetta (La) **S** ▽ 15 | 10 | 13 | fr211
41, rue Lepic, 18ᵉ (Abbesses/Blanche), 01 42 23 41 70;
fax 01 42 23 41 70

◪ With a pleasant terrace for summer dining and a Montmartre address near the house where Van Gogh once lived, this Italian feeds both trattoria-loving tourists and habitués who give decent marks to its food and "jovial" service; but some lament that it's "become à la mode" these days while tightwads carp about "expensive" dishes.

Safran (Le) – | – | – | M
29, rue d'Argenteuil, 1ᵉʳ (Pyramides), 01 42 61 25 30
Between the Opéra and Palais Royal, chef Caroll Sinclair's latest salutes its namesake spice with a pretty dining room in saffron tones; the kitchen turns out Gallic home cooking made with organic ingredients, and the few surveyors who have tried it thus far find it "likable for its originality", even if the cooking sometimes "misses" the mark.

Saint Amarante (Le) 19 | 11 | 16 | fr236
4, rue Biscornet, 12ᵉ (Bastille), 01 43 43 00 08
■ "Exceptional for this neighborhood" say boosters of this low-key bistro steps from the Bastille serving "fine" traditional fare highlighted by daily chalkboard specials; "very welcoming owners" are another reason it's considered a "wonderful local place."

Saint Pourçain (Le) ▽ 15 | 12 | 13 | fr214
234, rue du Faubourg-St-Antoine, 12ᵉ (Nation),
01 43 70 83 22
■ Small Traditional French between the Bastille and Nation that's appreciated for its "good regional cuisine from the Cantal" area and meats from Limousin; it's a worthy stop year-round, but connoisseurs claim the "rich" fare is especially satisfying in winter.

Saint Vincent (Le) ▽ 20 | 13 | 15 | fr244
26, rue de la Croix-Nivert, 15ᵉ (Cambronne), 01 47 34 14 94;
fax 01 45 66 02 80
◪ "Down-home" French fare comes in "copious" portions ("ideal for a sumo wrestler") at this Lyonnaise bistro near the Ecole Militaire in the 15th; in contrast to the "hearty" eats, some find the welcome a little thin: "a smile, please."

Salle à Manger (La) **S** – | – | – | E
Hôtel Raphael, 17, av. Kléber, 16ᵉ, 01 53 64 32 11;
fax 01 53 64 32 02
As discreet and elegant as the Hôtel Raphael itself, its dining room has a suitably hushed air ("you could hear a pin drop") and refined French cuisine courtesy of chef Philip Delahaye; while few can argue with the excellent service and "handsome", well-upholstered setting, naysayers find prices high for what's on the plate.

San Valero
18 | 14 | 14 | fr310

209 ter, av. Charles de Gaulle, Neuilly-sur-Seine (Pont de Neuilly), 01 46 24 07 87; fax 01 47 47 83 17

◪ For a quick trip south of the (French) border, head west to this family-run Spaniard in Neuilly; cheerleaders call it a good place to "discover the fine flavors of Spanish cuisine" and also toast its "interesting" wines, but a few are less impressed by the cooking and find the "bourgeois" decor a little "cold" and the tabs a bit hard to swallow.

Sarladais (Le)
▽ 16 | 11 | 15 | fr301

2, rue de Vienne, 8ᵉ (St-Augustin), 01 45 22 23 62; fax 01 45 22 23 62

■ The food may be on the "heavy" side, but that doesn't faze fans of this Traditional French near Saint-Augustin church in the 8th, where the faithful come for "classic Southwestern French specialties" (foie gras, confit, truffles, cassoulet) and wines (Buzet, Cahors); regulars relish the good service and ignore the rather nondescript decor.

Saudade
▽ 16 | 13 | 17 | fr268

34, rue des Bourdonnais, 1ᵉʳ (Châtelet-Les Halles), 01 42 36 03 65; fax 01 42 36 27 77

■ Even "if you don't like cod, you'll change your mind" after a meal here promise partisans of this patch of Portugal near Châtelet serving "cod in all its forms – a treat" plus other "authentic" dishes and "excellent ports"; with "original" decor accented by blue-and-white tiles, it's a "transporting" experience, though a few feel the fare could use more zip.

Sauvignon (Au)
▽ 14 | 12 | 12 | fr149

80, rue des Saints-Pères, 7ᵉ (Sèvres-Babylone), 01 45 48 49 02; fax 01 45 49 41 00

■ Near the Bon Marché department store in the 7th, this long-standing bar à vins draws a chic crowd that comes to graze on the likes of charcuterie and cheese on Poilâne bread, accompanied, of course, by "excellent wines"; advocates insist "the real Paris is here" and find it "perfect for a quick lunch", especially at a sidewalk table.

Savy (Chez)
▽ 16 | 9 | 16 | fr266

23, rue Bayard, 8ᵉ (Franklin D. Roosevelt), 01 47 23 46 98; fax 01 47 23 46 98

■ Good, solid French cuisine with an Auvergnat accent is dished up at this "bistro for white-collar workers" in front of the RTL radio station in the 8th; though it recently had a face-lift, few seem to notice, perhaps because they're so busy digging into sturdy classics such as the roast shoulder of lamb for two; just be advised that it's not cheap and "there's not much choice for light eaters."

Sawadee
▽ 19 | 10 | 16 | fr268

53, av. Emile Zola, 15ᵉ (Charles Michels), 01 45 77 68 90; fax 01 45 77 57 78

■ The decor consists largely of an aquarium and some houseplants, but that doesn't matter since this bustling, well-established Thai in the 15th is commended for its "delicious" fare – some insist it's the "best Thai value" in town; there's not much of a wine list, but service is fast and friendly.

Scheffer (Le)
14 | 11 | 14 | fr223

22, rue Scheffer, 16ᵉ (Trocadéro), 01 47 27 81 11

■ Despite the address in the smart 16th and the young trendsetters in the crowd, this is a traditional provincial-style bistro serving "simple", hearty homestyle eats in an unassuming plastic-tablecloth setting that's "very warm", if sometimes "noisy"; nostalgists note that such homey, "good-value" hideaways are "rare" these days.

Scusi
▽ 14 | 11 | 15 | fr262

10 bis, rue d'Artois, 8ᵉ (St-Philippe-du-Roule), 01 53 76 44 44

◪ "Agreeable cuisine" from a menu encompassing Italy and Provence is what admirers find at this trattoria with a tiny terrace in the 8th; the mix of dishes may explain why sticklers complain that it's "not very Italian", but to most it's a "pleasant" place even if it can be "a little hectic."

Sébillon Élysées ◑ S
14 | 11 | 14 | fr304

66, rue Pierre Charron, 8ᵉ (Franklin D. Roosevelt), 01 43 59 28 15; fax 01 43 59 30 00

■ Advocates argue that the "best lamb in Paris" may be the roasts carved by waiters beneath the brass chandeliers of this brasserie near the Champs-Elysées, offspring of the Neuilly original; if some claim it's "not equal" to its parent, few have serious complaints, perhaps because the wines are fine and most diners get exactly what they expect.

Sébillon Neuilly ◑ S
15 | 12 | 14 | fr306

20, av. Charles de Gaulle, Neuilly-sur-Seine (Porte Maillot), 01 46 24 71 31; fax 01 46 24 43 50

■ In the upscale 'burb of Neuilly near the Porte Maillot, this "noisy" brasserie is considered a "must" for its "sliced-in-front-of-you" roast lamb (a "Parisian legend") and fresh oysters; busy with businessfolk at lunch, it pulls in locals at night who consider it a "classic" that's always "true to form."

Sédillot
▽ 13 | 14 | 14 | fr198

2, rue Sédillot, 7ᵉ (Alma-Marceau/Ecole-Militaire), 01 45 51 95 82; fax 01 45 51 95 82

◪ A stylish art nouveau building in the 7th is home to this little neighborhood bistro that strikes some as a "charming, out-of-the-way" find, with "prix fixe menus that don't disappoint" and "very nice" service; others complain of "nondescript" fare, but given the relaxing atmosphere and reasonable prices, regulars don't seem to mind.

16 Haussmann (Le) ◑
15 | 16 | 15 | fr280

Hôtel Ambassador, 16, bd Haussmann, 9ᵉ (Chausée d'Antin/ Richelieu-Drouot), 01 44 83 40 58; fax 01 42 46 20 83
■ This attractive French in the Hôtel Ambassador on the Boulevard Haussmann is "cleverly decorated" in tones of ultramarine and ocher with Philippe Starck furnishings, and partisans find the food "beautiful" too, calling it "perfect for business meals"; not everyone agrees with those who judge it a "good value", however, and there are grumbles about "overwhelmed service" and "noise."

Senteurs de Provence (Aux)
▽ 18 | 14 | 18 | fr284

295, rue Lecourbe, 15ᵉ (Lourmel), 01 45 57 11 98; fax 01 45 58 66 84
■ *Bourride* (fish soup), *bar* (bass) and bouillabaisse are but three of the seafaring specialties at this refreshing Provençal ray of sunshine in the 15th; surveyors call the "excellent, copious" offerings "a delight" and like the service enough not to quibble over the cost.

Sept Quinze (Le)
▽ 19 | 13 | 20 | fr233

29, av. Lowendal, 15ᵉ (Cambronne), 01 43 06 23 06; fax 01 45 67 14 11
■ This trendy Mediterranean near the Ecole Militaire and UNESCO is building a following for its "inventive cuisine" (there's a menu change every two months) and "very good value"; despite nitpicking about "noise" and "too many tables", its "fine flavors", "original decor" and "warm, friendly atmosphere" help it draw a stylish crowd.

Shozan
19 | 17 | 16 | fr434

11, rue de La Trémoille, 8ᵉ (Alma-Marceau), 01 47 23 37 32; fax 01 47 23 67 30
■ A "successful blend" of French and Japanese cuisines – concocted, oddly enough, by a German-born chef – yields food that's "flavorful, light and full of invention" at this well-regarded hybrid in the 8th; "chic" decor by Christian Liaigre provides the backdrop as diners "discover new tastes", and while tabs are high, it's a "transporting" experience.

Signatures (Les) 🄢
– | – | – | M

Sofitel Champs-Elysées, 8, rue Jean Goujon, 8ᵉ (Champs-Elysées), 01 40 74 64 94; fax 01 40 74 64 94
The former Les Saveurs in the Sofitel Champs-Elysées has become this slightly less expensive but equally business-oriented restaurant, serving updated French fare with Mediterranean touches in a contemporary setting.

Signorelli
– | – | – | M

35, rue St-Honoré, 1ᵉʳ (Châtelet-Les Halles/Louvre-Rivoli), 01 40 13 91 41; fax 01 40 13 91 41
Not everyone knows this "real Italian" near Châtelet, but those who do appreciate its "flavorful" pastas, as well as its "pretty" setting and "welcoming" ambiance; "gentle prices" and a nice Italian wine list help make it worth discovering.

Sologne (La) ▽ 18 | 13 | 16 | fr281

164, av. Daumesnil, 12e (Daumesnil), 01 43 07 68 97; fax 01 43 44 66 23

■ "Excellent" cuisine including "well-prepared game" and specialties from the Sologne region earns solid marks for this Traditional French in the 12th; the "warmth" of its sure service and old-fashioned decor are also pleasing.

SORMANI 22 | 17 | 19 | fr503

4, rue du Général Lanrezac, 17e (Charles de Gaulle-Etoile), 01 43 80 13 91; fax 01 40 55 07 37

■ Arguably the "best Italian" in Paris, and perhaps "the most expensive" as well, this standout near the Champs-Elysées in the 17th is lauded for the "remarkable", "inventive" cuisine of Jean-Pascal Fayet, which is served by a pro staff in two small, elegant rooms; fine wines round out the pleasure, and if the bill threatens to spoil it, devotees say "too bad for the price – it's my favorite grand Italian."

Soufflé (Le) 16 | 11 | 15 | fr295

36, rue du Mont-Thabor, 1er (Concorde), 01 42 60 27 19; fax 01 42 60 54 98

■ Acolytes of this "temple of the soufflé" near the Place de la Concorde can now enjoy its "light", "flavorful" fare in a newly renovated setting with a "touch of chic"; if a few find the concept a bit droopy, more consider it a nice change of pace and a "good value."

Souletin (Le) ▽ 14 | 11 | 15 | fr225

6, rue La Vrillière, 1er (Bourse/Châtelet-Les Halles), 01 42 61 43 78; fax 01 42 61 43 78

◪ A hankering for *piperade* (a tomato and pepper–based dish) and other Basque bites can be satisfied at this bistro near the Place des Victoires; fans call it a "good, serious" place with an "agreeable ambiance", and though purists claim the cooking is "not authentic", it benefits from moderate prices and a decent wine list.

Soun [S] – | – | – | E

192, av Victor Hugo, 16e (Henri Martin), 01 45 04 04 31

The space that was once home to Le Vivarois in the 16th has gone Asian in cooking if not in atmosphere, serving pricey Chinese-Vietnamese fare in a setting that still retains its predecessor's '70s modern look; don't miss the Peking duck, served with ceremony in three courses.

Soupière (La) ▽ 20 | 13 | 19 | fr284

154, av. de Wagram, 17e (Wagram), 01 46 22 80 10; fax 01 46 22 27 09

■ This French storefront in the 17th is "always jammed" with fungi fanciers who can't get enough of its "excellent", "innovative" recipes showcasing wild mushrooms; though it's small and underdecorated, the "friendly" atmosphere, "attentive service" and moderate prices compensate.

Sousceyrac (A) 17 | 12 | 14 | fr357

35, rue Faidherbe, 11e (Charonne/Faidherbe-Chaligny), 01 43 71 65 30; fax 01 40 09 79 75

◪ According to devotees, this "homey, local" fixture in the 11th still serves "superb game" (kudos to the hare à la royale) and other "very good Southwestern French cuisine" enhanced by a "smiling welcome" and good wines; however, the setting is "very old-fashioned" and critics who cite "disappointing cassoulet" call it a case of "faded glory."

Spicy Restaurant ◐ [S] 11 | 14 | 12 | fr218

8, av. Franklin D. Roosevelt, 8e (Franklin D. Roosevelt/ St-Philippe-du-Roule), 01 56 59 62 59; fax 01 56 59 62 50

◪ The rotisserie fare may be "basic" (and, some argue, "not even spicy"), but this hot spot near the *rond-point* des Champs-Elysées draws a "young", stylish crowd that likes its "amusing" modern decor, "pretty waitresses", "reasonable prices" and "central" location; still, opponents dismiss it as a "factory" with "uninspiring cuisine."

SPOON, FOOD & WINE 19 | 18 | 18 | fr394

Sofitel Hôtel SAS Marignan, 14, rue de Marignan, 8e (Franklin D. Roosevelt), 01 40 76 34 44; fax 01 40 76 34 37

◪ Star chef Alain Ducasse's "restaurant of the 21st century" near the Champs-Elysées strikes most diners as an "original and very successful concept", offering an "exciting", "creative" menu of 'world food' with "interesting pick-your-own" options; also lauded are the "refreshing", "New York"–style decor and globe-trotting wine list, but outvoted critics "can't believe all the hype" and many are put off by the two-week (or more) wait to get in.

Square Trousseau (Le) ◐ [S] 15 | 16 | 14 | fr276

1, rue Antoine Vollon, 12e (Bastille/Ledru-Rollin), 01 43 43 06 00; fax 01 43 43 00 66

■ Media and fashion types in search of a square meal turn to this "lovely old bistro" in the 12th for rustic but "good-quality" dishes like swordfish carpaccio or goat-cheese ravioli, served in a setting that's so spot-on Parisian it's been used as a backdrop for ads; misgivings over "slow" service hardly detract from its "charm."

Stella Maris ▽ 22 | 16 | 20 | fr502

4, rue Arsène Houssaye, 8e (Charles de Gaulle-Etoile), 01 42 89 16 22; fax 01 42 89 16 01

■ Chef-owner Tateru Yoshino's training with master chef Joël Robuchon shows in the "superb menu" of rigorously executed French fare (with subtle Japanese touches) served at this small yet stylish spot near the Arc de Triomphe; though prices are high and the most striking aspect of the decor is the deco ironwork around the windows, its "incredible mix of ingredients" and "extremely kind" service leave most diners more than satisfied.

Stéphane Martin (Restaurant)   – – – M
67, rue des Entrepreneurs, 15ᵉ (Charles Michels/Commerce),
01 45 79 03 31; fax 01 45 79 44 69
The former home of L'Armoise in the 15th has been taken
over by Stéphane Martin; unlike some of the more modern
bistros moving into the area, it has a rustic setting, midpriced
prix fixe menus and fresh, lively market-based French dishes.

Stresa (Le)   17 12 14 fr444
7, rue Chambiges, 8ᵉ (Alma-Marceau), 01 47 23 51 62
▲ Celeb-hounds recommend this hideaway of French TV,
film and fashion stars near the Avenue Montaigne for its
"great people-watching" as well as its "good Italian cuisine",
but cynics note "glamour comes at a price", declaring it
"expensive", "cramped" and "snobbish"; in any case, it's a
certified "chic" scene.

Studio (The) ●S   ▽ 9 16 11 fr172
41, rue du Temple, 4ᵉ (Hôtel-de-Ville/Rambuteau), 01 42 74 10 38;
fax 01 42 77 19 90
▲ Its "unusual" courtyard setting in a historic Marais
building makes this Tex-Mex "superb" for outdoor dining,
even if urban cowboys can't get too excited about the
"standard" (some say "mediocre") chow; still, it's "ok for
brunch" and easy on the billfold.

Sud (Le)   15 21 14 fr292
91, bd Gouvion-St-Cyr, 17ᵉ (Porte Maillot), 01 45 74 02 77;
fax 01 45 74 35 36
▲ This little corner of Provence near the Porte Maillot does
a convincing imitation of that region's ambiance ("Paris
with crickets and olive trees" – even "on a rainy night"),
and though hedgers wish the Southern French fare were on
par with the "beautiful" setting, most find it "well prepared",
if a tad pricey; its fish dishes help make it a "nice change"
from meat-centric eateries.

Sushi One ●   ▽ 11 14 10 fr228
63, av Franklin D. Roosevelt, 8ᵉ (St. Philippe du Roule),
01 43 59 48 00; fax 01 43 59 48 01
▲ "Minimalist" Japanese near the Champs-Elysées that
opened in '99 with lots of media fanfare and the intention
of attracting a trendy crowd; the few surveyors who've
visited have mixed opinions on the food ("decent" vs.
"disappointing") and some find the decor "a bit cold."

Table d'Anvers (La) ●   21 13 15 fr547
2, place d'Anvers, 9ᵉ (Anvers), 01 48 78 35 21; fax 01 45 26 66 67
▲ "Imaginative cuisine at the foot of Montmartre" can be
found at Christian Conticini's Contemporary French; admirers
consider it "unfairly undersung", praising its "high-quality
food and wines" and "delicious desserts", outvoting critics
who feel it's slipping and "expensive"; both sides note service
lapses and few are enamored of the "passable" decor.

Table de Babette (La)   – | – | – | M

36, bd Robespierre, Poissy (Poissy), 01 39 65 52 52;
fax 01 47 45 76 09
The few surveyors who know this Caribbean in remote
Poissy praise its "high-quality" cuisine and "charming
service"; stay-at-home sorts say it's "too far" away, but
enthusiasts insist "you must at all costs discover it."

TAILLEVENT   28 | 26 | 28 | fr820

15, rue Lamennais, 8ᵉ (George V), 01 44 95 15 01; fax 01 42 25 95 18
■ "Perfection with a capital P" sums up this "luxurious"
"temple of gastronomy" near the Etoile that again ranks
No. 1 for Food, Service and Popularity; Michel del Burgo
(ex Le Bristol) has smoothly picked up where predecessor
Philippe Legendre left off, turning out "sparkling", "updated"
haute cuisine enhanced by a "superb wine list" and
"superlative service" – they "do everything but cut the
food and feed you"; simply put, it's "an absolute must."

Taïra   ▽ 23 | 11 | 17 | fr374

10, rue des Acacias, 17ᵉ (Argentine), 01 47 66 74 14;
fax 01 47 66 74 14
■ "The best fish restaurant in Paris" trumpets one fan of
this "small" Franco-Japanese behind the Etoile in the 17th;
the decor may be kind of "odd", but the ambiance is "warm",
the fish "fresh" and it's an "excellent value."

Taka   – | – | – | M

1, rue Véron, 18ᵉ (Abbesses), 01 42 23 74 16
Though not widely known by surveyors, this small, simple-
looking Japanese on the slopes of Montmartre just above
Pigalle is said to offer some of the "best Japanese" fare
around for "affordable" prices; it draws a clubby crowd of
arty regulars, which can make newcomers feel a bit lost,
but it's worth it for the tasty homestyle cooking; note that
it serves dinner only, with last orders at 10 PM.

Tan Dinh ⊟   20 | 11 | 19 | fr413

60, rue de Verneuil, 7ᵉ (Rue du Bac/Solférino), 01 45 44 04 84;
fax 01 45 44 36 93
■ The Vietnamese food is "terrific" and the "superb" wine
list "will have you rolling on the floor" at this restaurant
in the 7th near the Musée d'Orsay; run by a "very nice"
family, it strikes most as "fun" and "surprising", but some
wish they'd perk up the decor.

Tang   22 | 13 | 18 | fr377

125, rue de la Tour, 16ᵉ (Rue de la Pompe), 01 45 04 35 35;
fax 01 45 04 58 19
■ Some of the "best Chinese" fare in Paris can be found at
this neighborhood eatery in the 16th serving "outstanding"
food (with Thai touches too) that will "seduce even the
most recalcitrant"; it's "very pricey", though, and some
grumble about "minuscule" portions and "average" decor.

Tante Jeanne
_ _ _ M

116, bd Péreire, 17ᵉ (Péreire), 01 43 80 88 68; fax 01 47 66 53 02
Bernard Loiseau (of La Côte d'Or in Saulieu) extends his
Parisian family with this third *tante* (aunt), an elegant space
in the 17th serving bourgeois French fare in an off-white
setting dressed up with mirrors, chandeliers and modern
paintings; midpriced prix fixe menus and a terrace are pluses.

Tante Louise (Chez)
17 13 16 fr360

41, rue Boissy d'Anglas, 8ᵉ (Concorde/Madeleine),
01 42 65 06 85; fax 01 46 65 28 19
☑ "Old-fashioned" French between the Madeleine and the
Place de la Concorde that was taken over by Bernard
Loiseau of La Côte d'Or in Saulieu a few years ago; while
some laud its "delicious" Burgundian fare and "warm
service", others are let down given Loiseau's rep ("stay in
Saulieu – the capital doesn't agree with you"), but it's "good
for a business lunch" and the prix fixe is a "great buy."

Tante Marguerite
18 15 17 fr352

5, rue de Bourgogne, 7ᵉ (Assemblée Nationale/Invalides),
01 45 51 79 42; fax 01 47 53 79 56
☑ Another member of the Bernard Loiseau family, this
Traditional French near the Assemblée Nationale offers
"refined" cuisine in an "elegant", "airy" setting; admirers
also applaud the "charming" welcome and "remarkable"
value, but naysayers find the cooking "uneven."

Tastevin S
▽ 21 20 19 fr572

9, av Eglé, Maisons-Laffitte (Maisons-Laffitte RER),
01 39 62 11 67; fax 01 39 62 73 09
■ It's "traditional cuisine, for sure, but it borders on absolute
perfection" say admirers of this "slightly old-fashioned"
French located west of Paris in Maisons-Laffitte; the
"excellent" welcome, "attentive" service and "beautiful"
setting, especially in the garden, also earn high marks;
the one beef: "very high prices."

Taverne de Maître Kanter ●▶S
11 11 10 fr237

16, rue Coquillière, 1ᵉʳ (Châtelet-Les Halles/Louvre-Rivoli),
01 42 36 74 24; fax 01 42 21 42 31
☑ Approached with the right expectations, this Les Halles
brasserie does a "respectable" job, delivering "hearty
servings" of "good choucroute" and other "traditional" fare
at "decent" prices, albeit with below-average service.

Taverne Henri IV ⌀
12 14 13 fr162

13, place du Pont-Neuf, 1ᵉʳ (Pont-Neuf), 01 43 54 27 90
■ "I can sit for hours and soak up the atmosphere" sighs one
devotee of this wine bar on the Ile de la Cité, "one of the
loveliest" locales in Paris; the food is "respectable", ditto
the prices, and as you'd expect, there's a "good selection
of wines"; it's popular with the legal crowd from the nearby
courthouse and fans of 'old-France' ambiance.

Taverne Kronenbourg (La) ◑ 🅢   12 | 13 | 13 | fr237

24, bd des Italiens, 9ᵉ (Opéra/Richelieu-Drouot),
01 55 33 10 00; fax 01 55 33 10 09

◤ For "choucroute before or after a movie" nearby, this big, "traditional" brasserie near the Opéra will do just fine; it's "a bit of a factory" but "pleasant" enough, with "fast service", "reasonable" prices and an appealing woody setting.

Télégraphe (Le) ◑ 🅢   14 | 19 | 14 | fr306

41, rue de Lille, 7ᵉ (Rue du Bac), 01 42 92 03 04; fax 01 42 92 02 77

■ Surveyors adore the "surprising", "original" decor of this "nicely redone" Belle Epoque townhouse behind the Musée d'Orsay; alas, the French fare and service "don't reach the same level" and the tab's not cheap, but diners are "pleasantly seduced" by the setting and it's "excellent for Sunday lunch in the garden."

Temps des Cerises (Le) ◑   11 | 11 | 11 | fr155

18, rue Butte-aux-Cailles, 13ᵉ (Place d'Italie), 01 45 89 69 48;
fax 01 43 67 60 91

■ This bistro in the picturesque Butte-aux-Cailles area of the 13th was founded as a workers' cooperative in the '60s, and while the cooking is hardly revolutionary, it's served in a "fun, cafeteria-like ambiance" at proletarian prices that make it a "good value."

Terminus Nord ◑ 🅢   14 | 18 | 15 | fr284

23, rue de Dunkerque, 10ᵉ (Gare du Nord), 01 42 85 05 15;
fax 01 40 16 13 98

◤ A "beautiful", "high-quality" brasserie that's "ideally placed for when you arrive [or leave] by Eurostar" say partisans of this Flo group outpost across from the Gare du Nord; critics may beef about "heavy" food and "noise", but with its "super" '20s decor, "rapid service" and moderate prices, it's a "haven" in an otherwise unpromising area.

Terrasse (La) 🅢   ▽ 14 | 16 | 14 | fr298

Hôtel Terrass, 12, rue Joseph de Maistre, 18ᵉ (Blanche/
Place de Clichy), 01 44 92 34 00; fax 01 42 52 29 11

■ "One of the most beautiful views of Paris" can be enjoyed from the "sublime" rooftop terrace of this hotel restaurant behind the Place de Clichy; there's less agreement on the French food ("flavorful" vs. "average"), but there's an affordable lunch prix fixe and the vista quells most complaints.

Terrasses du Palais (Les) ◑ 🅢   ▽ 18 | 17 | 16 | fr277

2, place de la Porte Maillot, 17ᵉ (Porte Maillot),
01 55 37 70 80; fax 01 55 37 70 88

■ The "melting pot" menu of "contemporary" International fare seems to work at this sprawling loftlike newcomer in the renovated Palais du Congrès convention center at the Porte Maillot; "trendy but not snobby", it has an appealing modern ambiance, "efficient", "friendly" servers ("pretty rare for this kind of place") and an attractively priced prix fixe.

Terroir (Le) ▽ 19 | 12 | 14 | fr289

11, bd Arago, 13e (Les Gobelins), 01 47 07 36 99

■ "Generous" portions of "good, basic, no froufrou" Traditional French fare that could have been cooked by "grandma" are served at this "real bistro for real men" (and, we presume, women) in the 13th near the Gobelins Tapestry works; the ambiance is "familial" and the owner is "fun", so it doesn't seem to matter if service can be "a bit slow" and "chaotic."

Thanksgiving [S] 13 | 10 | 13 | fr200

20, rue St-Paul, 4^e^ (St-Paul), 01 42 77 68 28; fax 01 42 77 70 83

■ Partisans "give thanks for decent American fare" at this "friendly" Marais source of "good-quality" Cajun-Creole fare plus the likes of "lox, bagels and eggs Benedict at brunch"; some gripe about "small portions" of "ersatz" N'Awlins eats, but most agree it's one of the "top American" picks in Paris, and kids are welcome too, "no problem."

Thoumieux ◐ [S] 13 | 13 | 13 | fr243

Hôtel Thoumieux, 79, rue St-Dominique, 7^e^ (Invalides/La Tour-Maubourg), 01 47 05 49 75; fax 01 47 05 36 96

◪ "Monumental cassoulet" and other "traditional" French Southwestern fare earn praise at this "noisy", "chic" brasserie veteran overlooking the Invalides in the 7th; dissenters claim it "relies on its reputation", but most feel it delivers "what you expect": "honest", "hearty" fare in a delightful, "old Parisian atmosphere."

Timgad (Le) [S] 20 | 19 | 18 | fr386

21, rue Brunel, 17^e^ (Argentine), 01 45 74 23 70; fax 01 40 68 76 46

■ A veritable "institution of couscous", this Moroccan in the 17th behind the Etoile is said to serve one of "the best" versions of that dish in Paris plus other "authentic" North African fare; "warm service" and "handsome decor" add to its appeal, but a few doubters feel it's "resting on its laurels" and all agree it's "pretty pricey."

Tire-Bouchon (Le) 20 | 14 | 19 | fr237

62, rue des Entrepreneurs, 15^e^ (Charles Michels), 01 40 59 09 27; fax 01 40 59 09 27

■ This "darling little restaurant" might not look like much, but reviewers shout "bravo" for the "great value" and "friendly", "assured" service; with "admirable" cooking and "good wines", it's "undoubtedly one of the best addresses in the 15th", but one regular advises "don't get there too late" or they may be out of certain dishes.

Tong Yen ◐ [S] 15 | 11 | 16 | fr363
1 bis, rue Jean Mermoz, 8e (Franklin D. Roosevelt), 01 42 25 04 23; fax 01 45 63 51 57
◪ "You're sure to see a star" at this "chic", "pricey", "celestial Chinese" off the Champs-Elysées run by the ever-smiling Thérèse Luong, who is said to seat "VIPs" on the ground floor, "regulars and Parisians upstairs"; fans say it offers "good" food in a "discreet" atmosphere, but others deem it "overrated": "Thérèse", opines one diner, "should play less golf and spend more time in the kitchen."

Tonnelle Saintongeaise (La) ▽ 14 | 14 | 12 | fr254
32, bd Vital Bouhot, Neuilly-sur-Seine (Pont-de-Levallois), 01 46 24 43 15; fax 01 46 24 36 33
■ An "oasis of calm" is how surveyors see this "elegant", "relaxing" Traditional French on the fashionable Ile de la Jatte in Neuilly; the food is "consistently good", prices are "reasonable" and the shaded terrace is "very pleasant" in summer, leading admirers to ask "why leave Paris for the weekend when happiness" is just a "few minutes" away?

Toque (La) ▽ 19 | 13 | 12 | fr275
16, rue de Tocqueville, 17e (Villiers), 01 42 27 97 75; fax 01 47 63 97 69
■ Surveyors tip their toques to this intimate French in the 17th near Villiers, praising its "high-quality" food, "well-chosen wines" and "luminous setting"; since it's "an enjoyable place to spend an evening" and a "good value" to boot, "reservations are recommended."

Totem (Le) ◐ [S] 9 | 21 | 11 | fr262
Musée de l'Homme, 17, place du Trocadéro, 16e (Trocadéro), 01 47 27 28 29; fax 01 47 27 53 01
■ A "marvelous terrace" with an "exceptional" view of the Eiffel Tower is the big draw at this fashionable, "lively" French in the Musée de l'Homme at Trocadéro; sadly, the cooking and service fail to live up to the "dream location", but "the view is so superb you forget what's on the plate" and it's also "good for a drink" or "informal lunch."

Toupary (Le) ◐ 11 | 23 | 12 | fr324
La Samaritaine, 2, quai du Louvre, 1er (Pont-Neuf), 01 40 41 29 29; fax 01 42 33 96 79
◪ "Sublime panorama, banal cuisine" is the consensus on this French perched atop the Samaritaine department store in the 1st; while the "unforgettable view" and attractive "modern" decor outshine the food and service, it can be a good place to "bring a romantic conquest" or an out-of-towner, and there's a well-priced lunch prix fixe; P.S. one clean-freak suggests they need to "wash the windows."

TOUR D'ARGENT (LA) S
23 | 28 | 24 | fr791

15-17, quai de la Tournelle, 5ᵉ (Cardinal Lemoine/Pont Marie), 01 43 54 23 31; fax 01 44 07 12 04

■ "In a class by itself": this "historic" "mecca of Classic French gastronomy", run by the "smiling" Claude Terrail, offers "the duck of your life", "extraordinary" wines, "helpful" service and a "superb" view of Notre Dame (hence its No. 2 Decor ranking); given its reputation and cost, it's no surprise if some are let down ("the magic is tarnished", for "tourists"), but it's hard to "imagine Paris without it"; N.B. the prix fixe lunch is a "godsend."

Tournesol (Le)
▽ 13 | 16 | 12 | fr303

2, av. de Lamballe, 16ᵉ (Passy), 01 45 25 95 94; fax 01 45 25 43 09

■ A "hip place where you eat well" is the word on this newcomer in the 16th near Passy drawing a fashionable young crowd with its "original" cooking; a few complainers find it "smoky" and "mediocre for the price", but "the terrace in summer can seduce you."

Toutoune (Chez) S
14 | 9 | 12 | fr266

5, rue de Pontoise, 5ᵉ (Maubert-Mutualité), 01 43 26 56 81; fax 01 40 46 80 34

■ Newcomers to owner Toutoune's flower-filled Provençal bistro on the Left Bank dub it a "discovery", but it's been around for over 20 years, pleasing those who know it with its "good, consistent" cuisine and unusual touches such as "soup offered at the beginning of the meal"; if some feel a meal can take too "long" and quality has slipped a bit, most have no complaints.

TRAIN BLEU (LE) S
14 | 27 | 15 | fr365

Gare de Lyon, 12ᵉ (Gare de Lyon), 01 43 43 09 06; fax 01 43 43 97 96

■ "Sumptuous", "step-back-in-time" Belle Epoque decor (classified as a historic monument) makes this brasserie in the Gare de Lyon perfect for "nostalgia" or a "romantic" "tête-à-tête"; some find the cooking "improved" of late while others say it "could be better" and claim service "breaks all records for slowness", but it's a must-see and lovely "for a drink."

Trentaquattro ●S
▽ 20 | 17 | 16 | fr319

34, rue de Bourgogne, 7ᵉ (Assemblée Nationale/Varenne), 01 45 55 80 75

☑ No longer as trendy as when it opened several years ago, this "preppy" Italian in the 7th near the Assemblée Nationale elicits mixed reactions, perhaps because it has "gone through a lot of changes in cuisine and management style"; the menu now features creative dishes such as risotto with cèpes, rose petals and blueberries, but some find the decor a little "gloomy" and prices a little high.

Tricotin ◐ [S] — | — | — | I

15, av. de Choisy, 13e (Porte de Choisy), 01 45 84 74 44
This "easy-to-get-to" Chinese at the tip of Chinatown is "crowded" with patrons who say it serves "fresh", "honest" food; the nonexistent decor doesn't matter since you eat "very well" for a very low price.

TROIS MARCHES (LES) [S] 24 | 25 | 23 | fr690

Hôtel Trianon Palace, 1, bd de la Reine, Versailles (Versailles Rive Droite), 01 39 50 13 21; fax 01 30 21 01 25
■ "The place to dine in Versailles" say admirers of Gérard Vié's "luxurious" haute cuisine restaurant in the Trianon Palace Hôtel; "remarkable" food, a "wine list to bring you to your knees" and a "lovely" setting (with terrace) next to the gardens of Versailles make for an "exceptional" experience, and if it seems that only "wealthy foreigners" can afford it, most think the "prices are justified."

Troquet (Le) 19 | 6 | 14 | fr222

21, rue François Bonvin, 15e (Sèvres-Lecourbe), 01 45 66 89 00; fax 01 45 66 89 83
■ This Paris bistro scene earns high marks for the "excellent, original cuisine" of Christian Etchebest, offered via "good-value" prix fixe menus in a simple space in the 15th; the decor "could stand redoing", but the "excellent welcome" and service, plus the food, ensure that it's "usually full."

Trou Gascon (Au) 22 | 13 | 19 | fr423

40, rue Taine, 12e (Daumesnil), 01 43 44 34 26; fax 01 43 07 80 55
■ "More fun and less expensive" than his famed Carré des Feuillants say devotees of Alain Dutournier's original venue in the 12th near Daumesnil, deemed a "must" for "excellent Southwestern French cuisine" including "the best cassoulet of my existence"; the "elegant Belle Epoque room, gracious staff" and "serious wine list" are also attractions, as are prices that are "reasonable for the quality."

Troyon (Le) 17 | 10 | 16 | fr295

4, rue Troyon, 17e (Charles de Gaulle-Etoile), 01 40 68 99 40; fax 01 40 68 99 57
■ "Bravo" for this "fast, good, affordable" contemporary bistro near the Etoile where chef Jean-Marc Notelet whips up a "refreshing menu" of "thoughtful", "inventive" dishes, including a "chocolate cake that's worth the trip"; service is "likable", but some find portions a bit "stingy."

Truffe Noire (La) 18 | 10 | 16 | fr436

2, place Parmentier, Neuilly-sur-Seine (Porte Maillot), 01 46 24 94 14; fax 01 46 27 37 02
■ "Gastronomically speaking, the best address in Neuilly" say those partial to this French near the Porte Maillot serving a menu laced with "lots of truffles"; the decor doesn't make a big impression, but with "thoughtful service" and a "classic wine list", it's "a good place to relax."

Truffière (La) S
▽ 19 | 15 | 15 | fr307
4, rue Blainville, 5ᵉ (Cardinal Lemoine/Place Monge),
01 46 33 29 82; fax 01 46 33 64 74

■ This Latin Quarter French near the Panthéon offers "excellent food" in a "romantic setting" – a 17th-century building with a pretty arched-ceiling cellar and fireplace; it "really pleases foreign guests" and partisans say it's "one of the very few good restaurants open on Sunday night."

Truite Vagabonde (La) S
▽ 17 | 13 | 13 | fr324
17, rue des Batignolles, 17ᵉ (Place de Clichy/Rome),
01 43 87 77 80; fax 01 43 87 31 50

■ "Time has stood still" at this "very pleasant" neighborhood French near the Place de Clichy in the 17th; the cooking "is not extraordinary, just very good" (if "a bit expensive"), and though the decor is a little "sad", the atmosphere is "cozy."

Trumilou (Le) S
▽ 12 | 9 | 12 | fr192
84, quai de l'Hôtel-de-Ville, 4ᵉ (Hôtel-de-Ville/Pont-Marie),
01 42 77 63 98; fax 01 48 04 91 89

◪ Not far from the Hôtel de Ville overlooking the Seine is this rustic bistro frequented by "students", "tourists" and others on a shoestring budget; the "basic" cooking is "not the best", but it's "decent", the price is right and the atmosphere is "very warm and welcoming."

Tsé-Yang S
17 | 20 | 16 | fr397
25, av. Pierre 1er de Serbie, 16ᵉ (Alma-Marceau/Iéna),
01 47 20 70 22; fax 01 49 52 03 68

■ This "high-class Chinese" in the 16th is "perhaps the best" of its kind in Paris, offering "delicious" food (including praiseworthy Peking duck) in a "luxurious" setting where diners actually "have space"; but it's "pricey" and jet-setters sniff it's not on a par with its New York cousin.

Tsukizi S
– | – | – | M
2 bis, rue des Ciseaux, 6ᵉ (Mabillon/St-Germain-des-Prés),
01 43 54 65 19

Only a few surveyors know this tiny (room for 22) Japanese with nondescript decor on the Left Bank behind Saint-Germain-des-Prés, but they nominate it as "best" of its kind in Paris, with special praise for the sushi, which is made behind a counter in full view of everyone; the well-heeled crowd includes plenty of Japanese.

Ty Coz
17 | 10 | 15 | fr341
35, rue St-Georges, 9ᵉ (St-Georges), 01 48 78 42 95;
fax 01 48 78 34 61

■ Longtime regulars say this "calm" seafooder in the 9th "hasn't changed" "for 20 years", praising its "excellent", "well-prepared" fare with a Breton accent; but some think the "retro" decor could benefit from change, and there also are complaints that it's "too expensive for what it is."

Vagenende ●⬛   12 20 12 fr278
*142, bd St-Germain, 6ᵉ (Mabillon/Odéon), 01 43 26 68 18;
fax 01 40 51 73 38*

◪ This "ravishing" Belle Epoque brasserie in Saint-Germain "shouldn't be for tourists only" say admirers of its "authentic" turn-of-the-century decor and bargain prix fixe menu; while the "simple" food "isn't on a par with the setting", the latter is so magnetic that diners "let themselves be drawn" in by it over and over again.

Van Gogh   ▽ 18 17 15 fr391
*2, quai Aulagnier, Asnières-sur-Seine (Mairie de Clichy),
01 47 91 05 10; fax 01 47 93 00 93*

◼ "Well-located on the banks of the Seine" just north of the city in Asnières, this French is "ideal for a business lunch", especially "in summer" on its lovely terrace, where one might not mind lingering if service is "slow"; prices are "pretty high", but you get "quality" cuisine and a "worthy wine list" for your money.

Vaudeville (Le) ●⬛   13 16 15 fr285
*29, rue Vivienne, 2ᵉ (Bourse), 01 40 20 04 62;
fax 01 49 27 08 78*

◼ "Pretty", "very Parisian" brasserie (part of the Flo group) across from the stock exchange, with art deco decor, "good, basic" food and a "lively" ambiance; it's an "excellent value" and handy "pre- or post-theater" since "you don't have to reserve and there's almost always room"; even those unimpressed by the cooking say the ambiance and service "make you forget you're eating assembly-line fare."

Vendanges (Les)   – – – M
*40, rue Friant, 14ᵉ (Porte d'Orléans), 01 45 39 59 98;
fax 01 45 39 74 13*

"The decor has changed, but happily, not the cuisine" say admirers of this little bistro near the Porte d'Orléans, where chefs Philippe Joubin and Philippe Leroux offer dishes that are expressly conceived to marry well with wine (of which there's a good selection), including salmon with anise-scented ratatouille and a fricassee of veal in *vin jaune* sauce; well-priced prix fixe menus are a plus.

Véranda (La) ●⬛   7 13 6 fr288
*40, av. George V, 8ᵉ (George V), 01 53 57 49 49;
fax 01 47 20 22 19*

◪ This big, "trendy" Italian near the Champs-Elysées with a round dining room and central cupola is "anything but Italian" according to some, but it works as a place "to be seen" or "have a drink" "before hitting a nightclub"; while critics clout "mediocre", "pricey" cuisine and decor that's "aging badly", it's "one of those places where what counts is saying you've been there."

Verre Bouteille (Le) ◑🆂 | 14 | 10 | 11 | fr213 |

5, bd Gouvion-St-Cyr, 17ᵉ (Porte de Champerret),
01 47 63 39 99; fax 01 47 63 07 02
85, av. des Ternes, 17ᵉ (Porte Maillot), 01 45 74 01 02;
fax 01 47 63 07 02

■ "Excellent steak tartare" (chopped by knife) and good wines are highlights at this bistro duo in the 17th; both are "pleasant" neighborhood places and night owls appreciate the late hours (until 5 AM) at the Ternes branch, but service "isn't always on a par" with the rest ("a little smile", please) and oenophiles say it's "too bad smoke masks the nose of certain wines."

Viaduc Café (Le) ◑🆂 | 10 | 15 | 10 | fr188 |

43, av. Daumesnil, 12ᵉ (Bastille/Gare de Lyon), 01 44 74 70 70;
fax 01 44 74 70 71

◪ The "superb setting" – a brick-walled, big-windowed space under the arches of an old railway viaduct – keeps people coming back to this "very pleasant" spot near the Bastille; though the bistro fare is "ordinary", it won't break the bank and the ambiance is "amusing"; P.S. check out the "copious" Sunday jazz brunch.

Vieille (Chez la) | 18 | 13 | 16 | fr366 |

1, rue Bailleul, 1ᵉʳ (Louvre-Rivoli), 01 42 60 15 78;
fax 01 42 33 85 71

■ "A Parisian institution", this "excellent" bistro in Les Halles may be "a little pricey" but it's a "sure bet" for "wonderful bourgeois cuisine" of "exemplary authenticity"; "the only thing missing is space" (it's tiny) and, some might add, decor.

Vieille Fontaine Rôtisserie (La) 🆂 | 17 | 20 | 15 | fr311 |

8, av. Grétry, Maisons-Laffitte (Poissy RER), 01 39 62 01 78;
fax 01 39 62 13 43

■ François Clerc (of Les Bouchons fame) is behind this "delightful" French set in a private mansion overlooking "quiet gardens" in Maisons-Laffitte; "inventive" cuisine and "superb decor" make for "romantic" dining, and the prix fixe menus are "reasonable" to boot; P.S. there's a "pleasant terrace" in summer.

Vieux Bistro (Le) 🆂 | 19 | 14 | 18 | fr285 |

14, rue du Cloître-Notre-Dame, 4ᵉ (Cité/St-Michel),
01 43 54 18 95; fax 01 44 07 35 63

■ This "cozy bistro" "right next to Notre Dame" may be in a "very touristy location", but that doesn't detract from its "intimate" atmosphere, "warm" welcome and "very good", "rich" fare ("not for dieters"); regulars say don't miss the "unequaled" beef fillet and be sure to "ask for a table in the back."

Vieux Métiers de France (Les) S 16 | 13 | 14 | fr331
13, bd Auguste Blanqui, 13ᵉ (Place d'Italie), 01 45 88 90 03;
fax 01 45 80 73 80
◪ According to partisans, this Traditional French in the 13th is "a little straight-laced" but provides "very good" food in a "calm, relaxing" setting with medieval-themed decor; dissenters call for "a little more effort with the cooking, please" and some judge it "overpriced", but there are moderately priced prix fixe menus.

Village d'Ung et Li Lam ◐S ▽ 16 | 17 | 18 | fr236
10, rue Jean Mermoz, 8ᵉ (Franklin D. Roosevelt),
01 42 25 99 79; fax 01 42 25 12 06
■ An "oasis of flavor and good humor" that will "transport you to unknown destinations" is how one carried-away fan describes this Asian off the Champs-Elysées; while others are a bit more restrained, the consensus is that the Thai-Chinese food is "excellent" and "modestly priced", service is "friendly" and the decor "original" (check out the ceiling aquarium).

Villaret (Le) ◐ 22 | 12 | 17 | fr267
13, rue Ternaux, 11ᵉ (Parmentier), 01 43 57 89 76;
fax 01 43 57 89 69
■ "You have to look hard" to find this simple-looking bistro "deep in the 11th" near Parmentier "where good restaurants are in short supply", but it rewards the search with a changing menu of "excellent", "inventive" cuisine and "friendly" (or is it "slightly arrogant"?) service; "good value" is another reason it's "worth a stop."

Vincent (Chez) ▽ 21 | 10 | 16 | fr257
5, rue du Tunnel, 19ᵉ (Botzaris/Buttes-Chaumont),
01 42 02 22 45
■ "My find of the year" clamors one diner who isn't alone in admiring this "very good traditional Italian" "at the ends of the earth" near the Buttes-Chaumont in the 19th; "huge portions" of "savory" food and a "jovial", "authentic" ambiance make it a "celebration", provided you manage to snag a table; the moderately priced tasting menu earns a special mention.

Vinci (Le) ▽ 17 | 13 | 18 | fr293
23, rue Paul Valéry, 16ᵉ (Boissière/Victor Hugo),
01 45 01 68 18; fax 01 45 01 60 37
■ Surveyors say this "very small Italian" near the Arc de Triomphe has "improved considerably" under new management; though some think the menu could use more variety, portions are almost "too big" and most consider it a "good value"; however, the "dark atmosphere behind drawn blinds" seems out of sync with Italian cuisine.

Vin des Rues (Au) ▽ 15 | 9 | 11 | fr216

21, rue Boulard, 14e (Denfert-Rochereau), 01 43 22 19 78; fax 01 43 22 19 78

■ Those who've hesitated to revisit this "typical Parisian bistro" in the 14th since former owner Jean Chanrion retired can take heart: "happily, the new owners haven't changed a thing"; expect "excellent" food, "good wines" (bravos for the Beaujolais) and "authentic" ambiance; N.B. dinner is only served Wednesday, Friday and Saturday.

Vinea Café (Le) ◐ [S] ▽ 9 | 17 | 13 | fr190

26-28, Cour St-Emilion, 12e (Cour St-Emilion), 01 44 74 09 09; fax 01 44 74 06 66

■ "Terrific outdoor seating" and trendy modern decor are the main draws at this cafe in a newly developing section of southeastern Paris across from the national library; located where wine wholesalers once received their shipments, it's "handy before a movie" nearby, but nonlocals ask "is it worth the trip to this remote" corner?

Vin et Marée [S] 16 | 10 | 14 | fr264

71, av. de Suffren, 7e (La Motte-Picquet-Grenelle), 01 47 83 27 12; fax 01 42 06 62 35

276, bd Voltaire, 11e (Nation), 01 43 72 31 23; fax 01 40 09 05 24 ◐

108, av. du Maine, 14e (Gaîté), 01 43 20 29 50; fax 01 43 27 84 11 ◐

183, bd Murat, 16e (Porte St-Cloud), 01 46 47 91 39; fax 01 46 47 69 07

■ A fine "fish fiesta" awaits at this "unpretentious" seafood chain offering "generous portions" of "impeccably fresh", "simply prepared" fish at very "reasonable" prices; service is "always smiling" and regulars advise "leave room for the baba au rhum" – it's big enough for two; the only sour note is decor that some find "depressing."

Vin sur Vin 16 | 13 | 17 | fr429

20, rue de Monttessuy, 7e (Alma-Marceau), 01 47 05 14 20; fax 01 47 05 14 20

■ "One of Paris' gems" say devotees of this comfy wine-oriented French near the Eiffel Tower serving "excellent food" to go with its "fabulous wine list"; service is "very pleasant" and it's one of the rare small restaurants "content to leave plenty of room between tables."

VIOLON D'INGRES (LE) 24 | 16 | 20 | fr536

135, rue St-Dominique, 7e (Ecole-Militaire), 01 45 55 15 05; fax 01 45 55 48 42

◪ Christian Constant (ex Crillon Hôtel) has "reached a good cruising speed" at his "elegant" French in the 7th, turning out "inventive", "refined" fare that shows his "love and enthusiasm for food"; while that's not a unanimous view – critics call it "overrated" and cite "pricey" wines and "so-so" decor – most consider it a "high-class" "value", with extra praise for the "warm, professional service" and "superb" tasting menu.

Virgin Café ◐ [S] 10 | 10 | 8 | fr181

Virgin Megastore, 52-60, av. Champs-Elysées, 8e (Franklin D. Roosevelt), 01 42 89 46 81; fax 01 49 53 50 41

◪ "Trendy" cafe in the Virgin Megastore that works for a "quick lunch" or break from CD-scoping, offering "decent" bistro-style eats in a "noisy", "modern" setting overlooking the Champs-Elysées; it's "not too expensive" and the good "people-watching" is free.

Vivario – | – | – | I

6, rue Cochin, 5e (Maubert-Mutualité), 01 43 25 08 19; fax 01 43 29 51 05

"A marvelous surprise" say admirers of this tiny Latin Quarter Corsican with an old-fashioned setting; it may be "inconsistent, but when it's good it's wonderful", not to mention affordable; "ask for the goat – it's worth the trip."

Voltaire (Le) 18 | 17 | 18 | fr410

27, quai Voltaire, 7e (Rue du Bac), 01 42 61 17 49

◪ "Excellent, traditional cuisine" keeps an "elegant" crowd coming back to this "reassuring but never boring" bistro veteran set in the one-time home of Voltaire on the banks of the Seine in Saint-Germain; "the bill isn't modest", but that doesn't seem to bother habitués; try the tables in the back for quiet conversation.

Vong (Chez) ◐ [S] 18 | 21 | 17 | fr353

10, rue de la Grande-Truanderie, 1er (Etienne Marcel/Les Halles), 01 40 26 09 36; fax 01 42 33 38 15

■ "Refined, melt-in-the-mouth" Chinese (and Vietnamese) fare is what admirers find at this upscale Asian near Les Halles; maybe "you're paying for" the exotic setting and "attentive service", but it's "worth it"; a few outvoted dissenters find it "overrated" and carp about "no spice" and "minuscule portions."

Vong (Chez) ◐ 19 | 17 | 16 | fr338

27, rue du Colisée, 8e (Franklin D. Roosevelt), 01 43 59 77 12; fax 01 43 59 59 27

■ A "good Chinese for a snobby clientele" is one way to look at this "calm, serious" source of Chinese and Vietnamese fare near the Champs-Elysées; "constant quality" and a "lovely" setting explain why regulars "always return with pleasure" despite "high prices."

Wadja ▽ 19 | 14 | 18 | fr235

10, rue de la Grande-Chaumière, 6e (Vavin), 01 46 33 02 02

■ "Good food", good wine and "good value" make this bistro a "nice neighborhood place" in the heart of bustling Montparnasse; it pulls an arty youngish crowd, plus lots of foreigners, which creates a convivial if noisy atmosphere; big eaters say the portions "might leave you hungry", but the very modestly priced prix fixe menus certainly won't leave you broke.

Wally Le Saharien
19 | 16 | 17 | fr320

36, rue Rodier, 9ᵉ (Anvers), 01 42 85 51 90; fax 01 45 86 08 35

■ Devotees of dry couscous (a Saharan specialty served without broth or vegetables) say this North African in the 9th near Anvers serves "the best in town"; since portions are "copious", the ambiance is "excellent" and Wally is a real "character", not to mention a couscous and *mechoui* [roast lamb] maven, fans find it easy to "forget the cost."

Wepler ◖ⓢ
14 | 12 | 13 | fr272

14, place de Clichy, 18ᵉ (Place de Clichy), 01 45 22 53 24; fax 01 44 70 07 50

◪ Stick with the aquatic stuff and you're likely to be happy at this crowded, "classic" brasserie overlooking the Place de Clichy; it's "a must" for "fresh" seafood platters and "exceptional oysters", but critics say the rest of the menu is "disappointing", also knocking the "old-fashioned" decor and service that can be "efficient" or "interminable."

Willi's Wine Bar
17 | 12 | 14 | fr262

13, rue des Petits Champs, 1ᵉʳ (Bourse/Palais Royal-Musée du Louvre), 01 42 61 05 09; fax 01 47 03 36 93

■ Drink up the "cosmopolitan" anglophone ambiance at this upscale but "fun" bar à vins near the Place des Victoires in the 1st, and while you're at it, sip some "remarkable" wines; run by Englishman Mark Williamson, it also offers "delicious" bistro fare, which keeps regulars "coming back" despite the "crowded", "noisy" quarters and "slow" service.

Wok Restaurant
– | – | – | I

25, rue de Taillandiers, 11ᵉ (Bastille/Voltaire), 01 55 28 88 77; fax 01 55 28 88 78

This Asian newcomer to the trendy Bastille area is built around an "original idea": diners choose their own ingredients and then watch as chefs stir-fry their dish; it's "noisy" with "antiseptic decor" and service that can be "too relaxed", but it's hard to argue with the tab and it's amusing "with friends", since the young crowd mingles easily; N.B. come early or brace for endless waits to get your meal cooked.

Woolloomooloo ⓢ
10 | 10 | 10 | fr204

36, bd Henri IV, 4ᵉ (Bastille), 01 42 72 32 11; fax 01 42 72 32 21

◪ You won't find many Parisian restaurants specializing in grilled kangaroo, which may be reason enough to check out this Australian near the Bastille; the menu is certainly "original", if "uneven", the ambiance is "pleasant" and there's a good selection of wines from down under, but as ratings attest, not everybody is a mate.

Yvan ◐   17 | 17 | 16 | fr392
1 bis, rue Jean Mermoz, 8ᵉ (Franklin D. Roosevelt),
01 43 59 18 40; fax 01 42 89 30 95
☑ Filled with "pretty artwork" and "beautiful bouquets", chef-owner Yvan's stylish French just off the Rond-Point of the Champs-Elysées has been a long-running "trendy" scene; though some claim the cooking suffers when the "mythic" owner isn't around, most consider it a high-class "best buy" thanks to "always interesting", "inventive" prix fixe menus; still, there are complaints about "slow" service and "affectation."

Yvan, Petit (Le) ◐   16 | 13 | 14 | fr256
1 bis, rue Jean Mermoz, 8ᵉ (Franklin D. Roosevelt),
01 42 89 49 65; fax 01 42 89 30 95
☑ Yvan's next-door annex is "more fun and less snobby", drawing a "young, funky crowd" with its "noisy, bustling" ambiance and prix fixe menus offering "interesting" bistro fare at prices that are "moderate" given the locale near the Champs-Elysées; outvoted critics say "insipid" food and "capricious service" can equal an "eternal wait for very little"; note: it gets "pretty crazy" at night.

Yves Quintard   ▽ 22 | 19 | 19 | fr309
99, rue Blomet, 15ᵉ (Vaugirard), 01 42 50 22 27;
fax 01 42 50 22 27
■ In the heart of the 15th near Vaugirard, this "little, refined French" offers "excellent" food at "good-value prices" in a "handsomely decorated" room; Mme. Quintard "welcomes you warmly", and while there's a grumble or two about "small portions" and unmet expectations, enthusiasts feel it "should be better known."

Zebra Square ◐Ⓢ   11 | 16 | 10 | fr270
3, place Clément-Ader, 16ᵉ (Mirabeau), 01 44 14 91 91;
fax 01 45 20 46 41
☑ "Trendy" (maybe "too trendy") French in the 16th near the Maison de la Radio that's more appreciated for its "original", "ultramodern" decor and watchable crowd than for its food ("expensive", "not exceptional"); even so, it's a "place to be seen" and "good for drinks" or a "copious" Sunday brunch.

Zéphyr (Le)   ▽ 15 | 15 | 14 | fr221
1, rue du Jourdain, 20ᵉ (Jourdain), 01 46 36 65 81;
fax 01 43 58 00 06
■ A "very pleasant" option in a "neighborhood on the rise" say those who know this bistro with appealing '30s decor in the 20th; while it doesn't blow everyone away, admirers describe it as "hip, retro, inexpensive and good."

Zeyer (Le) ◐🄢
10 | 11 | 11 | fr252

62, rue d'Alésia, 14ᵉ (Alésia), 01 45 40 43 88;
fax 01 45 40 64 51

◪ Maybe you shouldn't "go out of your way" for it, but "as far as ultraclassic brasseries go", this one in the Alésia quarter of Montparnasse is "perfectly recommendable" as a "solid neighborhood place"; "you get what you expect", including good shellfish and, alas, service that's sometimes "not up to snuff."

Zinzins (Les)
▽ 13 | 10 | 12 | fr186

6, rue des Colonnes, 2ᵉ (Bourse/Richelieu-Drouot),
01 40 20 90 50; fax 01 40 20 97 05

■ Numbers-crunchers from the nearby stock exchange like to cash in on the "good prix fixe lunch" deal at this Italian in the 2nd, which is also liked for its "friendly ambiance" and "super service, especially in the evening"; the food gets decent marks and it's the kind of good-natured place that puts patrons in the mood to "laugh a lot."

Zygomates (Les)
▽ 18 | 14 | 15 | fr217

7, rue de Capri, 12ᵉ (Daumesnil/Michel Bizot),
01 40 19 93 04; fax 01 44 73 46 63

■ With an "atypical" setting in a former butcher shop, "fast, friendly" service and "excellent", "reasonably priced" food, this French near Daumesnil has all the attributes of "a very good little neighborhood place"; those who find the decor "depressing" can console themselves with the good wine selection.

Indexes

CUISINES

African

(See also Moroccan)
Entoto (13e)
Gazelle (17e)
Impala Lounge (8e)

American

Buffalo Grill (3e, 5e, 9e, 10e, 13e,
    14e, 15e, 17e, 19e)
Chicago Meatpackers (1er)
Chicago Pizza Pie Factory (8e)
Coffee Parisien (6e, 16e)
Joe Allen (1er)
Pacific Eiffel (15e)
Planet Hollywood (8e)
Spoon, Food & Wine (8e)
Thanksgiving (4e)

Armenian

Diamantaires (9e)

Asian

Asian (8e)
Blue Elephant (11e)
Buddha Bar (8e)
Diep (Chez) (8e)
Erawan (15e)
Kambodgia (16e)
Poste (9e)
Soun (16e)
Tan Dinh (7e)
Tang (16e)
Village d'Ung et Li Lam (8e)

Australian

Woolloomooloo (4e)

Belgian

Bouillon Racine (6e)
Graindorge (17e)
Léon de Bruxelles (1er, 4e, 6e, 8e,
    9e, 11e, 14e, 15e, 17e)

British/Irish

Bertie's (16e)
Carr's (1er)
Juvenile's (1er)
Kitty O'Sheas (2e)
Willi's Wine Bar (1er)

Cambodian

Coin des Gourmets (5e)

Caribbean

Flamboyant (14e)
Marais-Cage (3e)
Table de Babette (Poissy)

Caviar

Caviar Kaspia (8e)
Comptoir du Saumon (4e, 8e, 15e, 17e)
Daru (8e)
Flora Danica (8e)
Maison du Caviar (8e)
Maison Prunier (16e)
Petrossian (7e)

Central European

Paprika (9e)
Patrick Goldenberg (17e)

Chinese

Chen (15e)
China Club (12e)
China Town Belleville (10e)
China Town Olympiades (13e)
Davé (1er)
Délices de Szechuen (7e)
Diep (Chez) (8e)
FocLy (Neuilly)
Lao Tseu (7e)
Mandarin (8e)
Mandarin de Neuilly (Neuilly)
Mirama (5e)
New Nioullaville (11e)
Ngo (16e)
Nouveau Village Tao-Tao (13e)
Passy Mandarin (2e, 16e)
Président (11e)
Soun (16e)
Tang (16e)
Tong Yen (8e)
Tricotin (13e)
Tsé-Yang (16e)
Village d'Ung et Li Lam (8e)
Vong (1er, 8e)
Wok Restaurant (11e)

Eclectic/International

Ailleurs (8e)
Auberge du Clou (9e)
Barfly (8e)
Barramundi (9e)
Bermuda Onion (15e)
Bon (16e)
Cou de la Girafe (8e)

Diable des Lombards (1er)
Doobie's (8e)
Epicure 108 (17e)
Man Ray (8e)
Poste (9e)
Relais du Parc (16e)
Spicy Restaurant (8e)
Spoon, Food & Wine (8e)
Taïra (17e)
Zebra Square (16e)

French: Bistro (Contemporary)

Absinthe (1er)
Affriolé (7e)
Ardoise (1er)
Avant Goût (13e)
Bistro d'Hubert (15e)
Bistrot de l'Etoile Lauriston (16e)
Bistrot de l'Etoile Niel (17e)
Bistrot de l'Etoile Troyon (17e)
Bon Accueil (7e)
Bookinistes (6e)
Bouchons de Fr. Clerc (5e, 8e, 15e, 16e, 17e)
Brézolles (6e)
Butte Chaillot (16e)
Café Beaubourg (4e)
Café Bleu (8e)
Café d'Angel (17e)
Café de la Musique (19e)
Café Faubourg (8e)
Café Marly (1er)
C'Amelot (11e)
Casa del Habano (6e)
Cave de l'Os à Moelle (15e)
Cave Gourmande (19e)
Clos des Gourmets (7e)
Coude Fou (4e)
Dame Jeanne (11e)
Dauphin (1er)
Detourbe Duret (16e)
Durand Dupont (Neuilly)
Epi Dupin (6e)
Fabrique (11e)
Floridita (16e)
Fumoir (1er)
Georges (4e)
Jean (9e)
Kiosque (16e)
Marie et Fils (6e)
Montalembert (7e)
Nemrod (6e)
Os à Moelle (15e)
Petit Plat (15e)

Petit Poucet (Le) (Levallois)
Prune (10e)
P'tit Troquet (7e)
Quai Ouest (St-Cloud)
Régalade (14e)
River Café (Issy-les-Moulineaux)
Robe et le Palais (1er)
Rôtisserie Monsigny (2e)
Rue Balzac (8e)
16 Haussmann (9e)
Signatures (8e)
Stéphane Martin (15e)
Troyon (17e)
Viaduc Café (12e)
Vinea Café (12e)
Virgin Café (8e)
Wadja (6e)
Zéphyr (20e)

French: Bistro (Traditional)

A et M Le Bistrot (16e, 17e)
Agape (15e)
Allard (6e)
Allobroges (20e)
Ambassade du Sud-Ouest (7e)
Ami Louis (3e)
Ami Pierre (11e)
André (8e)
Aristide (17e)
Assassins (6e)
Astier (11e)
Auberge Bressane (7e)
Auberge du Champ de Mars (7e)
Babylone (7e)
Bacchantes (9e)
Baracane (4e)
Beaujolais d'Auteuil (16e)
Bec Rouge (8e)
Benoît (4e)
Berry's (8e)
Berthoud (5e)
Biche au Bois (12e)
Bistro 121 (15e)
Bistro de Gala (9e)
Bistro de la Grille (6e)
Bistro de l'Olivier (8e)
Bistro des Deux Théâtres (9e)
Bistro du 17ème (17e)
Bistro Melrose (17e)
Bistrot d'à Côté (5e, 17e, Neuilly)
Bistrot d'Albert (17e)
Bistrot d'Alex (6e)
Bistrot d'André (15e)
Bistrot de Breteuil (7e)

Bistrot de l'Université (7e)
Bistrot de Marius (8e)
Bistrot de Paris (7e)
Bistrot d'Henri (6e)
Bistrot du Louvre (2e)
Bistrot du Peintre (11e)
Bistrot St. Ferdinand (17e)
Bistrot St. James (Neuilly)
Bouclard (18e)
Boulangerie (20e)
Café Charbon (11e)
Café de Flore (6e)
Café de l'Industrie (11e)
Café de Mars (7e)
Café Indigo (8e)
Café la Jatte (Neuilly)
Café Les Deux Magots (6e)
Café Louis Philippe (4e)
Café Max (7e)
Caméléon (6e)
Camille (3e)
Carpe Diem (Neuilly)
Cartet Restaurant (11e)
Catherine (9e)
Caveau du Palais (1er)
Cave Drouot (9e)
Caves Pétrissans (17e)
Champ de Mars (7e)
Chardenoux (11e)
Charpentiers (6e)
Chez Eux (7e)
Cigale (7e)
Clément (2e, 4e, 8e, 14e, 15e, 17e,
    Bougival, Boulogne)
Clémentine (2e)
Clovis (1er)
Clown Bar (11e)
Comptoir des Sports (6e)
Côté 7ème (7e)
Crus de Bourgogne (2e)
Denise (1er)
Diane (6e)
Dos de la Baleine (4e)
Driver's (16e)
Ebauchoir (12e)
Epi d'Or (1er)
Escargot Montorgueil (1er)
Etrier (18e)
Filoche (15e)
Fins Gourmets (7e)
Flambée (12e)
Fontaine de Mars (7e)
Fous d'en Face (4e)
Fred (17e)
Gavroche (2e)

Georges (2e)
Georges Porte Maillot (17e)
Gérard (Neuilly)
Gourmets des Ternes (8e)
Grille Montorgueil (2e)
Grille St-Honoré (1er)
Grizzli (4e)
Janou (3e)
Je Thé...Me (15e)
Joséphine "Chez Dumonet" (6e)
Languedoc (5e)
Léon (17e)
Lescure (1er)
Lozère (6e)
Lyonnais (2e)
Ma Bourgogne (4e, 8e)
Maître Paul (6e)
Marcel (6e)
Marie-Louise (18e)
Marlotte (6e)
Mathusalem (16e)
Mère Agitée (14e)
Michel (10e)
Moissonnier (5e)
Monttessuy (7e)
Moulin à Vent "Chez Henri" (5e)
Natacha (14e)
Nénesse (3e)
Noces de Jeannette (2e)
O à la Bouche (14e)
Oeillade (7e)
Omar (3e)
Opportun (14e)
Os à Moelle (15e)
Parc aux Cerfs (6e)
Paul (1er, 11e, 13e)
Pauline (1er)
Pento (5e)
Perraudin (5e)
Petit Coin de la Bourse (2e)
Petite Chaise (7e)
Petite Cour (La) (6e)
Petites Sorcières (14e)
Petit Keller (11e)
Petit Mâchon (1er, 15e)
Petit Marguery (13e)
Petit Riche (9e)
Petit St. Benoît (6e)
Philosophes (4e)
Pied de Fouet (7e)
Pierre (15e)
Plage Parisienne (15e)
Polidor (6e)
Poquelin (1er)
Pouilly Reuilly (Le Pré-St-Gervais)

Poule au Pot (1er)
Quincy (12e)
Réconfort (3e)
Relais Beaujolais (9e)
Relais de l'Entrecôte (6e, 8e)
Relais de Venise (17e)
Réminet (5e)
Rendez-vous/Camionneurs (14e)
Rendez-vous/Chauffeurs (18e)
René (5e)
Restaurant (18e)
Rest. des Beaux Arts (6e)
Rest. des Chauffeurs (16e)
Rest. Jean Bouin (16e)
Rest. La Zygothèque (13e)
Ribe (7e)
Robert et Louise (3e)
Roi du Pot-au-Feu (9e)
Rond de Serviette (6e)
Rouge Vif (7e)
Rubis (1er)
Saint Amarante (12e)
Saint Pourçain (12e)
Saint Vincent (15e)
Savy (8e)
Scheffer (16e)
Sédillot (7e)
Souletin (Le) (1er)
Square Trousseau (12e)
Temps des Cerises (13e)
Tire-Bouchon (15e)
Tournesol (16e)
Toutoune (5e)
Troquet (15e)
Trumilou (4e)
Vendanges (14e)
Verre Bouteille (17e)
Vieille (1er)
Vieux Bistro (4e)
Villaret (11e)
Vin des Rues (14e)
Voltaire (7e)
Yvan, Petit (8e)
Zygomates (12e)

French: Brasserie

Alcazar (6e)
Alsace (8e)
Antiquaires (7e)
Arbuci (6e)
Auberge Dab (16e)
Ballon des Ternes (17e)
Baumann Ternes (17e)
Bœuf Couronné (19e)
Bœuf sur le Toit (8e)
Bofinger (4e)
Brasserie Balzar (5e)
Brasserie de la Poste (16e)
Brasserie de l'Ile St. Louis (4e)
Brasserie du Louvre (1er)
Brasserie Flo (10e)
Brasserie Lipp (6e)
Brasserie Lorraine (8e)
Brasserie Lutétia (6e)
Brasserie Mollard (8e)
Brasserie Munichoise (1er)
Brasserie Stella (16e)
Café de la Paix (9e)
Café de l'Esplanade (Le) (7e)
Café du Commerce (15e)
Café Ruc (1er)
Café Runtz (2e)
Chien qui Fume (1er)
Chope d'Alsace (6e)
Closerie des Lilas (6e)
Club Matignon (8e)
Congrès (17e)
Coupole (14e)
Dagorno (19e)
Drugstore Champs-Elysées (8e)
Flandrin (16e)
Flore en l'Ile (4e)
Francis (8e)
Gallopin (2e)
Gare (16e)
Gauloise (15e)
Gégène (Joinville)
Grand Café des Capucines (9e)
Grand Colbert (2e)
Grandes Marches (12e)
Jenny (3e)
Julien (10e)
Marty (5e)
Mascotte (8e)
Muniche (6e)
Petit Bofinger (4e, 9e, 17e, Neuilly)
Petit Lutétia (6e)
Petit Victor Hugo (16e)
Petit Zinc (6e)
Pharamond (1er)
Pied de Cochon (1er)
Procope (6e)
Rech (17e)
Sébillon Élysées (8e)
Sébillon Neuilly (Neuilly)
Taverne de Maître Kanter (1er)
Taverne Kronenbourg (9e)
Terminus Nord (10e)
Terrasse (18e)
Thoumieux (7e)

Train Bleu (12e)
Vagenende (6e)
Vaudeville (2e)
Wepler (18e)
Zebra Square (16e)
Zeyer (14e)

French: Cheese

Ambassade d'Auvergne (3e)
Androuët (8e)
Ferme St-Hubert (8e)
Montparnasse 25 (14e)
Soufflé (1er)

French: Classic

Abélard (5e)
Aiguière (11e)
Altitude 95 (7e)
Ampère (17e)
Amphyclès (17e)
Anacréon (13e)
Appart' (8e)
Armand au Palais Royal (1er)
Assiette (14e)
Atelier Maître Albert (5e)
Auberge Nicolas Flamel (3e)
Avenue (8e)
Bar des Théâtres (8e)
Bar Vendôme (1er)
Basilic (7e)
Beauvilliers (A.) (18e)
Beudant (17e)
Bistrot du Sommelier (8e)
Bistrot Papillon (9e)
Bon Saint Pourçain (6e)
Braisière (17e)
Bristol (8e)
Bûcherie (5e)
Café de Vendôme (1er)
Café Flo (9e)
Café Terminus (8e)
Café Véry (1er)
Camélia (Bougival)
Cap Seguin (Boulogne)
Catounière (Neuilly)
Cave de l'Os à Moelle (15e)
Cazaudehore La Forestière
    (Saint-Germain-en-Laye)
Céladon (2e)
Célébrités (15e)
Cercle Ledoyen (8e)
Cévennes (15e)
Chalet des Iles (16e)
Chartier (9e)
Chat Grippé (6e)
Chiberta (8e)

Christine (6e)
Clément (2e, 4e, 8e, 14e, 15e, 17e,
    Bougival, Boulogne)
Cloche d'Or (9e)
Closerie des Lilas (6e)
Clovis (Le) (8e)
Coconnas (4e)
Comédiens (9e)
Communautés (Puteaux)
Comptoir du Saumon (4e, 8e, 15e, 17e)
Comte de Gascogne (Boulogne)
Contre-Allée (14e)
Coq/Maison Blanche (St-Ouen)
Costes (1er)
Côte de Bœuf (17e)
Cottage Marcadet (18e)
Coupe-Chou (5e)
Cuisinier François (16e)
Dame Tartine (4e, 12e)
Débarcadère (17e)
Deux Canards (10e)
Drouant (2e)
Entracte (18e)
Entrecôte (7e)
Entrepôt (14e)
En Ville (6e)
Etoile (8e)
Fabrice (1er)
Ferme de Boulogne (Boulogne)
Ferme des Mathurins (8e)
Ferme St-Simon (7e)
Fermette Marbeuf 1900 (8e)
Fernandises (11e)
Fins Gourmets (7e)
Florimond (7e)
Fontaines (5e)
Fouquet's (8e)
Françoise (7e)
Galoche d'Aurillac (11e)
Gamin de Paris (4e)
Gastroquet (15e)
Gaudriole (1er)
Germaine (7e)
Gitane (15e)
Gourmet de l'Isle (4e)
Grande Armée (16e)
Grande Cascade (16e)
Grille (10e)
Guinguette de Neuilly (Neuilly)
Guirlande de Julie (3e)
Hédiard (8e)
Homero (8e)
Improviste (17e)
Jacky (Chez) (13e)
Jacques Cagna (6e)

Jamin (16ᵉ)
Jardin (8ᵉ)
Jardin des Cygnes (8ᵉ)
Jardins de Bagatelle (16ᵉ)
Jules Verne (7ᵉ)
Lapérouse (6ᵉ)
Laurent (8ᵉ)
Léna et Mimile (5ᵉ)
Maison (5ᵉ)
Maison Courtine (14ᵉ)
Mandragore (19ᵉ)
Manufacture (Issy-les-Moulineaux)
Marie-Louise (18ᵉ)
Maupertu (7ᵉ)
Maxence (6ᵉ)
Maxim's (Orly)
Mère Agitée (14ᵉ)
Meurice (1ᵉʳ)
Michel Courtalhac (7ᵉ)
Michel Rostang (17ᵉ)
Monde des Chimères (4ᵉ)
Monsieur Lapin (14ᵉ)
Montparnasse 25 (14ᵉ)
Morot-Gaudry (15ᵉ)
Muses (9ᵉ)
Nénesse (3ᵉ)
Obélisque (8ᵉ)
Orangerie (4ᵉ)
Ormes (16ᵉ)
Pactole (5ᵉ)
Pamphlet (3ᵉ)
Paris (6ᵉ)
Paul Chêne (16ᵉ)
Pavillon des Princes (16ᵉ)
Pavillon Elysée (8ᵉ)
Pavillon Montsouris (14ᵉ)
Pavillon Puebla (19ᵉ)
Père Claude (15ᵉ)
Petit Colombier (17ᵉ)
Petite Tour (16ᵉ)
Petit Laurent (7ᵉ)
Petit Prince de Paris (5ᵉ)
Petit Rétro (16ᵉ)
Pichet (8ᵉ)
Pied de Cochon (1ᵉʳ)
"Pierre" A la Fontaine (2ᵉ)
Pierre au Palais Royal (1ᵉʳ)
Pluvinel (1ᵉʳ)
Port du Salut (5ᵉ)
Potager du Roy (Versailles)
Pressoir (12ᵉ)
Récamier (7ᵉ)
Rech (17ᵉ)
Relais Chablisien (1ᵉʳ)
Relais de Sèvres (15ᵉ)

Relais Louis XIII (6ᵉ)
Relais Plaza (8ᵉ)
Repaire de Cartouche (11ᵉ)
Rest. de la Tour (15ᵉ)
Rest. du Musée d'Orsay (7ᵉ)
Rest. du Palais Royal (1ᵉʳ)
Rest. Opéra (9ᵉ)
Rôtisserie (Levallois)
Rôtisserie d'Armaillé (17ᵉ)
Rôtisserie d'en Face (6ᵉ)
Rotonde (6ᵉ)
Salle à Manger (16ᵉ)
Sologne (12ᵉ)
Soufflé (1ᵉʳ)
Soupière (17ᵉ)
Stéphane Martin (15ᵉ)
Tante Jeanne (17ᵉ)
Tante Louise (8ᵉ)
Tante Marguerite (7ᵉ)
Tastevin (Maisons-Laffitte)
Terrasse (18ᵉ)
Terroir (13ᵉ)
Tonnelle Saintongeaise (Neuilly)
Totem (16ᵉ)
Toupary (1ᵉʳ)
Truite Vagabonde (17ᵉ)
Vieille Fontaine Rôtisserie (La)
    (Maisons-Laffitte)
Vieux Métiers de France (13ᵉ)
Vin sur Vin (7ᵉ)
Violon d'Ingres (7ᵉ)
Zygomates (12ᵉ)

French: Haute Cuisine

Alain Ducasse (8ᵉ)
Ambassadeurs (8ᵉ)
Ambroisie (4ᵉ)
Apicius (17ᵉ)
Arpège (7ᵉ)
Astor (8ᵉ)
Bristol (8ᵉ)
Carré des Feuillants (1ᵉʳ)
Cinq (8ᵉ)
Elysées du Vernet (8ᵉ)
Espadon (1ᵉʳ)
Faugeron (16ᵉ)
Gérard Besson (1ᵉʳ)
Grand Véfour (1ᵉʳ)
Guy Savoy (17ᵉ)
Jacques Cagna (6ᵉ)
Jamin (16ᵉ)
Lasserre (8ᵉ)
Laurent (8ᵉ)
Ledoyen (8ᵉ)
Lucas Carton (8ᵉ)

Maxim's (8ᵉ)
Meurice (1ᵉʳ)
Michel Rostang (17ᵉ)
Pierre Gagnaire (8ᵉ)
Pré Catelan (16ᵉ)
Relais d'Auteuil (16ᵉ)
Rest. Opéra (9ᵉ)
Taillevent (8ᵉ)
Tour d'Argent (5ᵉ)
Trois Marches (Versailles)

French: New

Amadéo (4ᵉ)
Amognes (11ᵉ)
Amuse Bouche (14ᵉ)
Argenteuil (1ᵉʳ)
Arpège (7ᵉ)
Astor (8ᵉ)
Atelier Berger (1ᵉʳ)
Atelier Gourmand (17ᵉ)
Bamboche (7ᵉ)
Bath's (8ᵉ)
Béatilles (17ᵉ)
Bonne Table (14ᵉ)
Bourdonnais (7ᵉ)
Bristol (8ᵉ)
Café M (8ᵉ)
Carré des Feuillants (1ᵉʳ)
Cartes Postales (1ᵉʳ)
Céladon (2ᵉ)
Clos Morillons (15ᵉ)
Colette (1ᵉʳ)
Dînée (15ᵉ)
Excuse (4ᵉ)
Faucher (17ᵉ)
Fontaine d'Auteuil (16ᵉ)
Grange Batelière (9ᵉ)
Grenadin (8ᵉ)
Guy Savoy (17ᵉ)
Hangar (3ᵉ)
Il Baccello (17ᵉ)
Impatient (17ᵉ)
Jumeaux (11ᵉ)
Macéo (1ᵉʳ)
Maison Blanche (8ᵉ)
Maison de l'Amérique (7ᵉ)
Pergolèse (16ᵉ)
Philippe Detourbe (15ᵉ)
Pierre Gagnaire (8ᵉ)
Restaurant W (8ᵉ)
Rocher Gourmand (8ᵉ)
Rôtisserie (Levallois)
Safran (1ᵉʳ)
Shozan (8ᵉ)
Table d'Anvers (9ᵉ)

Télégraphe (7ᵉ)
Terrasse (18ᵉ)
Toque (17ᵉ)
Truffière (5ᵉ)
Van Gogh (Asnières)
Yvan (8ᵉ)
Yves Quintard (15ᵉ)

French: Regional

Alsace/Jura
Alsace (8ᵉ)
Alsaco (9ᵉ)
Bec Rouge (8ᵉ)
Café Runtz (2ᵉ)
Chope d'Alsace (6ᵉ)
Epicure 108 (17ᵉ)
Fabrique (11ᵉ)
Jenny (3ᵉ)
Léna et Mimile (5ᵉ)
Maître Paul (6ᵉ)
Taverne Kronenbourg (9ᵉ)

Auvergne
Ambassade d'Auvergne (3ᵉ)
Bath's (8ᵉ)
Chantairelle (5ᵉ)
Clovis (1ᵉʳ)
Galoche d'Aurillac (11ᵉ)
Lozère (6ᵉ)
Mascotte (8ᵉ)
Nemrod (6ᵉ)
Savy (8ᵉ)

Aveyron
Auberge Aveyronnaise (12ᵉ)

Basque
Ami Jean (7ᵉ)
Auberge Etchégorry (13ᵉ)
Bascou (3ᵉ)
Casa Alcalde (15ᵉ)
Dauphin (1ᵉʳ)
Plancha (11ᵉ)
P'tit Troquet (7ᵉ)
Souletin (Le) (1ᵉʳ)

Berry
Berry's (8ᵉ)
Quincy (12ᵉ)

Brittany/Charente
Cagouille (14ᵉ)
Crêperie de Josselin (14ᵉ)
Divellec (7ᵉ)
Michel (10ᵉ)
Ty Coz (9ᵉ)

Burgundy
Bourguignon du Marais (4ᵉ)
Crus de Bourgogne (2ᵉ)
Ferme des Mathurins (8ᵉ)
Ma Bourgogne (4ᵉ, 8ᵉ)
Pierre (15ᵉ)
Récamier (7ᵉ)
Relais Chablisien (1ᵉʳ)
Tante Jeanne (17ᵉ)
Tante Louise (8ᵉ)
Tante Marguerite (7ᵉ)

Corsica
Alivi (4ᵉ)
Casa Corsa (6ᵉ)
Paris Main d'Or (11ᵉ)
Vivario (5ᵉ)

Lyons
Assiette Lyonnaise (1ᵉʳ, 8ᵉ)
Auberge Bressane (7ᵉ)
Bellecour (7ᵉ)
Bistrot d'Alex (6ᵉ)
Bons Crus (1ᵉʳ)
Cartet Restaurant (11ᵉ)
Fred (17ᵉ)
Lyonnais (2ᵉ)
Marcel (6ᵉ)
Moissonnier (5ᵉ)
Monttessuy (7ᵉ)
Paul (13ᵉ)
Petit Mâchon (1ᵉʳ, 15ᵉ)
René (5ᵉ)
Rôtisserie du Beaujolais (5ᵉ)
Saint Vincent (15ᵉ)

Mediterranean/Provence
Aimant du Sud (13ᵉ)
Bastide Odéon (6ᵉ)
Bistro de l'Olivier (8ᵉ)
Bistrot d'Albert (17ᵉ)
Bistrot d'Alex (6ᵉ)
Campagne et Provence (5ᵉ)
Casa Olympe (9ᵉ)
Coco et sa Maison (17ᵉ)
Côté Soleil (1ᵉʳ)
Elysées du Vernet (8ᵉ)
Janou (3ᵉ)
Languedoc (5ᵉ)
Marines (17ᵉ)
Olivades (7ᵉ)
Pavillon des Princes (16ᵉ)
Persiennes (8ᵉ)
Quinson (15ᵉ)
Réconfort (3ᵉ)
Senteurs de Provence (15ᵉ)

Sept Quinze (15ᵉ)
Signatures (8ᵉ)
Sud (17ᵉ)
Toutoune (5ᵉ)
Truffe Noire (Neuilly)

Normandy
Fernandises (11ᵉ)
Pharamond (1ᵉʳ)

Southwest
Ambassade du Sud-Ouest (7ᵉ)
Auberge Etchégorry (13ᵉ)
Auberge Landaise (9ᵉ)
Aub. Pyrénées Cévennes (L') (11ᵉ)
Baracane (4ᵉ)
Café Faubourg (8ᵉ)
Carré des Feuillants (1ᵉʳ)
Chez Eux (7ᵉ)
Comte de Gascogne (Boulogne)
Dauphin (1ᵉʳ)
Espace Sud-Ouest (8ᵉ, 10ᵉ, 14ᵉ, 15ᵉ)
Fermette du Sud-Ouest (1ᵉʳ)
Flambée (12ᵉ)
Florimond (7ᵉ)
Fontaine de Mars (7ᵉ)
Grand Louvre (1ᵉʳ)
Grizzli (4ᵉ)
Hélène Darroze (6ᵉ)
Il était une Oie (17ᵉ)
Jacquot de Bayonne (12ᵉ)
Joséphine "Chez Dumonet" (6ᵉ)
Oulette (12ᵉ)
Quercy (9ᵉ)
Régalade (14ᵉ)
Rest. du Marché (15ᵉ)
Sarladais (8ᵉ)
Sousceyrac (A) (11ᵉ)
Thoumieux (7ᵉ)
Trou Gascon (12ᵉ)
Truffe Noire (Neuilly)
Truffière (5ᵉ)

French: Seafood
Aristippe (1ᵉʳ)
Auberge des Dolomites (17ᵉ)
Augusta (17ᵉ)
Bar à Huîtres (3ᵉ, 5ᵉ, 14ᵉ)
Bar au Sel (7ᵉ)
Bistrot d'à Côté (5ᵉ, 17ᵉ, Neuilly)
Bistrot de Marius (8ᵉ)
Bistrot du Dôme (4ᵉ, 14ᵉ)
Boucholeurs (1ᵉʳ)
Cagouille (14ᵉ)
Cap Seguin (Boulogne)
Cap Vernet (8ᵉ)

Charlot - Roi/Coquillages (9ᵉ)
Coco de Mer (5ᵉ)
Comptoir/Saumon (4ᵉ, 8ᵉ, 15ᵉ, 17ᵉ)
Dessirier (17ᵉ)
Divellec (7ᵉ)
Dôme (14ᵉ)
Duc (14ᵉ)
Ecaille et Plume (7ᵉ)
Espadon Bleu (6ᵉ)
Filoche (15ᵉ)
Francis (8ᵉ)
Frégate (12ᵉ)
Gaya, L'Estaminet (1ᵉʳ)
Gaya Rive Gauche (7ᵉ)
Glénan (7ᵉ)
Goumard (1ᵉʳ)
Huitrier (17ᵉ)
Iles Marquises (14ᵉ)
Jarasse (Neuilly)
Luna (8ᵉ)
Maison Prunier (16ᵉ)
Marée (8ᵉ)
Marée de Versailles (Versailles)
Marines (17ᵉ)
Marius (16ᵉ)
Marius et Janette (8ᵉ)
Méditerranée (6ᵉ)
Moniage Guillaume (14ᵉ)
Ostréade (15ᵉ)
Paul Minchelli (7ᵉ)
Petit Navire (5ᵉ)
Petit Niçois (7ᵉ)
Petrossian (7ᵉ)
Pétrus (17ᵉ)
Pichet (8ᵉ)
Plage Parisienne (15ᵉ)
Port Alma (16ᵉ)
Quinson (15ᵉ)
Senteurs de Provence (15ᵉ)
Stella Maris (8ᵉ)
Sud (17ᵉ)
Taïra (17ᵉ)
Ty Coz (9ᵉ)
Vin et Marée (7ᵉ, 11ᵉ, 14ᵉ, 16ᵉ)

French: Shellfish

Alcazar (6ᵉ)
Alsace (8ᵉ)
Arbuci (6ᵉ)
Auberge Dab (16ᵉ)
Ballon des Ternes (17ᵉ)
Bar à Huîtres (3ᵉ, 5ᵉ, 14ᵉ)
Bistrot de Marius (8ᵉ)
Bofinger (4ᵉ)
Brasserie Flo (10ᵉ)

Brasserie Lorraine (8ᵉ)
Brasserie Lutétia (6ᵉ)
Brasserie Mollard (8ᵉ)
Cagouille (14ᵉ)
Cap Vernet (8ᵉ)
Charlot - Roi/Coquillages (9ᵉ)
Chien qui Fume (1ᵉʳ)
Chope d'Alsace (6ᵉ)
Club Matignon (8ᵉ)
Congrès (17ᵉ)
Coupole (14ᵉ)
Dagorno (19ᵉ)
Dessirier (17ᵉ)
Dôme (14ᵉ)
Goumard (1ᵉʳ)
Huitrier (17ᵉ)
Jarasse (Neuilly)
Maison Prunier (16ᵉ)
Marius et Janette (8ᵉ)
Marty (5ᵉ)
Petit Lutétia (6ᵉ)
Petit Riche (9ᵉ)
Petit Zinc (6ᵉ)
Pétrus (17ᵉ)
Pichet (8ᵉ)
Rech (17ᵉ)
Sébillon Élysées (8ᵉ)
Sébillon Neuilly (Neuilly)
Taverne Kronenbourg (9ᵉ)
Vagenende (6ᵉ)
Wepler (18ᵉ)
Zeyer (14ᵉ)

French: Steakhouse

Anahï (3ᵉ)
Bœuf Couronné (19ᵉ)
Charpentiers (6ᵉ)
Chez Eux (7ᵉ)
Dagorno (19ᵉ)
Denise (1ᵉʳ)
Entrecôte (7ᵉ)
Gavroche (2ᵉ)
Gourmets des Ternes (8ᵉ)
Hippopotamus (1ᵉʳ, 2ᵉ, 4ᵉ, 5ᵉ, 6ᵉ,
      8ᵉ, 14ᵉ, Puteaux)
Mascotte (8ᵉ)
Opportun (14ᵉ)
Relais de l'Entrecôte (6ᵉ, 8ᵉ)
Relais de Venise (17ᵉ)
René (5ᵉ)
Robert et Louise (3ᵉ)
Rôtisserie (Levallois)
Rôtisserie d'Armaillé (17ᵉ)
Rôtisserie d'en Face (6ᵉ)

Rôtisserie du Beaujolais (5e)
Rôtisserie Monsigny (2e)

French: Tearoom

Angelina (1er)
Antiquaires (7e)
A Priori Thé (2e)
Arbre à Cannelle (2e, 5e)
Bernardaud (8e)
Cour de Rohan (6e)
Dalloyau (6e, 8e, 15e)
Deux Abeilles (7e)
Enfants Gâtés (4e)
Je Thé...Me (15e)
Ladurée (8e, 9e)
Loir dans la Théière (4e)
Mariage Frères (4e, 6e, 8e)
Muscade (1er)

French: Wine Bar/Bistro

Bacchantes (9e)
Baron Rouge (12e)
Bons Crus (1er)
Bourguignon du Marais (4e)
Café du Passage (11e)
Cloche des Halles (1er)
Dix Vins (15e)
Ecluse (6e, 8e, 11e, 17e)
Enoteca (4e)
Escale (4e)
Griffonnier (8e)
Jacques Mélac (11e)
Juvenile's (1er)
Ma Bourgogne (8e)
Mauzac (5e)
Oenothèque (9e)
Passage (11e)
Sauvignon (7e)
Taverne Henri IV (1er)
Vin sur Vin (7e)
Willi's Wine Bar (1er)

German

Brasserie Munichoise (1er)

Greek

Délices d'Aphrodite (5e)
Diamantaires (9e)
Mavrommatis (5e)

Hamburger

Chicago Meatpackers (1er)
Coffee Parisien (6e, 16e)
Joe Allen (1er)
Planet Hollywood (8e)

Health Food

Bon (16e)
Ferme (1er)
Grenier de Notre Dame (5e)
Safran (1er)

Indian

Annapurna (8e)
Indra (8e)
Lalqila (15e)
Maharajah (5e)
New Jawad (7e)
Ravi (7e)

Italian

Bartolo (6e)
Bauta (6e)
Beato (7e)
Bellini (16e)
Ca d'Oro (1er)
Cafetière (6e)
Caffé Toscano (7e)
Cailloux (13e)
Casa Bini (6e)
Cherche Midi (6e)
Conti (16e)
Cosi (6e)
Da Mimmo (10e)
Emporio Armani Caffé (6e)
Enoteca (4e)
Fellini (1er, 15e)
Findi (8e)
Finzi (8e)
Fontanarosa (15e)
Gildo (7e)
Giulio Rebellato (16e)
Grand Venise (15e)
I Golosi (9e)
Il Barone (14e)
Il Carpaccio (8e)
Il Cortile (1er)
Il Ristorante (17e)
Il Sardo (9e)
Livio (Neuilly)
Moulin/Galette Graziano (18e)
Ostéria (4e)
Paolo Petrini (17e)
Paparazzi (9e)
Perron (7e)
Petit Mabillon (6e)
Romantica (Clichy)
Rughetta (18e)
Scusi (8e)
Signorelli (1er)
Sormani (17e)

Stresa (8ᵉ)
Trentaquattro (7ᵉ)
Véranda (8ᵉ)
Vincent (19ᵉ)
Vinci (16ᵉ)
Zinzins (2ᵉ)

Japanese
Benkay (15ᵉ)
Foujita (1ᵉʳ)
Higuma (1ᵉʳ)
Inagiku (5ᵉ)
Isami (4ᵉ)
Isse (2ᵉ)
Kinugawa (1ᵉʳ, 8ᵉ)
Lô Sushi (8ᵉ)
Orient-Extrême (6ᵉ)
Shozan (8ᵉ)
Sushi One (8ᵉ)
Taka (18ᵉ)
Tsukizi (6ᵉ)

Jewish
Jo Goldenberg (4ᵉ)
Marianne (4ᵉ)
Patrick Goldenberg (17ᵉ)
Pitchi Poï (4ᵉ)

Latin American
Anahï (3ᵉ)
Anahuacalli (5ᵉ)
Barrio Latino (12ᵉ)
Churrasco (17ᵉ)
Milonga (6ᵉ)
Palanquin (6ᵉ)

Lebanese
Al Dar (5ᵉ, 16ᵉ)
Al Diwan (8ᵉ)
Byblos Café (16ᵉ)
Fakhr el Dine (8ᵉ, 16ᵉ)
Noura (6ᵉ)
Noura Pavillon (16ᵉ)

Mexican
Anahuacalli (5ᵉ)
Ay!! Caramba!! (19ᵉ)

Middle Eastern
Persiennes (8ᵉ)

Moroccan
Al Mounia (16ᵉ)
Amazigh (16ᵉ)
Atlas (5ᵉ)
Caroubier (15ᵉ)
Comptoir Paris-Marrakech (1ᵉʳ)

El Mansour (8ᵉ)
Etoile Marocaine (8ᵉ)
Mansouria (11ᵉ)
Maroc (1ᵉʳ)
Omar (3ᵉ)
Oum el Banine (16ᵉ)
Pied de Chameau (4ᵉ)
404 (3ᵉ)
Timgad (17ᵉ)
Wally Le Saharien (9ᵉ)

Pizza
Bartolo (6ᵉ)
Chicago Pizza Pie Factory (8ᵉ)
Da Mimmo (10ᵉ)
Paparazzi (9ᵉ)

Portuguese
Albert (6ᵉ)
Juvenile's (1ᵉʳ)
Saudade (1ᵉʳ)

Russian
Daru (8ᵉ)
Dominique (6ᵉ)
Maison du Caviar (8ᵉ)
Petrossian (7ᵉ)

Sandwich Shop
Café Véry (1ᵉʳ)
Cosi (6ᵉ)
Dame Tartine (4ᵉ, 12ᵉ)
Ferme (1ᵉʳ)
Lina's (1ᵉʳ, 2ᵉ, 6ᵉ, 8ᵉ, 9ᵉ, 12ᵉ, 17ᵉ,
   Neuilly, Puteaux)
Scusi (8ᵉ)

Scandinavian
Café des Lettres (7ᵉ)
Comptoir du Saumon (4ᵉ, 8ᵉ, 15ᵉ, 17ᵉ)
Copenhague (8ᵉ)
Flora Danica (8ᵉ)
Petite Sirène (9ᵉ)
Petrossian (7ᵉ)

Seychelles
Coco de Mer (5ᵉ)

Spanish
Casa Alcalde (15ᵉ)
Casa Tina (16ᵉ)
Catalogne (La) (6ᵉ)
El Picador (17ᵉ)
Fogón Saint Julien (5ᵉ)
Juvenile's (1ᵉʳ)
Olé Bodéga! (12ᵉ)

Pavillon Puebla (19ᵉ)
Plancha (11ᵉ)
Rosimar (16ᵉ)
San Valero (Neuilly)

Tex-Mex
Indiana Café (2ᵉ, 3ᵉ, 6ᵉ, 8ᵉ, 9ᵉ, 11ᵉ, 14ᵉ)
Studio (4ᵉ)

Thai
Baan-Boran (1er)
Bains (3ᵉ)
Blue Elephant (11ᵉ)
Chieng Mai (5ᵉ)
Erawan (15ᵉ)
Khun Akorn (11ᵉ)
Lao Siam (19ᵉ)
Livingstone (1er)

Sawadee (15ᵉ)
Village d'Ung et Li Lam (8ᵉ)

Vegetarian
Bon (16ᵉ)
Enfants Gâtés (4ᵉ)
Grenier de Notre Dame (5ᵉ)

Vietnamese
Baie d'Ha Long (16ᵉ)
Coin des Gourmets (5ᵉ)
Kim Anh (15ᵉ)
Kim Lien (5ᵉ)
Lac-Hong (16ᵉ)
Palanquin (6ᵉ)
Soun (16ᵉ)
Tan Dinh (7ᵉ)
Vong (1er)

LOCATIONS
(by arrondissement)

1st arrondissement
Absinthe
Angelina
Ardoise
Argenteuil
Aristippe
Armand au Palais Royal
Assiette Lyonnaise
Atelier Berger
Baan-Boran
Bar Vendôme
Bons Crus
Boucholeurs
Brasserie du Louvre
Brasserie Munichoise
Ca d'Oro
Café de Vendôme
Café Marly
Café Ruc
Café Véry
Carré des Feuillants
Carr's
Cartes Postales
Caveau du Palais
Chicago Meatpackers
Chien qui Fume
Cloche des Halles
Clovis
Colette
Comptoir Paris-Marrakech
Costes
Côté Soleil
Dauphin
Davé
Denise
Diable des Lombards
Epi d'Or
Escargot Montorgueil
Espadon
Fabrice
Fellini
Ferme
Fermette du Sud-Ouest
Foujita
Fumoir
Gaudriole
Gaya, L'Estaminet
Gérard Besson
Goumard
Grand Louvre
Grand Véfour

Grille St-Honoré
Higuma
Hippopotamus
Il Cortile
Joe Allen
Juvenile's
Kinugawa
Léon de Bruxelles
Lescure
Lina's
Livingstone
Macéo
Maroc
Meurice
Muscade
Paul
Pauline
Petit Mâchon
Pharamond
Pied de Cochon
Pierre au Palais Royal
Pluvinel
Poquelin
Poule au Pot
Relais Chablisien
Rest. du Palais Royal
Robe et le Palais
Rubis
Safran
Saudade
Signorelli
Soufflé
Souletin (Le)
Taverne de Maître Kanter
Taverne Henri IV
Toupary
Vieille
Vong
Willi's Wine Bar

2nd arrondissement
A Priori Thé
Arbre à Cannelle
Bistrot du Louvre
Café Runtz
Céladon
Clément
Clémentine
Crus de Bourgogne
Drouant
Gallopin

Gavroche
Georges
Grand Colbert
Grille Montorgueil
Hippopotamus
Indiana Café
Isse
Kitty O'Sheas
Lina's
Lyonnais
Noces de Jeannette
Passy Mandarin
Petit Coin de la Bourse
"Pierre" A la Fontaine
Rôtisserie Monsigny
Vaudeville
Zinzins

3rd arrondissement

Ambassade d'Auvergne
Ami Louis
Anahï
Auberge Nicolas Flamel
Bains
Bar à Huîtres
Bascou
Buffalo Grill
Camille
Guirlande de Julie
Hangar
Indiana Café
Janou
Jenny
Marais-Cage
Nénesse
Omar
Pamphlet
404
Réconfort
Robert et Louise

4th arrondissement

Alivi
Amadéo
Ambroisie
Baracane
Benoît
Bistrot du Dôme
Bofinger
Bourguignon du Marais
Brasserie de l'Ile St. Louis
Café Beaubourg
Café Louis Philippe
Clément
Coconnas
Comptoir du Saumon

Coude Fou
Dame Tartine
Dos de la Baleine
Enfants Gâtés
Enoteca
Escale
Excuse
Flore en l'Ile
Fous d'en Face
Gamin de Paris
Georges
Gourmet de l'Isle
Grizzli
Hippopotamus
Isami
Jo Goldenberg
Léon de Bruxelles
Loir dans la Théière
Ma Bourgogne
Mariage Frères
Marianne
Monde des Chimères
Orangerie
Ostéria
Petit Bofinger
Philosophes
Pied de Chameau
Pitchi Poï
Studio
Thanksgiving
Trumilou
Vieux Bistro
Woolloomooloo

5th arrondissement

Abélard
Al Dar
Anahuacalli
Arbre à Cannelle
Atelier Maître Albert
Atlas
Bar à Huîtres
Berthoud
Bistrot d'à Côté
Bouchons de Fr. Clerc
Brasserie Balzar
Bûcherie
Buffalo Grill
Campagne et Provence
Chantairelle
Chieng Mai
Coco de Mer
Coin des Gourmets
Coupe-Chou
Délices d'Aphrodite

Fogón Saint Julien
Fontaines
Grenier de Notre Dame
Hippopotamus
Inagiku
Kim Lien
Languedoc
Léna et Mimile
Maharajah
Maison
Marty
Mauzac
Mavrommatis
Mirama
Moissonnier
Moulin à Vent "Chez Henri"
Pactole
Palenque
Pento
Perraudin
Petit Navire
Petit Prince de Paris
Port du Salut
Réminet
René
Rôtisserie du Beaujolais
Tour d'Argent
Toutoune
Truffière
Vivario

6th arrondissement

Albert
Alcazar
Allard
Arbuci
Assassins
Bartolo
Bastide Odéon
Bauta
Bistro de la Grille
Bistrot d'Alex
Bistrot d'Henri
Bon Saint Pourçain
Bookinistes
Bouillon Racine
Brasserie Lipp
Brasserie Lutétia
Brézolles
Café de Flore
Café Les Deux Magots
Cafetière
Caméléon
Casa Bini
Casa Corsa

Casa del Habano
Catalogne (La)
Charpentiers
Chat Grippé
Cherche Midi
Chope d'Alsace
Christine
Closerie des Lilas
Coffee Parisien
Comptoir des Sports
Cosi
Cour de Rohan
Dalloyau
Diane
Dominique
Ecluse
Emporio Armani Caffé
En Ville
Epi Dupin
Espadon Bleu
Hélène Darroze
Hippopotamus
Indiana Café
Jacques Cagna
Joséphine "Chez Dumonet"
Lapérouse
Léon de Bruxelles
Lina's
Lozère
Maître Paul
Marcel
Mariage Frères
Marie et Fils
Marlotte
Maxence
Méditerranée
Milonga
Muniche
Nemrod
Noura
Orient-Extrême
Palanquin
Parc aux Cerfs
Paris
Petite Cour (La)
Petit Lutétia
Petit Mabillon
Petit St. Benoît
Petit Zinc
Polidor
Procope
Relais de l'Entrecôte
Relais Louis XIII
Rest. des Beaux Arts
Rond de Serviette

Rôtisserie d'en Face
Rotonde
Tsukizi
Vagenende
Wadja

7th arrondissement

Affriolé
Altitude 95
Ambassade du Sud-Ouest
Ami Jean
Antiquaires
Arpège
Auberge Bressane
Auberge du Champ de Mars
Babylone
Bamboche
Bar au Sel
Basilic
Beato
Bellecour
Bistrot de Breteuil
Bistrot de l'Université
Bistrot de Paris
Bon Accueil
Bourdonnais
Café de l'Esplanade (Le)
Café de Mars
Café des Lettres
Café Max
Caffé Toscano
Champ de Mars
Chez Eux
Cigale
Clos des Gourmets
Côté 7ème
Délices de Szechuen
Deux Abeilles
Divellec
Ecaille et Plume
Entrecôte
Ferme St-Simon
Fins Gourmets
Florimond
Fontaine de Mars
Françoise
Gaya Rive Gauche
Germaine
Gildo
Glénan
Jules Verne
Lao Tseu
Maison de l'Amérique
Maupertu
Michel Courtalhac

Montalembert
Monttessuy
New Jawad
Oeillade
Olivades
Paul Minchelli
Perron
Petite Chaise
Petit Laurent
Petit Niçois
Petrossian
Pied de Fouet
P'tit Troquet
Ravi
Récamier
Rest. du Musée d'Orsay
Ribe
Rouge Vif
Sauvignon
Sédillot
Tan Dinh
Tante Marguerite
Télégraphe
Thoumieux
Trentaquattro
Vin et Marée
Vin sur Vin
Violon d'Ingres
Voltaire

8th arrondissement

Ailleurs
Alain Ducasse
Al Diwan
Alsace
Ambassadeurs
André
Androuët
Annapurna
Appart'
Asian
Assiette Lyonnaise
Astor
Avenue
Bar des Théâtres
Barfly
Bath's
Bec Rouge
Bernardaud
Berry's
Bistro de l'Olivier
Bistrot de Marius
Bistrot du Sommelier
Bœuf sur le Toit
Bouchons de Fr. Clerc

Brasserie Lorraine
Brasserie Mollard
Bristol
Buddha Bar
Café Bleu
Café Faubourg
Café Indigo
Café M
Café Terminus
Cap Vernet
Caviar Kaspia
Cercle Ledoyen
Chiberta
Chicago Pizza Pie Factory
Cinq
Clément
Clovis (Le)
Club Matignon
Comptoir du Saumon
Copenhague
Cou de la Girafe
Dalloyau
Daru
Diep (Chez)
Doobie's
Drugstore Champs-Elysées
Ecluse
El Mansour
Elysées du Vernet
Espace Sud-Ouest
Etoile
Etoile Marocaine
Fakhr el Dine
Ferme des Mathurins
Ferme St-Hubert
Fermette Marbeuf 1900
Findi
Finzi
Flora Danica
Fouquet's
Francis
Gourmets des Ternes
Grenadin
Griffonnier
Hédiard
Hippopotamus
Homero
Il Carpaccio
Impala Lounge
Indiana Café
Indra
Jardin
Jardin des Cygnes
Kinugawa
Ladurée

Lasserre
Laurent
Ledoyen
Léon de Bruxelles
Lina's
Lô Sushi
Lucas Carton
Luna
Ma Bourgogne
Maison Blanche
Maison du Caviar
Mandarin
Man Ray
Marée
Mariage Frères
Marius et Janette
Mascotte
Maxim's
Obélisque
Pavillon Elysée
Persiennes
Pichet
Pierre Gagnaire
Planet Hollywood
Relais de l'Entrecôte
Relais Plaza
Restaurant W
Rocher Gourmand
Rue Balzac
Sarladais
Savy
Scusi
Sébillon Élysées
Shozan
Signatures
Spicy Restaurant
Spoon, Food & Wine
Stella Maris
Stresa
Sushi One
Taillevent
Tante Louise
Tong Yen
Véranda
Village d'Ung et Li Lam
Virgin Café
Vong
Yvan
Yvan, Petit

9th arrondissement
Alsaco
Auberge du Clou
Auberge Landaise
Bacchantes

Barramundi
Bistro de Gala
Bistro des Deux Théâtres
Bistrot Papillon
Buffalo Grill
Café de la Paix
Café Flo
Casa Olympe
Catherine
Cave Drouot
Charlot - Roi/Coquillages
Chartier
Cloche d'Or
Comédiens
Diamantaires
Grand Café des Capucines
Grange Batelière
I Golosi
Il Sardo
Indiana Café
Jean
Ladurée
Léon de Bruxelles
Lina's
Muses
Oenothèque
Paparazzi
Paprika
Petit Bofinger
Petite Sirène
Petit Riche
Poste
Quercy
Relais Beaujolais
Rest. Opéra
Roi du Pot-au-Feu
16 Haussmann
Table d'Anvers
Taverne Kronenbourg
Ty Coz
Wally Le Saharien

10th arrondissement
Brasserie Flo
Buffalo Grill
China Town Belleville
Da Mimmo
Deux Canards
Espace Sud-Ouest
Grille
Julien
Michel
Prune
Terminus Nord

11th arrondissement
Aiguière
Ami Pierre
Amognes
Astier
Auberge Pyrénées Cévennes (L')
Bistrot du Peintre
Blue Elephant
Café Charbon
Café de l'Industrie
Café du Passage
C'Amelot
Cartet Restaurant
Chardenoux
Clown Bar
Dame Jeanne
Ecluse
Fabrique
Fernandises
Galoche d'Aurillac
Indiana Café
Jacques Mélac
Jumeaux
Khun Akorn
Léon de Bruxelles
Mansouria
New Nioullaville
Paris Main d'Or
Passage
Paul
Petit Keller
Plancha
Président
Repaire de Cartouche
Sousceyrac (A)
Villaret
Vin et Marée
Wok Restaurant

12th arrondissement
Auberge Aveyronnaise
Baron Rouge
Barrio Latino
Biche au Bois
China Club
Dame Tartine
Ebauchoir
Flambée
Frégate
Grandes Marches
Jacquot de Bayonne
Lina's
Olé Bodéga!
Oulette
Pressoir

Quincy
Saint Amarante
Saint Pourçain
Sologne
Square Trousseau
Train Bleu
Trou Gascon
Viaduc Café
Vinea Café
Zygomates

13th arrondissement
Aimant du Sud
Anacréon
Auberge Etchégorry
Avant Goût
Buffalo Grill
Cailloux
China Town Olympiades
Entoto
Jacky
Nouveau Village Tao-Tao
Paul
Petit Marguery
Rest. La Zygothèque
Temps des Cerises
Terroir
Tricotin
Vieux Métiers de France

14th arrondissement
Amuse Bouche
Assiette
Bar à Huîtres
Bistrot du Dôme
Bonne Table
Buffalo Grill
Cagouille
Clément
Contre-Allée
Coupole
Crêperie de Josselin
Dôme
Duc
Entrepôt
Espace Sud-Ouest
Flamboyant
Hippopotamus
Il Barone
Iles Marquises
Indiana Café
Léon de Bruxelles
Maison Courtine
Mère Agitée
Moniage Guillaume
Monsieur Lapin

Montparnasse 25
Natacha
O à la Bouche
Opportun
Pavillon Montsouris
Petites Sorcières
Régalade
Rendez-vous/Camionneurs
Vendanges
Vin des Rues
Vin et Marée
Zeyer

15th arrondissement
Agape
Benkay
Bermuda Onion
Bistro 121
Bistro d'Hubert
Bistrot d'André
Bouchons de Fr. Clerc
Buffalo Grill
Café du Commerce
Caroubier
Casa Alcalde
Cave de l'Os à Moelle
Célébrités
Cévennes
Chen
Clément
Clos Morillons
Comptoir du Saumon
Dalloyau
Dînée
Dix Vins
Erawan
Espace Sud-Ouest
Fellini
Filoche
Fontanarosa
Gastroquet
Gauloise
Gitane
Grand Venise
Je Thé...Me
Kim Anh
Lalqila
Léon de Bruxelles
Morot-Gaudry
Os à Moelle
Ostréade
Pacific Eiffel
Père Claude
Petit Mâchon
Petit Plat

Philippe Detourbe
Pierre
Plage Parisienne
Quinson
Relais de Sèvres
Rest. de la Tour
Rest. du Marché
Saint Vincent
Sawadee
Senteurs de Provence
Sept Quinze
Stéphane Martin
Tire-Bouchon
Troquet
Yves Quintard

16th arrondissement
A et M Le Bistrot
Al Dar
Al Mounia
Amazigh
Auberge Dab
Baie d'Ha Long
Beaujolais d'Auteuil
Bellini
Bertie's
Bistrot de l'Etoile Lauriston
Bon
Bouchons de Fr. Clerc
Brasserie de la Poste
Brasserie Stella
Butte Chaillot
Byblos Café
Casa Tina
Chalet des Iles
Coffee Parisien
Conti
Cuisinier François
Detourbe Duret
Driver's
Fakhr el Dine
Faugeron
Flandrin
Floridita
Fontaine d'Auteuil
Gare
Giulio Rebellato
Grande Armée
Grande Cascade
Jamin
Jardins de Bagatelle
Kambodgia
Kiosque
Lac-Hong
Maison Prunier

Marius
Mathusalem
Ngo
Noura Pavillon
Ormes
Oum el Banine
Passy Mandarin
Paul Chêne
Pavillon des Princes
Pergolèse
Petite Tour
Petit Rétro
Petit Victor Hugo
Port Alma
Pré Catelan
Relais d'Auteuil
Relais du Parc
Rest. des Chauffeurs
Rest. Jean Bouin
Rosimar
Salle à Manger
Scheffer
Soun
Tang
Totem
Tournesol
Tsé-Yang
Vinci
Vin et Marée
Zebra Square

17th arrondissement
A et M Le Bistrot
Ampère
Amphyclès
Apicius
Aristide
Atelier Gourmand
Auberge des Dolomites
Augusta
Ballon des Ternes
Baumann Ternes
Béatilles
Beudant
Bistro du 17ème
Bistro Melrose
Bistrot d'à Côté
Bistrot d'Albert
Bistrot de l'Etoile Niel
Bistrot de l'Etoile Troyon
Bistrot St. Ferdinand
Bouchons de Fr. Clerc
Braisière
Buffalo Grill
Café d'Angel

Caves Pétrissans
Churrasco
Clément
Coco et sa Maison
Comptoir du Saumon
Congrès
Côte de Bœuf
Débarcadère
Dessirier
Ecluse
El Picador
Epicure 108
Faucher
Fred
Gazelle
Georges Porte Maillot
Graindorge
Guy Savoy
Huitrier
Il Baccello
Il était une Oie
Il Ristorante
Impatient
Improviste
Léon
Léon de Bruxelles
Lina's
Marines
Michel Rostang
Paolo Petrini
Patrick Goldenberg
Petit Bofinger
Petit Colombier
Pétrus
Rech
Relais de Venise
Rôtisserie d'Armaillé
Sormani
Soupière
Sud

Taïra
Tante Jeanne
Terrasses du Palais
Timgad
Toque
Troyon
Truite Vagabonde
Verre Bouteille

18th arrondissement

Beauvilliers (A.)
Bouclard
Cottage Marcadet
Entracte
Etrier
Marie-Louise
Moulin/Galette Graziano
Rendez-vous/Chauffeurs
Restaurant
Rughetta
Taka
Terrasse
Wepler

19th arrondissement

Ay!! Caramba!!
Bœuf Couronné
Buffalo Grill
Café de la Musique
Cave Gourmande
Dagorno
Lao Siam
Mandragore
Pavillon Puebla
Vincent

20th arrondissement

Allobroges
Boulangerie
Zéphyr

OUTLYING AREAS

Asnières-sur-Seine
Van Gogh

Bougival
Camélia
Clément

Boulogne-Billancourt
Cap Seguin
Clément
Comte de Gascogne
Ferme de Boulogne

Clichy
Romantica

Issy-les-Moulineaux
Ile
Manufacture
River Café

Joinville-le-Pont
Gégène

Le Pré-St-Gervais
Pouilly Reuilly

Levallois-Perret
Petit Poucet (Le)
Rôtisserie

Maisons-Laffitte
Tastevin
Vieille Fontaine Rôtisserie (La)

Neuilly-sur-Seine
Bistrot d'à Côté
Bistrot St. James
Café la Jatte
Carpe Diem
Catounière
Durand Dupont
FocLy
Gérard
Guinguette de Neuilly
Jarasse
Lina's
Livio
Mandarin de Neuilly
Petit Bofinger
San Valero
Sébillon Neuilly

Tonnelle Saintongeaise
Truffe Noire

Orly
Maxim's

Poissy
Table de Babette

Puteaux
Communautés
Hippopotamus
Lina's

Saint-Cloud
Quai Ouest

Saint-Germain-en-Laye
Cazaudehore La Forestière

Saint-Ouen
Coq/Maison Blanche

Versailles
Marée de Versailles
Potager du Roy
Trois Marches

SPECIAL FEATURES AND APPEALS

Breakfast
(All hotels and the
following standouts)
A Priori Thé (2ᵉ)
Arbuci (6ᵉ)
Bernardaud (8ᵉ)
Brasserie Balzar (5ᵉ)
Café Beaubourg (4ᵉ)
Café Bleu (8ᵉ)
Café de Flore (6ᵉ)
Café de la Musique (19ᵉ)
Café Indigo (8ᵉ)
Café Les Deux Magots (6ᵉ)
Café Marly (1ᵉʳ)
Café Ruc (1ᵉʳ)
Cave Drouot (9ᵉ)
Chalet des Iles (16ᵉ)
Chien qui Fume (1ᵉʳ)
Clément (2ᵉ, 4ᵉ, 8ᵉ, 14ᵉ, 15ᵉ, 17ᵉ)
Cloche des Halles (1ᵉʳ)
Closerie des Lilas (6ᵉ)
Colette (1ᵉʳ)
Congrès (17ᵉ)
Coupole (14ᵉ)
Dalloyau (6ᵉ, 8ᵉ, 15ᵉ)
Deux Abeilles (7ᵉ)
Diable des Lombards (1ᵉʳ)
Drugstore Champs-Elysées (8ᵉ)
Emporio Armani Caffé (6ᵉ)
Escale (4ᵉ)
Flandrin (16ᵉ)
Flore en l'Ile (4ᵉ)
Fontaines (5ᵉ)
Fouquet's (8ᵉ)
Grande Armée (16ᵉ)
Janou (3ᵉ)
Jardins de Bagatelle (16ᵉ)
Ladurée (8ᵉ)
Loir dans la Théière (4ᵉ)
Ma Bourgogne (4ᵉ)
Mauzac (5ᵉ)
Pacific Eiffel (15ᵉ)
Pavillon Puebla (19ᵉ)
Pied de Cochon (1ᵉʳ)
Planet Hollywood (8ᵉ)
Procope (6ᵉ)
Restaurant W (8ᵉ)
Taverne de Maître Kanter (1ᵉʳ)
Terminus Nord (10ᵉ)
Train Bleu (12ᵉ)
Vaudeville (2ᵉ)
Viaduc Café (12ᵉ)
Virgin Café (8ᵉ)

Brunch
(Best of many)
Alcazar (6ᵉ)
Al Diwan (8ᵉ)
Appart' (8ᵉ)
A Priori Thé (2ᵉ)
Bermuda Onion (15ᵉ)
Brasserie du Louvre (1ᵉʳ)
Café Beaubourg (4ᵉ)
Café Bleu (8ᵉ)
Café de la Musique (19ᵉ)
Café de Mars (7ᵉ)
Café des Lettres (7ᵉ)
Café Indigo (8ᵉ)
Carr's (1ᵉʳ)
Clovis (Le) (8ᵉ)
Comptoir Paris-Marrakech (1ᵉʳ)
Costes (1ᵉʳ)
Cour de Rohan (6ᵉ)
Dalloyau (6ᵉ, 8ᵉ, 15ᵉ)
Débarcadère (17ᵉ)
Diable des Lombards (1ᵉʳ)
Doobie's (8ᵉ)
Durand Dupont (Neuilly)
Enfants Gâtés (4ᵉ)
Fabrique (11ᵉ)
Flore en l'Ile (4ᵉ)
Fumoir (1ᵉʳ)
Grande Armée (16ᵉ)
Kiosque (16ᵉ)
Ladurée (8ᵉ)
Loir dans la Théière (4ᵉ)
Mariage Frères (8ᵉ)
Mauzac (5ᵉ)
Pacific Eiffel (15ᵉ)
Planet Hollywood (8ᵉ)
Quai Ouest (St-Cloud)
Rech (17ᵉ)
River Café (Issy-les-Moulineaux)
Studio (4ᵉ)
Thanksgiving (4ᵉ)
Véranda (8ᵉ)
Viaduc Café (12ᵉ)
Virgin Café (8ᵉ)
Zebra Square (16ᵉ)

Business Dining
Ailleurs (8ᵉ)
Alain Ducasse (8ᵉ)
Ambassadeurs (8ᵉ)
Ambroisie (4ᵉ)
Ami Louis (3ᵉ)
Amognes (11ᵉ)

Ampère (17e)
Amphyclès (17e)
André (8e)
Androuët (8e)
Antiquaires (7e)
Apicius (17e)
Appart' (8e)
Aristide (17e)
Armand au Palais Royal (1er)
Arpège (7e)
Assiette (14e)
Astor (8e)
Atelier Gourmand (17e)
Auberge Bressane (7e)
Auberge Dab (16e)
Auberge Nicolas Flamel (3e)
Augusta (17e)
Avenue (8e)
Baie d'Ha Long (16e)
Bamboche (7e)
Bar au Sel (7e)
Bar Vendôme (1er)
Basilic (7e)
Bastide Odéon (6e)
Baumann Ternes (17e)
Béatilles (17e)
Beaujolais d'Auteuil (16e)
Beauvilliers (A.) (18e)
Bellecour (7e)
Benkay (15e)
Berry's (8e)
Bertie's (16e)
Bistro de Gala (9e)
Bistro de l'Olivier (8e)
Bistro des Deux Théâtres (9e)
Bistro d'Hubert (15e)
Bistrot d'à Côté (5e, 17e, Neuilly)
Bistrot d'Albert (17e)
Bistrot d'Alex (6e)
Bistrot de l'Etoile Lauriston (16e)
Bistrot de l'Etoile Niel (17e)
Bistrot de l'Etoile Troyon (17e)
Bistrot de Marius (8e)
Bistrot du Sommelier (8e)
Bistrot St. Ferdinand (17e)
Bistrot St. James (Neuilly)
Blue Elephant (11e)
Bœuf Couronné (19e)
Bookinistes (6e)
Bouchons/Fr. Clerc (8e, 15e, 17e)
Bourdonnais (7e)
Braisière (17e)
Brasserie Balzar (5e)
Brasserie du Louvre (1er)
Brasserie Flo (10e)

Brasserie Lipp (6e)
Brasserie Lorraine (8e)
Brasserie Mollard (8e)
Brézolles (6e)
Bristol (8e)
Bûcherie (5e)
Café Bleu (8e)
Café de Vendôme (1er)
Café Faubourg (8e)
Café Indigo (8e)
Café M (8e)
Café Marly (1er)
Café Terminus (8e)
Cagouille (14e)
Camélia (Bougival)
Cap Seguin (Boulogne)
Cap Vernet (8e)
Carpe Diem (Neuilly)
Carré des Feuillants (1er)
Cartes Postales (1er)
Casa del Habano (6e)
Catounière (Neuilly)
Caves Pétrissans (17e)
Cazaudehore La Forestière
   (Saint-Germain-en-Laye)
Céladon (2e)
Célébrités (15e)
Cercle Ledoyen (8e)
Charlot - Roi/Coquillages (9e)
Charpentiers (6e)
Chen (15e)
Cherche Midi (6e)
Chez Eux (7e)
Chiberta (8e)
Chieng Mai (5e)
Cinq (8e)
Clos Morillons (15e)
Clovis (1er)
Clovis (Le) (8e)
Comte de Gascogne (Boulogne)
Congrès (17e)
Conti (16e)
Copenhague (8e)
Coq/Maison Blanche (St-Ouen)
Costes (1er)
Côte de Bœuf (17e)
Côté 7ème (7e)
Cou de la Girafe (8e)
Cuisinier François (16e)
Dagorno (19e)
Dessirier (17e)
Detourbe Duret (16e)
Diep (Chez) (8e)
Dînée (15e)
Divellec (7e)

Dôme (14ᵉ)
Drouant (2ᵉ)
Duc (14ᵉ)
Durand Dupont (Neuilly)
Ecaille et Plume (7ᵉ)
Elysées du Vernet (8ᵉ)
Emporio Armani Caffé (6ᵉ)
En Ville (6ᵉ)
Epi Dupin (6ᵉ)
Espadon Bleu (6ᵉ)
Etoile (8ᵉ)
Fakhr el Dine (8ᵉ, 16ᵉ)
Faucher (17ᵉ)
Faugeron (16ᵉ)
Fellini (1ᵉʳ, 15ᵉ)
Ferme de Boulogne (Boulogne)
Ferme des Mathurins (8ᵉ)
Ferme St-Simon (7ᵉ)
Fermette Marbeuf 1900 (8ᵉ)
Findi (8ᵉ)
Finzi (8ᵉ)
Flambée (12ᵉ)
Flandrin (16ᵉ)
Flora Danica (8ᵉ)
Floridita (16ᵉ)
Florimond (7ᵉ)
FocLy (Neuilly)
Fontaine d'Auteuil (16ᵉ)
Fouquet's (8ᵉ)
Francis (8ᵉ)
Françoise (7ᵉ)
Fred (17ᵉ)
Gallopin (2ᵉ)
Gastroquet (15ᵉ)
Gauloise (15ᵉ)
Gaya, L'Estaminet (1ᵉʳ)
Gaya Rive Gauche (7ᵉ)
Georges (2ᵉ)
Georges Porte Maillot (17ᵉ)
Gérard Besson (1ᵉʳ)
Gitane (15ᵉ)
Glénan (7ᵉ)
Goumard (1ᵉʳ)
Gourmets des Ternes (8ᵉ)
Graindorge (17ᵉ)
Grand Colbert (2ᵉ)
Grande Armée (16ᵉ)
Grande Cascade (16ᵉ)
Grandes Marches (12ᵉ)
Grand Louvre (1ᵉʳ)
Grand Véfour (1ᵉʳ)
Grange Batelière (9ᵉ)
Grenadin (8ᵉ)
Grille St-Honoré (1ᵉʳ)
Guy Savoy (17ᵉ)

Hédiard (8ᵉ)
Huitrier (17ᵉ)
Il Barone (14ᵉ)
Il Carpaccio (8ᵉ)
Il Cortile (1ᵉʳ)
Il Ristorante (17ᵉ)
Indra (8ᵉ)
Isse (2ᵉ)
Jacques Cagna (6ᵉ)
Jamin (16ᵉ)
Jarasse (Neuilly)
Jardin (8ᵉ)
Joséphine "Chez Dumonet" (6ᵉ)
Jules Verne (7ᵉ)
Kambodgia (16ᵉ)
Kinugawa (1ᵉʳ, 8ᵉ)
Kiosque (16ᵉ)
Ladurée (8ᵉ)
Lapérouse (6ᵉ)
Lasserre (8ᵉ)
Laurent (8ᵉ)
Ledoyen (8ᵉ)
Lucas Carton (8ᵉ)
Luna (8ᵉ)
Ma Bourgogne (8ᵉ)
Maison du Caviar (8ᵉ)
Maison Prunier (16ᵉ)
Mandarin (8ᵉ)
Mandarin de Neuilly (Neuilly)
Mansouria (11ᵉ)
Manufacture (Issy-les-Moulineaux)
Marée (8ᵉ)
Marines (17ᵉ)
Marius (16ᵉ)
Marius et Janette (8ᵉ)
Marty (5ᵉ)
Mathusalem (16ᵉ)
Maxence (6ᵉ)
Maxim's (8ᵉ, Orly)
Méditerranée (6ᵉ)
Meurice (1ᵉʳ)
Michel Rostang (17ᵉ)
Moniage Guillaume (14ᵉ)
Montalembert (7ᵉ)
Morot-Gaudry (15ᵉ)
Muses (9ᵉ)
Noces de Jeannette (2ᵉ)
Obélisque (8ᵉ)
Oenothèque (9ᵉ)
Olivades (7ᵉ)
Orangerie (4ᵉ)
Oulette (12ᵉ)
Paolo Petrini (17ᵉ)
Paris (6ᵉ)
Passy Mandarin (2ᵉ, 16ᵉ)

Paul Chêne (16e)
Pauline (1er)
Paul Minchelli (7e)
Pavillon Elysée (8e)
Pergolèse (16e)
Petit Bofinger (4e)
Petit Colombier (17e)
Petite Tour (16e)
Petit Laurent (7e)
Petit Lutétia (6e)
Petit Marguery (13e)
Petit Poucet (Le) (Levallois)
Pichet (8e)
Pierre au Palais Royal (1er)
Pierre Gagnaire (8e)
Pluvinel (1er)
Port Alma (16e)
Pré Catelan (16e)
Pressoir (12e)
Quai Ouest (St-Cloud)
Quincy (12e)
Ravi (7e)
Récamier (7e)
Relais d'Auteuil (16e)
Relais de Sèvres (15e)
Relais du Parc (16e)
Relais Plaza (8e)
René (5e)
Rest. du Marché (15e)
Rest. Jean Bouin (16e)
Rest. Opéra (9e)
Rest. W (8e)
River Café (Issy-les-Moulineaux)
Rôtisserie (Levallois)
Rôtisserie d'Armaillé (17e)
Rôtisserie Monsigny (2e)
San Valero (Neuilly)
Savy (8e)
Scusi (8e)
Sébillon Élysées (8e)
Sébillon Neuilly (Neuilly)
16 Haussmann (9e)
Shozan (8e)
Signatures (8e)
Sormani (17e)
Sousceyrac (A) (11e)
Stella Maris (8e)
Stresa (8e)
Sud (17e)
Table d'Anvers (9e)
Taillevent (8e)
Taïra (17e)
Tan Dinh (7e)
Tang (16e)
Tante Jeanne (17e)

Tante Louise (8e)
Tante Marguerite (7e)
Taverne de Maître Kanter (1er)
Télégraphe (7e)
Terminus Nord (10e)
Terrasse (18e)
Tong Yen (8e)
Tonnelle Saintongeaise (Neuilly)
Toque (17e)
Tour d'Argent (5e)
Train Bleu (12e)
Trentaquattro (7e)
Trois Marches (Versailles)
Trou Gascon (12e)
Troyon (17e)
Truffe Noire (Neuilly)
Tsé-Yang (16e)
Ty Coz (9e)
Vaudeville (2e)
Vendanges (14e)
Véranda (8e)
Vieille (1er)
Vieux Bistro (4e)
Vieux Métiers de France (13e)
Vin et Marée (11e, 14e, 16e)
Violon d'Ingres (7e)
Vong (8e)
Yvan (8e)
Zebra Square (16e)

Caters
(Best of many)
Ailleurs (8e)
Amphyclès (17e)
Anahuacalli (5e)
A Priori Thé (2e)
Asian (8e)
Atelier Gourmand (17e)
Auberge du Clou (9e)
Baan-Boran (1er)
Baumann Ternes (17e)
Bistro 121 (15e)
Bistrot de l'Etoile Niel (17e)
Bistrot du Louvre (2e)
Bookinistes (6e)
Butte Chaillot (16e)
Caffé Toscano (7e)
Casa Tina (16e)
Coco de Mer (5e)
Coffee Parisien (6e, 16e)
Coin des Gourmets (5e)
Coq/Maison Blanche (St-Ouen)
Dalloyau (6e, 8e, 15e)
Diep (Chez) (8e)
Dînée (15e)

Dos de la Baleine (4ᵉ)
Fabrice (1ᵉʳ)
Fakhr el Dine (8ᵉ, 16ᵉ)
Faucher (17ᵉ)
Findi (8ᵉ)
Glénan (7ᵉ)
Jacky (Chez) (13ᵉ)
Jo Goldenberg (4ᵉ)
Ladurée (8ᵉ, 9ᵉ)
Lalqila (15ᵉ)
Livio (Neuilly)
Maison Prunier (16ᵉ)
Mandarin (8ᵉ)
Maroc (1ᵉʳ)
Mavrommatis (5ᵉ)
Milonga (6ᵉ)
Noura Pavillon (16ᵉ)
Ormes (16ᵉ)
Oum el Banine (16ᵉ)
Passy Mandarin (2ᵉ, 16ᵉ)
Pauline (1ᵉʳ)
Petit Mâchon (1ᵉʳ, 15ᵉ)
Pied de Chameau (4ᵉ)
Relais Louis XIII (6ᵉ)
Rosimar (16ᵉ)
Soupière (17ᵉ)
Thanksgiving (4ᵉ)
Thoumieux (7ᵉ)
Troyon (17ᵉ)
Vong (1ᵉʳ, 8ᵉ)
Wally Le Saharien (9ᵉ)

Dancing/Entertainment

(Check days, times and performers for entertainment; D=dancing; best of many)
Abélard (5ᵉ) (classical)
Alcazar (6ᵉ) (music)
Al Diwan (8ᵉ) (music)
Amadéo (4ᵉ) (opera)
Annapurna (8ᵉ) (sitar)
Arbuci (6ᵉ) (D/jazz)
Asian (8ᵉ) (DJ)
Assassins (6ᵉ) (piano)
Aub. Nicolas Flamel (3ᵉ) (theater)
Ay!! Caramba!! (19ᵉ) (music)
Barfly (8ᵉ) (DJ)
Barramundi (9ᵉ) (DJ)
Barrio Latino (12ᵉ) (Latin music)
Bar Vendôme (1ᵉʳ) (harp/piano)
Bistrot de l'Etoile Lauriston (16ᵉ) (magician)
Bœuf sur le Toit (8ᵉ) (bass/piano)
Bookinistes (6ᵉ) (magician)
Bouillon Racine (6ᵉ) (piano)

Café de la Musique (19ᵉ) (D/jazz/world)
Café Faubourg (8ᵉ) (D)
Cap Seguin (Boulogne) (piano)
Cap Vernet (8ᵉ) (magic)
Carr's (1ᵉʳ) (Celtic)
Casa Alcalde (15ᵉ) (Spanish)
Chicago Pizza Pie Factory (8ᵉ) (DJ)
China Club (12ᵉ) (jazz)
China Town Belleville (10ᵉ) (D/karaoke)
China Town Olympiades (13ᵉ) (karaoke)
Closerie des Lilas (6ᵉ) (piano)
Costes (1ᵉʳ) (DJ)
Côté Soleil (1ᵉʳ) (singer/piano)
Deux Canards (10ᵉ) (piano)
Diamantaires (9ᵉ) (music)
Elysées du Vernet (8ᵉ) (harp/piano)
Entrepôt (14ᵉ) (music)
Espadon (1ᵉʳ) (violins)
Fabrique (11ᵉ) (DJ)
Flamboyant (14ᵉ) (music)
Françoise (7ᵉ) (jazz)
Gégène (Joinville) (D)
Georges Porte Maillot (17ᵉ) (piano)
Grille (10ᵉ) (gypsy)
Impala Lounge (8ᵉ) (DJ)
Jardins de Bagatelle (16ᵉ) (D)
Jenny (3ᵉ) (D)
Jo Goldenberg (4ᵉ) (gypsy)
Jules Verne (7ᵉ) (piano)
Kitty O'Sheas (2ᵉ) (Irish)
Lasserre (8ᵉ) (piano)
Maroc (1ᵉʳ) (dancers)
Maxim's (8ᵉ) (D)
Milonga (6ᵉ) (Argentine)
Olé Bodéga! (12ᵉ) (Spanish)
Pacific Eiffel (15ᵉ) (music)
Paprika (9ᵉ) (Hungarian)
Pavillon des Princes (16ᵉ) (D)
Pied de Chameau (4ᵉ) (D/belly dancers)
Poquelin (1ᵉʳ) (classical)
Poste (9ᵉ) (music)
Relais Plaza (8ᵉ) (piano)
Saudade (1ᵉʳ) (fado)
Télégraphe (7ᵉ) (jazz)
Timgad (17ᵉ) (music)
Viaduc Café (12ᵉ) (jazz brunch)
Vinea Café (12ᵉ) (jazz)

Dining Alone

(Other than hotels)

Abélard (5e)
Agape (15e)
Alcazar (6e)
Al Dar (16e)
Al Diwan (8e)
Allard (6e)
Al Mounia (16e)
Alsaco (9e)
Ambassade d'Auvergne (3e)
Ami Jean (7e)
Anacréon (13e)
Anahuacalli (5e)
Arbuci (6e)
Argenteuil (1er)
Aristide (17e)
Armand au Palais Royal (1er)
Asian (8e)
Assiette Lyonnaise (1er, 8e)
Auberge des Dolomites (17e)
Avenue (8e)
Baie d'Ha Long (16e)
Ballon des Ternes (17e)
Baracane (4e)
Bar à Huîtres (3e, 5e, 14e)
Bar au Sel (7e)
Bar des Théâtres (8e)
Basilic (7e)
Baumann Ternes (17e)
Beato (7e)
Beaujolais d'Auteuil (16e)
Bellecour (7e)
Beudant (17e)
Biche au Bois (12e)
Bistro 121 (15e)
Bistro de Gala (9e)
Bistro de l'Olivier (8e)
Bistro des Deux Théâtres (9e)
Bistro du 17ème (17e)
Bistrot d'à Côté (5e, 17e, Neuilly)
Bistrot de l'Etoile Lauriston (16e)
Bistrot de l'Etoile Niel (17e)
Bistrot de l'Etoile Troyon (17e)
Bistrot de l'Université (7e)
Bistrot de Marius (8e)
Bistrot de Paris (7e)
Bistrot d'Henri (6e)
Bistrot du Louvre (2e)
Bistrot du Peintre (11e)
Bistrot St. Ferdinand (17e)
Bœuf Couronné (19e)
Bœuf sur le Toit (8e)
Bofinger (4e)
Bon Accueil (7e)

Bon Saint Pourçain (6e)
Bons Crus (1er)
Braisière (17e)
Brasserie Lorraine (8e)
Brasserie Mollard (8e)
Brasserie Munichoise (1er)
Brasserie Stella (16e)
Bûcherie (5e)
Ca d'Oro (1er)
Café Beaubourg (4e)
Café Charbon (11e)
Café de Flore (6e)
Café de la Musique (19e)
Café de l'Industrie (11e)
Café de Mars (7e)
Café des Lettres (7e)
Café du Passage (11e)
Café Les Deux Magots (6e)
Café Louis Philippe (4e)
Café Marly (1er)
Café Ruc (1er)
Café Runtz (2e)
Café Terminus (8e)
Cafetière (6e)
Café Véry (1er)
Cagouille (14e)
Caméléon (6e)
Campagne et Provence (5e)
Cap Seguin (Boulogne)
Carpe Diem (Neuilly)
Carr's (1er)
Casa del Habano (6e)
Catherine (9e)
Catounière (Neuilly)
Cave Drouot (9e)
Caviar Kaspia (8e)
Cévennes (15e)
Champ de Mars (7e)
Chantairelle (5e)
Chardenoux (11e)
Charlot - Roi/Coquillages (9e)
Charpentiers (6e)
Chat Grippé (6e)
Chicago Meatpackers (1er)
Chieng Mai (5e)
Chien qui Fume (1er)
Chope d'Alsace (6e)
Cigale (7e)
Clément (2e, 4e, 8e, 14e, 15e, 17e)
Cloche d'Or (9e)
Clos des Gourmets (7e)
Closerie des Lilas (6e)
Clovis (1er)
Clown Bar (11e)
Coconnas (4e)

Coffee Parisien (6e)
Coin des Gourmets (5e)
Colette (1er)
Comptoir du Saumon (4e, 8e, 15e, 17e)
Congrès (17e)
Cosi (6e)
Côté Soleil (1er)
Coude Fou (4e)
Coupole (14e)
Crêperie de Josselin (14e)
Dagorno (19e)
Dame Tartine (12e)
Délices d'Aphrodite (5e)
Délices de Szechuen (7e)
Deux Canards (10e)
Diamantaires (9e)
Diep (Chez) (8e)
Divellec (7e)
Dominique (6e)
Dos de la Baleine (4e)
Drugstore Champs-Elysées (8e)
Ecluse (6e, 8e, 11e, 17e)
Entoto (13e)
Entracte (18e)
Entrecôte (7e)
En Ville (6e)
Epi d'Or (1er)
Epi Dupin (6e)
Erawan (15e)
Escale (4e)
Escargot Montorgueil (1er)
Espadon Bleu (6e)
Etoile (8e)
Etoile Marocaine (8e)
Etrier (18e)
Excuse (4e)
Fakhr el Dine (8e, 16e)
Fellini (1er, 15e)
Ferme de Boulogne (Boulogne)
Ferme des Mathurins (8e)
Ferme St-Hubert (8e)
Ferme St-Simon (7e)
Fermette du Sud-Ouest (1er)
Fernandises (11e)
Findi (8e)
Fins Gourmets (7e)
Finzi (8e)
Flambée (12e)
Flandrin (16e)
Flore en l'Ile (4e)
Floridita (16e)
Fontaines (5e)
Fouquet's (8e)
Fous d'en Face (4e)
Françoise (7e)

Gallopin (2e)
Gaudriole (1er)
Gauloise (15e)
Gaya, L'Estaminet (1er)
Georges (2e)
Gérard (Neuilly)
Giulio Rebellato (16e)
Glénan (7e)
Goumard (1er)
Gourmet de l'Isle (4e)
Grand Café des Capucines (9e)
Grand Colbert (2e)
Grande Armée (16e)
Grandes Marches (12e)
Grenadin (8e)
Grizzli (4e)
Hédiard (8e)
Higuma (1er)
Huitrier (17e)
I Golosi (9e)
Il Barone (14e)
Ile (Issy-les-Moulineaux)
Il était une Oie (17e)
Inagiku (5e)
Indiana Café (2e)
Indra (8e)
Isami (4e)
Isse (2e)
Jacky (Chez) (13e)
Jacques Mélac (11e)
Jean (9e)
Jenny (3e)
Je Thé...Me (15e)
Joe Allen (1er)
Joséphine "Chez Dumonet" (6e)
Jumeaux (11e)
Juvenile's (1er)
Kim Lien (5e)
Kinugawa (1er)
Kitty O'Sheas (2e)
Ladurée (8e)
Languedoc (5e)
Lao Tseu (7e)
Ledoyen (8e)
Léna et Mimile (5e)
Léon de Bruxelles (1er, 4e)
Lina's (8e)
Livio (Neuilly)
Loir dans la Théière (4e)
Lô Sushi (8e)
Lucas Carton (8e)
Luna (8e)
Lyonnais (2e)
Ma Bourgogne (4e)
Macéo (1er)

Maison Prunier (16ᵉ)
Maître Paul (6ᵉ)
Mandarin (8ᵉ)
Mandarin de Neuilly (Neuilly)
Marcel (6ᵉ)
Marée (8ᵉ)
Mariage Frères (8ᵉ)
Marianne (4ᵉ)
Marie-Louise (18ᵉ)
Marius et Janette (8ᵉ)
Marlotte (6ᵉ)
Marty (5ᵉ)
Mauzac (5ᵉ)
Maxence (6ᵉ)
Maxim's (Orly)
Michel Courtalhac (7ᵉ)
Mirama (5ᵉ)
Monttessuy (7ᵉ)
Moulin à Vent "Chez Henri" (5ᵉ)
Muniche (6ᵉ)
Nemrod (6ᵉ)
Nénesse (3ᵉ)
New Jawad (7ᵉ)
Ngo (16ᵉ)
Noces de Jeannette (2ᵉ)
Noura (6ᵉ)
Oeillade (7ᵉ)
Oenothèque (9ᵉ)
Olé Bodéga! (12ᵉ)
Opportun (14ᵉ)
Pacific Eiffel (15ᵉ)
Palanquin (6ᵉ)
Palenque (5ᵉ)
Pamphlet (3ᵉ)
Paparazzi (9ᵉ)
Parc aux Cerfs (6ᵉ)
Passage (11ᵉ)
Passy Mandarin (2ᵉ, 16ᵉ)
Patrick Goldenberg (17ᵉ)
Paul Minchelli (7ᵉ)
Pavillon Puebla (19ᵉ)
Père Claude (15ᵉ)
Perraudin (5ᵉ)
Perron (7ᵉ)
Petit Bofinger (4ᵉ)
Petit Coin de la Bourse (2ᵉ)
Petite Chaise (7ᵉ)
Petites Sorcières (14ᵉ)
Petit Lutétia (6ᵉ)
Petit Mabillon (6ᵉ)
Petit Mâchon (1ᵉʳ)
Petit Niçois (7ᵉ)
Petit Plat (15ᵉ)
Petit Rétro (16ᵉ)
Petit St. Benoît (6ᵉ)

Petit Victor Hugo (16ᵉ)
Pétrus (17ᵉ)
Pichet (8ᵉ)
Pied de Cochon (1ᵉʳ)
Pied de Fouet (7ᵉ)
Pierre (15ᵉ)
Polidor (6ᵉ)
Poquelin (1ᵉʳ)
Poule au Pot (1ᵉʳ)
Ravi (7ᵉ)
Rech (17ᵉ)
René (5ᵉ)
Rest. des Chauffeurs (16ᵉ)
Rond de Serviette (6ᵉ)
Rôtisserie (Levallois)
Rôtisserie d'Armaillé (17ᵉ)
Rôtisserie Monsigny (2ᵉ)
Rouge Vif (7ᵉ)
Rubis (1ᵉʳ)
Sarladais (8ᵉ)
Saudade (1ᵉʳ)
Sauvignon (7ᵉ)
Savy (8ᵉ)
Scheffer (16ᵉ)
Sébillon Élysées (8ᵉ)
Sébillon Neuilly (Neuilly)
Senteurs de Provence (15ᵉ)
Sologne (12ᵉ)
Tan Dinh (7ᵉ)
Tang (16ᵉ)
Tante Jeanne (17ᵉ)
Tante Louise (8ᵉ)
Tante Marguerite (7ᵉ)
Taverne de Maître Kanter (1ᵉʳ)
Taverne Henri IV (1ᵉʳ)
Taverne Kronenbourg (9ᵉ)
Télégraphe (7ᵉ)
Terminus Nord (10ᵉ)
Thanksgiving (4ᵉ)
Tire-Bouchon (15ᵉ)
Toutoune (5ᵉ)
Train Bleu (12ᵉ)
Trentaquattro (7ᵉ)
Trou Gascon (12ᵉ)
Truffe Noire (Neuilly)
Truffière (5ᵉ)
Tsé-Yang (16ᵉ)
Tsukizi (6ᵉ)
Ty Coz (9ᵉ)
Vagenende (6ᵉ)
Vendanges (14ᵉ)
Verre Bouteille (17ᵉ)
Viaduc Café (12ᵉ)
Vieux Bistro (4ᵉ)
Vincent (19ᵉ)

Vin et Marée (11ᵉ, 14ᵉ, 16ᵉ)
Virgin Café (8ᵉ)
Wally Le Saharien (9ᵉ)
Wepler (18ᵉ)
Willi's Wine Bar (1ᵉʳ)
Yvan, Petit (8ᵉ)
Zeyer (14ᵉ)

Expense Account

Alain Ducasse (8ᵉ)
Ambassadeurs (8ᵉ)
Ambroisie (4ᵉ)
Ami Louis (3ᵉ)
Amphyclès (17ᵉ)
Apicius (17ᵉ)
Aristippe (1ᵉʳ)
Armand au Palais Royal (1ᵉʳ)
Arpège (7ᵉ)
Assiette (14ᵉ)
Astor (8ᵉ)
Beauvilliers (A.) (18ᵉ)
Benkay (15ᵉ)
Benoît (4ᵉ)
Braisière (17ᵉ)
Brasserie Lipp (6ᵉ)
Bristol (8ᵉ)
Café Faubourg (8ᵉ)
Café M (8ᵉ)
Carpe Diem (Neuilly)
Carré des Feuillants (1ᵉʳ)
Cartes Postales (1ᵉʳ)
Caves Pétrissans (17ᵉ)
Caviar Kaspia (8ᵉ)
Cazaudehore La Forestière
   (Saint-Germain-en-Laye)
Céladon (2ᵉ)
Célébrités (15ᵉ)
Charlot - Roi/Coquillages (9ᵉ)
Chen (15ᵉ)
Chiberta (8ᵉ)
Clos Morillons (15ᵉ)
Clovis (1ᵉʳ)
Clovis (Le) (8ᵉ)
Comte de Gascogne (Boulogne)
Copenhague (8ᵉ)
Coq/Maison Blanche (St-Ouen)
Côte de Bœuf (17ᵉ)
Dagorno (19ᵉ)
Dessirier (17ᵉ)
Dînée (15ᵉ)
Divellec (7ᵉ)
Dôme (14ᵉ)
Drouant (2ᵉ)
Duc (14ᵉ)
Elysées du Vernet (8ᵉ)

Espadon (1ᵉʳ)
Etoile (8ᵉ)
Faucher (17ᵉ)
Faugeron (16ᵉ)
Ferme des Mathurins (8ᵉ)
Ferme St-Simon (7ᵉ)
Flora Danica (8ᵉ)
Floridita (16ᵉ)
Fontaine d'Auteuil (16ᵉ)
Frégate (12ᵉ)
Gaya, L'Estaminet (1ᵉʳ)
Gaya Rive Gauche (7ᵉ)
Georges (2ᵉ)
Georges Porte Maillot (17ᵉ)
Gérard Besson (1ᵉʳ)
Glénan (7ᵉ)
Goumard (1ᵉʳ)
Grande Armée (16ᵉ)
Grande Cascade (16ᵉ)
Grand Louvre (1ᵉʳ)
Grenadin (8ᵉ)
Grille St-Honoré (1ᵉʳ)
Guy Savoy (17ᵉ)
Hélène Darroze (6ᵉ)
Huitrier (17ᵉ)
Il Carpaccio (8ᵉ)
Il Cortile (1ᵉʳ)
Il Ristorante (17ᵉ)
Indra (8ᵉ)
Isse (2ᵉ)
Jacques Cagna (6ᵉ)
Jamin (16ᵉ)
Jardin (8ᵉ)
Jardins de Bagatelle (16ᵉ)
Joséphine "Chez Dumonet" (6ᵉ)
Jules Verne (7ᵉ)
Kambodgia (16ᵉ)
Kinugawa (8ᵉ)
Lasserre (8ᵉ)
Laurent (8ᵉ)
Ledoyen (8ᵉ)
Luna (8ᵉ)
Maison Prunier (16ᵉ)
Marée (8ᵉ)
Marines (17ᵉ)
Marius et Janette (8ᵉ)
Mathusalem (16ᵉ)
Maxence (6ᵉ)
Maxim's (8ᵉ, Orly)
Meurice (1ᵉʳ)
Michel Rostang (17ᵉ)
Moniage Guillaume (14ᵉ)
Montparnasse 25 (14ᵉ)
Morot-Gaudry (15ᵉ)
Muses (9ᵉ)

Obélisque (8e)
Oenothèque (9e)
Orangerie (4e)
Oulette (12e)
Paolo Petrini (17e)
Paris (6e)
Paul Chêne (16e)
Pauline (1er)
Paul Minchelli (7e)
Pavillon Elysée (8e)
Pergolèse (16e)
Petit Colombier (17e)
Petite Tour (16e)
Petit Marguery (13e)
Pétrus (17e)
Pichet (8e)
Pierre Gagnaire (8e)
Port Alma (16e)
Pré Catelan (16e)
Pressoir (12e)
Quincy (12e)
Ravi (7e)
Récamier (7e)
Relais d'Auteuil (16e)
Relais de Sèvres (15e)
Relais Plaza (8e)
Rest. du Marché (15e)
Rest. Opéra (9e)
Rest. W (8e)
Romantica (Clichy)
San Valero (Neuilly)
16 Haussmann (9e)
Sormani (17e)
Sousceyrac (A) (11e)
Stella Maris (8e)
Stresa (8e)
Table d'Anvers (9e)
Taillevent (8e)
Tang (16e)
Tante Jeanne (17e)
Tante Louise (8e)
Tante Marguerite (7e)
Tonnelle Saintongeaise (Neuilly)
Tour d'Argent (5e)
Tournesol (16e)
Trois Marches (Versailles)
Trou Gascon (12e)
Truffe Noire (Neuilly)
Tsé-Yang (16e)
Vieille (1er)
Violon d'Ingres (7e)

Family Appeal
Agape (15e)
Allard (6e)

Alsaco (9e)
Ambassade d'Auvergne (3e)
Ambassade du Sud-Ouest (7e)
Ami Jean (7e)
Anahuacalli (5e)
Arbuci (6e)
Assassins (6e)
Assiette Lyonnaise (1er, 8e)
Astier (11e)
Atelier Maître Albert (5e)
Auberge Aveyronnaise (12e)
Auberge des Dolomites (17e)
Auberge Etchégorry (13e)
Avant Goût (13e)
Babylone (7e)
Baracane (4e)
Bartolo (6e)
Beaujolais d'Auteuil (16e)
Berthoud (5e)
Bistro 121 (15e)
Bistro de Gala (9e)
Bistro de la Grille (6e)
Bistro d'Hubert (15e)
Bistro du 17ème (17e)
Bistrot d'Alex (6e)
Bistrot d'André (15e)
Bistrot de l'Université (7e)
Bistrot d'Henri (6e)
Bistrot du Louvre (2e)
Bon Saint Pourçain (6e)
Bons Crus (1er)
Boucholeurs (1er)
Brasserie de l'Ile St. Louis (4e)
Ca d'Oro (1er)
Café de Mars (7e)
Café du Commerce (15e)
Café Louis Philippe (4e)
Café Max (7e)
Café Runtz (2e)
Caméléon (6e)
C'Amelot (11e)
Camille (3e)
Cartet Restaurant (11e)
Casa Alcalde (15e)
Catherine (9e)
Catounière (Neuilly)
Caveau du Palais (1er)
Cazaudehore La Forestière
    (Saint-Germain-en-Laye)
Cévennes (15e)
Champ de Mars (7e)
Chantairelle (5e)
Charlot - Roi/Coquillages (9e)
Charpentiers (6e)
Chez Eux (7e)

Chicago Meatpackers (1er)
Chien qui Fume (1er)
Chope d'Alsace (6e)
Cigale (7e)
Clément (2e, 4e, 8e, 14e, 15e, 17e)
Clos des Gourmets (7e)
Coin des Gourmets (5e)
Cosi (6e)
Côté Soleil (1er)
Coude Fou (4e)
Da Mimmo (10e)
Délices d'Aphrodite (5e)
Denise (1er)
Entoto (13e)
En Ville (6e)
Epi d'Or (1er)
Epi Dupin (6e)
Erawan (15e)
Escale (4e)
Espace Sud-Ouest (14e)
Espadon Bleu (6e)
Etrier (18e)
Excuse (4e)
Fabrique (11e)
Fellini (1er, 15e)
Ferme des Mathurins (8e)
Ferme St-Hubert (8e)
Fermette du Sud-Ouest (1er)
Fernandises (11e)
Fins Gourmets (7e)
Flambée (12e)
Fogón Saint Julien (5e)
Fontaines (5e)
Fous d'en Face (4e)
Gauloise (15e)
Gavroche (2e)
Georges (2e)
Georges Porte Maillot (17e)
Gérard (Neuilly)
Germaine (7e)
Gitane (15e)
Giulio Rebellato (16e)
Gourmet de l'Isle (4e)
Graindorge (17e)
Grizzli (4e)
Guinguette de Neuilly (Neuilly)
Hippopotamus (1er, 4e, 5e, 6e, 8e, 14e, Puteaux)
Il Barone (14e)
Improviste (17e)
Jacky (Chez) (13e)
Jacques Mélac (11e)
Jean (9e)
Jenny (3e)
Je Thé...Me (15e)

Joséphine "Chez Dumonet" (6e)
Kitty O'Sheas (2e)
Languedoc (5e)
Léna et Mimile (5e)
Léon de Bruxelles (1er, 4e)
Livio (Neuilly)
Lyonnais (2e)
Ma Bourgogne (8e)
Marcel (6e)
Marie-Louise (18e)
Marlotte (6e)
Marty (5e)
Mavrommatis (5e)
Mère Agitée (14e)
Michel Courtalhac (7e)
Mirama (5e)
Moissonnier (5e)
Monde des Chimères (4e)
Monsieur Lapin (14e)
Monttessuy (7e)
Moulin à Vent "Chez Henri" (5e)
Nemrod (6e)
Nénesse (3e)
Noces de Jeannette (2e)
Oeillade (7e)
Olivades (7e)
Opportun (14e)
Palenque (5e)
Pamphlet (3e)
Paprika (9e)
Parc aux Cerfs (6e)
Paris Main d'Or (11e)
Patrick Goldenberg (17e)
Paul (11e, 13e)
Pento (5e)
Père Claude (15e)
Perraudin (5e)
Petit Coin de la Bourse (2e)
Petite Chaise (7e)
Petit Lutétia (6e)
Petit Navire (5e)
Petit Niçois (7e)
Petit Rétro (16e)
Petit St. Benoît (6e)
Pied de Fouet (7e)
Pierre (15e)
Polidor (6e)
Poquelin (1er)
Poule au Pot (1er)
Quincy (12e)
Quinson (15e)
Régalade (14e)
Relais de Venise (17e)
Rendez-vous/Chauffeurs (18e)
René (5e)

Repaire de Cartouche (11e)
Rest. des Chauffeurs (16e)
Robert et Louise (3e)
Roi du Pot-au-Feu (9e)
Rond de Serviette (6e)
Rôtisserie du Beaujolais (5e)
Saint Pourçain (12e)
Sarladais (8e)
Savy (8e)
Scheffer (16e)
Sébillon Élysées (8e)
Sébillon Neuilly (Neuilly)
Senteurs de Provence (15e)
Sologne (12e)
Souletin (Le) (1er)
Stéphane Martin (15e)
Taverne de Maître Kanter (1er)
Temps des Cerises (13e)
Terminus Nord (10e)
Terroir (13e)
Thoumieux (7e)
Tire-Bouchon (15e)
Tonnelle Saintongeaise (Neuilly)
Tricotin (13e)
Troquet (15e)
Truffière (5e)
Trumilou (4e)
Vendanges (14e)
Verre Bouteille (17e)
Vieux Bistro (4e)
Vin des Rues (14e)
Vivario (5e)
Wally Le Saharien (9e)

Fireplace

Atelier Maître Albert (5e)
Auberge du Champ de Mars (7e)
Auberge du Clou (9e)
Bistrot d'Henri (6e)
Bon (16e)
Brasserie Munichoise (1er)
Carr's (1er)
Cazaudehore La Forestière
   (Saint-Germain-en-Laye)
China Club (12e)
Comptoir des Sports (6e)
Coq/Maison Blanche (St-Ouen)
Costes (1er)
Coupe-Chou (5e)
Diamantaires (9e)
Elysées du Vernet (8e)
Georges (4e)
Il Barone (14e)
Ile (Issy-les-Moulineaux)
Jarasse (Neuilly)

Je Thé...Me (15e)
Moniage Guillaume (14e)
Montalembert (7e)
Orangerie (4e)
Pactole (5e)
Paris Main d'Or (11e)
Pavillon Montsouris (14e)
Petit Colombier (17e)
Petit Poucet (Le) (Levallois)
Petit Victor Hugo (16e)
Plage Parisienne (15e)
Pluvinel (1er)
Pré Catelan (16e)
Quai Ouest (St-Cloud)
Rest. Jean Bouin (16e)
River Café (Issy-les-Moulineaux)
Robert et Louise (3e)
Romantica (Clichy)
Sud (17e)
Tastevin (Maisons-Laffitte)
Truffière (5e)

Game in Season

Aiguière (11e)
Allobroges (20e)
Ami Jean (7e)
Ami Louis (3e)
Amognes (11e)
Ampère (17e)
Anacréon (13e)
André (8e)
Ardoise (1er)
Argenteuil (1er)
Armand au Palais Royal (1er)
Arpège (7e)
Assiette (14e)
Astier (11e)
Atelier Berger (1er)
Atelier Gourmand (17e)
Auberge Bressane (7e)
Auberge Nicolas Flamel (3e)
Avant Goût (13e)
Bamboche (7e)
Bascou (3e)
Benoît (4e)
Berry's (8e)
Bertie's (16e)
Beudant (17e)
Biche au Bois (12e)
Bistrot d'à Côté (5e, 17e, Neuilly)
Bistrot d'Alex (6e)
Bistrot de l'Etoile Lauriston (16e)
Bistrot de l'Etoile Niel (17e)
Bistrot de l'Etoile Troyon (17e)
Bistrot de Paris (7e)

Bistrot d'Henri (6e)
Bistrot du Louvre (2e)
Bon Accueil (7e)
Brasserie de la Poste (16e)
Bristol (8e)
Café Faubourg (8e)
Camélia (Bougival)
Carré des Feuillants (1er)
Cartes Postales (1er)
Catherine (9e)
Céladon (2e)
Cévennes (15e)
Chardenoux (11e)
Charpentiers (6e)
Cinq (8e)
Clos des Gourmets (7e)
Clos Morillons (15e)
Clovis (Le) (8e)
Cottage Marcadet (18e)
Cou de la Girafe (8e)
Cuisinier François (16e)
Detourbe Duret (16e)
Diane (6e)
Dînée (15e)
Ecaille et Plume (7e)
Elysées du Vernet (8e)
Espadon (1er)
Etoile (8e)
Etrier (18e)
Excuse (4e)
Faucher (17e)
Ferme des Mathurins (8e)
Ferme St-Simon (7e)
Françoise (7e)
Gaudriole (1er)
Gérard Besson (1er)
Graindorge (17e)
Grande Cascade (16e)
Jamin (16e)
Jean (9e)
Lucas Carton (8e)
Lyonnais (2e)
Marie-Louise (18e)
Marty (5e)
Maxence (6e)
Michel (10e)
Michel Rostang (17e)
Moissonnier (5e)
Montparnasse 25 (14e)
Monttessuy (7e)
Morot-Gaudry (15e)
Oeillade (7e)
Oulette (12e)
Pamphlet (3e)
Parc aux Cerfs (6e)

Paul (11e, 13e)
Paul Chêne (16e)
Pavillon Elysée (8e)
Perraudin (5e)
Petit Colombier (17e)
Petite Tour (16e)
Petit Marguery (13e)
Petit Riche (9e)
Pierre (15e)
Poquelin (1er)
Potager du Roy (Versailles)
P'tit Troquet (7e)
Quincy (12e)
Récamier (7e)
Relais de Sèvres (15e)
Relais Louis XIII (6e)
Repaire de Cartouche (11e)
Rest. du Marché (15e)
Rest. du Palais Royal (1er)
Rocher Gourmand (8e)
Rôtisserie du Beaujolais (5e)
Saint Amarante (12e)
Sologne (12e)
Sousceyrac (A) (11e)
Stella Maris (8e)
Table d'Anvers (9e)
Taillevent (8e)
Temps des Cerises (13e)
Tour d'Argent (5e)
Troquet (15e)
Trou Gascon (12e)
Truffe Noire (Neuilly)
Vieux Bistro (4e)
Vieux Métiers de France (13e)
Villaret (11e)
Yves Quintard (15e)
Zéphyr (20e)

Historic Interest
(date of building and/or
restaurant)
1292 Escargot Montorgueil (1er)
1580 Auberge Nicolas Flamel (3e)
1582 Tour d'Argent (5e)
1600 Ambroisie (4e)
1600 Monde des Chimères (4e)
1605 Coconnas (4e)
1650 Petit Prince de Paris (5e)
1680 Gaudriole (1er)
1680 Guirlande de Julie (3e)
1680 Jacques Cagna (6e)
1680 Petite Chaise (7e)
1680 Relais Louis XIII (6e)
1680 Taverne Henri IV (1er)
1686 Procope (6e)

1700 Côté Soleil (1er)	1900 Brasserie Flo (10e)
1700 Coupe-Chou (5e)	1900 Café Charbon (11e)
1750 Armand au Palais Royal (1er)	1900 Café Runtz (2e)
1760 Grand Véfour (1er)	1900 Fermette Marbeuf 1900 (8e)
1766 Lapérouse (6e)	1900 Fontaine de Mars (7e)
1780 Ambassadeurs (8e)	1900 Gauloise (15e)
1780 Obélisque (8e)	1900 Grande Cascade (16e)
1780 Paul (13e, 1er, 11e)	1900 Grille St-Honoré (1er)
1780 Rest. du Palais Royal (1er)	1900 Joséphine "Chez
1807 Rest. Opéra (9e)	Dumonet" (6e)
1840 Café Louis Philippe (4e)	1900 Lyonnais (2e)
1840 Grand Colbert (2e)	1900 Omar (3e)
1845 Polidor (6e)	1900 Pauline (1er)
1850 Coq/Maison Blanche (St-Ouen)	1900 Petit Lutétia (6e)
1850 Rest. des Beaux Arts (6e)	1900 Petit Rétro (16e)
1854 Charpentiers (6e)	1900 Rest. du Musée d'Orsay (7e)
1854 Petit Riche (9e)	1900 Square Trousseau (12e)
1862 Café de la Paix (9e)	1901 Petit St. Benoît (6e)
1862 Ladurée (8e)	1901 Train Bleu (12e)
1865 Dagorno (19e)	1902 Grizzli (4e)
1870 Arbre à Cannelle (2e)	1903 Perraudin (5e)
1870 Bœuf Couronné (19e)	1903 Pierre (15e)
1870 Meurice (1er)	1904 Chardenoux (11e)
1871 Ledoyen (8e)	1904 Vagenende (6e)
1872 Goumard (1er)	1905 Bons Crus (1er)
1872 Poste (9e)	1905 Bouillon Racine (6e)
1876 Gallopin (2e)	1906 Rendez-vous/Chauffeurs (18e)
1876 Grange Batelière (9e)	1909 Bistrot d'André (15e)
1880 Brasserie Balzar (5e)	1910 Dôme (14e)
1880 Brasserie Lipp (6e)	1910 Elysées du Vernet (8e)
1880 Drouant (2e)	1910 Janou (3e)
1880 Pavillon Montsouris (14e)	1910 Télégraphe (7e)
1880 Pavillon Puebla (19e)	1910 Trou Gascon (12e)
1880 Pré Catelan (16e)	1912 Benoît (4e)
1881 Café Terminus (8e)	1913 Marty (5e)
1885 Alain Ducasse (8e)	1914 Sébillon Neuilly (Neuilly)
1885 Café Les Deux Magots (6e)	1918 Daru (8e)
1885 Pluvinel (1er)	1919 Clown Bar (11e)
1888 Espadon (1er)	1919 Lescure (1er)
1889 Altitude 95 (7e)	1919 Marcel (6e)
1889 Maxim's (8e)	1920 Closerie des Lilas (6e)
1890 Lucas Carton (8e)	1920 Paris (6e)
1890 Petit Coin de la Bourse (2e)	1921 Café du Commerce (15e)
1890 Trois Marches (Versailles)	1923 Sousceyrac (A) (11e)
1891 Jules Verne (7e)	1923 Thoumieux (7e)
1892 Café de Flore (6e)	1924 Ami Louis (3e)
1893 Aristide (17e)	1924 Bristol (8e)
1893 Laurent (8e)	1925 Biche au Bois (12e)
1894 Chalet des Iles (16e)	1925 Guinguette de Neuilly
1895 Brasserie Mollard (8e)	(Neuilly)
1895 Grand Café des Capucines (9e)	1925 Maison Prunier (16e)
1895 Wepler (18e)	1925 Rech (17e)
1898 Pavillon Elysée (8e)	1925 Terminus Nord (10e)
1899 Fouquet's (8e)	1925 Vaudeville (2e)
1900 Brasserie de l'Ile St. Louis (4e)	1926 Georges Porte Maillot (17e)

1927 Brasserie Lorraine (8ᵉ)
1927 Coupole (14ᵉ)
1928 Cazaudehore La Forestière
(Saint-Germain-en-Laye)
1928 Cloche d'Or (9ᵉ)
1928 Dominique (6ᵉ)
1928 Petit Colombier (17ᵉ)
1929 Diamantaires (9ᵉ)
1929 Tante Louise (8ᵉ)
1930 Allard (6ᵉ)
1930 Bœuf sur le Toit (8ᵉ)
1930 Brasserie Stella (16ᵉ)
1930 Georges (2ᵉ)
1930 Mathusalem (16ᵉ)
1930 Petit Zinc (6ᵉ)
1930 Roi du Pot-au-Feu (9ᵉ)
1932 Crus de Bourgogne (2ᵉ)
1932 Jarasse (Neuilly)
1932 Jenny (3ᵉ)
1935 Epi d'Or (1ᵉʳ)
1935 Languedoc (5ᵉ)
1935 Poule au Pot (1ᵉʳ)
1936 Cartet Restaurant (11ᵉ)
1936 Ecaille et Plume (7ᵉ)
1936 Relais Plaza (8ᵉ)
1940 Flandrin (16ᵉ)
1940 Galoche d'Aurillac (11ᵉ)
1944 Robert et Louise (3ᵉ)
1945 Lasserre (8ᵉ)
1945 Méditerranée (6ᵉ)
1945 Quinson (15ᵉ)

Hotel Dining

Alain Ducasse (8ᵉ)
Ambassadeurs (8ᵉ)
Antiquaires (7ᵉ)
Astor (8ᵉ)
Bar Vendôme (1ᵉʳ)
Benkay (15ᵉ)
Bertie's (16ᵉ)
Bourdonnais (7ᵉ)
Brasserie du Louvre (1ᵉʳ)
Brasserie Lutétia (6ᵉ)
Bristol (8ᵉ)
Café de la Paix (9ᵉ)
Café de Vendôme (1ᵉʳ)
Café Faubourg (8ᵉ)
Café M (8ᵉ)
Café Terminus (8ᵉ)
Céladon (2ᵉ)
Célébrités (15ᵉ)
Cinq (8ᵉ)
Clovis (Le) (8ᵉ)
Costes (1ᵉʳ)
Elysées du Vernet (8ᵉ)

Espadon (1ᵉʳ)
Il Carpaccio (8ᵉ)
Il Cortile (1ᵉʳ)
Jardin (8ᵉ)
Jardin des Cygnes (8ᵉ)
Meurice (1ᵉʳ)
Montalembert (7ᵉ)
Montparnasse 25 (14ᵉ)
Muses (9ᵉ)
Obélisque (8ᵉ)
Paris (6ᵉ)
Pierre Gagnaire (8ᵉ)
Pluvinel (1ᵉʳ)
Relais de Sèvres (15ᵉ)
Relais du Parc (16ᵉ)
Relais Plaza (8ᵉ)
Rest. Opéra (9ᵉ)
Rest. W (8ᵉ)
Salle à Manger (16ᵉ)
16 Haussmann (9ᵉ)
Signatures (8ᵉ)
Spoon, Food & Wine (8ᵉ)
Terrasse (18ᵉ)
Thoumieux (7ᵉ)
Trois Marches (Versailles)

"In" Places

A et M Le Bistrot (16ᵉ, 17ᵉ)
Ailleurs (8ᵉ)
Alain Ducasse (8ᵉ)
Alcazar (6ᵉ)
Allobroges (20ᵉ)
Anahï (3ᵉ)
Appart' (8ᵉ)
Asian (8ᵉ)
Avant Goût (13ᵉ)
Bains (3ᵉ)
Barfly (8ᵉ)
Barrio Latino (12ᵉ)
Bermuda Onion (15ᵉ)
Bistrot du Peintre (11ᵉ)
Bookinistes (6ᵉ)
Buddha Bar (8ᵉ)
Butte Chaillot (16ᵉ)
Café Beaubourg (4ᵉ)
Café Charbon (11ᵉ)
Café de Flore (6ᵉ)
Café de la Musique (19ᵉ)
Café de l'Industrie (11ᵉ)
Café du Passage (11ᵉ)
Café la Jatte (Neuilly)
Café Marly (1ᵉʳ)
Café Ruc (1ᵉʳ)
Cafetière (6ᵉ)
C'Amelot (11ᵉ)

Casa Bini (6ᵉ)
Casa Olympe (9ᵉ)
Catherine (9ᵉ)
Cherche Midi (6ᵉ)
China Club (12ᵉ)
Coco et sa Maison (17ᵉ)
Coffee Parisien (6ᵉ, 16ᵉ)
Colette (1ᵉʳ)
Contre-Allée (14ᵉ)
Costes (1ᵉʳ)
Cou de la Girafe (8ᵉ)
Da Mimmo (10ᵉ)
Dauphin (1ᵉʳ)
Davé (1ᵉʳ)
Doobie's (8ᵉ)
Driver's (16ᵉ)
Durand Dupont (Neuilly)
Emporio Armani Caffé (6ᵉ)
Enoteca (4ᵉ)
Epi Dupin (6ᵉ)
Etoile (8ᵉ)
Fabrique (11ᵉ)
Flandrin (16ᵉ)
Fontaine de Mars (7ᵉ)
Fumoir (1ᵉʳ)
Gare (16ᵉ)
Grande Armée (16ᵉ)
Homero (8ᵉ)
I Golosi (9ᵉ)
Ile (Issy-les-Moulineaux)
Impala Lounge (8ᵉ)
Kambodgia (16ᵉ)
Kiosque (16ᵉ)
Lô Sushi (8ᵉ)
Macéo (1ᵉʳ)
Maison (5ᵉ)
Man Ray (8ᵉ)
Mansouria (11ᵉ)
Manufacture (Issy-les-Moulineaux)
Marie et Fils (6ᵉ)
Méditerranée (6ᵉ)
Natacha (14ᵉ)
O à la Bouche (14ᵉ)
Olé Bodéga! (12ᵉ)
Omar (3ᵉ)
Orient-Extrême (6ᵉ)
Os à Moelle (15ᵉ)
Ostéria (4ᵉ)
Petit Poucet (Le) (Levallois)
Plage Parisienne (15ᵉ)
Poste (9ᵉ)
Prune (10ᵉ)
P'tit Troquet (7ᵉ)
Quai Ouest (St-Cloud)
404 (3ᵉ)
Régalade (14ᵉ)
River Café (Issy-les-Moulineaux)
Shozan (8ᵉ)

Spicy Restaurant (8ᵉ)
Square Trousseau (12ᵉ)
Stresa (8ᵉ)
Studio (4ᵉ)
Taka (18ᵉ)
Télégraphe (7ᵉ)
Totem (16ᵉ)
Troquet (15ᵉ)
Véranda (8ᵉ)
Viaduc Café (12ᵉ)
Voltaire (7ᵉ)
Wadja (6ᵉ)
Willi's Wine Bar (1ᵉʳ)
Zebra Square (16ᵉ)

Jacket/Tie Recommended

Astor (8ᵉ)
Beauvilliers (A.) (18ᵉ)
Bristol (8ᵉ)
Carré des Feuillants (1ᵉʳ)
Drouant (2ᵉ)
Faugeron (16ᵉ)
Gérard Besson (1ᵉʳ)
Guy Savoy (17ᵉ)
Jules Verne (7ᵉ)
Laurent (8ᵉ)
Ledoyen (8ᵉ)
Lucas Carton (8ᵉ)
Maison Blanche (8ᵉ)
Pierre Gagnaire (8ᵉ)
Pré Catelan (16ᵉ)

Jacket/Tie Required

Alain Ducasse (8ᵉ)
Ambassadeurs (8ᵉ)
Ambroisie (4ᵉ)
Cinq (8ᵉ)
Espadon (1ᵉʳ)
Grand Véfour (1ᵉʳ)
Lasserre (8ᵉ)
Maxim's (8ᵉ)
Taillevent (8ᵉ)
Tour d'Argent (5ᵉ)

July/August Dining

(July and August are the traditional vacation months for Parisian restaurants. Below is a partial list of places open during this period. As dates may change, call in advance to confirm.)
Absinthe (1ᵉʳ)
Alcazar (6ᵉ)
Ambassadeurs (8ᵉ)
Amphyclès (17ᵉ)

Arpège (7ᵉ)
Avenue (8ᵉ)
Beauvilliers (A.) (18ᵉ)
Bœuf sur le Toit (8ᵉ)
Bofinger (4ᵉ)
Bourdonnais (7ᵉ)
Brasserie Balzar (5ᵉ)
Brasserie du Louvre (1ᵉʳ)
Brasserie Lipp (6ᵉ)
Bristol (8ᵉ)
Bûcherie (5ᵉ)
Buddha Bar (8ᵉ)
Café de Vendôme (1ᵉʳ)
Café Marly (1ᵉʳ)
Café Ruc (1ᵉʳ)
China Club (12ᵉ)
Cinq (8ᵉ)
Closerie des Lilas (6ᵉ)
Colette (1ᵉʳ)
Coupole (14ᵉ)
Divellec (7ᵉ)
Dôme (14ᵉ)
Emporio Armani Caffé (6ᵉ)
Espadon (1ᵉʳ)
Fouquet's (8ᵉ)
Gérard Besson (1ᵉʳ)
Grand Colbert (2ᵉ)
Grandes Marches (12ᵉ)
Il Cortile (1ᵉʳ)
Jardin (8ᵉ)
Jules Verne (7ᵉ)
Juvenile's (1ᵉʳ)
Laurent (8ᵉ)
Macéo (1ᵉʳ)
Man Ray (8ᵉ)
Mansouria (11ᵉ)
Méditerranée (6ᵉ)
Meurice (1ᵉʳ)
Pauline (1ᵉʳ)
Pavillon Montsouris (14ᵉ)
Pré Catelan (16ᵉ)
Procope (6ᵉ)
Récamier (7ᵉ)
Rest. du Palais Royal (1ᵉʳ)
Table d'Anvers (9ᵉ)
Tour d'Argent (5ᵉ)
Train Bleu (12ᵉ)
Vaudeville (2ᵉ)
Willi's Wine Bar (1ᵉʳ)

Late Late – After 12:30

(All hours are AM;
* check locations)
Alcazar (6ᵉ) (1)
Al Diwan (8ᵉ) (1)

André (8ᵉ) (1)
Arbuci (6ᵉ) (2)
Asian (8ᵉ) (1)
Auberge Dab (16ᵉ) (2)
Baan-Boran (1ᵉʳ) (2)
Bar à Huîtres (1)*
Bar des Théâtres (8ᵉ) (2)
Barfly (8ᵉ) (1)
Bellecour (7ᵉ) (1:30)
Bistro Melrose (17ᵉ) (1)
Bœuf sur le Toit (8ᵉ) (1)
Bofinger (4ᵉ) (1)
Brasserie Flo (10ᵉ) (1:30)
Brasserie Lipp (6ᵉ) (1)
Brasserie Lorraine (8ᵉ) (2:45)
Buffalo Grill (1)*
Café Beaubourg (4ᵉ) (1)
Café Bleu (8ᵉ) (3)
Café de Flore (6ᵉ) (1)
Café de la Musique (19ᵉ) (2)
Café du Passage (11ᵉ) (2)
Café Marly (1ᵉʳ) (2)
Café Ruc (1ᵉʳ) (1)
C'Amelot (11ᵉ) (1)
Catalogne (La) (6ᵉ) (1)
Caviar Kaspia (8ᵉ) (1)
Charlot - Roi/Coquillages (9ᵉ) (1)
Chicago Meatpackers (1ᵉʳ) (1)
Chicago Pizza Pie Factory (8ᵉ) (1)
Chien qui Fume (1ᵉʳ) (2)
China Town Belleville (10ᵉ) (1:30)
Chope d'Alsace (6ᵉ) (2)
Clément (1)*
Cloche d'Or (9ᵉ) (4)
Comptoir Paris-Marrakech (1ᵉʳ) (1)
Costes (1ᵉʳ) (1)
Coupe-Chou (5ᵉ) (1)
Coupole (14ᵉ) (2)
Débarcadère (17ᵉ) (1)
Denise (Chez) (1ᵉʳ) (7)
Dominique (6ᵉ) (1)
Drugstore Champs-Elysées (8ᵉ) (2)
Ecluse (1)*
Espace Sud-Ouest (1)*
Flore en l'Ile (4ᵉ) (2)
Francis (8ᵉ) (1)
Gamin de Paris (4ᵉ) (2)
Gavroche (2ᵉ) (1:30)
Grand Colbert (2ᵉ) (1)
Hippopotamus (1)*
Indiana Café (1)*
Jenny (3ᵉ) (1)
Joe Allen (1ᵉʳ) (1)

Julien (10ᵉ) (1:30)
Léon de Bruxelles (1)*
Livingstone (1ᵉʳ) (1)
Ma Bourgogne (4ᵉ) (1)
Maison du Caviar (8ᵉ) (1)
Mauzac (5ᵉ) (2)
Milonga (6ᵉ) (1)
New Nioullaville (11ᵉ) (1)
Noura (6ᵉ) (1)
Olé Bodéga! (12ᵉ) (2)
Paparazzi (9ᵉ) (1)
Petit Bofinger (1)
Philosophes (4ᵉ) (1)
Pied de Chameau (4ᵉ) (2)
"Pierre" A la Fontaine (2ᵉ) (12:30)
Plancha (11ᵉ) (1:30)
Planet Hollywood (8ᵉ) (1)
Poste (9ᵉ) (1:30)
Poule au Pot (1ᵉʳ) (5)
Président (11ᵉ) (2)
Procope (6ᵉ) (1)
Rotonde (6ᵉ) (1)
Taverne Kronenbourg (9ᵉ) (2)
Terminus Nord (10ᵉ) (1)
Vagenende (6ᵉ) (1)
Vaudeville (2ᵉ) (1)
Véranda (8ᵉ) (1)
Verre Bouteille (17ᵉ) (5)
Viaduc Café (12ᵉ) (3)
Villaret (11ᵉ) (1)
Vong (1ᵉʳ) (12:30)
Wepler (18ᵉ) (1)
Yvan (8ᵉ) (1)
Yvan, Petit (8ᵉ) (1)
Zebra Square (16ᵉ) (1)

Meet for a Drink
(Most top hotels and the
following standouts)
Alain Ducasse (8ᵉ)
Alcazar (6ᵉ)
Asian (8ᵉ)
Bar des Théâtres (8ᵉ)
Barfly (8ᵉ)
Baron Rouge (12ᵉ)
Bons Crus (1ᵉʳ)
Bouillon Racine (6ᵉ)
Buddha Bar (8ᵉ)
Café Beaubourg (4ᵉ)
Café Charbon (11ᵉ)
Café de Flore (6ᵉ)
Café de la Musique (19ᵉ)
Café de la Paix (9ᵉ)
Café de l'Industrie (11ᵉ)
Café du Passage (11ᵉ)

Café Les Deux Magots (6ᵉ)
Café Marly (1ᵉʳ)
Café Ruc (1ᵉʳ)
Café Véry (1ᵉʳ)
Carr's (1ᵉʳ)
Casa del Habano (6ᵉ)
Cave Drouot (9ᵉ)
China Club (12ᵉ)
Cloche des Halles (1ᵉʳ)
Closerie des Lilas (6ᵉ)
Clown Bar (11ᵉ)
Colette (1ᵉʳ)
Coupole (14ᵉ)
Dalloyau (6ᵉ, 8ᵉ, 15ᵉ)
Doobie's (8ᵉ)
Drugstore Champs-Elysées (8ᵉ)
Ecluse (6ᵉ, 8ᵉ, 11ᵉ, 17ᵉ)
Enoteca (4ᵉ)
Escale (4ᵉ)
Etoile (8ᵉ)
Fabrique (11ᵉ)
Floridita (16ᵉ)
Fouquet's (8ᵉ)
Fumoir (1ᵉʳ)
Gavroche (2ᵉ)
Grande Armée (16ᵉ)
Griffonnier (8ᵉ)
Jacques Mélac (11ᵉ)
Juvenile's (1ᵉʳ)
Kitty O'Sheas (2ᵉ)
Ladurée (8ᵉ)
Loir dans la Théière (4ᵉ)
Ma Bourgogne (4ᵉ)
Macéo (1ᵉʳ)
Man Ray (8ᵉ)
Mauzac (5ᵉ)
Nemrod (6ᵉ)
Oenothèque (9ᵉ)
Olé Bodéga! (12ᵉ)
Passage (11ᵉ)
Poste (9ᵉ)
Rubis (1ᵉʳ)
Sauvignon (7ᵉ)
Taverne Henri IV (1ᵉʳ)
Train Bleu (12ᵉ)
Viaduc Café (12ᵉ)
Willi's Wine Bar (1ᵉʳ)
Zebra Square (16ᵉ)

Modish Intelligentsia
Absinthe (1ᵉʳ)
A et M Le Bistrot (16ᵉ)
Ampère (17ᵉ)
Anahï (3ᵉ)
Appart' (8ᵉ)

Assiette (14e)
Auberge Nicolas Flamel (3e)
Avant Goût (13e)
Bamboche (7e)
Bar des Théâtres (8e)
Bartolo (6e)
Bascou (3e)
Bastide Odéon (6e)
Bermuda Onion (15e)
Bistro de Gala (9e)
Bistro des Deux Théâtres (9e)
Bistrot d'Alex (6e)
Bistrot de l'Etoile Lauriston (16e)
Bistrot de l'Etoile Niel (17e)
Bistrot de l'Etoile Troyon (17e)
Bistrot de l'Université (7e)
Bistrot d'Henri (6e)
Bistrot du Peintre (11e)
Bon Accueil (7e)
Bon Saint Pourçain (6e)
Bookinistes (6e)
Bouillon Racine (6e)
Brasserie Balzar (5e)
Brasserie Lipp (6e)
Buddha Bar (8e)
Butte Chaillot (16e)
Café Beaubourg (4e)
Café de Flore (6e)
Café de la Musique (19e)
Café de l'Industrie (11e)
Café des Lettres (7e)
Café Marly (1er)
Café Ruc (1er)
Cafetière (6e)
Caffé Toscano (7e)
Cagouille (14e)
C'Amelot (11e)
Camille (3e)
Casa Bini (6e)
Casa del Habano (6e)
Casa Olympe (9e)
Catherine (9e)
Caviar Kaspia (8e)
Cercle Ledoyen (8e)
Chardenoux (11e)
Cherche Midi (6e)
Chieng Mai (5e)
China Club (12e)
Closerie des Lilas (6e)
Clown Bar (11e)
Coco et sa Maison (17e)
Coin des Gourmets (5e)
Colette (1er)
Comptoir Paris-Marrakech (1er)
Contre-Allée (14e)

Cosi (6e)
Costes (1er)
Coude Fou (4e)
Cou de la Girafe (8e)
Coupole (14e)
Dame Jeanne (11e)
Da Mimmo (10e)
Davé (1er)
Débarcadère (17e)
Denise (1er)
Diane (6e)
Dôme (14e)
Dominique (6e)
Doobie's (8e)
Durand Dupont (Neuilly)
Ebauchoir (12e)
Emporio Armani Caffé (6e)
Epi Dupin (6e)
Fabrique (11e)
Fernandises (11e)
Flandrin (16e)
Fogón Saint Julien (5e)
Fontaine de Mars (7e)
Fouquet's (8e)
Fumoir (1er)
Gare (16e)
Gauloise (15e)
Georges (2e)
Grande Armée (16e)
Grille (10e)
Hangar (3e)
I Golosi (9e)
Il Barone (14e)
Impala Lounge (8e)
Inagiku (5e)
Isami (4e)
Isse (2e)
Jacques Mélac (11e)
Janou (3e)
Jean (9e)
Joséphine "Chez Dumonet" (6e)
Jumeaux (11e)
Kambodgia (16e)
Kinugawa (1er, 8e)
Kiosque (16e)
Loir dans la Théière (4e)
Lô Sushi (8e)
Luna (8e)
Macéo (1er)
Maison (5e)
Mansouria (11e)
Manufacture (Issy-les-Moulineaux)
Marais-Cage (3e)
Mariage Frères (8e)
Marianne (4e)

Marie et Fils (6e)
Marlotte (6e)
Marty (5e)
Méditerranée (6e)
Mère Agitée (14e)
Michel (10e)
Moulin à Vent "Chez Henri" (5e)
Natacha (14e)
Nénesse (3e)
Oeillade (7e)
Omar (3e)
Orient-Extrême (6e)
Ostéria (4e)
Pamphlet (3e)
Passage (11e)
Paul (11e, 13e)
Petites Sorcières (14e)
Petit Mabillon (6e)
Petit Poucet (Le) (Levallois)
Petit St. Benoît (6e)
Plage Parisienne (15e)
Plancha (11e)
Port du Salut (5e)
Poste (9e)
Quai Ouest (St-Cloud)
404 (3e)
Récamier (7e)
Réconfort (3e)
Réminet (5e)
Rendez-vous/Chauffeurs (18e)
Restaurant (18e)
Rest. du Palais Royal (1er)
River Café (Issy-les-Moulineaux)
Rôtisserie d'en Face (6e)
Rouge Vif (7e)
Saint Pourçain (12e)
Sauvignon (7e)
Scheffer (16e)
Shozan (8e)
Spicy Restaurant (8e)
Square Trousseau (12e)
Stresa (8e)
Taka (18e)
Tan Dinh (7e)
Télégraphe (7e)
Temps des Cerises (13e)
Véranda (8e)
Viaduc Café (12e)
Vieux Bistro (4e)
Villaret (11e)
Vincent (19e)
Voltaire (7e)
Zebra Square (16e)
Zygomates (12e)

Noteworthy Newcomers (35)
Aimant du Sud (13e)
Antiquaires (7e)
Atelier Berger (1er)
Auberge du Clou (9e)
Baan-Boran (1er)
Barramundi (9e)
Bath's (8e)
Bon (16e)
Café de l'Esplanade (Le) (7e)
Cailloux (13e)
Casa Corsa (6e)
Cave de l'Os à Moelle (15e)
Cave Gourmande (19e)
Cinq (8e)
Comédiens (9e)
En Ville (6e)
Ferme (1er)
Georges (4e)
Hélène Darroze (6e)
Homero (8e)
Il Baccello (17e)
Impala Lounge (8e)
Jacquot de Bayonne (12e)
Maison Courtine (14e)
Petrossian (7e)
Rest. La Zygothèque (13e)
Rue Balzac (8e)
Safran (1er)
Signatures (8e)
Soun (16e)
Stéphane Martin (15e)
Tante Jeanne (17e)
Terrasses du Palais (17e)
Tournesol (16e)
Wok Restaurant (11e)

Outdoor Dining
(G=garden; T=terrace;
W=waterside; best of many)
Abélard (5e) (T)
Absinthe (1er) (T)
A et M Le Bistrot (16e, 17e) (T)
Aimant du Sud (13e) (T)
Al Dar (16e) (T)
Alivi (4e) (T)
Alsace (8e) (T)
Amadéo (4e) (T)
Ambassade du Sud-Ouest (7e) (T)
Amognes (11e) (T)
Ampère (17e) (T)
André (8e) (T)
A Priori Thé (2e) (T)
Arbre à Cannelle (2e) (T)
Arbuci (6e) (T)

Argenteuil (1er) (T)
Aristide (17e) (T)
Assiette Lyonnaise (1er) (T)
Astier (11e) (T)
Auberge Bressane (7e) (T)
Auberge Etchégorry (13e) (T)
Ballon des Ternes (17e) (T)
Bar à Huîtres (5e, 14e) (T)
Bar au Sel (7e) (T)
Bartolo (6e) (T)
Bar Vendôme (1er) (T)
Basilic (7e) (T)
Baumann Ternes (17e) (T)
Beaujolais d'Auteuil (16e) (T)
Beauvilliers (A.) (18e) (T)
Bermuda Onion (15e) (T)
Bistro de la Grille (6e) (T)
Bistro d'Hubert (15e) (T)
Bistro du 17ème (17e) (T)
Bistrot d'à Côté (5e, 17e, Neuilly) (T)
Bistrot d'Albert (17e) (T)
Bistrot d'André (15e) (T)
Bistrot de l'Etoile Niel (17e) (T)
Bistrot du Dôme (14e) (T)
Bistrot du Louvre (2e) (T)
Bistrot du Peintre (11e) (T)
Bistrot St. Ferdinand (17e) (T)
Bon Accueil (7e) (T)
Bon Saint Pourçain (6e) (T)
Bouchons de Fr. Clerc (17e) (T)
Brasserie Balzar (5e) (T)
Brasserie de la Poste (16e) (T)
Brasserie de l'Ile St. Louis (4e) (T)
Brasserie du Louvre (1er) (T)
Brasserie Lorraine (8e) (T)
Brasserie Stella (16e) (T)
Bristol (8e) (G,T)
Bûcherie (5e) (T)
Butte Chaillot (16e) (T)
Ca d'Oro (1er) (T)
Café Beaubourg (4e) (T)
Café Charbon (11e) (T)
Café de Flore (6e) (T)
Café de la Musique (19e) (T)
Café des Lettres (7e) (T)
Café de Vendôme (1er) (T)
Café du Passage (11e) (T)
Café la Jatte (Neuilly) (T)
Café Les Deux Magots (6e) (G,T)
Café Louis Philippe (4e) (T)
Café Marly (1er) (T)
Café Ruc (1er) (T)
Café Véry (1er) (G,T)
Cagouille (14e) (T)
Camille (3e) (T)

Cap Seguin (Boulogne) (T,W)
Cap Vernet (8e) (T)
Casa Alcalde (15e) (T)
Caveau du Palais (1er) (T)
Caves Pétrissans (17e) (T)
Cazaudehore La Forestière
    (Saint-Germain-en-Laye) (G)
Cercle Ledoyen (8e) (G,T)
Chalet des Iles (16e) (T,W)
Champ de Mars (7e) (T)
Chantairelle (5e) (G)
Charpentiers (6e) (T)
Cherche Midi (6e) (T)
Chicago Meatpackers (1er) (T)
Chien qui Fume (1er) (T)
Chope d'Alsace (6e) (T)
Churrasco (17e) (T)
Cigale (7e) (T)
Cinq (8e) (T)
Clément (2e, 4e, 8e, 14e, 17e,
    Bougival) (T)
Cloche des Halles (1er) (T)
Clos des Gourmets (7e) (T)
Closerie des Lilas (6e) (T)
Clovis (1er) (T)
Clown Bar (11e) (T)
Club Matignon (8e) (T)
Coconnas (4e) (T)
Coffee Parisien (16e) (T)
Coin des Gourmets (5e) (T)
Comptoir du Saumon (4e, 8e, 15e,
    17e) (T)
Comte de Gascogne (Boulogne) (G)
Congrès (17e) (T)
Contre-Allée (14e) (T)
Costes (1er) (T)
Côté 7ème (7e) (T)
Cou de la Girafe (8e) (T)
Cour de Rohan (6e) (T)
Crêperie de Josselin (14e) (T)
Crus de Bourgogne (2e) (T)
Dalloyau (6e, 15e) (T)
Dame Jeanne (11e) (T)
Dame Tartine (12e) (T)
Da Mimmo (10e) (T)
Daru (8e) (T)
Dauphin (1er) (T)
Délices d'Aphrodite (5e) (T)
Délices de Szechuen (7e) (T)
Dessirier (17e) (T)
Detourbe Duret (16e) (T)
Deux Abeilles (7e) (T)
Diable des Lombards (1er) (T)
Diep (Chez) (8e) (T)
Dominique (6e) (T)

Drugstore Champs-Elysées (8e) (T)
Durand Dupont (Neuilly) (G,T)
Ebauchoir (12e) (T)
El Mansour (8e) (T)
Entracte (18e) (T)
Entrepôt (14e) (T)
Escargot Montorgueil (1er) (T)
Espace Sud-Ouest (14e, 15e) (T)
Espadon (1er) (G,T)
Fabrique (11e) (T)
Faucher (17e) (T)
Ferme St-Hubert (8e) (T)
Fermette du Sud-Ouest (1er) (T)
Fermette Marbeuf 1900 (8e) (T)
Findi (8e) (T)
Flambée (12e) (T)
Flandrin (16e) (T)
Flora Danica (8e) (G,T)
Flore en l'Ile (4e) (T)
Fontaine de Mars (7e) (T)
Fontaines (5e) (T)
Fontanarosa (15e) (T)
Fouquet's (8e) (T)
Fous d'en Face (4e) (T)
Francis (8e) (T)
Françoise (7e) (T)
Fred (17e) (T)
Fumoir (1er) (T)
Gallopin (2e) (T)
Gare (16e) (T)
Gaudriole (1er) (T)
Gauloise (15e) (T)
Gégène (Joinville) (T,W)
Georges Porte Maillot (17e) (T)
Gérard (Neuilly) (T)
Gitane (15e) (T)
Gourmets des Ternes (8e) (T)
Grand Café des Capucines (9e) (T)
Grande Armée (16e) (T)
Grande Cascade (16e) (G,S)
Grandes Marches (12e) (T)
Grange Batelière (9e) (T)
Grenadin (8e) (T)
Grenier de Notre Dame (5e) (T)
Grille Montorgueil (2e) (T)
Grille St-Honoré (1er) (T)
Grizzli (4e) (T)
Guinguette/Neuilly (Neuilly) (T,W)
Guirlande de Julie (3e) (T)
Hangar (3e) (T)
Hippopotamus (2e, 4e, 5e, 6e,
   Puteaux) (T)
Il Cortile (1er) (T)
Ile (Issy-les-Moulineaux) (G,T,W)
Improviste (17e) (T)

Indiana Café (6e, 8e, 11e, 2e, 3e) (T)
Jacques Mélac (11e) (T)
Janou (3e) (T)
Jarasse (Neuilly) (T)
Jardin (8e) (T)
Jardin des Cygnes (8e) (G,T)
Jardins de Bagatelle (16e) (T)
Jenny (3e) (G,T)
Je Thé...Me (15e) (T)
Joe Allen (1er) (T)
Jo Goldenberg (4e) (T)
Joséphine "Chez Dumonet" (6e) (T)
Kim Lien (5e) (T)
Kiosque (16e) (T)
Kitty O'Sheas (2e) (T)
Ladurée (8e) (T)
Lao Tseu (7e) (T)
Laurent (8e) (G,T)
Ledoyen (8e) (G)
Léna et Mimile (5e) (T)
Léon de Bruxelles (6e) (T)
Lescure (1er) (T)
Livio (Neuilly) (G,T)
Ma Bourgogne (4e) (T)
Maharajah (5e) (T)
Maison Blanche (8e) (T)
Maison Courtine (14e) (T)
Maison de l'Amérique (7e) (G)
Manufacture
   (Issy-les-Moulineaux) (T)
Marcel (6e) (T)
Marianne (4e) (T)
Marie et Fils (6e) (T)
Marines (17e) (T)
Marius et Janette (8e) (T)
Marlotte (6e) (T)
Marty (5e) (T)
Mascotte (8e) (T)
Maupertu (7e) (T)
Mauzac (5e) (T)
Méditerranée (6e) (T)
Michel (10e) (T)
Moniage Guillaume (14e) (T)
Montalembert (7e) (T)
Monttessuy (7e) (T)
Morot-Gaudry (15e) (T)
Moulin à Vent "Chez Henri" (5e) (T)
Moulin/Galette Graziano (18e) (G,T)
Muniche (6e) (T)
Muscade (1er) (G,T)
Nemrod (6e) (T)
Noura (6e) (G)
O à la Bouche (14e) (T)
Olivades (7e) (T)
Os à Moelle (15e) (T)

Pacific Eiffel (15ᵉ) (T)
Pactole (5ᵉ) (T)
Paparazzi (9ᵉ) (T)
Parc aux Cerfs (6ᵉ) (T)
Patrick Goldenberg (17ᵉ) (T)
Paul (1ᵉʳ, 11ᵉ, 13ᵉ) (T)
Pavillon des Princes (16ᵉ) (G)
Pavillon Elysée (8ᵉ) (T)
Pavillon Montsouris (14ᵉ) (G)
Pavillon Puebla (19ᵉ) (T)
Père Claude (15ᵉ) (T)
Perraudin (5ᵉ) (T)
Persiennes (8ᵉ) (T)
Petit Bofinger (17ᵉ) (T)
Petite Cour (La) (6ᵉ) (G,T)
Petite Sirène (9ᵉ) (T)
Petit Lutétia (6ᵉ) (T)
Petit Mâchon (1ᵉʳ, 15ᵉ) (T)
Petit Plat (15ᵉ) (T)
Petit Poucet (Le) (Levallois) (G)
Petit St. Benoît (6ᵉ) (T)
Petit Victor Hugo (16ᵉ) (T)
Petit Zinc (6ᵉ) (T)
Philosophes (4ᵉ) (T)
Pichet (8ᵉ) (T)
Pied de Cochon (1ᵉʳ) (T)
"Pierre" A la Fontaine (2ᵉ) (T)
Pitchi Poï (4ᵉ) (T)
Plage Parisienne (15ᵉ) (T,W)
Pluvinel (1ᵉʳ) (G)
Poule au Pot (1ᵉʳ) (T)
Pré Catelan (16ᵉ) (G,T)
Prune (10ᵉ) (T)
Quai Ouest (St-Cloud) (T,W)
Relais Chablisien (1ᵉʳ) (T)
Relais du Parc (16ᵉ) (G,T)
Réminet (5ᵉ) (T)
Rendez-vous/Camionneurs (14ᵉ) (T)
René (5ᵉ) (T)
Rest. des Chauffeurs (16ᵉ) (T)
Rest. du Marché (15ᵉ) (T)
Rest. du Palais Royal (1ᵉʳ) (G)
Rest. Jean Bouin (16ᵉ) (G)
Rest. La Zygothèque (13ᵉ) (T)
Ribe (7ᵉ) (T)
River Café
   (Issy-les-Moulineaux) (W)
Robe et le Palais (1ᵉʳ) (T)
Roi du Pot-au-Feu (9ᵉ) (T)
Romantica (Clichy) (T)
Rond de Serviette (6ᵉ) (T)
Rughetta (18ᵉ) (T)
Saint Pourçain (12ᵉ) (T)
Salle à Manger (16ᵉ) (T)
Sauvignon (7ᵉ) (T)

Savy (8ᵉ) (T)
Scusi (8ᵉ) (T)
Sédillot (7ᵉ) (T)
16 Haussmann (9ᵉ) (T)
Senteurs de Provence (15ᵉ) (T)
Sept Quinze (15ᵉ) (T)
Signatures (8ᵉ) (T)
Sologne (12ᵉ) (T)
Soupière (17ᵉ) (T)
Square Trousseau (12ᵉ) (T)
Stresa (8ᵉ) (T)
Studio (4ᵉ) (T)
Sud (17ᵉ) (T)
Sushi One (8ᵉ) (T)
Table de Babette (Poissy) (T)
Tastevin (Maisons-Laffitte) (G)
Taverne de Maître Kanter (1ᵉʳ) (T)
Taverne Kronenbourg (9ᵉ) (T)
Télégraphe (7ᵉ) (T)
Terroir (13ᵉ) (T)
Tonnelle Saintongeaise (Neuilly) (T)
Totem (16ᵉ) (T)
Tournesol (16ᵉ) (T)
Trois Marches (Versailles) (T)
Troquet (15ᵉ) (T)
Trumilou (4ᵉ) (T)
Vagenende (6ᵉ) (T)
Van Gogh (Asnières) (T)
Vaudeville (2ᵉ) (T)
Verre Bouteille (17ᵉ) (T)
Vieux Bistro (4ᵉ) (T)
Vieux Métiers de France (13ᵉ) (T)
Vin des Rues (14ᵉ) (T)
Vin et Marée (11ᵉ) (T)
Vivario (5ᵉ) (T)
Vong (1ᵉʳ) (T)
Woolloomooloo (4ᵉ) (T)
Zebra Square (16ᵉ) (T)
Zéphyr (20ᵉ) (T)
Zinzins (2ᵉ) (T)

Outstanding View

Altitude 95 (7ᵉ)
Café Marly (1ᵉʳ)
Chalet des Iles (16ᵉ)
Etoile (8ᵉ)
Flore en l'Ile (4ᵉ)
Francis (8ᵉ)
Gégène (Joinville)
Georges (2ᵉ)
Grande Cascade (16ᵉ)
Grand Véfour (1ᵉʳ)
Jardins de Bagatelle (16ᵉ)
Jules Verne (7ᵉ)
Ledoyen (8ᵉ)

Maison Blanche (8e)
Maupertu (7e)
Morot-Gaudry (15e)
Pavillon Puebla (19e)
Rest. du Musée d'Orsay (7e)
Totem (16e)
Toupary (1er)
Tour d'Argent (5e)
Trois Marches (Versailles)

Parking/Valet

A et M Le Bistrot (16e, 17e)
Ailleurs (8e)
Alain Ducasse (8e)
Ambassadeurs (8e)
Ambroisie (4e)
Ampère (17e)
Amphyclès (17e)
Apicius (17e)
Arpège (7e)
Asian (8e)
Astor (8e)
Bains (3e)
Barrio Latino (12e)
Benkay (15e)
Bertie's (16e)
Bistro 121 (15e)
Bistro du 17ème (17e)
Bistrot d'à Côté (5e, 17e, Neuilly, 17e)
Bistrot de l'Etoile Niel (17e)
Bistrot de l'Etoile Troyon (17e)
Bistrot de Marius (8e)
Bistrot de Paris (7e)
Bistrot St. Ferdinand (17e)
Bœuf sur le Toit (8e)
Bourdonnais (7e)
Brasserie Flo (10e)
Brasserie Lorraine (8e)
Bristol (8e)
Buddha Bar (8e)
Café de Vendôme (1er)
Café Faubourg (8e)
Café Indigo (8e)
Café la Jatte (Neuilly)
Café M (8e)
Café Terminus (8e)
Cap Seguin (Boulogne)
Carré des Feuillants (1er)
Caviar Kaspia (8e)
Cazaudehore La Forestière
   (Saint-Germain-en-Laye)
Céladon (2e)
Célébrités (15e)
Cercle Ledoyen (8e)
Chiberta (8e)

Cinq (8e)
Closerie des Lilas (6e)
Clovis (Le) (8e)
Coco et sa Maison (17e)
Comte de Gascogne (Boulogne)
Copenhague (8e)
Coq/Maison Blanche (St-Ouen)
Costes (1er)
Cou de la Girafe (8e)
Dagorno (19e)
Dalloyau (6e, 15e, 8e)
Débarcadère (17e)
Dessirier (17e)
Diep (Chez) (8e)
Divellec (7e)
Doobie's (8e)
Drouant (2e)
El Mansour (8e)
Elysées du Vernet (8e)
Espadon (1er)
Espadon Bleu (6e)
Fakhr el Dine (8e, 16e)
Faucher (17e)
Faugeron (16e)
Fellini (15e)
Flandrin (16e)
Floridita (16e)
Fouquet's (8e)
Françoise (7e)
Gare (16e)
Georges Porte Maillot (17e)
Grand Colbert (2e)
Grande Armée (16e)
Grande Cascade (16e)
Grand Véfour (1er)
Grand Venise (15e)
Grille (10e)
Guy Savoy (17e)
Hédiard (8e)
Homero (8e)
Il Carpaccio (8e)
Il Cortile (1er)
Ile (Issy-les-Moulineaux)
Jacques Cagna (6e)
Jarasse (Neuilly)
Jardin (8e)
Jardin des Cygnes (8e)
Jardins de Bagatelle (16e)
Jenny (3e)
Jules Verne (7e)
Julien (10e)
Kiosque (16e)
Lapérouse (6e)
Lasserre (8e)
Ledoyen (8e)

Lucas Carton (8ᵉ)
Maison Blanche (8ᵉ)
Maison du Caviar (8ᵉ)
Maison Prunier (16ᵉ)
Man Ray (8ᵉ)
Marius (16ᵉ)
Marius et Janette (8ᵉ)
Marty (5ᵉ)
Maxence (6ᵉ)
Maxim's (8ᵉ)
Méditerranée (6ᵉ)
Meurice (1ᵉʳ)
Michel Rostang (17ᵉ)
Montalembert (7ᵉ)
Montparnasse 25 (14ᵉ)
Moulin/Galette Graziano (18ᵉ)
Muses (9ᵉ)
Noura (6ᵉ)
Olé Bodéga! (12ᵉ)
Orangerie (4ᵉ)
Pacific Eiffel (15ᵉ)
Pactole (5ᵉ)
Paris (6ᵉ)
Paul Chêne (16ᵉ)
Pavillon Elysée (8ᵉ)
Pavillon Montsouris (14ᵉ)
Pergolèse (16ᵉ)
Persiennes (8ᵉ)
Petit Poucet (Le) (Levallois)
Petrossian (7ᵉ)
Pétrus (17ᵉ)
Pied de Chameau (4ᵉ)
Pierre au Palais Royal (1ᵉʳ)
Pierre Gagnaire (8ᵉ)
Plage Parisienne (15ᵉ)
Pluvinel (1ᵉʳ)
Poste (9ᵉ)
Pré Catelan (16ᵉ)
Pressoir (12ᵉ)
Quai Ouest (St-Cloud)
Relais d'Auteuil (16ᵉ)
Relais de Sèvres (15ᵉ)
Relais du Parc (16ᵉ)
Relais Plaza (8ᵉ)
Rest. Jean Bouin (16ᵉ)
Rest. Opéra (9ᵉ)
Rest. W (8ᵉ)
River Café (Issy-les-Moulineaux)
Romantica (Clichy)
Rôtisserie d'en Face (6ᵉ)
Rue Balzac (8ᵉ)
Salle à Manger (16ᵉ)
Scusi (8ᵉ)
Sébillon Neuilly (Neuilly)
16 Haussmann (9ᵉ)

Signatures (8ᵉ)
Spoon, Food & Wine (8ᵉ)
Sushi One (8ᵉ)
Taillevent (8ᵉ)
Télégraphe (7ᵉ)
Terrasses du Palais (17ᵉ)
Tong Yen (8ᵉ)
Tonnelle Saintongeaise (Neuilly)
Toupary (1ᵉʳ)
Tour d'Argent (5ᵉ)
Trois Marches (Versailles)
Truffe Noire (Neuilly)
Véranda (8ᵉ)
Village d'Ung et Li Lam (8ᵉ)
Vin et Marée (7ᵉ, 11ᵉ, 16ᵉ, 14ᵉ)
Violon d'Ingres (7ᵉ)
Vong (1ᵉʳ, 8ᵉ)
Yvan (8ᵉ)
Yvan, Petit (8ᵉ)
Zebra Square (16ᵉ)

Parties & Private Rooms
(* indicates private rooms
available; best of many)
Absinthe (1ᵉʳ)*
A et M Le Bistrot (17ᵉ)
Affriolé (7ᵉ)
Aiguière (11ᵉ)*
Ailleurs (8ᵉ)
Alcazar (6ᵉ)*
Al Dar (5ᵉ)
Al Mounia (16ᵉ)*
Alsace (8ᵉ)*
Amadéo (4ᵉ)*
Amazigh (16ᵉ)
Ambassade d'Auvergne (3ᵉ)*
Amphyclès (17ᵉ)*
Anahï (3ᵉ)*
Angelina (1ᵉʳ)*
Annapurna (8ᵉ)
A Priori Thé (2ᵉ)
Arbre à Cannelle (2ᵉ)*
Arbuci (6ᵉ)*
Ardoise (1ᵉʳ)*
Argenteuil (1ᵉʳ)*
Aristippe (1ᵉʳ)*
Arpège (7ᵉ)*
Asian (8ᵉ)*
Assiette Lyonnaise (1ᵉʳ)*
Astor (8ᵉ)*
Atelier Berger (1ᵉʳ)*
Atelier Gourmand (17ᵉ)*
Atelier Maître Albert (5ᵉ)*
Atlas (5ᵉ)*
Auberge Aveyronnaise (12ᵉ)*

Auberge Dab (16e)*
Auberge Landaise (9e)*
Avenue (8e)*
Baie d'Ha Long (16e)*
Bains (3e)
Bamboche (7e)*
Bar à Huîtres (5e)*
Bar des Théâtres (8e)
Barfly (8e)
Barramundi (9e)
Bastide Odéon (6e)*
Baumann Ternes (17e)*
Beauvilliers (A.) (18e)*
Bellini (16e)
Benkay (15e)*
Bertie's (16e)*
Beudant (17e)*
Bistro 121 (15e)*
Bistrot d'Alex (6e)*
Bistrot de l'Etoile Niel (17e)*
Bistrot de l'Etoile Troyon (17e)*
Bistrot de Paris (7e)*
Bistrot du Sommelier (8e)*
Bistrot St. Ferdinand (17e)*
Bistrot St. James (Neuilly)
Blue Elephant (11e)
Bœuf Couronné (19e)
Bofinger (4e)*
Bookinistes (6e)
Bouillon Racine (6e)*
Boulangerie (20e)
Bourdonnais (7e)*
Brasserie Flo (10e)
Brasserie Lorraine (8e)*
Brasserie Lutétia (6e)
Brasserie Mollard (8e)*
Brasserie Munichoise (1er)*
Brézolles (6e)*
Bristol (8e)*
Bûcherie (5e)*
Butte Chaillot (16e)*
Café Bleu (8e)*
Café d'Angel (17e)
Café de la Musique (19e)
Café du Commerce (15e)*
Café du Passage (11e)
Café Faubourg (8e)*
Café Flo (9e)*
Café Louis Philippe (4e)*
Café M (8e)
Café Marly (1er)*
Café Ruc (1er)
Café Runtz (2e)*
Café Terminus (8e)*
Café Véry (1er)

Cagouille (14e)*
Camélia (Bougival)*
Cap Seguin (Boulogne)*
Carré des Feuillants (1er)*
Carr's (1er)*
Casa del Habano (6e)*
Casa Tina (16e)
Catalogne (La) (6e)*
Caveau du Palais (1er)*
Cave Drouot (9e)
Caves Pétrissans (17e)*
Cazaudehore La Forestière
    (Saint-Germain-en-Laye)*
Céladon (2e)*
Célébrités (15e)*
Chalet des Iles (16e)*
Champ de Mars (7e)*
Charlot - Roi/Coquillages (9e)*
Chen (15e)*
Chez Eux (7e)*
Chiberta (8e)*
Chicago Meatpackers (1er)
Chien qui Fume (1er)
China Club (12e)
China Town Olympiades (13e)*
Chope d'Alsace (6e)
Cigale (7e)*
Cloche d'Or (9e)
Clovis (1er)
Clovis (Le) (8e)*
Club Matignon (8e)*
Coco de Mer (5e)*
Coco et sa Maison (17e)*
Coconnas (4e)
Coffee Parisien (16e)
Coin des Gourmets (5e)*
Communautés (Puteaux)*
Comptoir des Sports (6e)*
Comptoir du Saumon (15e)*
Contre-Allée (14e)
Coq/Maison Blanche (St-Ouen)*
Côté 7ème (7e)
Côté Soleil (1er)*
Coupe-Chou (5e)*
Coupole (14e)
Crus de Bourgogne (2e)*
Dalloyau (8e)*
Dame Jeanne (11e)*
Dauphin (1er)*
Dessirier (17e)*
Diamantaires (9e)
Dînée (15e)
Dôme (14e)*
Dominique (6e)
Doobie's (8e)*

Drouant (2e)
Durand Dupont (Neuilly)*
Ecaille et Plume (7e)*
Ecluse (11e, 17e)
El Picador (17e)
Elysées du Vernet (8e)*
Enoteca (4e)
Entoto (13e)
Entrecôte (7e)*
Entrepôt (14e)
En Ville (6e)*
Escargot Montorgueil (1er)*
Espadon Bleu (6e)*
Etoile (8e)
Etoile Marocaine (8e)
Excuse (4e)
Fabrice (1er)*
Fakhr el Dine (16e)*
Faugeron (16e)*
Fellini (1er)*
Ferme de Boulogne (Boulogne)*
Ferme St-Simon (7e)
Fernandises (11e)*
Findi (8e)*
Fins Gourmets (7e)*
Flandrin (16e)
Fontaine d'Auteuil (16e)
Fouquet's (8e)*
Fous d'en Face (4e)
Françoise (7e)*
Galoche d'Aurillac (11e)*
Gauloise (15e)
Gaya, L'Estaminet (1er)*
Gazelle (17e)
Gégène (Joinville)
Goumard (1er)*
Grand Café des Capucines (9e)
Grande Cascade (16e)*
Grandes Marches (12e)
Grand Louvre (1er)*
Grand Véfour (1er)
Grenadin (8e)*
Grille Montorgueil (2e)*
Grille St-Honoré (1er)*
Grizzli (4e)
Guy Savoy (17e)*
Homero (8e)
Huitrier (17e)*
Il Carpaccio (8e)*
Il Cortile (1er)*
Ile (Issy-les-Moulineaux)*
Iles Marquises (14e)*
Impatient (17e)*
Jacques Cagna (6e)*
Jamin (16e)*

Jarasse (Neuilly)*
Jardin (8e)*
Jardin des Cygnes (8e)*
Jardins de Bagatelle (16e)*
Jean (9e)*
Jenny (3e)*
Je Thé...Me (15e)*
Jo Goldenberg (4e)*
Joséphine "Chez Dumonet" (6e)*
Khun Akorn (11e)*
Kinugawa (1er)*
Kiosque (16e)
Ladurée (8e)*
Lalqila (15e)
Lapérouse (6e)*
Lasserre (8e)*
Laurent (8e)*
Ledoyen (8e)*
Léon (17e)*
Léon de Bruxelles (6e)*
Livingstone (1er)*
Livio (Neuilly)*
Lucas Carton (8e)*
Lyonnais (2e)*
Ma Bourgogne (8e)*
Macéo (1er)*
Maharajah (5e)
Maison Blanche (8e)
Maison Courtine (14e)*
Maison de l'Amérique (7e)*
Maison Prunier (16e)*
Maître Paul (6e)*
Mandarin (8e)
Mandarin de Neuilly (Neuilly)
Mansouria (11e)*
Marais-Cage (3e)*
Marée (8e)*
Marie-Louise (18e)
Marius et Janette (8e)*
Marlotte (6e)
Maroc (1er)*
Marty (5e)*
Mavrommatis (5e)*
Maxim's (8e, Orly)*
Méditerranée (6e)*
Mère Agitée (14e)*
Meurice (1er)*
Michel (10e)
Michel Courtalhac (7e)*
Michel Rostang (17e)*
Milonga (6e)
Moniage Guillaume (14e)*
Montalembert (7e)*
Montparnasse 25 (14e)*
Morot-Gaudry (15e)*

New Jawad (7ᵉ)
Ngo (16ᵉ)*
Noces de Jeannette (2ᵉ)*
Noura (6ᵉ)*
Olivades (7ᵉ)*
Pacific Eiffel (15ᵉ)*
Pactole (5ᵉ)*
Palanquin (6ᵉ)*
Paris (6ᵉ)
Passy Mandarin (2ᵉ)*
Patrick Goldenberg (17ᵉ)*
Paul (11ᵉ)
Paul Chêne (16ᵉ)*
Pauline (1er)*
Paul Minchelli (7ᵉ)*
Pavillon des Princes (16ᵉ)*
Pavillon Elysée (8ᵉ)*
Pavillon Montsouris (14ᵉ)*
Pavillon Puebla (19ᵉ)*
Pergolèse (16ᵉ)*
Persiennes (8ᵉ)*
Petit Coin de la Bourse (2ᵉ)*
Petit Colombier (17ᵉ)*
Petite Chaise (7ᵉ)*
Petite Cour (La) (6ᵉ)*
Petit Rétro (16ᵉ)*
Petit Riche (9ᵉ)*
Petit Victor Hugo (16ᵉ)
Petit Zinc (6ᵉ)*
Pétrus (17ᵉ)*
Pied de Chameau (4ᵉ)*
Pied de Cochon (1er)*
"Pierre" A la Fontaine (2ᵉ)*
Pierre Gagnaire (8ᵉ)*
Plage Parisienne (15ᵉ)*
Planet Hollywood (8ᵉ)*
Pluvinel (1er)*
Port du Salut (5ᵉ)*
Poste (9ᵉ)*
Pouilly Reuilly (Le Pré-St-Gervais)
Poule au Pot (1er)*
Pressoir (12ᵉ)*
Procope (6ᵉ)*
Quai Ouest (St-Cloud)
Quercy (9ᵉ)*
Quinson (15ᵉ)*
Rech (17ᵉ)*
Réconfort (3ᵉ)*
Relais Louis XIII (6ᵉ)*
Réminet (5ᵉ)*
Repaire de Cartouche (11ᵉ)
Rest. La Zygothèque (13ᵉ)*
Rest. du Marché (15ᵉ)*
Rest. du Musée d'Orsay (7ᵉ)*
Rest. du Palais Royal (1er)*

Rest. Jean Bouin (16ᵉ)
Rest. W (8ᵉ)
Ribe (7ᵉ)
Rocher Gourmand (8ᵉ)
Romantica (Clichy)*
Rond de Serviette (6ᵉ)*
Rôtisserie (Levallois)
Rôtisserie Monsigny (2ᵉ)
Rotonde (6ᵉ)*
Rue Balzac (8ᵉ)*
Salle à Manger (16ᵉ)*
Sarladais (8ᵉ)*
Sawadee (15ᵉ)
16 Haussmann (9ᵉ)
Shozan (8ᵉ)*
Signatures (8ᵉ)*
Signorelli (1er)*
Sologne (12ᵉ)
Sormani (17ᵉ)*
Soufflé (1er)*
Sousceyrac (A) (11ᵉ)*
Square Trousseau (12ᵉ)*
Stella Maris (8ᵉ)*
Stéphane Martin (15ᵉ)*
Studio (4ᵉ)*
Sushi One (8ᵉ)
Table d'Anvers (9ᵉ)*
Taillevent (8ᵉ)*
Tan Dinh (7ᵉ)*
Tante Louise (8ᵉ)
Tante Marguerite (7ᵉ)*
Taverne de Maître Kanter (1er)
Télégraphe (7ᵉ)*
Terminus Nord (10ᵉ)*
Terrasse (18ᵉ)*
Terrasses du Palais (17ᵉ)*
Thanksgiving (4ᵉ)*
Thoumieux (7ᵉ)*
Tonnelle Saintongeaise
  (Neuilly)*
Toupary (1er)
Tour d'Argent (5ᵉ)*
Trentaquattro (7ᵉ)*
Truffière (5ᵉ)*
Trumilou (4ᵉ)*
Tsé-Yang (16ᵉ)*
Vagenende (6ᵉ)
Van Gogh (Asnières)*
Viaduc Café (12ᵉ)
Vieille (1er)*
Vieux Métiers de France (13ᵉ)*
Village d'Ung et Li Lam (8ᵉ)*
Vinci (16ᵉ)*
Vinea Café (12ᵉ)*
Vin et Marée (11ᵉ, 14ᵉ)

Virgin Café (8ᵉ)
Vivario (5ᵉ)
Vong (1ᵉʳ, 8ᵉ)*
Wally Le Saharien (9ᵉ)*
Zebra Square (16ᵉ)*
Zeyer (14ᵉ)*
Zinzins (2ᵉ)*

People-Watching
A et M Le Bistrot (16ᵉ)
Ailleurs (8ᵉ)
Alcazar (6ᵉ)
Anahï (3ᵉ)
Asian (8ᵉ)
Barfly (8ᵉ)
Blue Elephant (11ᵉ)
Bon (16ᵉ)
Brasserie Stella (16ᵉ)
Buddha Bar (8ᵉ)
Café de Flore (6ᵉ)
Café de la Paix (9ᵉ)
Café Faubourg (8ᵉ)
Café Indigo (8ᵉ)
Café Les Deux Magots (6ᵉ)
Casa Bini (6ᵉ)
Colette (1ᵉʳ)
Costes (1ᵉʳ)
Da Mimmo (10ᵉ)
Doobie's (8ᵉ)
Emporio Armani Caffé (6ᵉ)
Espadon (1ᵉʳ)
Etoile (8ᵉ)
Fumoir (1ᵉʳ)
Gare (16ᵉ)
Grande Armée (16ᵉ)
Guy Savoy (17ᵉ)
Ile (Issy-les-Moulineaux)
Ladurée (8ᵉ, 9ᵉ)
Lô Sushi (8ᵉ)
Lucas Carton (8ᵉ)
Macéo (1ᵉʳ)
Maison (5ᵉ)
Maison Blanche (8ᵉ)
Man Ray (8ᵉ)
Marie et Fils (6ᵉ)
Natacha (14ᵉ)
Orangerie (4ᵉ)
Paul Minchelli (7ᵉ)
Relais Plaza (8ᵉ)
Sormani (17ᵉ)
Stresa (8ᵉ)
Taillevent (8ᵉ)
Véranda (8ᵉ)
Voltaire (7ᵉ)

Power Scene
A et M Le Bistrot (16ᵉ)
Alain Ducasse (8ᵉ)
Ambassadeurs (8ᵉ)
Ambroisie (4ᵉ)
Ami Louis (3ᵉ)
Amphyclès (17ᵉ)
Apicius (17ᵉ)
Arpège (7ᵉ)
Assiette (14ᵉ)
Astor (8ᵉ)
Auberge Bressane (7ᵉ)
Bar des Théâtres (8ᵉ)
Bar Vendôme (1ᵉʳ)
Bastide Odéon (6ᵉ)
Beato (7ᵉ)
Beauvilliers (A.) (18ᵉ)
Bellecour (7ᵉ)
Benoît (4ᵉ)
Bertie's (16ᵉ)
Bourdonnais (7ᵉ)
Brasserie Balzar (5ᵉ)
Brasserie Lipp (6ᵉ)
Brasserie Stella (16ᵉ)
Bristol (8ᵉ)
Café de Flore (6ᵉ)
Café des Lettres (7ᵉ)
Café Faubourg (8ᵉ)
Café Les Deux Magots (6ᵉ)
Café Marly (1ᵉʳ)
Cagouille (14ᵉ)
Carré des Feuillants (1ᵉʳ)
Casa Bini (6ᵉ)
Caviar Kaspia (8ᵉ)
Céladon (2ᵉ)
Cercle Ledoyen (8ᵉ)
Cherche Midi (6ᵉ)
Chiberta (8ᵉ)
Closerie des Lilas (6ᵉ)
Comte de Gascogne (Boulogne)
Copenhague (8ᵉ)
Costes (1ᵉʳ)
Dessirier (17ᵉ)
Dînée (15ᵉ)
Divellec (7ᵉ)
Dôme (14ᵉ)
Drouant (2ᵉ)
Duc (14ᵉ)
Elysées du Vernet (8ᵉ)
Epi Dupin (6ᵉ)
Espadon (1ᵉʳ)
Etoile (8ᵉ)
Faucher (17ᵉ)
Faugeron (16ᵉ)
Ferme St-Simon (7ᵉ)

Fins Gourmets (7e)
Flandrin (16e)
Fouquet's (8e)
Gare (16e)
Gauloise (15e)
Georges (2e, 4e)
Georges Porte Maillot (17e)
Grande Armée (16e)
Grande Cascade (16e)
Grand Véfour (1er)
Guy Savoy (17e)
Il Carpaccio (8e)
Jamin (16e)
Jarasse (Neuilly)
Joséphine "Chez Dumonet" (6e)
Jules Verne (7e)
Ladurée (8e)
Lasserre (8e)
Laurent (8e)
Ledoyen (8e)
Lucas Carton (8e)
Maison (5e)
Maison Blanche (8e)
Maison Prunier (16e)
Marée (8e)
Marie et Fils (6e)
Marius (16e)
Meurice (1er)
Michel Courtalhac (7e)
Michel Rostang (17e)
Montalembert (7e)
Natacha (14e)
Orangerie (4e)
Oulette (12e)
Paris (6e)
Pauline (1er)
Paul Minchelli (7e)
Pavillon Montsouris (14e)
Pergolèse (16e)
Petit Poucet (Le) (Levallois)
Petit Colombier (17e)
Petit Laurent (7e)
Petit Marguery (13e)
Pétrus (17e)
Pichet (8e)
Pied de Fouet (7e)
Pierre au Palais Royal (1er)
Pierre Gagnaire (8e)
Pré Catelan (16e)
Récamier (7e)
Relais d'Auteuil (16e)
Relais Plaza (8e)
Sormani (17e)
Stresa (8e)
Taillevent (8e)

Tan Dinh (7e)
Tante Marguerite (7e)
Tour d'Argent (5e)
Trois Marches (Versailles)
Violon d'Ingres (7e)
Voltaire (7e)

Quick Fix

Alcazar (6e)
Alsaco (9e)
Angelina (1er)
A Priori Thé (2e)
Arbre à Cannelle (2e, 5e)
Babylone (7e)
Baron Rouge (12e)
Bernardaud (8e)
Bons Crus (1er)
Bouillon Racine (6e)
Café Beaubourg (4e)
Café d'Angel (17e)
Café de Flore (6e)
Café de la Musique (19e)
Café de l'Industrie (11e)
Café de Mars (7e)
Café du Commerce (15e)
Café Faubourg (8e)
Café Flo (9e)
Café Les Deux Magots (6e)
Café M (8e)
Café Véry (1er)
Carr's (1er)
Cave Drouot (9e)
Cave Gourmande (19e)
Caviar Kaspia (8e)
Chartier (9e)
Chicago Meatpackers (1er)
Chicago Pizza Pie Factory (8e)
Cloche des Halles (1er)
Closerie des Lilas (6e)
Clown Bar (11e)
Coffee Parisien (6e, 16e)
Colette (1er)
Comptoir du Saumon (4e, 8e, 15e, 17e)
Cosi (6e)
Cour de Rohan (6e)
Crêperie de Josselin (14e)
Dalloyau (6e, 8e, 15e)
Dame Tartine (12e)
Deux Abeilles (7e)
Diable des Lombards (1er)
Drugstore Champs-Elysées (8e)
Ecluse (6e, 8e, 11e, 17e)
Emporio Armani Caffé (6e)
Enfants Gâtés (4e)
Enoteca (4e)

Entrecôte (7e)
Escale (4e)
Ferme St-Hubert (8e)
Flore en l'Ile (4e)
Foujita (1er)
Fumoir (1er)
Grande Armée (16e)
Griffonnier (8e)
Hédiard (8e)
Higuma (1er)
Indiana Café (2e, 3e, 6e, 8e, 9e, 11e, 14e)
Isami (4e)
Jacques Mélac (11e)
Jacquot de Bayonne (12e)
Joe Allen (1er)
Juvenile's (1er)
Ladurée (8e)
Léon de Bruxelles (1er, 4e, 6e, 8e,
    9e, 11e, 14e, 15e, 17e)
Lina's (1er, 2e, 6e, 8e, 9e, 12e, 17e,
    Neuilly, Puteaux)
Loir dans la Théière (4e)
Mariage Frères (8e)
Marianne (4e)
Mauzac (5e)
Mirama (5e)
Montalembert (7e)
Muscade (1er)
Nemrod (6e)
Ostréade (15e)
Pacific Eiffel (15e)
Paparazzi (9e)
Patrick Goldenberg (17e)
Rest. du Musée d'Orsay (7e)
Rubis (1er)
Sauvignon (7e)
Signorelli (1er)
Taverne Henri IV (1er)
Thanksgiving (4e)
Tournesol (16e)
Tricotin (13e)
Tsukizi (6e)
Virgin Café (8e)

Quiet Conversation

Abélard (5e)
Affriolé (7e)
Agape (15e)
Aiguière (11e)
Alain Ducasse (8e)
Al Dar (5e, 16e)
Allard (6e)
Allobroges (20e)
Al Mounia (16e)
Alsaco (9e)

Amadéo (4e)
Amazigh (16e)
Ambassade d'Auvergne (3e)
Ambassade du Sud-Ouest (7e)
Ambassadeurs (8e)
Ambroisie (4e)
Ami Louis (3e)
Amognes (11e)
Amphyclès (17e)
Amuse Bouche (14e)
Anacréon (13e)
Anahï (3e)
Anahuacalli (5e)
Angelina (1er)
Annapurna (8e)
Antiquaires (7e)
Apicius (17e)
Appart' (8e)
A Priori Thé (2e)
Arbre à Cannelle (2e, 5e)
Ardoise (1er)
Argenteuil (1er)
Aristide (17e)
Aristippe (1er)
Armand au Palais Royal (1er)
Arpège (7e)
Asian (8e)
Assiette (14e)
Assiette Lyonnaise (1er, 8e)
Astor (8e)
Atelier Berger (1er)
Atlas (5e)
Auberge Aveyronnaise (12e)
Auberge Bressane (7e)
Auberge Dab (16e)
Auberge des Dolomites (17e)
Auberge Etchégorry (13e)
Auberge Landaise (9e)
Auberge Nicolas Flamel (3e)
Avenue (8e)
Baan-Boran (1er)
Baie d'Ha Long (16e)
Bamboche (7e)
Baracane (4e)
Bar au Sel (7e)
Bar des Théâtres (8e)
Bartolo (6e)
Bar Vendôme (1er)
Bascou (3e)
Basilic (7e)
Bastide Odéon (6e)
Bath's (8e)
Bauta (6e)
Béatilles (17e)
Beato (7e)

Beaujolais d'Auteuil (16e)
Beauvilliers (A.) (18e)
Bellecour (7e)
Bellini (16e)
Benoît (4e)
Bernardaud (8e)
Berry's (8e)
Berthoud (5e)
Bertie's (16e)
Beudant (17e)
Bistro 121 (15e)
Bistro de Gala (9e)
Bistro de l'Olivier (8e)
Bistro des Deux Théâtres (9e)
Bistro d'Hubert (15e)
Bistrot d'à Côté (5e, 17e, Neuilly)
Bistrot d'Albert (17e)
Bistrot d'Alex (6e)
Bistrot d'André (15e)
Bistrot de l'Etoile Lauriston (16e)
Bistrot de l'Etoile Niel (17e)
Bistrot de l'Université (7e)
Bistrot de Marius (8e)
Bistrot de Paris (7e)
Bistrot d'Henri (6e)
Bistrot du Louvre (2e)
Bistrot du Sommelier (8e)
Bistrot St. James (Neuilly)
Blue Elephant (11e)
Bœuf sur le Toit (8e)
Bofinger (4e)
Bon Accueil (7e)
Bon Saint Pourçain (6e)
Boucholeurs (1er)
Bouchons de Fr. Clerc (5e, 8e, 15e, 16e, 17e)
Bourdonnais (7e)
Brézolles (6e)
Bristol (8e)
Bûcherie (5e)
Ca d'Oro (1er)
Café de la Paix (9e)
Café des Lettres (7e)
Café de Vendôme (1er)
Café Faubourg (8e)
Café la Jatte (Neuilly)
Café Les Deux Magots (6e)
Café Louis Philippe (4e)
Café Marly (1er)
Café Runtz (2e)
Cafetière (6e)
Café Véry (1er)
Caffé Toscano (7e)
Cagouille (14e)
Caméléon (6e)

Camélia (Bougival)
Campagne et Provence (5e)
Cap Vernet (8e)
Carré des Feuillants (1er)
Cartes Postales (1er)
Cartet Restaurant (11e)
Casa Bini (6e)
Casa del Habano (6e)
Catherine (9e)
Catounière (Neuilly)
Caveau du Palais (1er)
Cave Drouot (9e)
Caves Pétrissans (17e)
Caviar Kaspia (8e)
Cazaudehore La Forestière
   (Saint-Germain-en-Laye)
Céladon (2e)
Célébrités (15e)
Cercle Ledoyen (8e)
Cévennes (15e)
Chalet des Iles (16e)
Chantairelle (5e)
Chardenoux (11e)
Charpentiers (6e)
Chat Grippé (6e)
Chen (15e)
Chez Eux (7e)
Chiberta (8e)
Chieng Mai (5e)
Chien qui Fume (1er)
China Club (12e)
Chope d'Alsace (6e)
Cigale (7e)
Cloche d'Or (9e)
Clos des Gourmets (7e)
Clos Morillons (15e)
Clovis (Le) (8e)
Clown Bar (11e)
Coconnas (4e)
Coin des Gourmets (5e)
Contre-Allée (14e)
Copenhague (8e)
Coq/Maison Blanche (St-Ouen)
Costes (1er)
Côté 7ème (7e)
Côté Soleil (1er)
Cottage Marcadet (18e)
Coude Fou (4e)
Coupe-Chou (5e)
Coupole (14e)
Cour de Rohan (6e)
Crus de Bourgogne (2e)
Cuisinier François (16e)
Dagorno (19e)
Délices d'Aphrodite (5e)

Délices de Szechuen (7e)
Dessirier (17e)
Detourbe Duret (16e)
Deux Abeilles (7e)
Deux Canards (10e)
Diamantaires (9e)
Diane (6e)
Diep (Chez) (8e)
Dînée (15e)
Divellec (7e)
Dôme (14e)
Dos de la Baleine (4e)
Drouant (2e)
Durand Dupont (Neuilly)
Ecaille et Plume (7e)
Ecluse (6e, 8e, 11e, 17e)
El Mansour (8e)
Elysées du Vernet (8e)
Enoteca (4e)
Entoto (13e)
Entracte (18e)
En Ville (6e)
Epi d'Or (1er)
Epi Dupin (6e)
Erawan (15e)
Escargot Montorgueil (1er)
Espadon (1er)
Espadon Bleu (6e)
Etoile (8e)
Etoile Marocaine (8e)
Etrier (18e)
Excuse (4e)
Fakhr el Dine (8e, 16e)
Faucher (17e)
Faugeron (16e)
Fellini (1er, 15e)
Ferme des Mathurins (8e)
Ferme St-Simon (7e)
Fermette du Sud-Ouest (1er)
Fermette Marbeuf 1900 (8e)
Fins Gourmets (7e)
Finzi (8e)
Flambée (12e)
Flandrin (16e)
Flora Danica (8e)
Floridita (16e)
FocLy (Neuilly)
Fogón Saint Julien (5e)
Fontaine de Mars (7e)
Fouquet's (8e)
Fred (17e)
Fumoir (1er)
Gamin de Paris (4e)
Gaudriole (1er)
Gauloise (15e)

Gaya, L'Estaminet (1er)
Gaya Rive Gauche (7e)
Gégène (Joinville)
Georges (2e)
Gérard Besson (1er)
Giulio Rebellato (16e)
Glénan (7e)
Goumard (1er)
Gourmet de l'Isle (4e)
Graindorge (17e)
Grand Colbert (2e)
Grand Louvre (1er)
Grand Véfour (1er)
Grand Venise (15e)
Grange Batelière (9e)
Grenadin (8e)
Grenier de Notre Dame (5e)
Grille (10e)
Grille St-Honoré (1er)
Grizzli (4e)
Guirlande de Julie (3e)
Guy Savoy (17e)
Huitrier (17e)
I Golosi (9e)
Il Baccello (17e)
Il Barone (14e)
Il Carpaccio (8e)
Il Cortile (1er)
Ile (Issy-les-Moulineaux)
Iles Marquises (14e)
Il était une Oie (17e)
Il Ristorante (17e)
Impala Lounge (8e)
Improviste (17e)
Inagiku (5e)
Isse (2e)
Jacky (Chez) (13e)
Jacques Cagna (6e)
Jamin (16e)
Jarasse (Neuilly)
Jardins de Bagatelle (16e)
Jean (9e)
Jenny (3e)
Joséphine "Chez Dumonet" (6e)
Jules Verne (7e)
Jumeaux (11e)
Kambodgia (16e)
Khun Akorn (11e)
Kim Anh (15e)
Kinugawa (1er)
Languedoc (5e)
Lao Tseu (5e)
Lapérouse (6e)
Laurent (8e)
Ledoyen (8e)

Léna et Mimile (5e)
Loir dans la Théière (4e)
Lozère (6e)
Lucas Carton (8e)
Lyonnais (2e)
Ma Bourgogne (4e, 8e)
Maison (5e)
Maison de l'Amérique (7e)
Maison du Caviar (8e)
Maison Prunier (16e)
Maître Paul (6e)
Man Ray (8e)
Mansouria (11e)
Marcel (6e)
Mariage Frères (4e, 6e, 8e)
Marie-Louise (18e)
Marines (17e)
Marius (16e)
Marlotte (6e)
Marty (5e)
Mathusalem (16e)
Maupertu (7e)
Mavrommatis (5e)
Maxence (6e)
Maxim's (8e, Orly)
Méditerranée (6e)
Meurice (1er)
Michel Courtalhac (7e)
Michel Rostang (17e)
Moissonnier (5e)
Monde des Chimères (4e)
Moniage Guillaume (14e)
Monsieur Lapin (14e)
Montalembert (7e)
Montparnasse 25 (14e)
Monttessuy (7e)
Morot-Gaudry (15e)
Moulin à Vent "Chez Henri" (5e)
Moulin/Galette Graziano (18e)
Muscade (1er)
Nénesse (3e)
New Jawad (7e)
Noura (6e)
Obélisque (8e)
Oeillade (7e)
Oenothèque (9e)
Opportun (14e)
Orangerie (4e)
Orient-Extrême (6e)
Oulette (12e)
Oum el Banine (16e)
Pactole (5e)
Palanquin (6e)
Pamphlet (3e)
Paolo Petrini (17e)

Paprika (9e)
Parc aux Cerfs (6e)
Paris (6e)
Passy Mandarin (2e, 16e)
Paul (1er)
Pauline (1er)
Paul Minchelli (7e)
Pavillon Elysée (8e)
Pavillon Montsouris (14e)
Pavillon Puebla (19e)
Perron (7e)
Petit Poucet (Le) (Levallois)
Petit Bofinger (4e, 17e, Neuilly)
Petit Colombier (17e)
Petite Cour (La) (6e)
Petites Sorcières (14e)
Petite Tour (16e)
Petit Laurent (7e)
Petit Lutétia (6e)
Petit Mâchon (1er, 15e)
Petit Marguery (13e)
Petit Niçois (7e)
Petit Plat (15e)
Petit Prince de Paris (5e)
Petit Rétro (16e)
Petit Riche (9e)
Petit St. Benoît (6e)
Petit Zinc (6e)
Petrossian (7e)
Pichet (8e)
Pied de Fouet (7e)
Pierre (15e)
Pierre Gagnaire (8e)
Plage Parisienne (15e)
Pluvinel (1er)
Port Alma (16e)
Port du Salut (5e)
Potager du Roy (Versailles)
Poule au Pot (1er)
Pré Catelan (16e)
Pressoir (12e)
P'tit Troquet (7e)
Quincy (12e)
Quinson (15e)
Récamier (7e)
Relais d'Auteuil (16e)
Relais du Parc (16e)
Relais Louis XIII (6e)
Relais Plaza (8e)
Réminet (5e)
René (5e)
Repaire de Cartouche (11e)
Rest. de la Tour (15e)
Rest. des Chauffeurs (16e)
Rest. du Marché (15e)

Rest. du Palais Royal (1er)
Rest. Opéra (9e)
Rest. W (8e)
Ribe (7e)
Roi du Pot-au-Feu (9e)
Romantica (Clichy)
Rond de Serviette (6e)
Rosimar (16e)
Rôtisserie du Beaujolais (5e)
Rôtisserie Monsigny (2e)
Rouge Vif (7e)
Safran (1er)
Sarladais (8e)
Saudade (1er)
Sauvignon (7e)
Savy (8e)
Sawadee (15e)
Scheffer (16e)
Sébillon Élysées (8e)
Sébillon Neuilly (Neuilly)
Sédillot (7e)
16 Haussmann (9e)
Senteurs de Provence (15e)
Sept Quinze (15e)
Sologne (12e)
Sormani (17e)
Soufflé (1er)
Souletin (Le) (1er)
Soupière (17e)
Sousceyrac (A) (11e)
Spoon, Food & Wine (8e)
Stella Maris (8e)
Stéphane Martin (15e)
Stresa (8e)
Sushi One (8e)
Table d'Anvers (9e)
Taillevent (8e)
Taïra (17e)
Taka (18e)
Tan Dinh (7e)
Tante Louise (8e)
Taverne de Maître Kanter (1er)
Taverne Henri IV (1er)
Télégraphe (7e)
Terroir (13e)
Thanksgiving (4e)
Timgad (17e)
Tire-Bouchon (15e)
Tonnelle Saintongeaise (Neuilly)
Toque (17e)
Totem (16e)
Toupary (1er)
Tour d'Argent (5e)
Train Bleu (12e)
Trentaquattro (7e)

Trois Marches (Versailles)
Trou Gascon (12e)
Truffe Noire (Neuilly)
Tsé-Yang (16e)
Ty Coz (9e)
Vagenende (6e)
Vendanges (14e)
Verre Bouteille (17e)
Viaduc Café (12e)
Vieux Bistro (4e)
Vieux Métiers de France (13e)
Village d'Ung et Li Lam (8e)
Villaret (11e)
Vincent (19e)
Vinci (16e)
Vin et Marée (7e, 11e, 14e, 16e)
Violon d'Ingres (7e)
Voltaire (7e)
Vong (8e)
Wally Le Saharien (9e)
Willi's Wine Bar (1er)
Yvan, Petit (8e)
Zygomates (12e)

Romantic

Aiguière (11e)
Alain Ducasse (8e)
Allard (6e)
Allobroges (20e)
Al Mounia (16e)
Ambassadeurs (8e)
Ambroisie (4e)
Ami Louis (3e)
Anahï (3e)
Annapurna (8e)
Armand au Palais Royal (1er)
Atlas (5e)
Auberge Nicolas Flamel (3e)
Beauvilliers (A.) (18e)
Bellini (16e)
Berthoud (5e)
Blue Elephant (11e)
Bon Saint Pourçain (6e)
Brasserie Balzar (5e)
Brasserie Flo (10e)
Brasserie Lipp (6e)
Café de Flore (6e)
Café de la Paix (9e)
Café Les Deux Magots (6e)
Café Louis Philippe (4e)
Café Marly (1er)
Carré des Feuillants (1er)
Catherine (9e)
Caviar Kaspia (8e)

Cazaudehore La Forestière
  (Saint-Germain-en-Laye)
Chalet des Iles (16e)
Chardenoux (11e)
China Club (12e)
Closerie des Lilas (6e)
Clos Morillons (15e)
Coconnas (4e)
Comptoir Paris-Marrakech (1er)
Costes (1er)
Coupe-Chou (5e)
Diane (6e)
El Mansour (8e)
Elysées du Vernet (8e)
Epi d'Or (1er)
Espadon (1er)
Etoile (8e)
Etoile Marocaine (8e)
Faugeron (16e)
Fellini (1er, 15e)
Fermette Marbeuf 1900 (8e)
Fouquet's (8e)
Fred (17e)
Gamin de Paris (4e)
Gaudriole (1er)
Gégène (Joinville)
Gérard Besson (1er)
Goumard (1er)
Grande Cascade (16e)
Grand Véfour (1er)
Grange Batelière (9e)
Grille St-Honoré (1er)
Guirlande de Julie (3e)
Guy Savoy (17e)
Homero (8e)
Ile (Issy-les-Moulineaux)
Jacques Cagna (6e)
Jamin (16e)
Jardins de Bagatelle (16e)
Joséphine "Chez Dumonet" (6e)
Jules Verne (7e)
Kambodgia (16e)
Ladurée (8e)
Lapérouse (6e)
Lasserre (8e)
Ledoyen (8e)
Lucas Carton (8e)
Maison (5e)
Maison Blanche (8e)
Maison Courtine (14e)
Maison de l'Amérique (7e)
Maison du Caviar (8e)
Maison Prunier (16e)
Mansouria (11e)
Marty (5e)

Mavrommatis (5e)
Maxim's (8e)
Meurice (1er)
Michel Rostang (17e)
Monde des Chimères (4e)
Moniage Guillaume (14e)
Morot-Gaudry (15e)
Moulin/Galette Graziano (18e)
Obélisque (8e)
Orangerie (4e)
Oum el Banine (16e)
Pactole (5e)
Palanquin (6e)
Paris (6e)
Paul (1er, 11e)
Pauline (1er)
Paul Minchelli (7e)
Pavillon Elysée (8e)
Pavillon Montsouris (14e)
Pavillon Puebla (19e)
Petit Poucet (Le) (Levallois)
Petit Colombier (17e)
Petite Cour (La) (6e)
Petit Lutétia (6e)
Petit Prince de Paris (5e)
Petit Riche (9e)
Petit St. Benoît (6e)
Petit Zinc (6e)
Pierre Gagnaire (8e)
Port Alma (16e)
Pré Catelan (16e)
P'tit Troquet (7e)
404 (3e)
Relais Louis XIII (6e)
Relais Plaza (8e)
Rest. du Palais Royal (1er)
Rest. Opéra (9e)
Romantica (Clichy)
Safran (1er)
Shozan (8e)
Sormani (17e)
Square Trousseau (12e)
Stella Maris (8e)
Taillevent (8e)
Télégraphe (7e)
Timgad (17e)
Tonnelle Saintongeaise (Neuilly)
Toupary (1er)
Tour d'Argent (5e)
Train Bleu (12e)
Trou Gascon (12e)
Tsé-Yang (16e)
Vagenende (6e)
Vaudeville (2e)
Vong (8e)

Saturday – Best Bets

(B=brunch; L=lunch;
D=dinner; plus all hotels
and most Asians)

Alcazar (6e) (L,D)
Allard (6e) (L,D)
Ambassade d'Auvergne (3e) (L,D)
Ambroisie (4e) (L,D)
Ami Louis (3e) (L,D)
Amognes (11e) (D)
Amphyclès (17e) (D)
Anacréon (13e) (L,D)
André (8e) (L,D)
Androuët (8e) (D)
Appart' (8e) (L,D)
Ardoise (1er) (D)
Armand au Palais Royal (1er) (D)
Assiette (14e) (L,D)
Atelier Berger (1er) (L,D)
Atelier Maître Albert (5e) (L,D)
Auberge du Clou (9e) (L,D)
Avant Goût (13e) (L,D)
Avenue (8e) (L,D)
Bar des Théâtres (8e) (L,D)
Barrio Latino (12e) (L,D)
Bastide Odéon (6e) (L,D)
Beauvilliers (A.) (18e) (L,D)
Benoît (4e) (L,D)
Bistro des Deux Théâtres (9e) (L,D)
Bistro d'Hubert (15e) (L,D)
Bistrot du Peintre (11e) (L,D)
Bœuf sur le Toit (8e) (L,D)
Bofinger (4e) (L,D)
Bon (16e) (L,D)
Bookinistes (6e) (D)
Bouillon Racine (6e) (L,D)
Brasserie Balzar (5e) (L,D)
Brasserie de l'Ile St. Louis (4e) (L,D)
Brasserie Flo (10e) (L,D)
Brasserie Lipp (6e) (L,D)
Brasserie Lorraine (8e) (L,D)
Brasserie Mollard (8e) (L,D)
Brasserie Stella (16e) (B,L,D)
Brézolles (6e) (D)
Bûcherie (5e) (L,D)
Butte Chaillot (16e) (L,D)
Café Beaubourg (4e) (B,L,D)
Café de la Musique (19e) (B,L,D)
Café de l'Esplanade (Le) (7e) (L,D)
Café du Commerce (15e) (L,D)
Café la Jatte (Neuilly) (L,D)
Café Les Deux Magots (6e) (L,D)
Café Marly (1er) (L,D)
Café Ruc (1er) (L,D)
Café Terminus (8e) (L,D)
Cagouille (14e) (L,D)
Cailloux (13e) (L,D)
Cap Vernet (8e) (L,D)
Carré des Feuillants (1er) (D)
Cave de l'Os à Moelle (15e) (L,D)
Cercle Ledoyen (8e) (L,D)
Chardenoux (11e) (D)
Chartier (9e) (L,D)
Chen (15e) (L,D)
Cherche Midi (6e) (L,D)
Chez Eux (7e) (L,D)
Chiberta (8e) (L,D)
Chien qui Fume (1er) (L,D)
Cinq (8e) (L)
Cloche des Halles (1er) (L)
Clos des Gourmets (7e) (L,D)
Closerie des Lilas (6e) (L,D)
Clown Bar (11e) (L,D)
Colette (1er) (L)
Coupe-Chou (5e) (L,D)
Coupole (14e) (L,D)
Duc (14e) (D)
Ecaille et Plume (7e) (L,D)
Emporio Armani Caffé (6e) (L,D)
Enoteca (4e) (L,D)
Escargot Montorgueil (1er) (L,D)
Etoile (8e) (D)
Faugeron (16e) (D)
Ferme des Mathurins (8e) (L,D)
Fermette Marbeuf 1900 (8e) (L,D)
Flore en l'Ile (4e) (B,L,D)
Florimond (7e) (D)
Fogón Saint Julien (5e) (L,D)
Fouquet's (8e) (L,D)
Francis (8e) (L,D)
Fumoir (1er) (L,D)
Gare (16e) (L,D)
Gauloise (15e) (L,D)
Gavroche (2e) (L,D)
Gégène (Joinville) (L,D)
Georges (2e, 4e) (L,D)
Georges Porte Maillot (17e) (L,D)
Gérard Besson (1er) (D)
Goumard (1er) (L,D)
Grand Café des Capucines (9e)
  (L,D)
Grand Colbert (2e) (L,D)
Grande Armée (16e) (L,D)
Grande Cascade (16e) (L,D)
Grandes Marches (12e) (L,D)
Grand Venise (15e) (L,D)
Guinguette de Neuilly (Neuilly)
  (L,D)
Guy Savoy (17e) (L,D)
Hélène Darroze (6e) (L,D)

Homero (8e) (D)
I Golosi (9e) (L)
Il Baccello (17e) (D)
Ile (Issy-les-Moulineaux) (L,D)
Jacques Cagna (6e) (D)
Jacques Mélac (11e) (L,D)
Janou (3e) (L,D)
Jarasse (Neuilly) (L,D)
Jardins de Bagatelle (16e) (L,D)
Joe Allen (1er) (B,L,D)
Jo Goldenberg (4e) (B,L,D)
Jules Verne (7e) (L,D)
Julien (10e) (L,D)
Juvenile's (1er) (L,D)
Lapérouse (6e) (L,D)
Lasserre (8e) (L,D)
Laurent (8e) (D)
Lucas Carton (8e) (D)
Ma Bourgogne (4e) (D)
Macéo (1er) (L,D)
Maison (5e) (L,D)
Maison Blanche (8e) (D)
Maison du Caviar (8e) (L,D)
Maison Prunier (16e) (L,D)
Mansouria (11e) (L,D)
Marée (8e) (D)
Marianne (4e) (L,D)
Marius et Janette (8e) (L,D)
Maxim's (8e) (L,D)
Méditerranée (6e) (L,D)
Michel (10e) (L,D)
Michel Rostang (17e) (D)
Moissonnier (5e) (L,D)
Moulin/Galette Graziano (18e) (L,D)
O à la Bouche (14e) (L,D)
Olivades (7e) (D)
Omar (3e) (L,D)
Orangerie (4e) (D)
Os à Moelle (15e) (L,D)
Oulette (12e) (D)
Paul (11e) (L,D)
Paul Minchelli (7e) (L,D)
Pavillon Elysée (8e) (L,D)
Pavillon Montsouris (14e) (L,D)
Pavillon Puebla (19e) (L,D)
Petit Marguery (13e) (L,D)
Petit Riche (9e) (L,D)
Petrossian (7e) (L,D)
Pétrus (17e) (L,D)
Pharamond (1er) (L,D)
Pied de Cochon (1er) (B,L,D)
Pierre au Palais Royal (1er) (L,D)
Polidor (6e) (L,D)

Pouilly Reuilly (Le Pré-St-Gervais) (L,D)
Pré Catelan (16e) (L,D)
Procope (6e) (L,D)
Quai Ouest (St-Cloud) (L,D)
404 (3e) (B,L,D)
Récamier (7e) (L,D)
Régalade (14e) (L,D)
Relais d'Auteuil (16e) (D)
Relais Louis XIII (6e) (L,D)
René (5e) (L,D)
Repaire de Cartouche (11e) (L,D)
Rest. du Marché (15e) (L,D)
River Café (Issy-les-Moulineaux) (L,D)
Rue Balzac (8e) (L,D)
Square Trousseau (12e) (L,D)
Stella Maris (8e) (D)
Stéphane Martin (15e) (L,D)
Sud (17e) (L,D)
Table d'Anvers (9e) (D)
Terminus Nord (10e) (L,D)
Terrasses du Palais (17e) (L,D)
Totem (16e) (L,D)
Toupary (1er) (L,D)
Tour d'Argent (5e) (L,D)
Toutoune (5e) (L,D)
Train Bleu (12e) (L,D)
Trou Gascon (12e) (D)
Troyon (17e) (L,D)
Ty Coz (9e) (L,D)
Vagenende (6e) (L,D)
Vaudeville (2e) (L,D)
Véranda (8e) (L,D)
Vieux Bistro (4e) (L,D)
Violon d'Ingres (7e) (L,D)
Voltaire (7e) (L,D)
Wally Le Saharien (9e) (L,D)
Willi's Wine Bar (1er) (L,D)
Woolloomooloo (4e) (L,D)
Yvan (8e) (D)
Zebra Square (16e) (B,L,D)

Sunday – Best Bets
(B=brunch; L=lunch; D=dinner; plus all hotels and most Asians)
Alcazar (6e) (B,L,D)
Al Dar (5e, 16e) (L,D)
Al Diwan (8e) (L,D)
Alivi (4e) (L,D)
Alsace (8e) (L,D)
Altitude 95 (7e) (L,D)
Ambassade d'Auvergne (3e) (L,D)
Ami Louis (3e) (L,D)

Anahï (3e) (D)
André (8e) (L,D)
Angelina (1er) (L)
Appart' (8e) (B,L,D)
A Priori Thé (2e) (B,L)
Asian (8e) (B,D)
Assiette (14e) (L,D)
Atlas (5e) (L,D)
Auberge Bressane (7e) (L,D)
Avenue (8e) (L,D)
Ballon des Ternes (17e) (L,D)
Bar à Huîtres (3e, 5e, 14e) (L,D)
Bar au Sel (7e) (L,D)
Bar des Théâtres (8e) (L,D)
Barfly (8e) (B,L,D)
Baron Rouge (12e) (L,D)
Barrio Latino (12e) (B,L,D)
Basilic (7e) (L,D)
Baumann Ternes (17e) (L,D)
Beaujolais d'Auteuil (16e) (L,D)
Benoît (4e) (L,D)
Bermuda Onion (15e) (B,L,D)
Bistro des Deux Théâtres (9e) (L,D)
Bistro d'Hubert (15e) (L,D)
Bistrot de Paris (7e) (L,D)
Bistrot du Peintre (11e) (L,D)
Blue Elephant (11e) (L,D)
Bœuf sur le Toit (8e) (L,D)
Bofinger (4e) (L,D)
Bon (16e) (L,D)
Bookinistes (6e) (D)
Bouillon Racine (6e) (L,D)
Brasserie Balzar (5e) (L,D)
Brasserie de la Poste (16e) (L,D)
Brasserie de l'Ile St. Louis (4e) (L,D)
Brasserie Flo (10e) (L,D)
Brasserie Lipp (6e) (L,D)
Brasserie Lorraine (8e) (L,D)
Brasserie Mollard (8e) (L,D)
Brasserie Stella (16e) (B,L,D)
Bûcherie (5e) (L,D)
Buddha Bar (8e) (D)
Butte Chaillot (16e) (L,D)
Café Beaubourg (4e) (B,L,D)
Café Charbon (11e) (B,L,D)
Café de Flore (6e) (L,D)
Café de la Musique (19e) (B,L,D)
Café de la Paix (9e) (L,D)
Café de l'Esplanade (Le) (7e) (L,D)
Café la Jatte (Neuilly) (L,D)
Café Les Deux Magots (6e) (L,D)
Café Marly (1er) (L,D)
Café Ruc (1er) (L,D)
Cagouille (14e) (L,D)
Cap Vernet (8e) (L,D)

Catalogne (La) (6e) (L,D)
Cazaudehore La Forestière
   (Saint-Germain-en-Laye) (L,D)
Chalet des Iles (16e) (L,D)
Chartier (9e) (L,D)
Cherche Midi (6e) (L,D)
Chicago Meatpackers (1er) (L,D)
Chicago Pizza Pie Factory (8e) (L,D)
China Club (12e) (D)
Closerie des Lilas (6e) (L,D)
Coconnas (4e) (L,D)
Coffee Parisien (6e, 16e) (L,D)
Comptoir Paris-Marrakech (1er)
   (B,L,D)
Coupe-Chou (5e) (D)
Coupole (14e) (L,D)
Dalloyau (6e, 15e, 8e) (B,L)
Dôme (14e) (D)
Drugstore Champs-Elysées (8e)
   (L,D)
Enoteca (4e) (L,D)
Escargot Montorgueil (1er) (L,D)
Fermette Marbeuf 1900 (8e) (L,D)
Findi (8e) (B,D)
Finzi (8e) (D)
Flandrin (16e) (L,D)
Flora Danica (8e) (L,D)
Flore en l'Ile (4e) (B,L,D)
Fontaine de Mars (7e) (L,D)
Fouquet's (8e) (B,L,D)
Fous d'en Face (4e) (L,D)
Francis (8e) (L,D)
Françoise (7e) (L,D)
Fumoir (1er) (B,L,D)
Gare (16e) (L,D)
Gégène (Joinville) (L,D)
Georges (4e) (L,D)
Georges Porte Maillot (17e) (L,D)
Gérard (Neuilly) (L,D)
Gourmet de l'Isle (4e) (L,D)
Grand Colbert (2e) (L,D)
Grande Armée (16e) (L,D)
Grande Cascade (16e) (L,D)
Grandes Marches (12e) (L,D)
Grand Louvre (1er) (L,D)
Guirlande de Julie (3e) (L,D)
Hippopotamus (Puteaux, 1er, 2e,
   4e, 5e, 6e, 8e, 14e) (D)
Ile (Issy-les-Moulineaux) (L,D)
Impala Lounge (8e) (B,L,D)
Jardins de Bagatelle (16e) (L,D)
Joe Allen (1er) (B)
Jo Goldenberg (4e) (B,L,D)
Jules Verne (7e) (L,D)
Julien (10e) (L,D)

Kiosque (16e) (B,L,D)
Ladurée (8e, 8e) (B,L)
Languedoc (5e) (L,D)
Lapérouse (6e) (L,D)
Livio (Neuilly) (L,D)
Lô Sushi (8e) (L,D)
Maison du Caviar (8e) (L,D)
Man Ray (8e) (D)
Mansouria (11e) (L,D)
Mariage Frères (4e, 6e, 8e) (B,L)
Mavrommatis (5e) (L,D)
Méditerranée (6e) (L,D)
Moulin/Galette Graziano (18e)
  (L,D)
Orangerie (4e) (D)
Paolo Petrini (17e) (D)
Patrick Goldenberg (17e) (L,D)
Pavillon Montsouris (14e) (L,D)
Petit Poucet (Le) (Levallois) (L,D)
Petit Bofinger (4e, 9e, 17e,
  Neuilly) (L,D)
Petit Lutétia (6e) (L,D)
Pétrus (17e) (L,D)
Pied de Cochon (1er) (B,L,D)
Plage Parisienne (15e) (B,D)
Pré Catelan (16e) (L,D)
Prune (10e) (B)
Quai Ouest (St-Cloud) (B,L,D)
River Café
  (Issy-les-Moulineaux) (L,D)
Rue Balzac (8e) (L,D)
Spicy Restaurant (8e) (L,D)
Square Trousseau (12e) (L,D)
Studio (4e) (B,D)
Télégraphe (7e) (L,D)
Terminus Nord (10e) (L,D)
Terrasses du Palais (17e) (L,D)
Totem (16e) (L,D)
Tour d'Argent (5e) (L,D)
Train Bleu (12e) (L,D)
Vagenende (6e) (L,D)
Vaudeville (2e) (L,D)
Véranda (8e) (B,L,D)
Viaduc Café (12e) (B,D)
Zebra Square (16e) (B,L,D)

Singles Scene

Affriolé (7e)
Alcazar (6e)
André (8e)
Asian (8e)
Assassins (6e)
Bar des Théâtres (8e)
Barfly (8e)
Barrio Latino (12e)

Bar Vendôme (1er)
Bec Rouge (8e)
Bistro de la Grille (6e)
Bistrot d'à Côté (5e, 17e, Neuilly)
Bistrot d'Alex (6e)
Bistrot de l'Etoile Troyon (17e)
Bistrot de l'Université (7e)
Bistrot de Marius (8e)
Bistrot de Paris (7e)
Bistrot du Dôme (4e, 14e)
Bistrot du Louvre (2e)
Bistrot St. James (Neuilly)
Bofinger (4e)
Bookinistes (6e)
Brasserie Balzar (5e)
Brasserie Lipp (6e)
Brasserie Lorraine (8e)
Brasserie Lutétia (6e)
Buddha Bar (8e)
Café Beaubourg (4e)
Café Bleu (8e)
Café Charbon (11e)
Café d'Angel (17e)
Café de Flore (6e)
Café de la Paix (9e)
Café de l'Industrie (11e)
Café des Lettres (7e)
Café de Vendôme (1er)
Café du Commerce (15e)
Café Faubourg (8e)
Café Indigo (8e)
Café la Jatte (Neuilly)
Café Les Deux Magots (6e)
Café Marly (1er)
Café Runtz (2e)
Café Terminus (8e)
Cafetière (6e)
Caffé Toscano (7e)
Cagouille (14e)
Carr's (1er)
Cartet Restaurant (11e)
Casa del Habano (6e)
Catherine (9e)
Céladon (2e)
Charpentiers (6e)
Cherche Midi (6e)
China Club (12e)
Cloche des Halles (1er)
Cloche d'Or (9e)
Closerie des Lilas (6e)
Coffee Parisien (6e)
Comptoir des Sports (6e)
Contre-Allée (14e)
Costes (1er)
Dix Vins (15e)

Doobie's (8ᵉ)
Driver's (16ᵉ)
Duc (14ᵉ)
Durand Dupont (Neuilly)
Epi Dupin (6ᵉ)
Espadon Bleu (6ᵉ)
Etoile (8ᵉ)
Excuse (4ᵉ)
Fins Gourmets (7ᵉ)
Floridita (16ᵉ)
Fouquet's (8ᵉ)
Fred (17ᵉ)
Gégène (Joinville)
Georges Porte Maillot (17ᵉ)
Grande Armée (16ᵉ)
Ile (Issy-les-Moulineaux)
Juvenile's (1ᵉʳ)
Kiosque (16ᵉ)
Kitty O'Sheas (2ᵉ)
Lô Sushi (8ᵉ)
Maison (5ᵉ)
Man Ray (8ᵉ)
Marcel (6ᵉ)
Marlotte (6ᵉ)
Mascotte (8ᵉ)
Nemrod (6ᵉ)
Oenothèque (9ᵉ)
Olé Bodéga! (12ᵉ)
Opportun (14ᵉ)
Orient-Extrême (6ᵉ)
Passage (11ᵉ)
Petit Rétro (16ᵉ)
Petit St. Benoît (6ᵉ)
Pied de Fouet (7ᵉ)
Plage Parisienne (15ᵉ)
Poste (9ᵉ)
Prune (10ᵉ)
Quai Ouest (St-Cloud)
Relais Plaza (8ᵉ)
René (5ᵉ)
Rest. du Marché (15ᵉ)
River Café (Issy-les-Moulineaux)
Rouge Vif (7ᵉ)
Sarladais (8ᵉ)
Sauvignon (7ᵉ)
Scheffer (16ᵉ)
Sébillon Élysées (8ᵉ)
Sébillon Neuilly (Neuilly)
Taverne Henri IV (1ᵉʳ)
Véranda (8ᵉ)
Verre Bouteille (17ᵉ)
Vin sur Vin (7ᵉ)
Willi's Wine Bar (1ᵉʳ)

Sleepers
(Good to excellent food,
but little known)
Allobroges (20ᵉ)
Amognes (11ᵉ)
Atelier Gourmand (17ᵉ)
Avant Goût (13ᵉ)
Benkay (15ᵉ)
Biche au Bois (12ᵉ)
Bistrot d'Albert (17ᵉ)
Bonne Table (14ᵉ)
Clos des Gourmets (7ᵉ)
Comte de Gascogne (Boulogne)
Dînée (15ᵉ)
Ecaille et Plume (7ᵉ)
Faucher (17ᵉ)
Goumard (1ᵉʳ)
Graindorge (17ᵉ)
Grenadin (8ᵉ)
Grille (10ᵉ)
Il Sardo (9ᵉ)
Isami (4ᵉ)
Kim Anh (15ᵉ)
Lac-Hong (16ᵉ)
Lao Siam (19ᵉ)
Luna (8ᵉ)
Michel (10ᵉ)
Montparnasse 25 (14ᵉ)
Muses (9ᵉ)
Orangerie (4ᵉ)
Ostéria (4ᵉ)
Oulette (12ᵉ)
Pouilly Reuilly (Le Pré-St-Gervais)
Pressoir (12ᵉ)
Quercy (9ᵉ)
Quincy (12ᵉ)
Relais de Sèvres (15ᵉ)
Relais Louis XIII (6ᵉ)
Safran (1ᵉʳ)
Stella Maris (8ᵉ)
Table de Babette (Poissy)
Taïra (17ᵉ)
Taka (18ᵉ)
Tang (16ᵉ)
Tastevin (Maisons-Laffitte)
Villaret (11ᵉ)
Vincent (19ᵉ)
Yves Quintard (15ᵉ)

Special Occasion
Alain Ducasse (8ᵉ)
Alcazar (6ᵉ)
Ambassadeurs (8ᵉ)
Ambroisie (4ᵉ)
Ami Louis (3ᵉ)

Amphyclès (17e)
Apicius (17e)
Arpège (7e)
Astor (8e)
Beauvilliers (A.) (18e)
Benoît (4e)
Bristol (8e)
Carré des Feuillants (1er)
Caviar Kaspia (8e)
Cazaudehore La Forestière
   (Saint-Germain-en-Laye)
Céladon (2e)
Coupole (14e)
Daru (8e)
Dessirier (17e)
Dînée (15e)
Divellec (7e)
Dôme (14e)
Drouant (2e)
Duc (14e)
Espadon (1er)
Faucher (17e)
Faugeron (16e)
Fermette Marbeuf 1900 (8e)
Gérard Besson (1er)
Goumard (1er)
Grande Cascade (16e)
Grand Véfour (1er)
Guy Savoy (17e)
Jacques Cagna (6e)
Jamin (16e)
Jardins de Bagatelle (16e)
Jules Verne (7e)
Lapérouse (6e)
Lasserre (8e)
Laurent (8e)
Ledoyen (8e)
Lucas Carton (8e)
Macéo (1er)
Maison du Caviar (8e)
Mansouria (11e)
Michel Rostang (17e)
Morot-Gaudry (15e)
Orangerie (4e)
Oulette (12e)
Paris (6e)
Pauline (1er)
Paul Minchelli (7e)
Pavillon Montsouris (14e)
Pavillon Puebla (19e)
Petit Colombier (17e)
Pierre Gagnaire (8e)
Port Alma (16e)
Pré Catelan (16e)
Quai Ouest (St-Cloud)

Récamier (7e)
Relais Louis XIII (6e)
Sormani (17e)
Sousceyrac (A) (11e)
Stella Maris (8e)
Table d'Anvers (9e)
Taillevent (8e)
Taïra (17e)
Tan Dinh (7e)
Tour d'Argent (5e)
Trois Marches (Versailles)
Violon d'Ingres (7e)
Yvan (8e)

Teenagers & Other Youthful Spirits

Alcazar (6e)
Al Dar (5e, 16e)
Altitude 95 (7e)
Anahï (3e)
Anahuacalli (5e)
Appart' (8e)
Asian (8e)
Assassins (6e)
Avant Goût (13e)
Ay!! Caramba!! (19e)
Babylone (7e)
Barfly (8e)
Bermuda Onion (15e)
Bistro Melrose (17e)
Blue Elephant (11e)
Buddha Bar (8e)
Butte Chaillot (16e)
Ca d'Oro (1er)
Café Beaubourg (4e)
Café Charbon (11e)
Café d'Angel (17e)
Café de la Musique (19e)
Café de l'Industrie (11e)
Café la Jatte (Neuilly)
Café Max (7e)
Café Véry (1er)
Caffé Toscano (7e)
Carr's (1er)
Casa Alcalde (15e)
Chicago Meatpackers (1er)
Chicago Pizza Pie Factory (8e)
China Town Belleville (10e)
China Town Olympiades (13e)
Churrasco (17e)
Clément (2e, 4e, 8e, 14e, 15e, 17e,
   Bougival, Boulogne)
Clown Bar (11e)
Coco de Mer (5e)
Coco et sa Maison (17e)

Coffee Parisien (6e, 16e)
Comptoir des Sports (6e)
Cosi (6e)
Cou de la Girafe (8e)
Crêperie de Josselin (14e)
Dame Tartine (12e)
Da Mimmo (10e)
Débarcadère (17e)
Diable des Lombards (1er)
Doobie's (8e)
Driver's (16e)
Drugstore Champs-Elysées (8e)
Entrecôte (7e)
Escale (4e)
Fabrique (11e)
Gare (16e)
Gégène (Joinville)
Grenier de Notre Dame (5e)
Hangar (3e)
Higuma (1er)
Hippopotamus (1er, 2e, 4e, 5e, 6e,
    8e, 14e, Puteaux)
Indiana Café (2e, 3e, 6e, 8e, 9e, 11e, 14e)
Jean (9e)
Joe Allen (1er)
Juvenile's (1er)
Khun Akorn (11e)
Kiosque (16e)
Kitty O'Sheas (2e)
Lao Siam (19e)
Léon de Bruxelles (1er, 4e, 6e, 8e,
    9e, 11e, 14e, 15e, 17e)
Lina's (1er, 2e, 6e, 8e, 9e, 12e, 17e,
    Neuilly, Puteaux)
Livio (Neuilly)
Mandarin (8e)
Marie et Fils (6e)
New Nioullaville (11e)
Nouveau Village Tao-Tao (13e)
Olé Bodéga! (12e)
Omar (3e)
Paparazzi (9e)
Passy Mandarin (2e, 16e)
Petit Poucet (Le) (Levallois)
Plancha (11e)
Planet Hollywood (8e)
Polidor (6e)
Port du Salut (5e)
Président (11e)
Quai Ouest (St-Cloud)
Rest. des Beaux Arts (6e)
River Café (Issy-les-Moulineaux)
Signorelli (1er)
Spicy Restaurant (8e)
Square Trousseau (12e)

Studio (4e)
Taverne de Maître Kanter (1er)
Thanksgiving (4e)
Totem (16e)
Tricotin (13e)
Trumilou (4e)
Véranda (8e)
Viaduc Café (12e)
Village d'Ung et Li Lam (8e)
Vincent (19e)
Virgin Café (8e)
Yvan, Petit (8e)
Zebra Square (16e)
Zéphyr (20e)
Zinzins (2e)

Teflons
(Get lots of business, despite
so-so food, i.e. they have
other attractions that prevent
criticism from sticking)
Alcazar (6e)
Angelina (1er)
Appart' (8e)
Avenue (8e)
Bar à Huîtres (3e, 5e, 14e)
Bar des Théâtres (8e)
Barfly (8e)
Bermuda Onion (15e)
Bœuf sur le Toit (8e)
Brasserie Flo (10e)
Brasserie Lipp (6e)
Brasserie Lorraine (8e)
Buddha Bar (8e)
Café de Flore (6e)
Café la Jatte (Neuilly)
Café Marly (1er)
Clément (2e, 4e, 8e, 14e, 15e, 17e,
    Bougival, Boulogne)
Costes (1er)
Coupole (14e)
Fermette Marbeuf 1900 (8e)
Fouquet's (8e)
Gare (16e)
Hippopotamus (1er, 2e, 4e, 5e, 6e,
    8e, 14e, Puteaux)
Ladurée (8e, 9e)
Léon de Bruxelles (1er, 4e, 6e, 8e,
    9e, 11e, 14e, 15e, 17e)
Lina's (1er, 2e, 6e, 8e, 9e, 12e, 17e,
    Neuilly, Puteaux)
Livio (Neuilly)
Quai Ouest (St-Cloud)
Thoumieux (7e)

Train Bleu (12e)
Zebra Square (16e)

Theme Restaurant
Androuët (8e)
Asian (8e)
Baan-Boran (1er)
Barrio Latino (12e)
Bath's (8e)
Blue Elephant (11e)
Byblos Café (16e)
Casa Corsa (6e)
Casa del Habano (6e)
Casa Tina (16e)
Catalogne (La) (6e)
Chicago Meatpackers (1er)
Chicago Pizza Pie Factory (8e)
Churrasco (17e)
Clément (2e, 4e, 8e, 14e, 15e, 17e)
Comptoir Paris-Marrakech (1er)
Daru (8e)
Dauphin (1er)
Dominique (6e)
Driver's (16e)
Gégène (Joinville)
Il Sardo (9e)
Jacquot de Bayonne (12e)
Maison du Caviar (8e)
Man Ray (8e)
Olé Bodéga! (12e)
Pacific Eiffel (15e)
Paparazzi (9e)
Planet Hollywood (8e)

Transporting Experience
Alcazar (6e)
Al Diwan (8e)
Al Mounia (16e)
Alsaco (9e)
Androuët (8e)
Annapurna (8e)
Asian (8e)
Atlas (5e)
Benkay (15e)
Blue Elephant (11e)
Buddha Bar (8e)
Café Beaubourg (4e)
Café Charbon (11e)
Café Véry (1er)
Casa Tina (16e)
Caviar Kaspia (8e)
Chalet des Iles (16e)
Chantairelle (5e)
Chen (15e)
Coco de Mer (5e)
Copenhague (8e)

Costes (1er)
Dominique (6e)
El Mansour (8e)
Enoteca (4e)
Erawan (15e)
Etoile (8e)
Etoile Marocaine (8e)
Fakhr el Dine (8e, 16e)
Fogón Saint Julien (5e)
Gazelle (17e)
Gégène (Joinville)
Georges (4e)
Gérard (Neuilly)
Grande Armée (16e)
Grand Louvre (1er)
Guinguette de Neuilly (Neuilly)
Homero (8e)
Ile (Issy-les-Moulineaux)
Impala Lounge (8e)
Isami (4e)
Isse (2e)
Jarasse (Neuilly)
Jardins de Bagatelle (16e)
Jules Verne (7e)
Khun Akorn (11e)
Livingstone (1er)
Lô Sushi (8e)
Maison Courtine (14e)
Man Ray (8e)
Mansouria (11e)
Mavrommatis (5e)
Monsieur Lapin (14e)
New Nioullaville (11e)
Olé Bodéga! (12e)
Pavillon Montsouris (14e)
Pavillon Puebla (19e)
Pierre Gagnaire (8e)
Pré Catelan (16e)
Président (11e)
404 (3e)
Ravi (7e)
Saudade (1er)
Sud (17e)
Taïra (17e)
Tan Dinh (7e)
Timgad (17e)
Train Bleu (12e)
Tricotin (13e)
Tsé-Yang (16e)
Wok Restaurant (11e)
Woolloomooloo (4e)

Winning Wine List
Alain Ducasse (8e)
Ambassadeurs (8e)

Ambroisie (4e)
Arpège (7e)
Auberge Nicolas Flamel (3e)
Baron Rouge (12e)
Bistrot du Sommelier (8e)
Bons Crus (1er)
Bouchons de Fr. Clerc (5e, 8e, 15e, 17e)
Bristol (8e)
Café du Passage (11e)
Camélia (Bougival)
Carré des Feuillants (1er)
Catherine (9e)
Cave Drouot (9e)
Cazaudehore La Forestière (Saint-Germain-en-Laye)
Chiberta (8e)
Cloche des Halles (1er)
Clown Bar (11e)
Coude Fou (4e)
Ecluse (6e, 8e, 11e, 17e)
Elysées du Vernet (8e)
Enoteca (4e)
Espadon (1er)
Fous d'en Face (4e)
Gérard Besson (1er)
Grand Véfour (1er)
Griffonnier (8e)
Guy Savoy (17e)
I Golosi (9e)
Jacques Cagna (6e)
Jacques Mélac (11e)
Jamin (16e)
Jardin (8e)
Joséphine "Chez Dumonet" (6e)
Juvenile's (1er)
Laurent (8e)
Ledoyen (8e)
Lucas Carton (8e)
Macéo (1er)
Maxim's (8e)
Meurice (1er)
Michel (10e)
Michel Rostang (17e)

Montparnasse 25 (14e)
Oenothèque (9e)
Passage (11e)
Père Claude (15e)
Petit Riche (9e)
Pierre Gagnaire (8e)
Pressoir (12e)
Récamier (7e)
Rest. Opéra (9e)
Saudade (1er)
Sauvignon (7e)
Taillevent (8e)
Tan Dinh (7e)
Taverne Henri IV (1er)
Tire-Bouchon (15e)
Tour d'Argent (5e)
Trois Marches (Versailles)
Vieux Métiers de France (13e)
Vin sur Vin (7e)

Young Children

Altitude 95 (7e)
A Priori Thé (2e)
Bermuda Onion (15e)
Café Véry (1er)
Chalet des Iles (16e)
Chicago Meatpackers (1er)
Chicago Pizza Pie Factory (8e)
Clément (2e, 4e, 8e, 14e, 15e, 17e, Bougival, Boulogne)
Crêperie de Josselin (14e)
Dame Tartine (12e)
Drugstore Champs-Elysées (8e)
Guinguette de Neuilly (Neuilly)
Hippopotamus (1er, 2e, 4e, 5e, 6e, 8e, 14e, Puteaux)
Indiana Café (2e, 3e, 6e, 8e, 9e, 11e, 14e)
Léon de Bruxelles (1er, 4e, 6e, 8e, 9e, 15e)
Lina's (1er, 2e, 6e, 8e, 9e, 12e, 17e, Neuilly, Puteaux)
Pacific Eiffel (15e)
Planet Hollywood (8e)

NOTES

NOTES

May We Quote You?

Be a part of
ZAGAT SURVEY®

If you would like to participate in one of our
Surveys or be added to our mailing list,
please fill out this card and send it back to us.

☐ Mr. ☐ Mrs. ☐ Ms.
_____
Your Name

_____
Street Address   Apt #

_____
City   State   Zip

_____
e-mail Address

_____
Occupation

I'd like to be a surveyor for the following city:

_____

or a surveyor for U.S. Hotels, Resorts & Spas ☐

The city I visit most is: ———————————

My favorite restaurant is: ———————————

                          City

My favorite hotel is: ———————————

                          City

I eat roughly ——— lunches and dinners out per week.

☐ This book was a gift ☐ Bought by me ☐ Surveyor copy

The title of this book is: ———————————